# FLASHPOINT

A RICHARD KASAK BOOK

# FLASHPOINT

## Gay Male Sexual Writing

### EDITED BY MICHAEL BRONSKI

First Richard Kasak Book Edition 1996

First Printing April 1996

ISBN 1-56333-424-0

Author photo by Joshua Oppenheimer

Manufactured in the United States of America
Published by Masquerade Books, Inc.
801 Second Avenue
New York, N.Y. 10017

# FLASHPOINT

## Acknowledgments

No book, and particularly an anthology, materializes in a vacuum. Thanks to a large number of people is called for, the most prominent being: Michael Lowenthal for his unstinting support, sharp editorial eye, and endless good advice. Wickie Stamps for her endless suggestions of writers and her amazing ability to cut through the bullshit. Bill Andriette for his computer expertise. Jennifer Reut for her patience and publishing acumen. Chris Hogan for his friendship and advice on layout and formatting. Michele Karlsberg for her generosity and advice. And, even after the fact, Walta Borawski for twenty years of love and support.

Walta Borawski 1947–1994

Stan Leventhal 1952–1995

# *Introduction*

First some definitions: The words "smut," "porn," or "erotica" are fine, useful terms. But they are misleading. Each has a specific cultural meaning and intention, but they all ultimately obscure our understanding of the relationships between sexuality and writing, between desire and depiction. "Smut" has always been a derogatory term used by those who would denigrate explicit sexual writing. Its primary meaning is "a particle of dirt" or "a smudge made by soot, smoke, or dirt." "Smut" implies that sex is dirty and that we are soiled—smudged—by reading it. While many in the business of writing, publishing, or discussing sexual writings have gladly taken on the moniker of "smut peddlers"—the phrase has a nice 1950s tabloid exposé ring to it—even the reclaiming of the work in a pro-sex context has its limitations. The problem with "smut" is that it is a purely reactive word and gives little sense of the range, depth, or resonance of sexual writing.

"Porn," an abbreviation of "pornography," comes from two Greek words and means, literally, the "writings of whores." The word itself, however, is not Greek, but a Victorian invention. In his book *The Secret Museum*, Walter Kendrick details how the literary genre of "pornography" originated in late nineteenth-century England. As the public discussion of sex was becoming more and more common, it became necessary to specifically label and describe this discourse in an effort to contain it, to prevent it from becoming an accepted standard of everyday talk. As a result, "pornography" became the acknowledged place where sexual matters could be discussed and described. The problem with "porn" is that, at least in the popular imagination, it is simply about sex and does not do justice to the complexity of emotional and psychological contexts that inform our desires, longings, and activities.

"Pornography" eventually became a pejorative, rather than descriptive, term and, in recent years, the term "erotica" gained currency as value-free and more sex-positive. It had none of the negative cultural baggage that "pornography" carried with it, and implicitly conveyed a sense of health and happiness. There was never anything dirty about "erotica." And that was the problem. The late John Preston claimed that "erotica" was merely the acceptable middle-class word for "pornography," and that such euphemisms were, at best, misleading and, at worst, sex-negative. The problem with "erotica" is that, by insisting on giving equal weight to emotional and psychological experiences, it is frequently seen as minimizing the sexual.

Perhaps we have all of these differing—and at times conflicting—terms for sexual writing because it is difficult to ascertain how exactly sexuality fits into our own lives, our imaginations, and our experiences. Our culture does not encourage—and in some cases actively discourages—our thinking, talking, and writing about sex. That is why we even have a separate category of sexual writing—whether we call it smut, porn, or erotica. The stories in *Flashpoint: Gay Male Sexual Writing* deal with a whole range of sexual activities, feelings, imaginations, and circumstances. Some are closer to smut, others to erotica. The point of *Flashpoint* isn't to categorize its contents into separate, clearly labeled sexual genres, each with its own set of definitions and parameters, but rather to find the connecting threads, the underlying similarities. The cultural demand that writings about sexuality be strictly and securely labeled is simply the end result of the fact that we are constantly told that we must isolate and segregate our sexual lives from our "real" lives.

Gay male writing about sex is not a new phenomenon. The ancient Babylonian epic, *Gilgamesh*, contains clear expressions of male sexual desire and bonding. The story of the love between David and Jonathan shows that even the Bible has its share of gay male sexual writing as well. Petronius' *Satyricon* and Plato's *Symposium* were emblematic of their times, as well as vital in the formation of a modern homosexual identity—their idealized (and not so idealized) vision of male (homo)sexuality gave British Victorian writers and theorists such as John Addington Symonds and Edward Carpenter an opening to conceptualize and write about their desires. Homosexual porn was so prevalent in Great Britain during the Victorian era that even Oscar Wilde lent his hand in writing sections of the classic gay erotic novel, *Teleny*. The passionate letters of the monk Anselm, Abbot of Bec (later, Archbishop of Canterbury), to his beloved companion, William (written sometime around 1077), are examples of gay male sexual writing, as are the *Sonnets* of Michelangelo, written during the Italian Renaissance. The numerous small underground publications that found their way out of the darkness in the 1950s and '60s, and the burgeoning publication of mass-produced gay porn novels in the 1970s, are merely the newest manifestations of gay male sexual writing.

Every expression of gay male sexual writing is bound and limited, by its own cultural roots. While the situations are millennia apart, the passionate feelings in *Gilgamesh* are recognizable to gay men today, even though the work's content and form may be foreign to us. Early twentieth-century writings like Wilde's *Teleny* or A.E. Housman's coded erotic love poems to men are good examples of how cultural context can shape writings about gay male sexuality and desire. If you advance a little beyond the bounds of what is permitted in that culture—as Wilde and his co-writers did in *Teleny*—you are likely to be labeled a pornographer. If—like A.E. Housman—you find acceptable ways to portray gay male sexual desire, you might be called a genius. While the proscribed boundaries of what is acceptable and not acceptable (particularly in regard to sexually explicit subject matter) keep changing, there is another factor that must be considered: Is the writing truthful, does it honestly, authentically, represent the sexual, emotional, psychological, and physical aspects of gay male lives?

We live in a culture that now permits us to write—more explicitly than ever—about gay male sexuality. True, there is still censorship (the recent legal and judicial battles over gay and sexual information on the Internet is just one current example of an ongoing battle, as is the constant harassment of gay and lesbian bookstores both in Canada and the U.S.), but compared to five, ten, twenty, or fifty years ago, we are now living in a time in which gay male sexual writing is remarkably unrestrained. This new freedom is heady and exhilarating, and yet our sexual writing—be it smut, porn, or erotica—is not unbound from its cultural context. The important question is not simply "How explicit can we be?" (although sexual explicitness may be an important element in writing forthrightly), but rather "How honest can we be?" Gay men who read porn know that stories with the most explicit sexual details—"then he jammed his hard ten inches down my willing gullet as he was shoving three fingers into my pulsating asshole"—are not necessarily good, or even engaging. Without some element of truth, even the most salacious porn, startling detail piled upon startling detail, often feels fraudulent. It may give us a hard-on—and thus be efficient for jerking off—but it will not affect us in any other way....

The recent freedom to write and publish more openly sexual material has, ironically, created a situation in which we have a veritable cornucopia of sexual writing, but much of it is not very good. And while quantity is vital in marking social, political, and emotional gay male space, it should not be confused with quality. While even bad sexual writing—routine, predictable, badly paced and delivered—is an act of rebellion against the current political and social hegemony, it does not necessarily move us forward or significantly transform, or even inform, our lives. This raises important questions: What is the relationship between sexual writing and how we think and talk about sex in our lives? What is the connection between the sexual imagination and the act of literary creation? How do we manage—in a culture that hates and despises us and our desires—to talk and write honestly about our inner and public sexual lives?

British novelist and critic Brigid Brophy, in her massive and extraordinarily perceptive biography of gay novelist Ronald Firbank, discusses the intrinsic, unavoidable connections between writing and the imagination. "Pornography is simply a masturbation fantasy written down," she claims, and we can immediately see the truth and simplicity of the statement. But Brophy is not about to let us, or Western culture, off the hook so easily, and expands her argument to all creative fiction. If pornography is a transcribed—albeit in an altered and shaped form—masturbatory fantasy, then so is all fiction. For what is fiction writing—in short story or novel form—but a transcribed daydream. And, taking her cue from Freud, Brophy convinces us that all daydreaming is a direct offshoot of, and uses the same narrative and emotional underpinnings as, the masturbatory fantasy. While non-pornographic novels have a lot more on their minds than sex (as does a lot of writing we might label erotic or pornographic), it would be a mistake to think that the sexual impulse does not mightily inform the fiction of writers from Jane Austen to Tom Clancy, from Anthony Trollope to Danielle Steel.

It is difficult for anyone to be able to write authentic, emotionally honest, psychologically true, and sexually explicit experiences and fantasies in our culture; for gay men it is near miraculous. We are told, from our earliest years, to repress, hide, lie, and distort our gay desires. So is it any wonder that when gay men put pen to page—or fingers to keyboard—that they have a problem writing without hesitation or self-censorship? The bottom line is that it takes hard, often unnerving, work to write honestly about gay lives. The process by which gay men learn and continue to write honestly about our sexuality is an arduous one; before the writing has begun we must first be honest with ourselves. We must forthrightly face our sexual desires and feelings. This is harder than it might seem. It would be easy simply to transcribe a routine sexual fantasy—you want to fuck the policeman you saw earlier that day; you want to do it in the back of the police car while it is stuck in traffic; you want him to keep his hat on while you push his knees over his head—but it is much harder to get at the less-than-immediate emotions of the situation: What are your real feelings about police or men in authority? Is the fucking an act of revenge against an established homophobic institution? If your semi-public sexual activity is, in part, an act of humiliation, what does that say about your feelings about gay sex? Is it a rape fantasy, and what does that tell us about the relationship between sex, power, and violence in your fantasy life?

Writing honestly is not easy. Good writing about gay sexual desire and activities depends completely upon the writer's ability actively to pursue, mediate, and interrogate the endless labyrinths of his sexual imagination. Once the process has started, it is never-ending, for the sexual imagination is never static; unrepressed, it will flourish and thrive, shocking and surprising us with its often Byzantine and rebellious manifestations. Remember: self-repression of the imagination is an active, intentional act. It may be culturally induced and supported, but we must take responsibility for letting it shape and control our lives and minds. Writing—and thinking—as truthfully as we can is an act of resistance. Muriel Rukeyser, in her poem "The Speed of Darkness," wrote: "What would happen if one woman told the truth about her life?/The world would split open." Writing honestly about our sexuality and desire is a way of changing our lives as well as the world.

We are now facing new waves of social and political discrimination and repression—at once a confirmation of how far we have come in demanding our liberation, as well as a continuation of the hatred with which we have always had to live—but also the incalculable effects of AIDS on all of our lives. AIDS, whether we are personally living with it or not, affects our waking and sleeping hours, our thoughts, our work, our imaginations, our sexuality, and our writing. What is the effect of AIDS on sexual writing? It has heightened our awareness of the importance of writing about sexual topics. We can no longer view gay male sexuality or sexual activity with ease; it is no longer possible to contemplate sex—even in the realm of fantasy—without considering possible consequences. As our relationship to sex has become problematic, our relationship to sexual *fantasy* has become even more important. Sexual activities—even safe sexual activities—we might have considered exploring without a second (or even a first) thought fifteen years ago, we now view with suspicion and hesitate to perform.

Fantasy has always played a major role in the gay male sensibility —it has allowed us to imagine ourselves in a world that would deny our existence; to create, to invent contexts and social spheres for ourselves that allowed us to have lives and dreams. Sexual writings have traditionally played a huge role in the development and evolution of gay male sexuality. Michael Lowenthal notes in his introduction to *The Best of the Badboys:* "In reading someone else's fantasy, and in judging which parts do and don't turn me on, I am forced to own up to my innermost thoughts. Yes, I really do wish I could fuck the high school kid who bags groceries in the supermarket. Yes, I want to know what it feels like to whip somebody with my belt. Yes, sometimes I find it more erotic to watch a man with his pants on than with them off. The beauty of porn is that it allows you to experience a fantasy, even if you have no interest in the reality. When Aaron Travis writes about a slave being forced to drink piss, I feel the hot, bitter liquid gurgling in my throat—even though I honestly never want to try this experience. Porn allows me to rape, and to be raped—when I would never practice or desire sexual coercion in my real life."

Writing honestly about sexual activity and sexual fantasy in the age of AIDS is a way to assert the power of our desire and our imaginations over the disease. When AIDS enters into a piece of writing, it is often a way to control and mediate our relationship with the disease. When AIDS does not appear boldly in the text, it is nevertheless always there, lurking, and haunting the imaginations of both the reader and writer. The more honestly we face—and write about—our sexuality, the more honestly we are going to be able to face our fears and anxieties about AIDS.

And this brings us to the question of the connection between the sexual imagination and the act of literary creation, for good writing is obviously more than simply transcribing—no matter how faithfully or honestly—our fantasy, or actual, lives onto the page. What makes writing "good" is, to some degree, a mystery. What works for some readers does not work for others. Correct grammar might seem to be a prerequisite, except for those times that innovative grammar is both more "correct" and effective. One would think that good stories might have a beginning, middle, and an end, but in our post-modern world those very definitions are constantly disputed. Even the traditional ideas about narrative—it must tell a story, it should convey a moral or an emotion, it should be clear and sustained—no longer carry the weight they once did. If the traditional ideas about good writing are slowly disappearing from our critical vocabularies, it is because they no longer provide sound, clear guideposts to evaluating how literature reflects our real experience. This is particularly true of sexual writing. How do we evaluate a piece of sexual writing? In some ways the old labels—pornography, smut, erotica— made this easier for us. Smut or porn were good when they turned us on, when we had a physical reaction —a hard-on—while reading the piece. A Supreme Court Justice once remarked that he didn't know the definition of pornography, but he knew it when he saw it. Undoubtedly, what he actually meant to say was that when he felt a boner under his judicial robes, he knew he was looking at the real thing. And while this definition is useful—erections are surely an indicator that the libido has been engaged—it is perhaps limited.

Writing about sex and sexuality can do many things. It can turn us on. It can make us think. It can make us question our own sexual desires and fantasies. At its best it can force us to look at the world anew. In all these ways, sexual writing—particularly if it is truthful and honest—is no different from any other writing: it makes us see reality in a fresh and often revealing way.

The stories in this collection were chosen because they embodied what seemed to me some element of sexual honesty. Some of the pieces are traditional, realistic "porn" narratives; others are first-person tellings of "true-to-life" sexual adventures; there are pieces about obsessional romance and pieces that transmogrify sexual desire to violence or compulsion; there are stories that revel in their fantasy while others explore the often-tenuous connection between hard-core reality and the fantastic sexual imagination. I chose to call these narratives—and the book—"sexual writing" not only because I think the labels "porn" and "erotica" limit, or preconceptualize, our relationship to the work, but because I wanted to indicate that the pieces, while concerned with sex and eroticism, are connected to the broader realm of writing and literature.

As I read through the submissions for *Flashpoint*, I had three criteria in my mind: Does the story stir the imagination? Does it open our minds in new and surprising ways? Does it unfold new possibilities for, and in, our imagination? At their best ,the writings here do, I believe, reach a level of emotional and imaginative honesty that distinguishes them from other pieces of porn or erotica that rely on routine or simplistic formulas. It is possible that not all of the pieces here will give you an erection—erections, like preferences in movies and ice cream flavors, are engendered by the most idiosyncratic tastes—but they will all attempt to startle you out of sexual preconceptions, ignite your imagination, and—most importantly—make you think more openly and honestly about sex.

# The Transfiguration of Everyday Life

Gay people—and gay men in particular—have always been accused, by mainstream culture as well as conservative ideologues, of being *obsessed* with sex. And the reality is that it is true. We are obsessed with sex. And it's a good thing. Sexuality and eroticism are extraordinarily powerful forces in all of our lives and gay culture acknowledges and supports that. One of the important ways that our sexualities and our sexual perspectives are reinforced is through sexual writing. We often read to be transported from our everyday existence, and pornography, and other forms of sexual writing, perform this function very well. They let us engage in fantasies we might not have instigated ourselves, they encourage us to ruminate on sexual scenes and activities in which we do not usually partake, and they give us the vicarious pleasure of sexual excitement without the commitment of physical presence.

But sex—and sexual writing—can also allow us insights into the everyday world in which we are immersed. Much of the vitality and social power of gay culture is its preoccupation with sex. When we begin to view the ordinary through the lens of sexual experience, or a sexualized sensibility, it begins to look quite different. Mainstream culture is predicated upon repressing or denying sexuality—Freud hypothesizes this in *Civilization and Its Discontents;* Jesse Helms, Newt Gingrich, and their cronies see it as their political mandate—and gay culture, by its insistence on the importance of sexuality, challenges this. Gay culture and gay sexuality view the world from the position of an outsider, which grants us a privileged, critical critique of how the world works and how it might be changed. Each of these stories involves characters and situations that at first seem average, even mundane—an unhappy gay male relationship; a sexual encounter in the movie theater; a swim at the YMCA; a camping trip—but the texture and shape of the experiences are seen in a new light when viewed in the context of erotic and sexual feeling and action.

When Will Leber's story, "Sucked In"—involving an ACT UP demonstrator, a secret service agent, a loaded gun, and some heavy-duty, aggressive sex play—appeared in *Flesh and the Word 2* it caused a sensation. Leber mixed sex, violence, and queer rage in a crucible of power and politics, and the effects were unsettling and stimulating. Here in a new story, "The Comforts of Life," he brings the same incisive understanding of how sexual attraction, anger, and power feed off one another to his portrait of a troubled gay relationship. While the idea of fidelity is the ostensible "trouble" in Leber's characters' lives, his careful, detailed delineation of their unspoken sexual desires and fears is what gives the story its power.

Chris Bram's "New York 1942" (excerpted from his novel *Hold Tight*) tells the story of Hank Fayette, a gay sailor who, after he is caught in a gay brothel, ends up becoming a spy for Navy intelligence and the FBI during World War II. But Bram is interested in more than a playing out of a standard gay fantasy. In this excerpt, Hank has to face the ways in which his sexual desires for men are in direct conflict with the racism with which he was raised: he has no trouble breaking the social taboo of having sex with a man, but he cannot conceive of dancing with an African-

American. Sex here becomes the instigator of social consciousness, and Hank discovers that "thinking with his dick" might mean more than just having sex. By placing his concerns in a historical context, Bram forces us to look at how society and history, as well as individual lives, are affected by sexual desire and action. Although *Hold Tight* was published in 1988, the story is reprinted here to acknowledge and commemorate the continuing struggle of lesbians and gay men who are fighting to serve in the U.S. armed forces.

Philip Gambone's "YMCA" (an excerpt from his forthcoming novel *Pushing Off*) is a fine, detailed description of how the sexual imagination instills itself in our every waking moment. As Gambone's narrator swims his laps and showers at the YMCA, he reflects on the state of his life and the immediacies of everyday living. These mundane, passing wanderings often revolve around eroticism, and Gambone, who has always been an astute chronicler of gay male life, presents a striking portrait of how sexuality, infiltrating itself in the most uncommon places, transforms how we see and experience the world.

At first, "The Five of Us" looks like a traditional coming-of-age porn narrative—five friends go on a camping trip and end up having sex—but H. L. Wylie's deft telling of the story makes it more resonant than other, more formulaic, versions. His straightforward, plain-spoken storytelling convinces us not only of the story's sexual and emotional authenticity, but hits a profound cultural note that rings true. These are the boys from *Our Town* or a Sherwood Anderson story transposed to a homoerotic world of lust and playful sadism that feels as American as apple pie, Fourth of July nationalism, and incipient violence. U.S. literature has always had a dark side: maleness and violence are intrinsic to the classic American novel, and Wylie plays with the form—teasing us with it, turning us on; we are kept on the edge, unsure of what is going to happen next, or how we are to read the story. By overtly sexualizing the boys-in-the-wilderness theme, "The Five of Us" shocks, surprises, and allows us to view other, more familiar writing, in a new and radically different light.

# The Comforts of Life
*Will Leber*

Robert has always got an answer to everything. It can be damn annoying. Sometimes it makes me wonder why I love him.

I had set a beautiful table. Our gold-rimmed china, the real silver, long-stemmed crystal, starched napkins, and flickering candlelight. But now we sit amidst the aftermath of dinner, a crumb-strewn and wine-stained tablecloth rumpled up under dirty, not-yet-cleared dishes. Robert's sister, Sue, and her husband, Ed, have just spilled their guts. There is something wrong with Ed's sperm, and though they've tried for over a year, he can't get Sue pregnant. I am floored when Sue pops the question. "So Brian, we're still hoping to do it naturally." She smiles at me. "If we can get a little help from our friends."

"Brian?" Robert starts laughing.

"What's so funny?" I glare at him between the waning flames of the candles.

"I'm sorry, but the idea of you being a daddy...it just tickles me."

"This is not the way this conversation was supposed to go." Sue pushes away her dessert. "This is serious and it's between Brian and me!"

"Maybe we should leave." Ed downs the last of his wine.

"God, Sis, it's almost like incest," says Robert.

"I think we should talk about this another time." I touch Sue on the shoulder.

"Well, Sue," Robert sips his wine before going on, "it's no big deal if Brian doesn't do it. You can always go buy one in Russia or Romania."

After our guests depart, I stand at the sink and contemplate the floodlit garden while I soap off the plates and line them up in neat rows in the dishwasher. Robert plunks down another armload on the counter.

"You should be more considerate of your sister." I look at him over my shoulder.

"I think I am extremely accommodating." Robert hugs me around the waist from behind. "How many brothers would be willing to loan their boyfriend for stud service?"

"It's weird." I hoist the new stack of plates into the sink.

"You know, we should really think about getting that life insurance that I've been talking about." He hangs his head on my shoulder. I smell the red wine—Cabernet—on his breath.

"When are you going to quit beating that dead horse?"

"Sue and Ed are doing it, and they've only been together five years, half as long as us. We should do this, honeybuns. It's not about death anymore, it's a smart move for our retirement."

"We're only thirty-five for Godsakes! And they're doing it because they worry about supporting the baby if something should happen to them."

"If they ever have a baby."

"And anyway, Rob, they don't just give faggots big life insurance policies." I wiggle my butt in his crotch to remind him of who we are and what we do. "And I already told you I am not going to get tested."

"But Brian, if you decide to go through with this baby thing, you'll have to get tested. You have nothing to fear. It'll be negative. Mine was. You've done nothing that put you at risk."

I have not told Robert about my recent forays outside our relationship. I have not told him about my adventure in a sex club. I have not told him about yesterday:

*I decide to take our dog, Biscuit, for a walk in Golden Gate Park. I let Biscuit lead me on, his nose to the ground, out past the golf driving range to the soccer fields. I break the rules and let him run off the leash and dig at the gopher holes. As we walk down the path between the field and the road, we pass a mustached man sitting in a parked convertible. He says, "Hey! I love your retriever. Can I pet him?"*

"I'm going to go ahead with the policy." Robert kisses me on my neck. "I wish you would, too. It's for you, for us, for our security. Trust me."

"You always know what's best for us, don't you? You've got the savvy."

"Look around," Robert boasts. "What we've built together is no accident. We've just begun to enjoy all the comforts of life!"

*The guy jumps over the door frame out of the convertible. Very macho. His hair is black, trimmed close on the sides. A stub of sideburn extends to the bottom of his ears and a shock of hair wedges across his forehead. He squats down like a farmer and lets Biscuit smell his hand. "Good boy." He strokes the dog and looks up at me with a twinkle in his eye. "What's your name, mate?"*

*"Brian." I reach to shake his hand. It is meaty, firm.*

*"Cameron. It's a pleasure."*

*"Are you British? A tourist?" He is still holding my hand.*

*"Australian. I'm visiting friends."*

"At least you still enjoy my attentions." Robert's right hand is at my crotch. "How convenient—you're hard and I'm horny."

A plate slips from my soapy hands and shatters in the white porcelain sink. "Shit," I huff. "There goes the set of china."

"Don't worry about it," Robert rubs my neck. "I'll get another one at Macy's. Let's have sex." He turns me to face him and we kiss.

*We watch the dog race through the empty soccer field. Biscuit rolls over, scratching his back on the brilliant green grass with his feet pointed up in the air. Then he runs straight at us, veering off at the last moment and barking at us to pursue. I lunge forward as if I'll chase him. He runs off again. Cameron imitates the dog. He barks and runs toward me. I backpedal, fending him off. He catches me, stares into my eyes, and licks my nose.*

Biscuit comes to investigate the crash. He saunters into the kitchen from his fireside nap in the living room. He tilts his head at us quizzically, like dogs in TV commercials. He barks. Whenever we kiss, he barks. It's as though he is complaining because he isn't the center of attention. "Wanna go in the bedroom?" Robert asks.

"No, let's do it here." I run my wet hands through his hair. I sit up on the counter and wrap my legs around his waist. "It would be a little different." Biscuit woof-woofs.

"Out!" Robert slips from my legs and chases Biscuit and closes the kitchen door. He whimpers beyond it.

"You're suddenly in a feisty mood."

"I want to fuck your brains out." Robert lifts me from the counter piggyback-style, only I'm mounted on his chest instead of his back. He stares into my eyes and unexpectedly slaps my ass.

"Ouch! That hurt; what's got into you?" I jump to my feet.

"You said that we needed to spice up our sex life, right?"

"Yeah."

"So, you've been a bad boy, haven't you?" He spanks me again. "You like it?"

I find it arousing in a weird way. I think about the sex club, the park, that muscular waiter I slept with two years ago. I rub my erection against Robert's thigh. A shiver runs through me and I flash to a childhood memory of the time I stole a chocolate bar from the supermarket. I devoured it as I hid in the back seat between head-high grocery bags. I rolled the wrapper into a tiny ball and chucked the evidence out the window.

"I've been so bad," I say.

"Take down your pants, boy."

"Yes, sir."

"Push 'em down to your ankles. Take off your T-shirt and bend over and touch your toes."

"Yes, Daddy. Don't hurt me, Daddy. I didn't mean to do it, Daddy." I over-act a scenario I've seen many times on video, and wiggle my naked butt.

"You've been bad." The first skin-to-skin blow makes me throw back my head. He slaps me two, three, four times before he rests. He rubs my buns. The rubbing intensifies the burning sensation and makes the rest of my body feel cold. I get goose bumps and my nipples peak. "I want to fuck your little red butt. I'm going to go get a condom."

"Wait, I've got one in my pocket." I don't want him to leave and break the mood. "Let's do it on the table." My pants shackle my ankles as I shuffle across the tiled floor.

"I'd like to just butter up your butt like Marlon Brando in *Last Tango in Paris*." I lean against the edge of the kitchen table between the two caned chairs. It is a small, marble-topped bistro set that we bought because it reminded us of the sidewalk cafes in Paris. He squats down, reaches into my left pocket, and comes out with keys and two Trojans. "I love your buns. I love all the little soft blond hair. I love that it's blushing." He starts licking my crack with just the tip of his tongue. The point slips in and I reflexively tighten up.

"Let me in," he demands. "Let me lick it."

"That's not safe sex."

"You don't have anything."

"We don't know that." He stands back up and gives me a double-handed smack. His palms stick to my ass like buzzing flies to a glue strip.

"You do what I tell you, boy." Rob turns me to face him and shoves the condom in my hand. "Put it on me."

"Yes, Daddy." He thumbs my nipple. The dog starts to scratch at the door. "Go lie down, Biscuit!"

He unzips his khakis and lets them drop. His bobbing dick surprises me. "When did you quit wearing underwear?" I ask.

He smiles slyly and guides my hand to his cock. The little circle of latex won't budge at first, but suddenly gives and rolls over the ridge of his corona. The dog punctuates his scratching with yelps and whimpers.

*Cameron rubs his hard-on against my thigh. I look up at a blue sky battling the onset of the afternoon fog. A soft gray edge relentlessly proceeds from the ocean. It has nearly covered this end of the park, nearest the beach. There is a chill in the air. Biscuit dances at our feet.*

"What are we going to use for lube?" Rob asks between sloppy kisses.

"This," I answer and spit into my right hand.

"Nasty boy. Naughty boy."

"Help me up on the table."

He grips me by the ribs as I do a little leap and he guides me into a sitting position on the tabletop. The marble slab feels extremely cold on my red, bare bottom.

"What do you think about when I fuck you?" asks Rob. I try to ignore the question while I kick off my shoes and use my toes to push off my pants. "I asked you a question, boy."

"Fuck me." I put more saliva on my butthole. I bend my knees and rest the arches of my feet on his hipbones. I try to pull Rob to me by his arms and lose my balance. The table starts to go out from under me.

"This table is a little rickety." He catches me and sits me upright. "I like it."

"Here, hold on." He places my hands behind his neck and I interlace my fingers. He has a sixteen-inch neck. I know because I buy his dress shirts. His cockhead presses between my spread legs. He worms it into me. Slowly. "Tell me about your fantasies." He looks directly into my eyes. "Do you think about big, burly, football players fucking you after a hard workout?"

*Birds chirp in the pine tree off in the distance. "You're so handsome, mate." Cameron rubs my crotch while he kisses me. "I'd love to do it with you." His thick lips nibble at my nose.*

*"But we can't here. I have the dog." The fog has blanketed the sky.*

"*Tie up the dog. We could go in those bushes. Isn't that what they're famous for?*"

Rob is all the way inside me. I lie back on the frigid marble slab.

"Do you think about surfers?" Rob give me a hard thrust.

"I only think about you and your huge tool," I say, trying to sound raunchy.

"Do you think about blond lifeguards?"

"No, dark hair."

"Doing it in the back end of a pickup truck with a carpenter? Taking his hammer-head up you?" Robert pumps me, twists my nipples. He's got me. I feel my cock harden in my fist.

"No, in the bushes," I say.


"Why are you always cruising other guys when we're out together?" Rob hands me back my drink, which he's been holding while I went to the restroom. We are in a Castro Street video bar. A standing-room-only crowd of mostly white, under-thirty, preppy boys squeezes us.

"I can't help it if somebody talks to me," I say.

"He handed you his card." Robert glares at the guy. He sports a Cal Berkeley sweatshirt, a baseball cap, and thick, sensual lips.

"So what. I'll never call him. You can have it if you want it."

"Why would you want it?" Robert puffs up his chest and crosses his arms, and his biceps bulge forward. He's been going to the gym four days a week lately. We have become competitive. A way to battle age. A response to mid-life crisis. He's taken to wearing tight T-shirts and rolling the sleeves.

"Screw you. Some attractive man just talks to me and you go anal with jealousy."

"Lest I need to remind you," Robert gives me a goose, "you're the one who is anal in the family. And I'll remind you good, soon as we get home."

"It's got you revved up. Hasn't it?"

"What?"

"Your jealousy."

"I'm not jealous." Robert slips his hand into my rear jeans pocket, grabbing a handful of my butt. "What's this?" He comes out with a fistful of condoms, two pre-lubed and one flavored.

"I always carry them." I reach to take them back. "I don't know why." The men surrounding us let out a collective chuckle.

"You plan to have Mr. Berkeley fuck you?"

"Don't embarrass me, Robert."

"I tried to overlook how you always seem to have them on hand. But, Brian, let's be serious. There is only one reason that you need them. Is it someone I know? Or are you doing it with bar-trash?"

"So you think that I'm a slut and you're a saint?" I speak through gritted teeth directly in his ear. The young guy in a polo shirt to my right glances at us and moves away.

"Back to the condoms."

"You think I don't know that you fuck around when you are out on the road? Do you think that I am that naïve?"

"Don't be coy, Brian, I can feel it when I touch you. We've been together ten years, you know."

"Does the name Joseph sound familiar?" I down the last of my cocktail. "I found his name and number in your suit when I took it to the drycleaners. Is he your other woman?"

"Come on, Brian. I've told you before that all I've ever done is jerk off with a couple guys when I've been traveling. And always clean-cut guys who I'll never see again. Anything I've ever done is safe—always safe. And I've told you. That's our agreement, right? No secrets?"

"You're just jealous that I'm more popular." The men beside us pretend to hear nothing and stare at the screens.

"I hope you realize that if someone else screws you—it will kill me."

"I could use the insurance."

"It's not funny. Can't you see I've been going crazy? I've imagined all kinds of things. Is somebody fucking you? I need to know what my risk is!"

"So your concern is actuarial?" I spit out the words. "It's a damn risky world."

"So far, we've been spared, we've been lucky. Look where promiscuity got Tommy. Do you want to get AIDS?"

"How dare you accuse Tommy? He was no whore."

"Tell me!"

"I went to a sex club, okay? I chased naked men with huge dicks around and begged them to fuck me heavy and hard."

"How could you?" Robert elbows me out of his way, heading for the door. "How could you do this to us?" I watch him go.

"Excuse me, excuse me," I apologize to every video-entranced moron who stands in my way. I slink up to the bar and order a double.

It's much darker in this bar than in the video bar. It's smoky and just as packed. It's even harder to navigate the crowd. I step on toes as I head to get a drink. Someone feels me up as I slide past. I order a tequila shot and chase it with a beer. The fast lane to oblivion.

I think of Robert in the BMW speeding up to his favorite Pacific Heights haunt to sip martinis with the sweater set. Let him tell his sorrow to a sympathetic boy in tasseled loafers. I hope they go home to the boy's doorman building and watch the city lights while they sip from fluted glasses. I hope they relax on a leather sofa, Brahms in the background, and do it safely. I hope they mutually masturbate with flawless hands of unbroken skin. I hope their ooh-aah moment comes over them like a gentle breeze too weak to disturb the perfection of the boy's coiffeur.

It's a sexy crowd. Hot, evil-looking studs with goatees shoot pool. They bounce the sticks between their legs while contemplating their next shot. Lots of piercings: ears, a few noses, a couple eyebrows. There are collegiate types mixed in with the queers. A few guys in leather hoist a round of draft beers in the corner. A drag queen entertains from a bar stool, crosses her legs and blows smoke rings. I think about the cute queer-boy I jerked off with in Trouble. What a name for a sex club. Why didn't I tell

Robert the truth: that I'd done no sucking, no fucking—nothing so dangerous as he imagined?

I order another beer and loiter in the shadows. Maybe I should just go back to Trouble, let loose, and get it out of my system. I check my watch. It is past eleven.

A tap on my shoulder causes me to turn face-to-face with Cameron. He smiles broadly, "Fancy meeting you here." He takes my hand and pulls me into a circle of guys who look all of the same mold. They stand like dashboard puppets with torsos as rigid as painted wood and heads bobbing on springs.

"Don't be shy," Cameron says, and kisses me on the lips. I am surprised he is talking to me after I refused his advances two weeks ago in the park. "This is Brian." He presents me to the circle, and their heads bounce in turn as he calls their names. He stays close. His arm brushes mine.

"We're off to the disco," pipes up one of the gang. "Want to come?"

"Not tonight," I answer, and turn to say good-bye to Cameron.

"I'm going to hang out here a while, mates." Cameron winks and gives a thumbs-up to them as they file out. He steps in front of me to whisper something in his friend's ear, and he leans his butt against my crotch. I start to get hard.

With the coterie gone, he comes alive for me again. He wears a loose tank top. The large armholes expose the beef of his pectorals and barely conceal his nipples. The little brown circles are revealed momentarily as he moves his shoulders. My excitement blossoms. It is as if we were back in the park. I feel lightheaded.

"How about a shot?" I ask him.

"Sure, let's party," he says, and follows me to the bar.

There is a vacant stool and Cameron leans against its edge, half-seated. He turns so that I can muscle my way up to the bar. My hip rests between his legs.

"Bottoms up!" We clink the glasses and I down mine with my eyes closed. I feel Cameron's mustache scrape my lips and then his tongue slip in. I open and a warm rush of tequila washes between our sealed mouths. It's like fire. My free hand reaches for his crotch—grasps for the remembered excitement of his denim-constrained erection. We are twirling in the sunshine, flushed by the wind, heading for the bushes, and spinning out of control.

I finally swallow and open my eyes. I stare at a circle of neon advertising a brand of beer and blink at spotlights that illuminate lazy spirals of smoke. Cameron orders two beers. I hold my cold bottle by the base and rub the gooseneck lightly along Cameron's biceps. I catch the tip under the strap of his tank top and tickle his nipple with it.

"You make me shiver," he says and slips a knee inside my thigh. He rubs it against my erection.

"I'd rather make you sweat." I strike a pose: my head turned away at three-quarters, my shoulders back and tilted to the right, my beer held waist-high at a forty-five degree angle. Premeditatively cocky.

"So I'm finally going to get your pants down in the outback." Cameron chugs the last of his beer. "Let's go, mate. It's now or never. I go home tomorrow."

The cab circles a block off Market and heads toward downtown. We pass Polk Street. Cameron clamps my hand between his legs. We stop in front of a large gray building somewhere in the gritty Tenderloin district. Derelict drunks stumble down the sidewalk. I look up at the twisting ironwork of fire escapes clinging to the building's facade. The perspective makes me dizzy.

A long row of mailboxes lines the foyer. The building smells of onions and blood-stewed roasts. The elevator groans as it lifts us up and opens into a long, dim hallway.

Cameron ushers me through the door. I dodge a bicycle propped up against the wall. I look ahead into a tiny kitchen. Grimy dishes stick out of a sink of murky water like abandoned tires in a fetid swamp. Crusted glasses litter the drainboard. Cameron pulls a liquor bottle from out of the rubble. "Like a drink? More tequila?"

"Bring the bottle," I say and head into the adjoining living room. Tape cassettes and CDs are scattered across the floor. I step around the minefield and lie down on a futon in the center of the opposite wall. This is obviously where Cameron is crashing. He puts on some music and hands me the bottle before kneeling down on the lumpy bed.

I grab him by a nipple and he turns toward me. I am desperate to recapture the excitement that has brought us this far. I take a big swig of tequila, hold it in my mouth, and kiss him. Our tongues stir the tingling alcohol. I kiss him deeper and deeper. I gulp the liquor and suck his tongue. Our teeth gnash. The astringent, almost medicinal, taste of the alcohol emboldens me.

I set the bottle on the floor beside the futon and he lies on his back. I straddle his stomach on all fours, lapping at his mouth. I nibble at his nipples and he encourages me, "Oh yeah, oh yeah." I collapse down his length and rub against the hard mound of his crotch. I cannot distinguish the shaft from the head as I massage it through the tight jeans.

"Let's strip," he says between short gasps. We heave boots, T-shirts, pants, and socks over the side. He pulls off my underwear and presses naked against my butt. I wrestle him down onto his back and sprawl on top of him. He pinches both my tits at once and my cock jumps up. He squirms and rolls to his stomach. I feel him stretch out his arm and pull a box from under the table beside the bed. He rises up on his elbows and I hear him sniff. He holds a little vial to my nose.

"Want some?" he asks. I smell the poppers.

"No, I don't think so," I say, but I sniff anyway. He takes another hit and holds the bottle to my nostril. What can it hurt to get a little higher? I want that magic fog to cloud over me. As I inhale, the room grows hazy. I exist only where we touch. We float. I become Robert doing a Princeton rub to a blond-haired preppy. I am in the sex club dick-to-dick with that stud-boy. I'm in a locker room with the rude stars of a porn video. Cameron's hands, my hands, rub our bodies: more hands, more places than four hands can manage.

My body melds into this hot atmosphere of sensation. We are on our knees and he is behind me. I feel his cock, grown unimaginably huge, rub the crack of my ass. Then he is under me and beside me; we intertwine like serpents.

"Take another hit." He holds the cold rim of the bottle against my nose. "No," I hear a voice in the distance that sounds like mine. He squeezes my tits and I reciprocate, pinching his at arm's length. I lie down and he sits atop my stomach. My hand travels across his torso, over his pounding heart, and onto his dick. The head is the size and shape of a doorknob.

"I want to fuck," he says.

*We shouldn't. We need condoms. It's not safe. Not the first time. I'll let you fuck me. We'll be careful. Why not? I have condoms.* The voices confer off in a corner of the room.

I inhale instinctively each time the vial presses to my nose. *How do you want to do it? I don't usually get fucked. You want it. Fuck me. Yes. Yes. Yes.* The room is an oven. We melt and fuse and rise like baking bread. I enter him from above, force the air out of his lungs with a deep relentless plunge. He releases his breath with a scream. I'm inside him now. He twists and twitches. He rubs and rubs against me until the friction ignites. He viciously pinches my tits. We run across hot coals—mind over matter—sprinting for the other side. My cock becomes a flame-thrower. I spray fire into him and he launches incendiary missiles across the terrain between us. They explode on impact, hot blobs searing my chest and his. The conflagration spreads, and the flames consume us. We melt like plastic figures, collapse into a shrunken heap amidst the desolation of scorched earth.

Cameron lies on my arm, cutting off the circulation. A thousand pinpoints of pain prick my skin. His closed eyes seem more wrinkled, and the skin puffs up in charcoal rings beneath the sockets. A too-bright light shines from the hall. It exposes the disheveled room, the heaps of stinky laundry, the dark pools of stains in the carpet, the knotted bundles of our street clothes. I pull a wilted condom from the end of my dick. Why? I struggle to free my aching arm from Cameron's weight. Why? I stand and pull on my clothes.

"Where are you going?" Cameron stirs from the ashes. "Stay."

"I've got to go." I race for the door.

I wave down a yellow cab and give the driver my home address. I imagine Robert sitting up in the living room like an angry father. "What time is it?" I ask the cabbie.

"Just after two A.M."

"Thanks," I say and then I sneeze. Blood suddenly streams from my nose. My God, blood! I find a used tissue in my coat pocket and press it to the nostril. Damned poppers. Why? I'm panicked about blood and HIV and poppers and Robert. I can throw myself at Robert's feet, tell all, and beg for mercy. I can lie.

I stare at our burning porch light while I wait for change from the driver. I turn the key in the lock and swing the door open. Nothing is out of place. The reading lamp I turned on before leaving the house still illuminates the living room in a soft glow. The pillows are straight on the couch. There is not a fingerprint on the baby grand or a footprint on the Oriental rug. The seeming tranquility is shattered by Biscuit's insistent yelping. He scratches from inside the kitchen door. Robert can't be home. The sonofabitch is punishing me by tricking. I know it. How could he stay out all night? He knows I'll worry.

"It's okay, Biscuit," I call to the dog. "It's okay, baby." I carefully open the kitchen door and Biscuit frantically spins at my feet. He barks hysterically and refuses to calm down when I pet him. I see the message light flashing on the answering machine. I press playback. There are three messages. The machine's digital voice announces, "One."

"This is San Francisco General Hospital calling for Brian Collier. You are on the emergency call list in a Mr. Robert Jones's wallet. He has been mugged. Please call us..." The rest of the message blurs.

The machine beeps and announces, "Two."

"Brian, it's Sue. We're at SF General with Robert. He's been stabbed. He's lost a lot of blood. He's calling for you. Where are you?"

"Three."

"Brian, where the hell are you? We need you!"

I rush to the emergency room. It is full of crying babies and sighing adults. I wander through the spectacle and grab a woman in a white coat. "I need to find Robert Jones. He was stabbed. Where is he? How is he?"

"Who are you?" she asks.

"His lover," I answer. "Is he okay?"

"Come with me." She leads me through a locked door and down a hallway. We enter an automatic door marked INTENSIVE CARE.

Sue spots me coming down the hall and runs up to me, "Oh, Brian... It's been awful. I'm so glad you're here." Ed comes up beside her and they put me between them and wrap their arms around me. "He's resting now. He's going to make it," Sue reassures me with a tight hug.

"They cut him right up his gut." Ed looks me in the eye. "The paramedics said he kept saying to them, 'They were so well dressed!' He meant the gang that mugged him. Happened right off of Castro Street. Right in your own neighborhood. Can you believe it?"

"Can I see him?" I ask.

"Yes," answers Sue. "The nurses left us here with him. Come on."

The hospital scares me. My grandmother had an operation when I was a child and we waited for her outside the operating room. She died right after it and my mother blamed the institution. And I have visited too many friends in the hospital as they succumbed to AIDS. No wonder I think of them as places in which to die rather than recover.

Robert looks horrible. His face is bruised, predominately blue. He turns restlessly. His head moves from side to side. He says words to me that I can't quite make out. I hold his hand and kiss it.

"You're going to be fine," I say over and over until I realize I am saying it to comfort myself.

Robert's eyes open and he starts talking. I lean over him. I kiss his lips, just gently grazing the skin. His words suddenly become coherent, he says my name, "Brian."

"You're going to be fine," I say. I hold my ear just over his mouth.

"If I die...," he says.

"You're not going to die!" I squeeze his hand. He closes his eyes again. "I'm sorry." I hold Robert's palm to my lips and cry. "We should never have fought. It's all my fault. I love you. You're going to be fine. You're not going to die!"

"It's taken care of." His voice is weak. I watch a tear pool in each eye and roll down his cheek. "If I die..."

"You're not going to die!" I forget myself and start shaking him by the shoulders. I realize my mistake and just hold him tight.

He strains to get the words out. Sue and Ed draw close. "Brian," he reaches and grips my shoulder, "If I die, you'll be a millionaire!"

# New York 1942
*Christopher Bram*

Late one March afternoon in 1942, Seaman Second Class Hank Fayette entered the Lyric Theater on Forty-second Street.

The war was four months old. Hank was twenty. Tall and blond, a black pea coat buttoned over his uniform, he climbed the steps to the balcony two at a time, grinning like a kid at the gold ceiling, brass rails, and fancy carpet. There was nothing like this place back home in Beaumont, Texas.

Two sailors stood off to one side of the upstairs lobby and watched him pass. One nudged the other; the other shook his head. Hank wondered what they were considering, but he wanted nothing to do with them either. This was his very first day of liberty after two months at sea and he was sick of the navy. It was his first time in New York City and he wanted everything to be new. He'd spent all morning and most of the afternoon riding trolleys up and down this concrete beehive, getting a crick in his neck. There was something wonderfully unnatural about a place where buildings dwarfed the tallest tree. The city was straight out of the Planet Mongo in the funny papers.

The inside of the theater was as big as a circus tent, but the movie looked the same as movies in Beaumont, only taller. This was another one about the boy from the radio who talked through his nose. Hank almost turned around and went back out again, only he'd paid his four bits and there was no harm in staying long enough to see what happened. He stood at the back of the balcony, behind the partition, took off his bulky pea coat, and draped it over the partition. There were plenty of empty seats up here for the matinee, but theater seats never gave Hank enough room for his lanky legs. He tugged at the scratchy dress blues that pulled too tight across his butt and wondered if the guys had been only ragging him about this place. It was just a big old movie theater.

There was a sudden smell of cologne, sweet and boozy. Then the smell faded. Hank looked left and right. He saw the back of a man sliding off to the right. The pointy crown of the man's half-lit hat was turning, as though he'd been looking at Hank.

Hank glanced back at the movie—Henry Aldrich was getting scolded by his mother—then looked around the sloping balcony. Someone got up, walked up the aisle, then sat down again. So many Yankees wore those funny shoulders that Hank wasn't certain which were men and which were women in this light. He looked up at the staggered windows of the projection booth and the beam of light that occasionally twitched inside itself.

The smell of cologne returned, and hung there. Hank waited a moment. When he turned around, he found himself looking down on the spotless brim of a hat. The man stood only a foot away. Like most people, he was shorter than Hank.

The man looked up, his face slowly appearing beneath his hat. He had a smooth, friendly face and a red bow tie. "You're standing improperly," he whispered.

"Beg pardon?" said Hank. "Sir?"

"If you want to meet people, you should stand with your hands behind you."

The man sounded so well-meaning and knowledgeable, Hank

automatically took his big hands off the partition and placed them at his back in parade rest.

"And you're quite tall. You should hold them a little lower."

"Like this?"

"Let me see." The man stepped up behind Hank and pressed his crotch into Hank's hands.

The wool was ribbed and baggy. Hank cupped his hands around a loose bundle inside before he realized what he was doing. His heart began to race.

The man lightly cleared his throat. "Uh, you interested?"

Hank let go and spun around. He snatched the man's hat off his head so he could see him better. Strands of light from the movie flickered in the brilliantined hair while the man anxiously reached for his hat. He wasn't so old, maybe thirty, and not at all effeminate. Hank let him take the hat back, then reached down to feel the man's crotch from the front.

"Oh? Oh." The man pulled his brim back over his eyes, glanced around, reached down and touched Hank, tweaked him through the cloth. "I see," he whispered. "I don't suppose you have a place where we can go?"

Hank closed his eyes and shook his head. It felt so damn good to touch and be touched again. The cologne wasn't so strong once you got used to it.

"I live with my mother, you understand. But I have some friends downtown with a room we can use." He removed his hand and used it to take Hank's hand, rubbing a smooth thumb across the wide, hard palm. "Do you mind going downtown?"

"Hell, no!" Hank cried and pulled loose to grab his coat.

"Shhh, please. Discretion." But the man was smiling to himself as he nervously glanced around and nodded at the curtain over the exit.

Hank followed him out to the balcony lobby, where the two sailors still waited. "What did I tell you?" said one. "Trade."

The man didn't look at Hank, but walked quickly, trying to keep a step or two ahead of him. So even in the big city people were shy about this. Hank buttoned up his coat so he wouldn't show. He buried his eager hands in his coat pockets to stop himself from grabbing the man's arm or slapping him on the ass, he was so happy. His shipmates hadn't been teasing him when they joked about this movie house, laughing over why they wouldn't want to go there and why Hank might.

Out on the street it was almost spring, but a city kind of spring, just temperature. The other side of Forty-second Street was deeper in shadow now than it had been when Hank went inside, the penny arcade brighter. Gangs of sailors charged up and down the sidewalks, hooting and elbowing each other over every girl they saw, not understanding how much fun they could've had with themselves. Hank had understood since he was fourteen. Thumbing around the country or working at a C.C.C. camp, he had met plenty of others who understood, too. There had to be others on the *McCoy*, but living on a destroyer was worse than living in Beaumont. You had to live with them afterwards, which could get sticky if they started feeling guilty or, worse, all moony and calf-eyed. It should be as natural as eating, but people were funny and Hank did his best to get along with them. Most of his shipmates thought Hank was only joshing them or playing the dumb hick when he told them what he liked.

That Mongo skyscraper with the rounded corners stood at the far end of the street like a good idea. Hank's man stood at the curb, signaling for a taxi. The traffic was all trucks and taxicabs, with a lone streetcar nosing along like an old catfish. Finally, a square-roofed taxi pulled over and the man opened the door and signaled Hank to get in. "West Street and Gansevoort," he told the driver.

The man relaxed. He smiled at Hank, offered him a cigarette, then offered the driver one, too. "I thought our homesick boy in blue deserved a home-cooked meal," he told the driver. The men smoked cigarettes and talked about all the changes the war had brought about. The driver asked Hank all the usual civilian questions about home and ship and girlfriend. The man smirked to himself when Hank mentioned Mary Ellen, but he didn't understand.

They drove along a waterfront, the low sun flashing gold on the dusty windshield between the high warehouses and higher ships. It looked just like the area around the Brooklyn Navy Yard, where the *McCoy* was in dry dock. Suddenly, there was a long stretch of sunlight, and Hank saw the rounded metal ridge of a ship lying on its side in the river. "Poor *Normandie*," sighed the driver and said it was sabotage. The man said carelessness and stupidity; the two began to argue about how much they could trust the newspapers. The driver mentioned a house that had been raided in Brooklyn, where there were Nazi spies and all kinds of sick goings-on, but how the newspapers had to hush it up because they'd caught a Massachusetts senator there. The man abruptly changed the subject by asking Hank if he had any brothers or sisters.

The driver let them out beneath a highway on stilts, in front of a yellow brick warehouse whose cranes were loading another zigzag-painted ship. The man watched the taxi pull away, took Hank by the arm, and led him across the street, away from the river. "Almost there," said the man. "How long has it been? Two months? Oh, but this should be good."

"Hot damn," said Hank.

They walked up a cobblestoned side street, a long shed roof on one side, a snub-nosed truck parked on the other. Whatever the place was, it was closed for the day. Hank smelled chickens. There was a stack of poultry crates against one wall, a few feathers caught in the slats.

"Not the nicest neighborhood," the man admitted. "But what do we care, right?"

The street opened out on a square, a cobblestoned bay where five or six streets met at odd angles. Two flatbed trucks were parked in the middle. The entire side of a tall warehouse across the way was painted with an advertisement for Coca-Cola, the boy with the bottle-cap hat wearing a small window in his eye. There were houses on their side of the square, three of them wedged together in the narrow corner. The man went up the steps of the white frame house that needed painting and rang the bell. Hank stood back and wondered what the man looked like without his overcoat, then without any clothes at all.

A little slot behind a tarnished grill opened in the door.

"Hello, Mrs. Bosch," said the man. "Remember me?"

The slot closed and the door was opened by a horse-faced woman with a nose like a pickax. "Uf course I ree-member you. Mr. Jones? Or was it Smith? But come een, come een." She spoke in a weird singsong as she ushered them inside and closed the door. She wore an apron over her flowered housedress and smelled of cooked cabbage. "And you breeng one uf our luflee servicemen. How happy for you."

Hank was shocked to find a woman here. The women back home knew nothing about such things, which was only right. But Yankees were strange and this woman was foreign. Hank had never seen an uglier woman. She and the man weren't friends, but she seemed to know what they were here for.

"And you are smart to come earleee." Her voice went up at the end of each sentence. "There is another couple before you, but I think they are looking for courage and will let you go in front of them."

She took their coats and hats and hung them on a rack. The man hiked his trousers and winked at Hank. He looked nice and slim.

The woman opened a door to the right of the narrow stairway and Hank heard a radio. The man stayed back but Hank leaned forward, so he could see what was in there. It looked like an old lady's parlor, with a red-faced bald man and a pale boy sitting side by side on a flowery sofa. They kept their hands to themselves, demurely folded in their laps.

"How are we doing, Father? I mean...Mr. Jones," said the woman. "Will you mind if these two gentlemen go ahead and use the room?"

The bald man consented with a polite bow. He held up an empty glass. "Is it possible, Valeska...?"

"Uf course. For such a constant friend as you, anything. I will tell Juke." Pulling the door closed, she mumbled, "Drink me out of house and home, the hypocrite. So it is all yours. Leaving us with only one thing."

"Quite so," said the man, taking a billfold from inside his jacket. He handed her a bill while he looked at Hank, as if the money proved something. Hank was used to money changing hands for this. Sometimes people paid him; now and then, Hank even paid them. Money made some people more comfortable, but it was of no matter to Hank.

"And it has gone up a dollar since the last time," said the woman. "The war, you know."

The man smiled, shook his head, and gave her another dollar.

"Fine." She opened a door across the hall from the parlor and waved them inside. "I will be seeing you later. Enjoy."

The room was small, with scuffed linoleum patterned like a Turkish carpet, and cabbage roses on the wallpaper. It looked like any room in any boarding house, except the bed had no blankets, only sheets. When Hank heard the door click shut, he spun around and grabbed the man.

His hands were all over the man, inside the beltless trousers, under the shirttail, over soft cotton drawers and stiffening cock. The man kept his teeth together when Hank kissed him. He laughed when Hank got himself tangled up in the suspenders. The man unhooked the suspenders, stepped back, kicked off his shoes, and shed his trousers, then insisted on undressing Hank himself. He was already familiar with the uniform's complicated fly and thirteen buttons. Hank couldn't keep still; he touched and grabbed, undid the man's bow tie and shirt, yanked the man's drawers down so he could get a good look at him. Hank often had sex with clothes just opened or rearranged, like when he was hitchhiking or making do in a storage locker or the bushes, but what he really liked was stark nakedness, the way it had been those first times, when an aunt's hired hand had shown him what they could do together after their swim in the pasture pond, squirreling around in the warm, wet grass while cows watched. Girls were for marriage and families, guys for getting your ashes hauled.

In heaven and naked, Hank lay back and grinned while the man loved him with his mouth. Because he was paying, the man still seemed to think it was up to him to do everything, but Hank didn't mind lying still for this, a cool mouth and tongue admiring his cock. He held the man's crisp, brilliantined head with both hands, then stroked the man's neck and shoulders. Hank's hands were callused, so the man's skin felt very smooth. Hank slipped a bare foot beneath the man's stomach and brushed his leathery toes against the wispy hair and hard cock. With his other foot he stroked the man's bottom.

Hank wrestled the man up to him so he could feel more of him. After Hank's cock, the man didn't mind Hank's tongue in his mouth. He still wore his socks and garters, which Hank pried off with his big toe. The man had a city body, spongy where it wasn't bony, but the patches of warm, cool, and lukewarm skin felt good. Hank hummed and moaned and laughed without fear of who might hear them. They were safe here.

When Hank spat into his hand and reached between the man's legs, the man shook his head in a panic and said he didn't do that. So Hank got up on his knees, straddled the man, spat into his hand again, and did his own ass. The man watched in blank bewilderment, said he didn't like that either, then laughed and said, "You'll do anything, won't you?"

They ended up on their sides, curled into each other, their cocks in each other's mouths. Sucking while getting sucked was like having two people talk to you at once, but Hank enjoyed the game of doing to the man what the man did to him and, even upside down, the guy knew how to suck cock. The man was cut, so there was a round head with eaves and a smooth stalk to tongue. Hank pressed his foot against the cold wall and rocked himself into the man's mouth, his own full mouth murmuring and moaning around the man. Hank still wore his dog tags and they were thrown over his shoulder, jingling and rattling while the bedsprings creaked.

When it was time, Hank pulled his mouth back and let go with a string of yelps as it flew out of him. Before he finished, he was back on the man, twisting around to work his tongue against the best inch. The man was spitting and swallowing, trying to breathe again, but then he gave in to Hank, closed his eyes, and lay very still. Until the weight in Hank's mouth became harder than ever and, simultaneously, seemed to turn to water. The man finished with a shudder, gritting his teeth and sighing through his nose.

Hank wiped his mouth, climbed around, and stretched out beside the man. "Whew!" he said. "I needed that." He lay his leg over the man's legs and took a deep breath.

"Well," said the man. "You certainly seemed to enjoy it. How old are you?"

"Twenty." Hank gazed gratefully at his cock and the man's.

"I see. You've clearly been around. Uh, could you please let me up? We should be getting dressed."

"Naw. Let's stay like this. Wait a bit and have another go."

But the man was done for the day, maybe for the week. Beneath his politeness, he was slightly miserable. Still, better that than goo-goo eyes. Hank let him up and watched him wash off at the pitcher and basin on the dresser. His backside looked like dirty dough in the light of the bare bulb in the ceiling. Hank sprawled on the bed, hoping to change the man's mind, but the man didn't look at him until he was back in his suit.

"Is my bow straight?" he asked. There was no mirror in the room. He approached the bed and held out his hand. "That was thoroughly enjoyable," he said, shaking Hank's hand. "Good luck to you. Take care of yourself overseas." And he went out the door.

Hank smelled the brilliantine on the pillow one last time, then pitched himself out of the saggy bed. Yankees were no stranger than anyone else. The room was suddenly cold, the wash water colder. Hank quickly dressed, wet his hand, and flattened his hair. He wondered if there was time to find someone else before midnight, when he reported back to the Navy Yard.

There was nobody out in the hall. Then Hank saw a colored boy sitting on the stairs with a bundle of sheets in his lap. The boy slowly stood up. His hair was as straight and shiny as patent leather.

"You took your sweet time, honey," said the boy, only he sounded like a girl. He batted his eyes at Hank like a girl, and curled one corner of his mouth. "Miz Bosch!" he hollered. "The seafood's out!" He went into the room muttering, "See what kind of mess you and your girlfriend left me."

The horse-faced woman came out from the parlor. The radio was louder and someone inside was laughing. The woman grabbed a handful of sleeve at Hank's elbow. "Your friend is gone but you are welcomed to stay. I have a visitor who is having a paaaardy." She pulled Hank down so she could whisper, "You do not have to do anything. Just stand around and act like you are having a good time. There is food and beer. Yes?"

Hank didn't want to leave. He let the woman drag him through the door and heard her announce, "Look what I have. A saaaylor."

The bald man and pale boy still sat on the sofa, but there were new faces here. A laughing fat man with a mustache arranged food on a table: piles of sliced meat and cheese on sheets of delicatessen paper, a loaf of machine-sliced bread still in its wrapper, a handful of Hershey Bars. "Yes, welcome, welcome," the fat man boomed. "The more the merrier." Behind him stood a thin man with violet eyelids, hennaed hair, and hands like spatulas. He eyed Hank and smiled.

A soldier in khakis sat with one leg over the arm of the armchair in the corner. He seemed quite at home, and bored. He glanced at Hank with the same cool arrogance soldiers always showed for sailors.

"Yes, sir, a good time is worth all the ration stamps in the world," said the fat man. "Hey, Valeska. Where's that beer you promised?"

The horse-faced woman closed the door behind her, then immediately opened it again to tell the bald man the room was ready. The man and boy walked out, one behind the other, without a word.

"Thank God!" said the thin man when the door closed. "Now we can let our hair down."

"Now, now," said the fat man. "It's not her fault she's a priest. Just another victim of life's dirty tricks. Here, son. Help yourself to some of this fine salami. A growing boy like you must keep his strength up," he told Hank.

"He can help himself anytime to my salami," said the thin man.

Hank made himself two sandwiches while the men teased and flirted with him. Sex always left Hank hungry. He liked the men's friendly noise, but he didn't feel like touching them. The soldier, on the other hand, looked awfully good, even if he looked like the kind of guy who pretended to do it only for the money. Hank remembered how much money he had left and wondered how much the woman charged for use of the room. That would be a hoot, if he and the soldier went off together, leaving these two with their chocolate and salami. But the soldier only sat listlessly across his armchair, rocking his raised foot to the jingle that played on the radio.

The colored boy came in, carrying glasses and a pitcher of cloudy beer. Hank watched him more closely this time. He didn't mind the boy being colored—he liked that; it reminded him of home, but Hank had never seen a colored so womanly. The boy moved like a willow and swung his hips as he walked. Hank thought only whites, like the thin man, could be that way. The boy moved so gracefully he seemed boneless.

He set the pitcher on the table and caught Hank watching him. He did not look away but stared right back at Hank. He straightened up and perched the back of his hand on one hip. "What's the matter, Blondie? You a dinge queen?"

The fat man began to laugh.

"A what?" said Hank.

"If you ain't, don't go eyeballing me, Willy Cornbread," he sneered.

Uppity northern niggers: Hank couldn't make head or tail of them. He meant no harm by looking at the boy.

There was another program on the radio. New music came on, click-clickety and South American. It snapped the soldier to life.

He jumped up and began to jerk his knees and butt in time to the music. "Hey, Juke!" he called out to the colored boy. "Samba, Juke!"

The boy curled his lip at Hank and sashayed toward the soldier, already stepping with the guy as he approached him. They danced without touching at first, then the soldier actually took hold of the boy's hand and put his own hand on the boy's hip.

Hank couldn't believe it. The soldier looked Mexican or maybe Italian; he probably didn't know any better. But the fat man and thin man were amused, not shocked. And the two were good dancers, there was no denying that. The colored boy's baggy pants shimmied like a long skirt as he twitched inside them. The soldier's khakis tightened, went slack, then went tight again around his butt and front as he stepped to the music with all its extra beats.

"It must have been a sister who designed your uniforms," said the thin man as he passed Hank a glass of beer.

Hank watched the soldier and drank. The beer was homemade and tasted like wet bread. The soldier's hair was black and curly.

The song ended and the dancers finished with a twirl. Hank applauded with the fat man and thin man. Colored or no, it had looked like fun. Hank wanted to be able to dance like that. He set his glass down, wiped his mouth, and stepped in front of the soldier.

"Can you teach me that dance?"

The soldier was grinning over his samba. He grinned at Hank, then burst out laughing. "You, swab? I'd sooner dance with your cow, farmboy."

Hank was used to being taunted by Yankees, and there was nothing to gain by slugging the guy. "I can dance. Honest. Try me."

"No thanks, bub. I don't want my tootsies tromped on."

"You can dance with me."

It was the colored boy, looking up at Hank with a brazen smile.

He couldn't be serious. He was mocking Hank, sneering at the hick. His brown face was full of fight.

"This I gotta see," said the soldier, stepping back to the radio, tapping it as if that could hurry the program to the next song.

Hank just stood there.

"What's wrong, Blondie? You afraid you'll get soot on your hands?"

"No. Where I come from, whites don't dance with coloreds, that's all."

"Do tell. But do guys jazz with guys where you come from?"

"Sometimes." Hank didn't see what that had to do with it.

"But yeah. I know. You don't talk about it. While coons is something you talk about all the time. And that's all the diff. Come on, Blondie. Time you broke another golden rule."

More samba music was playing.

Juke did a box step to it, wiggled in a circle to it. "White dance. If this nigger can do it, you should too."

The boy was needling Hank, and Hank didn't like it, not in front of the others, especially the soldier. Maybe the soldier would like him if Hank showed he could dance with the boy. He moved his feet like Juke moved his.

"There you go, baby. Ain't so bad, is it?"

It wasn't, so long as Hank kept his eyes on Juke's two-toned shoes.

"Now move that tail of yours against the music. And step light. Shake that cowshit off your brogues. There you go, Blondie. Ain't you fine. Just like you and me was wiggling between the sheets."

Hank stopped dead.

Juke continued dancing. "What's the matter, baby?" No matter how sweetly he talked, his eyes had never lost their fight. "Oh, sorry. I forgot. You don't dig dinge. That's okay. I don't dig crackers."

"You're crapping me!"

"Am I ever, honey. And it feels so good."

Hank grabbed the front of Juke's shirt, but the boy was too small for Hank to hit. "Why you riding me like this? What did I do to you?"

Juke only pinched a smile at him, cool as ice.

The soldier rushed over. "Let the kid go," he said as he pushed his way between them. "Get your hands off him, you damn hill-billy."

"This is none of your damn business!" But Hank didn't want to hurt the boy; he only wanted to find out why the boy had it in for him. He released Juke, but Juke just stood there, not bothering to step behind the soldier.

"You want to pick on somebody your own size?" The soldier threw his shoulders back, pulling his uniform taut across his chest.

He was shorter than Hank but looked tough and muscular. He stood so close, Hank felt his breath when he spoke. Hank wanted to hit him and find what the body felt like. "Maybe I do. You want to step outside?"

"Maybe I do. Sucker!"

"Two big white boys," sang Juke. "Fighting over little old me."

"Shut up," said the soldier. "This is between me and him. Time you learned your lesson, hillbilly."

"I ain't no hillbilly, spick."

"I ain't no spick. I'm a wop, and proud of it."

"Oh, boys," said the fat man. "I do love it when the trade gets rough, but let's not go flying off the handle." The man stood beside them, gingerly patting the soldier on the back. "We're here to have fun. Juke? Bring these boys some beer."

Juke rocked on his hips a moment, then stepped over to the table. The soldier opened his fists and wiped his palms against his pants.

"And food? You haven't eaten a bite, Anthony. I know when I'm feeling ornery, there's nothing like a sandwich to calm me down." The man turned away to make the soldier a sandwich.

Hank and the soldier stood there, facing each other, catching their breath. Their bodies were still jumped into gear for a fight. Hank's muscles were humming; he ached to use them.

"You want to go off somewhere?" Hank whispered.

The soldier's jaw was still locked, but his eyes narrowed, surprised by the whisper. "To fight?" he asked.

"Nyaah. Not to fight." Once, it actually started in a fight, then, drunk and bruised, went one step better. Tonight, Hank wanted to skip the fight.

The soldier stared, then glanced at the others.

The thin man whispered and giggled something to the fat man.

Juke brought them their beer. "You're not going to let that fat queen talk you out of a fight, are you?" he whispered.

"Juke, fuck off," said the soldier.

The electric bell out in the hall rang. "Juke! The door!" the woman shouted in the distance.

"Shit. Ain't no Joe Louis here," sneered Juke and he left to answer the door.

"Oh, God," said the thin man. "Will it be more possibilities or more competition? And just when I made up my mind, too."

The soldier drank his beer and looked at Hank. "You're nuts," he said, but kindly.

Hank grinned. "What's that lady charge for a room? I'll buy."

"Yeah? Sheesh." The soldier shook his head in disbelief. "Like I was your whore? Uh uh. I'd go halves with you. Only I don't think the witch'll let us do it. She doesn't want to piss off her regulars."

"Is there somewhere else?"

"Maybe."

The two looked at each other and thought it over.

There were voices out in the hall, then something fell.

The door had been left open. Suddenly Juke was standing there, mouth and eyes wide open. He had already screamed, "It's the Shore Patrol!"

Hank wheeled around, but the only door was the one where the boy stood, and an arm with an armband and club had grabbed the boy's collar.

"Dammit to hell. Dammit to hell," the thin man hollered at the ceiling. "I'm sick of this."

"Fucking mother of God," the soldier shouted, jumped on the sofa, and tore down the heavy curtain. Hank jumped up beside him to help push up the window.

Someone grabbed Hank's ankles and yanked him off the sofa.

Hank jerked around and saw Juke gripping him while a Shore Patrol man pulled Juke backwards with a billy club across the boy's chest.

"Help me. Please," Juke pleaded. "I can't go back."

A woman screamed in the back of the house. The thin man stood there, cursing and spitting. The fat man stood with both hands raised over his head.

Hank swung his fist at the patrolman's face. The guy could not block the punch; his head jerked back and he let go of one end of his club. Juke scrambled over the sofa and jumped out the window the soldier had opened. The soldier had already jumped. Hank had his hands on the sill, a single light flared over a warehouse dock outside in the darkness, when someone grabbed the back flap of his jersey. Hank swung his fist and elbow behind him without looking.

Something hard banged his head. All at once, he was thinking every thought he had ever had: the excitement and burn of his first taste of liquor; his need to get through the window and back to his shipmates; his Baptist preacher's egg-smelling breath; his blinding anger during a fistfight with his father.

The thoughts slowed enough for Hank to notice he was on the floor now, sitting against the sofa. Everywhere were the canvas leggings of the Shore Patrol. Cold air poured through the open window behind him and there was scuffling outside. A man in a trench coat led the thin man, still cursing, out the door to the hall. And another man in a trenchcoat stood above Hank, a thin mustache across his upper lip, the hand at his crotch holding a square blue pistol.

Hank reached up to touch the pain on one side of his head.

"Don't move!" said the man, pointing the pistol straight at Hank's face. "You stinking fairy."

# YMCA
*Philip Gambone*

He began to ease himself into the pool. Goose bumps rose on his arms and legs. He never liked this part, the way the water inched up his thighs, chilling his crotch and belly. He sucked in his stomach, trying to pull away from the cold, wet assault. Sharp noises ricocheted off the walls: the sound of slapping water, the music from the lifeguard's radio, the sounds from the shower room every time someone opened the door. Listening to all this, he held himself there, stomach in, hands and arms pressed against the tiled edge behind him, his body hovering, half in and half out. Through his goggles, he could see the other swimmers. Among the seven or eight in the pool right now, he put himself in the middle as far as his body was concerned: hardly drop-down-dead-for (not like the guy in the next lane over), but not a floating watermelon either. His upper arms were firm, though he had to make a muscle to show off any bulk. His waist was an okay thirty-four. When he sucked in, he could make himself look even trimmer. As for his pectorals— "pecs" in the body lingo he was still learning—they were distinct enough, though hardly sculpted in the high relief he saw on some men here.

He braced his buttocks against the edge of the pool and brought his feet up, ankles together, toes pointed out, like a diver or a gymnast. In this position, his stomach looked pretty good, especially for a guy pushing forty. Sometimes, on the phone sex lines, he'd describe himself as having a "swimmer's body"; which wasn't really a lie, certainly not like the outrageous fabrications some guys would tell him over the phone. All in all, he guessed he had a decent body. A passable one. A body that still had a little something to it. On most days, he gave it a B+.

He relaxed his grip and lowered himself further into the water. The goose bumps rose again. And then he smiled: a B+. At Oakwood Country Day, some of his fellow teachers called him an easy grader. An encouraging grader, he would counter. Everyone needs a little encouragement.

He was up to his chest now, on tiptoes, his arms out to the side just above the water line, wriggling his fingers. He imagined he looked like a fledgling bird. He plunged his head under, then bobbed back up, letting his goggles clear. There were already two other swimmers in this lane, the medium lane, swimming their laps counterclockwise, up the right side and back down the left. He gauged their speed, waiting until one had gone midway down the right side and the other had reached the far end. Then, as the DJ on the lifeguard's radio announced the time—*Hey, Beantown, it's four twenty-three and we're gearing up for a fantastic weekend!* —Charlie pushed off.

He was always surprised at how effortless the first lengths felt. His strokes were easy and true, in graceful, athletic synchronicity, and suddenly he no longer felt like an awkward bird. *Hey, Beantown, it's four twenty-three and does Charlie Pellucca have fantastic form, or what?* In no time, it seemed, he had reached the other end of the pool. Quickly, he turned himself around and kicked off again.

For the past few months, he had been swimming at the YMCA, the big main branch on Huntington Avenue, just down from Symphony

Hall, the one he'd avoided for years. Three times a week, give or take a day, he'd show up after work and swim his half-hour routine, giving himself over to all the sensations he felt as he plied through this liquid world—to the light and color of the water, a slightly dingy aquamarine, not nearly as crystalline as the pool where Dennett swam these days; to the gray-green, mercury-vapor light overhead; to the way his torso twisted as he stroked; and to the images that would float up in his mind, pictures and ideas that his busy quotidian life usually crowded out.

He completed another length and turned again. He had never learned to negotiate one of those quick somersaulting flips like the one the swimmer ahead of him was doing. His own turns consisted of holding onto the edge of the pool with his left hand, bringing his legs up into a crouch, and pulling himself around, all the while fanning the water with his right hand. He'd learned to pull it off quite deftly. It almost looked like the real thing.

The guy in front of him had terrific buns. They were wrapped in a tight red Speedo that showed off the dimples in his cakes. And the way he kicked his legs: those well-muscled thighs and shapely calves. Charlie took in a big breath. He could swim five or six strokes without breathing, keeping his head under water, keeping the guy in sight. What was it about a man's legs that so turned him on? "A leg man": that's what his friend Arthur Hill called him. But if Charlie had to say, he'd call himself an everything man: a leg man, a face man, a blond-hair-and-blue-eyes man, a buns man, a basket man. He thought about Tap Callahan, the cute new guy on the maintenance staff at school, and wondered what kind of basket he had. With those baggy overalls he wore, it was hard to tell.

The guy in the red Speedo reached the end of the pool, did a perfect underwater flip, and headed back for the other side, all in one deft, graceful moment. Charlie got there a few seconds later, stopped long enough to catch his breath, then took off again. He swam like this for several more lengths, keeping Speedo's beautiful butt in sight. But he couldn't keep up the pace and eventually Speedo pulled far ahead. The other swimmer in their lane was fast, too. Charlie had to stop occasionally to let one or the other of them pass through.

Finally, Speedo took a breather. As Charlie approached the shallow end, he caught sight of Speedo standing against the wall. Even in the murky water, his suit was as red as the stormy weather beacon on top of the old Hancock tower. Charlie kept his head down, fixing his sights on Speedo's basket, swimming directly for it. Maybe he'd "accidentally" touch the guy, brush his crotch with his hand.

And then what?

His father used to sing a Neapolitan rhyme: *Quant' e bell' 'o mes' aoust'/Tutte le femmine senza bust'.* How lovely is the month of August/When all the women go without brassieres. Charlie used to be embarrassed when his father sang that ditty, but now—he was about the same age his father had been when he first heard Pop singing it—now it made perfect sense. It wasn't August but March, and the loveliness wasn't a pair of bobbing boobs, but this guy's dick underneath that tight red Speedo.

At the last possible moment, just as he would have plowed into Speedo's stomach, Charlie veered off, touched the end of the pool, and stood up. He stayed there a minute, panting athletically, trying to look exhilarated as he stared out down the length of the lane, concentrating—he hoped it seemed—on nothing but catching his breath. He didn't dare look at the guy. And then he stole a quick glance.

The rest of Speedo was as yummy as his buns and legs. He had a body *anyone* would call a swimmer's body: sleek, muscular arms; a small, tight waist; a nicely defined chest; and no body fat anywhere. Only his hair kept him from looking like one of those perfect California beach boys Charlie saw in the men's underwear catalogues. It was a mousy brown, in a kind of unruly crew cut that made him look a little like a street tough from Southie or Dorchester Irish, Charlie figured, which was always a pretty good guess in Boston. Guessing whether Speedo was gay or straight was trickier. It always had been for him.

Speedo kicked off again. Charlie waited a few seconds, took a deep breath, and followed.

As a kid, he'd not been athletic. And now, when he thought about why, he could come up with plenty of reasons: his father working six days a week at the dry cleaners and Sundays being for church and family dinners; or Nonna Gennaio declaring that sports were too rough, *troppo cafóne;* or his mother loading other activities, "cultural" ones, onto his plate—music lessons, art lessons, ballroom dancing classes. But none of these explanations fully convinced him. There was too much of the old absent father/dominant mother stuff there, a theory that didn't come close to describing what his childhood had felt like.

Only that one summer when his parents sent him to Dunster Academy for an enrichment program did he ever feel any keenness for athletics. There, along with his courses in American literature and music appreciation, he had learned how to play tennis and field a soccer ball. Still, with the end of that summer, his expertise and his interest had waned. It was not until he met Dennett— eleven summers later—that, in the first radiant happiness of being in love, he decided to give sports another try. That was the summer of 1980, the summer that together he and Denny had tried all sorts of things that neither of them had ever done before: a garden, a subscription to the Symphony, a weekend in Provincetown.

Back in those days, the gay gyms and health clubs had not yet hit Boston, not in the big way they did a few years later. But this hardly mattered, since he and Dennett had little interest in lifting weights or working with Nautilus machines. Sculpted bodies were not their thing: not for Dennett because, he said, there was little aerobic benefit in pumping iron; and not for Charlie because, though he didn't tell Dennett this, he couldn't imagine himself with a body that could call that kind of attention to itself. What they wanted, they told each other during that summer of 1980—Jesus, that summer he was still in his *twenties!*—was just some good, wholesome exercise. Just a way to keep in shape. And so, together, they had decided on swimming.

*Together.* There was a lot of magic in that word back then. The first year he was with Dennett, friends had complained that they never saw Charlie anymore. "You two do everything together now," they said.

"We're a couple," Charlie had answered, as if that explained it all. "I think it's important that we do stuff together." And together it was that they signed up at the YWCA.

Whenever anyone had asked them why the *YW,* they told them that it was more convenient than the YM; that the YW's pool was less crowded and the lap swimmers (mostly women) less likely to be aggressive and impatient with their slow, length-a-minute pace; and—this is what they always finally emphasized—that they could concentrate on their swimming and not be distracted by all the things that went on at the YM.

Now, eleven years later, Charlie tried to recall exactly what "things" he and Dennett used to hear. If there were specific stories, he couldn't remember them. Most likely, the ideas he'd picked up were all through innuendo. "Oh, yeah, the Y," someone would say, grinning, and everyone seemed to know what that meant. Back then, too, there was a song going around—"YMCA." Along with his friends, Charlie had chuckled and smirked at the lyrics, at the secret joke in those words about how much "fun" the Y was. But that song had given him one more reason to stay away.

And so, without ever discussing it, he and Dennett let each other know that the YM was not to their liking. For them, it remained as closed a world as those Brahmin gentlemen's clubs on Commonwealth Avenue: something other men joined. Not them. They would swim their chaste, wholesome laps at the YWCA. No one had ever written a song about *that.*

Suddenly, he veered into the flotation device, his arm knocking against someone in the slow lane. He stopped and clutched the float. Speedo swam by. Charlie let go of the line and tried to resume swimming, but it was hard to gain momentum when there wasn't a wall to kick off from. He felt himself sinking. He grabbed hold of the float again.

There was a story that had been going around Oakwood this week: One of the second-grade girls, when told how pretty she looked all dressed up for Grandparents Day, had exclaimed, "I don't want to look pretty!" And when her teacher said, "And what *do* you want to look like, Heather?" the little girl answered coyly, "I want to look sexy."

When the story passed through the faculty room, some of Charlie's colleagues had laughed, and others, Bonnie Becker included, said it was yet another example of the kind of message girls picked up from the prevailing sexist culture. Charlie understood both reactions. Later, at car-pool time, he had asked Bonnie, "Do you suppose there's a way to look sexy that isn't just capitulating to sexist culture?" It was the kind of question they'd been asking each other, on and off, for over twenty years.

He let go of the float and treaded water, trying to stabilize himself, but now one of the other swimmers in his lane had to stop in order not to bump into him. The guy looked miffed.

"Sorry," Charlie said, grabbing hold of the flotation line again.

The guy swam past. Charlie followed, dog-paddling his way to the other end and wondering if maybe even here, in the middle of the medium lane, he wasn't a bit out of his league.

The filter system at the YW had died back in January. At least a month to fix it, the attendant told Charlie the afternoon he showed up and found the pool closed.

"We'll give you an extension on your membership," she had said.

"What do I do in the meantime?" Charlie asked petulantly. In his eleven years of swimming at the YW, pool problems had been a frequent and annoying occurrence.

"What's the matter with the pool at the YMCA?" the woman had said. Almost as if that's where he really belonged.

All the way home that night, he had thought about it. What *was* the matter with the YM? Eleven years ago, he'd had visions of super-macho guys strutting through the locker rooms in skimpy towels, their muscles bulging, their looks competitive and unfriendly. He had assumed he would have been humiliated. Or had he *chosen* to feel that way? "Choice"—that big, adult word their therapist, Saul Rudginsky, had always emphasized.

It took him three days to tell Dennett he'd signed up at the YM. When he did, Dennett had made a face: skeptical and amused.

"It's the most convenient of all the pools I could use!" Charlie had protested. "It's just ten minutes from Oakwood."

Dennett smiled. It was like the smile Saul Rudginsky sometimes gave him, a smile that urged him to see he was *choosing* the YMCA, not just falling into it.

In the end, they opted for—chose—separate pools. Dennett signed up for a community membership at the University, out on Columbia Point. "Ten minutes from home," he noted.

A month later, when the YW's pool opened again, neither of them made any move to switch back.

His goggles were fogged now. It gave him an excuse to take another breather. Clutching the edge of the pool, he ran his finger around the inside of each lens to clear it. Speedo was at the other end, raising himself out of the water. Oh, those buns. They reminded him a little of Dennett's. "Grapefruit buns," Charlie used to call them.

He checked the time: four forty-six. Only seven minutes left. He was tempted to call it quits. He'd just swim to the other end. That would make about twenty-five minutes, and that was a decent workout. But as he swam, he couldn't shake the knowledge that it would be cheating. He didn't like to cheat, not really. He got to the other end and stopped again to readjust his goggles. Speedo was disappearing through the men's shower room door.

He checked the time again. Six more minutes. Speedo might still be in the shower six minutes from now. Charlie had seen that: guys leaving the pool well before he did, but still under the shower five, ten, even fifteen minutes later. He pushed off once more into the murky blue-green water.

At twenty-eight minutes, he quit. It was sloppy, he knew, but twenty-eight was close enough. He lifted his goggles onto his forehead, eased himself out of the pool, grabbed his towel, and headed for the shower room.

Speedo was there, his head bent under the nozzle, letting the fast, hard stream of water cascade over him. His red bathing suit was hanging limply on the faucet handle. Charlie selected a shower kitty-corner to Speedo's and turned it on. The burst of warm water felt good on his skin. He pulled his goggles down around his neck. It was sexier that way, this necklace of rubber and high-tech plastic. He'd seen the look in the underwear catalogues.

He slipped out of his bathing suit, a purple Speedo he'd bought in January when he first started coming here, and began to lather up. As he soaped himself, he stared blankly across the shower room, pretending to be in his own little world.

There were four other guys under the showers. He recognized two of them as afternoon regulars: a man who had to be in his seventies, with jowly cheeks and white skin. *Like a turkey in the meat bin at the supermarket*, he thought. The old man was standing under a shower head, slightly hunched over. When he turned around, Charlie could see brown moles and pink splotches on his back and flabby buttocks. Occasionally, perfunctorily, the man would pull on his penis, which was concealed by the folds of flesh that fell over his gut.

*This is what the body becomes*, Charlie thought.

The other regular was a man in his fifties, also paunchy, with a heavy growth of black hair all over his back and arms and butt. He was wearing a pair of black-framed glasses behind whose thick, water-spotted lenses his magnified eyes kept darting surreptitiously around the shower room.

Ever since he'd started swimming at the YM, Charlie had seen these two quite frequently. He always tried to avoid making eye contact with them. Their flabby asses and protruding bellies turned him off. Once, only half teasingly, Arthur Hill had accused him of being prejudiced against older men. "God, *Charlene*, what a chicken hawk you are!" Arthur had said. "What an ageist."

As he rinsed himself off, Charlie thought about that. Yes, he had a thing for younger men—for "cherubic blondes," as his first lover, Christopher Avon, used to call them. But did that make him an "ageist"? It embarrassed him to think so. Ageism was against his religion, so to speak.

He recalled a passage in one of Paul's letters—Romans, was it? or Ephesians?—about loving without discrimination, about loving in a way where outward appearances didn't count, where none of the world's criteria for meriting love counted. The point, Paul said, is that we are all brothers and sisters in Christ, loving one another for the Christ we encounter in each other.

During those two and a half years he had spent in the monastery, it had been easy to think like that. It's what had kept him from ever making a pass at Brother Gabriel. But here, in this incarnate world, where the body counted for so much…well, weren't the rules different? In some vague, unsystematic way, he still believed that it was wrong to objectify people sexually—he'd written a paper to that effect during his senior year at Boston College—but now he thought there should be room in his philosophy for celebrating the body, too. He liked to think of himself as a modern Catholic. A modern, homosexual Catholic, whatever that might mean. He wished he could have written a paper about *that* at B.C.

He didn't recognize the other two men: a guy with a baby face, curly red hair, and a hairless chest, and a tall black man with a shaved head. He guessed that Baby Face was in his mid-twenties, Black Man perhaps a few years older. Charlie could see that they would be considered attractive, though neither of them particularly appealed to him: red hair turned him off and so did shaved heads. Or was it the fact that the guy with the shaved head was black? Was he a racist? Could Arthur Hill accuse him of that, too? In his limited sexual experience, he'd never slept with a black man, not that that proved very much. Certainly in principle he was not a racist, and in principle, too, he was not averse to going to bed with a black man, if, that is, he ever dared to go to bed with another man again. Or was it just a question of when he would *choose* to?

By now, Baby Face and Black Man had begun playing with themselves, working themselves up into semi-erections for each other. Charlie pretended not to see, though he noticed that the two older regulars were watching everything, as nonchalantly as if they were on the sidelines watching a game of bocci. As for Speedo, he just kept on showering, his back turned away from them all.

Charlie soaped up again, careful not to touch his penis. And then, feeling slightly foolish, he rinsed off and lathered up a third time.

In the last three months, since he'd joined the YMCA, he'd done this a lot, lingering in the shower just to watch someone else. Sometimes he'd soap himself up and rinse off four, five, six times. Looking, that's all he did, though there was plenty of fooling around that went on in these showers. *Oh, yeah, the Y.* In three months he'd seen a lot. Once, a few weeks ago, there were seven or eight guys in the shower, and suddenly it became apparent that they were all there for just the same reason: As if on cue, every one of them had grabbed his dick and started jerking off. Terrified, Charlie had fled.

How the straight guys missed it, he didn't know. How could anyone fail to notice a guy soaping up his dick, stroking it to hardness? Did straight guys really not see that kind of stuff? Or had an unspoken truce been declared: Don't mess with us, we won't mess with you? How did you *learn* these things? Often these days he felt he was just missing what everyone else already knew.

By now, Baby Face and Black Man had full-blown hard-ons. Old Turkey Skin continued pulling on his still flaccid penis. The guy with the black glasses kept looking around. And Speedo still had his back to them all, displaying those lovely lobed buns. What was happening? *The question*, Saul Rudginsky used to ask him, *is what do you* want *to make happen?* Charlie didn't know what he wanted to make happen. He rinsed off.

And lathered up again.

Whenever he lingered in the showers like this—"loitering" was the term the law would use—he felt guilty. Not about the sex, not even about putting himself into the "occasion" for sex, the term the Church would use. It was all that hot water going down the drain. There were guys who regularly spent an hour under the showers. They were there when Charlie went into the pool, and still there when he returned. Meanwhile, the water, hundreds of gallons of it, all the way from the Quabbin Reservoir, continued to flow, pouring from the shower head onto his thrice-cleansed body, and from there, bouncing and splashing, onto the tile floor, where it collected in scummy backlogs at the drains, until eventually it ran down the pipes, through the sewers and out into Boston Harbor, the dirtiest harbor in the country, they said. Charlie thought about all this. And lingered.

Soon Baby Face and Black Man began jerking each other off. The next moment, Black Glasses moved to another shower head, one with a better view of the locker room. He was, Charlie understood, "spotting" for these guys, looking out for anyone coming along who might not take too kindly to this kind of activity. It was also an acknowledgment, Charlie saw, that he was being accepted as one of them, too, not an intruder but…well, what? an accomplice? a voyeur? a fellow waster of water? a brother in Christ?

Speedo finally turned around. He didn't have an erection. In fact, he seemed oblivious to what was going on. Oblivious or, more likely, not interested. It was fascinating watching a guy like Speedo, the way he could so easily hold out. Charlie admired the confidence that showed, the control and power in it, the way guys like Speedo always *chose* just what they wanted.

By now, other guys were beginning to come into the locker room. From the shower, Charlie could see them changing into workout gear and bathing suits. It was probably well after five. There would be a lot of coming and going now. Already another guy, a lithe Middle-Eastern–looking man, had entered the showers. Baby Face and Black Man left off briefly, each turning discreetly toward the wall. Charlie watched as the new guy selected a shower and turned on the faucet. The way he soaped himself up, it looked as if he was planning on sticking around a while.

Damn! Dennett was picking him up at five-fifteen. They had plans to go grocery shopping. With a quick, angry flip of his wrist, Charlie turned off the shower, grabbed his towel, and left. When he passed the sauna, he saw that guys were in there, too. Most likely doing stuff, he thought. It seemed as if no one had any obligations on this Friday afternoon but him.

In front of his locker, he began to towel himself off. He dried his feet especially carefully. Since he'd been coming here, he'd developed a fungus infection on one of his toes. The doctor he'd consulted told him these infections were difficult to get rid of. Charlie wondered what else you could pick up at the Y. Twice he'd seen guys in the shower with purple KS lesions on their legs.

He opened his locker and began to pull out his clothes. He dressed slowly, keeping an eye on the activity in the locker room. He took a long time putting on his sneakers, even to the point of untying and retying one of them.

As he was stuffing the last of his things into his gym bag, he saw Speedo finally coming out of the shower room. He was walking slowly but deliberately, the kind of saunter that shows off a body to its best advantage. His towel fell across one of his hard, firm pecs and down in front of his crotch, which he cupped with his right hand, rubbing himself dry.

From the seclusion of his row of lockers, Charlie watched him. Speedo strolled over to the dryers, punched the button, and began to dry his hair. He scrubbed at the short, unruly front plume of his crew cut, then turned around, facing away from the machine, hunkering down a bit, bending his knees and throwing his pelvis out so that the blast of hot air would catch the back of his head. His penis looked semi-tumescent, as if he'd just come away from sex. Then Baby Face came out of the shower area, briefly made eye contact with Speedo, and entered the sauna. When the dryer turned off, Speedo followed him.

For a brief, hopeless moment, Charlie considered undressing

again and following them into the sauna. *That* one, he wanted to yell at Speedo. *That* one? *What was the matter with me, huh?* What was it? His beaky nose? His thinning hair? Dennett used to kiss that nose—early on, when they were still having sex—kiss it, nibble on it, suck on it.

Five twenty-five. Shit. He hefted his gym bag again, and walked over to the water cooler, where he could get a view into the sauna room window. Speedo and Baby Face were sitting next to each other. Charlie took a drink, then made for the locker room door.

A blond guy was just entering. Short-cropped hair, pretty face, trim body—an older, more studiedly gay version of those cherubic blondes he used to go for back in college. The type who nowadays never gave him a second look. But as they passed, the blond flashed him a big, seductive smile. Charlie smiled back. He walked two more steps, then turned around. The blond turned, too, and was giving him another smile, a Definitely Interested smile.

Before Charlie could think what to do next, momentum and shyness had carried him out of the locker room. The lobby, where Dennett would be waiting, was down a long corridor. He still had time. For what? He stood there, questions flooding his head. Should he go back? Pretend he was just arriving and find himself a locker next to the blonde's? Should he make it that obvious? What would he say? What would his opening line be? And what exactly was it that he was interested in? *What did he want?*

*Most excuses are just a way of avoiding responsibility*, he heard Saul Rudginsky telling him.

*The wolf may give up his fur but never his inclination*, he heard his father saying.

*I'm glad I got all that stuff out of my system back in the seventies*, he heard Arthur Hill announcing.

*Turn away from the satisfactions of the flesh*, he heard St. Paul preaching.

*I want to look sexy*, he heard little Heather Buxton declaring.

*Play safe*, he heard the ads in the gay newspaper instructing.

*Whyy-Em-Cee-A*, he heard the Village People singing.

On the waves of all these voices, he was carried down the corridor and into the lobby, where he found Dennett, predictable, on-time, maddeningly steady Dennett—why couldn't he be late just once!—sitting in one of the easy chairs, reading a newspaper. He'd come directly from work, still dressed in his jacket and tie. His starched blue Oxford cloth shirt looked as crisp as when he'd put it on this morning, and his hair, that coal-black hair that eleven years ago Charlie had found so beautiful, despite his long history of going for blondes, that hair was meticulously groomed, every strand in order. Dennett. "Dennett the Lieutenant," Charlie sometimes called him because he could be so spiffy, so spit-and-polish. Dennett Sjostrommer. This man he loved. This man who could piss him off so much. This man for whom he'd pretty much lost all those locker room feelings.

"I was beginning to wonder if we'd gotten our signals crossed," Dennett said. Neatly, he folded up his paper and got up.

Last night, they'd had another fight. It had started over the garden, *something* about the garden, but then, like the dust balls collecting in the corners of their hallway, the argument had gathered up other stuff: money issues, house projects, how to spend the weekend. They'd gone to their respective bedrooms angry, and only spoken enough this morning to confirm that they would be rendezvousing at the Y to go grocery shopping. But now there was no hint of anger in Dennett's voice.

"Sorry," Charlie said. He glanced at his watch and then, trying not to show any sign of guilt, looked Dennett directly in the eye. Those blue, blue eyes. "So where do you want to do the shopping?"

"You know, every place is going to be jammed at this hour," Dennett said. "Why don't we go do something fun for a while—go have a drink or something—and then do the shopping?"

Charlie brightened. They almost never allowed themselves spontaneous time anymore. "Denny, I'd love to." Twenty-four hours ago he'd been ready for a divorce. "Where?"

They began trading off suggestions—Harvard Square, or one of the hotel bars in the Back Bay. The Copley Plaza perhaps.

"Too bad you're not wearing a jacket and tie," Dennett said, eyeing Charlie's teaching clothes—a sweater and sneakers and jeans. "We could have gone to the Ritz. We haven't been there in a long time."

Suddenly, over Dennett's shoulder, Charlie caught sight of the blond who'd cruised him in the locker room. He'd come out into the lobby, and it was clear, from the way he looked, that he'd been hoping Charlie would still be hanging around, clear from the expression on his face that he was disappointed to see Charlie talking to another guy. At forty-three, Dennett was still strikingly handsome. Charlie figured the blond felt outmatched. He saw him turn and disappear down the corridor to the locker room.

"How about that gay bar in the South End?" he asked Dennett, forcing himself not to look in the direction the blond was going.

"What gay bar?"

"The one with the restaurant and the cocktail piano."

"Why there?"

"I don't know. Because I feel like having some gay space." It was an expression, gay space, his teaching intern David Wulff used all the time.

"Haven't you had enough of that here?" The way Dennett said that made it sound as if he were gagging.

Charlie looked around the lobby as if to confirm Dennett's implication. It seemed innocuous enough to him. Nothing like what was going on inside that locker room. Dennett had never been in *there*.

"Okay, okay, so let's go to the Copley," he said. "You're sure I can get in like this?"

"It's a beautiful sweater," Dennett reassured him.

"It ought to be," Charlie agreed, happy to have something to be lighthearted about. "It's an Adeline Pellucca selection. My mother gave it to me for Christmas, remember?"

"I helped her pick it out, Bubellucca." Dennett flashed him a teasing smirk. "All your best clothes are either from your mother or me."

They walked out onto Huntington Avenue. The rush hour traffic was in full force.

"Which way?" Dennett asked, meaning where had Charlie parked his car.

"Up a few blocks." Charlie pointed to the left, toward Northeastern.

As they walked up Huntington Avenue, buttoning their coats against the raw March evening, Charlie thought about the blond, about what it would be like to be walking up the street with *him* right now. But no. He'd save the blond for tonight, when he was in bed. The blond and Speedo—tonight they'd replace that new maintenance man as his jerk-off material. For now, he'd put his attention to what was here and now: Friday evening. Dennett. A drink and then the grocery shopping. The beginning of the weekend. Chores. The house. The garden.

When he sighed, it only sounded like letting out a deep breath against the brisk, early spring air....

# The Five of Us
### *H. L. Wylie*

I hadn't been to Pompelly's glen for years. As I stood by the rushing water, admiring the familiar scent of woods and pine trees, I got a little nostalgic for the old days.

My hometown was pretty small. You had a choice: Get a girlfriend or play around with the other guys on the sly. Or both. I figured there was nothing wrong with having it both ways, because I always seemed to be incredibly horny. Going through school had turned into a joke. I was having much more fun cuddling up to my buddies during sleepovers. Even before that night, it had turned into a quest of sorts: how to ditch our girlfriends and seemingly have a boys' night out. The answer: Pompelly's glen, camping for an overnight.

All our girlfriends said no after we suggested what our plans were for the night. Girlfriends safely ditched, a case of beer, and my uncle's (stolen) Lucky Strikes had the making of a pretty butch camping expedition. We all decided to meet at my house so we could take one car. Kevin, Jeff, Halsey, Todd, and I were set. Since it was just over the bridge and a mile down the road, forgetting something wasn't a problem. After arriving, we all sent Todd back for our sleeping bags. Already I was starting to think this night held promise. I had been blowing Kevin and Halsey, but the other two had proven completely oblivious to past overtures. I thought that maybe the three of us could do some manly persuading later on.

Todd arrived with our sleeping bags and a stolen bottle of Canadian Club from my father's bar. As we walked down the path, my eyes fell upon Todd's perfect butt.

I was at the back of the pack watching everyone lumbering over fallen trees, rocks, and small mud holes. Each of my friends' bodies moved in its own certain style. Since I was following Todd, I can only tell you that the sight was most enjoyable. Todd played football. He was a defensive lineman. Our high school didn't promote the steroid-laden six-foot, four-inch, two-hundred-forty-pound players. Todd was about five feet nine inches and maybe weighed in at one hundred and eighty pounds. His blond hair reminded me of those California surfer dudes. Everyone commented on how his tanned skin matched his brown eyes. Todd was big on working out: His perfect bubble butt was the end result of serious lifting, and Todd's legs were a marvel to ogle. Most teenage guys build their chests up and seem to forget the legs.

As I followed him, Todd's muscular legs and butt were becoming a distraction. I was tripping over rocks and tree limbs. I definitely wasn't looking at my feet. I was staring a hole into Todd's shorts. Hoping that I would see more of Todd's body later on, I concentrated on not looking like an oaf and began to walk more carefully toward the campsite.

We settled for a place close to the water. That way, we could keep our precious beer cold under the running water. With the sleeping bags in place and our trusty plastic cover lean-to, we were ready to hang out.

The sun was just beginning to set. The beauty of the glen at dusk was always one of my favorite sights. It could take your breath away. As I sat there contemplating life in general, Kevin came over and sat next to me. He handed me a beer and asked what I was doing. "Where is everybody else?" I asked. Kevin went into this long explanation on how Todd was already throwing up. Todd had started right away into the Canadian Club, and before we were even done setting up camp, he was acting a little drunk. Todd drinks fast and gets drunk fast. Jeff and Halsey took him around the bend for a swim. I knew that once Todd went swimming he would sober up and join the party again.

Sitting close to Kevin always got me hard. Since I was occasionally having sex with him, the closeness was intoxicating. The first time I blew Kevin, I was amazed at the size of his dick. Not only was it very long, but it was incredibly thick. It surprised me because Kevin actually had the smallest build of any of us. His balls were also a sight. Large and round and absolutely hairless. In fact, the only hair on Kevin's body was around his dick. To this day I've always wondered how I ever got his huge dick all the way down my throat.

Kevin put his hand on my crotch and gave a long squeeze. My first reaction was to try to kiss him, but I hesitated too long. "We've got about a half hour before anyone comes back," he said. We were out of our clothes in no time. Having sixty-nined the last time with Kevin, I tried to get right into that position. With Kevin lying flat on the sleeping bag, I hovered over him ready to plunge at his dick. Right before I started to suck him off, I felt his tongue on my asshole.

It was like an electric shock had gone off inside my entire body. Kevin's tongue went crazy around my asshole while I went down on his ten-inch dick. Kevin must not have eaten for days, by the way he was slurping and chewing on my hole. His tongue was aggressive. I could tell that Kevin was way into this. I started grinding my ass up and down his face. "Eat my fucking ass, Kevin, this is going to be your only meal tonight." I thought that sounded pretty hot; it got me going on Kevin's dick like a wild man. I was sex hungry. I didn't even care how many times I gagged on his dick. He was fucking my mouth like crazy. His dick was so thick, my mouth was feeling like I had been in the dentist's chair for hours.

I hadn't realized that I could cum without actually jerking off. I started to tell Kevin that I was cumming. Kevin released his mouth grip on my hole, grabbed both my thighs, and lifted me so my dick was about two inches from his mouth. I immediately shot all over his face. I thought I was taking a piss. The sensation lasted for a long time. Kevin's face was covered from forehead to chin with little rivers of my spunk running off the sides of his face.

Kevin lowered me a little and proceeded to smash his cum-soaked face back to my asshole. Now Kevin was getting ready to shoot his load. As I concentrated on not gagging and taking all his juice, Kevin started slapping my asscheeks. The slaps were pretty hard. I could feel my asscheeks start to burn. At the exact time Kevin slipped his finger into my butt, he came into my mouth. I know that I swallowed five times. Kevin just wasn't stopping. I hung in there and even managed to get about another inch of his dick down my throat.

The rest of the group came back as Kevin and I were just sitting back down with our beers. I was feeling the heady rush of pure sex and loving it. Todd was looking better after his swim. At least he was talking and making sense. I did notice, however, that he was just in his underwear. He was sporting a semi-hard-on that looked quite impressive. I wanted to say something that would get the ball rolling into my own private fantasy orgy, but Jeff spoke up and ruined the moment. "Where are the cigarettes?" Jeff asked. I reached into my sleeping bag and passed the Lucky Strikes.

Halsey had gathered some wood for our fire and we all chipped in to get the campfire ready for the night. I don't know what five horny teenagers talk about, but my thoughts were elsewhere. I kept looking at Kevin, but he was playing that nonchalant act. Todd was getting pretty drunk again and Halsey was talking about his girlfriend. I did notice that Jeff had started to whittle a piece of wood while talking and joking. The piece of wood was pretty big and I was wondering why Jeff had picked this particular broken branch to whittle. As the fire was burning a steady red hue into everyone's face, I caught myself staring at him.

Jeff was, by far, the most handsome of the group. Dark brown wavy hair, crystal-cracked deep blue eyes. He was also the only one with a mustache. He was whittling fast. I watched the muscles in his arms move gracefully back and forth. I felt this feeling that I couldn't name back then. I know now: sensuous. The whole gliding motion of Jeff's arm going up and down was turning me on.

I stared at the piece of wood and slowly realized that it was starting to look a lot like Kevin's dick. The bark had been all shaved off and there was a pretty big knot at the very end of the branch. I was feeling no pain so I just let it fly. "You know, Jeff, that looks like Kevin's dick." I looked quickly at Kevin to see his reaction, but before he had time to register any response, Todd chimed in, "You know you're right, it does look like Kevin's dick."

There was this eerie silence that you only hear on school buses, when everyone stops talking at the same time.

"I'm not sure if it's bigger," Jeff said, putting the tip of the branch in his mouth, then sliding it out, "but Kevin's is much thicker." I sat there soaking all this in. I was just waiting for Halsey to chime in on another aspect of Kevin's dick. No response. So I asked him why he didn't say anything. Halsey let out a big sigh and said, "I think it's longer and thicker. Kevin's dick, that is." Todd and Jeff decided at the same time to go piss.

Out of the corner of my eye, I saw Jeff crouch down and grab the extra lean-to rope as he walked away.

Like Halsey had any reason to be jealous. His six-foot frame was muscular all over. Halsey was the hairiest of us all. His thick chest fur was fun to run your fingers through. I got an instant hard-on whenever my eyes followed the line of hair from his navel to his uncut dick. The first time I blew him, he had to show me how to carefully peel down the foreskin and gently lick around the tip of his dick. He said it was more sensitive because it was covered most of the time. Halsey's dick was almost as long as Kevin's, but nowhere near as thick.

Jeff appeared out of nowhere and sat next to the three of us around the campfire. I noticed that he had returned without Todd. Jeff stirred up the fire and spoke to Kevin, "I'd say it's time we get started." Kevin immediately jumped from his spot and started taking off all his clothes. Jeff and Halsey were not far behind. "Come on, David, your clothes, take them off," said Kevin. I needed no further prompting. In less than thirty seconds, I was staring at my friends' naked torsos.

Jeff, Kevin, and Halsey started to play with themselves. Jeff's dick was thick, but short. What made his dick memorable was that the head of his dick looked like a huge mushroom cap. I was in heaven. All I could think of was that this was where I wanted to be for the rest of my life. Everyone commented on Kevin's piece, but as I looked around at the other dicks, I realized that all our dicks were worthy of attention.

The three of them walked off toward the bend. I followed, thinking that we were all going for a swim. As we rounded the bend I noticed something on a big fallen tree. It was Todd. Jeff had tied his torso around this tree. Todd's hands were pulled around the tree limb and tied to his feet. The sight was almost too much to take. Todd had his underwear off and we all stood around staring at his exposed asshole. Todd's muscular legs were straining. Muscles I never knew legs had were undulating as Todd moved around. He appeared not to be struggling. It looked to me that Todd wanted to be tied up like this. His bubble butt was draped precisely over the middle of this fallen tree. His asshole was anybody's: open for business.

Jeff licked his finger and poked it up Todd's ass. Todd squirmed but was making no noise. "Looks like we have a prisoner for the night, guys," said Kevin. I was still looking at Jeff. His fingering technique had grown to three fingers up Todd's butt. "I can't take this waiting," said Kevin. He pulled Jeff's fingers out of Todd's asshole and just rammed his dick all the way in. Todd was pretty much gasping for air at this point. I blinked my eyes a few times just to make sure that I wasn't sleepwalking. Kevin was a wildman. His fucking was taking on a new dimension. He would pull his dick out to the point where you could see Todd's assring start to close. He'd spit on the tip of his dick and ram it back in, right up to his balls.

Todd was moaning pretty loudly, so Halsey knelt down on the leaves in front of Todd's face. One grab of Todd's hair and Halsey's dick was well into Todd's mouth. The moans were now muffled. It wasn't like we had to worry about the noise around there. No one was around for a couple of miles. Kevin's fucking was looking like a blur and he was ready to cum. He pulled out of Todd's asshole just enough so that Jeff and I could see the tip of his dick. We stood there staring at Todd's asshole, which was looking pretty worked over. Kevin came right on the outside of Todd's assring.

I was amazed at the volume, considering we had just spent our first load about an hour earlier. Kevin's cum splashed all over Todd's ass and lower back. "I'm going to shoot you guys, watch this," said Halsey. We leaned over Todd's torso just in time to see Halsey pull his dick out of Todd's mouth and cum all over his face. Todd looked a dog trying to drink from a hose. He wanted to drink Halsey's cum, but Halsey was about one inch out of reach. Todd's face had spunk in his eyes, on his cheeks, all over his face.

We stood there and watched Todd's body relax. He was covered from head to toe with Kevin's and Halsey's cum. Before anyone spoke, Jeff grabbed his whittled stick and shoved it up Todd's ass. He let go of the stick and all I could think about was how could anyone's ass take this much abuse. Now Todd looked like he was just speared by a pole vaulter. Jeff slowly moved the stick back and forth. He pulled the stick out and lowered his head to Todd's asshole. Jeff's tongue made a beeline to Todd's assring before it closed, like someone running for an elevator as the doors are closing. We watched Todd's ass clamp down onto Jeff's licking tongue. It looked like it was being sucked in like a vacuum. I thought that I was going to cum again without any assistance.

I told myself to calm down and enjoy the sights and sounds of my buddies fucking each other. Jeff was feasting on Todd's assring as Todd was trying to grind his butt up and down Jeff's face. Kevin looked at me and said, "Todd loves sucking dick, go fuck his mouth." I leaped over the tree and positioned myself on the ground right in front of Todd's face. I leaned forward to Todd's ear. "Are you all right?" I asked. Todd looked up at me and smiled. Halsey's cum was drying all over his face. The sight made me incredibly horny. I grabbed Todd's head and rammed my dick in his mouth so hard he gagged. What I lack in girth, I certainly make up in length. One lonely night, jerking off, I grabbed a ruler and measured eight and three quarter inches.

I wasn't aware of Todd's discomfort and proceeded to keep my dick in the back of his throat, fucking like there was no tomorrow. It didn't take very long before I felt my balls churning. "I'm going to cum, guys." My voice was husky; it sounded pretty sexy to me.

Kevin leaped over the tree. "Slide back," he ordered me. "Let me in between you guys." I slid back and realized that Kevin's ass was firmly placed in Todd's face and Kevin was now blowing me. That was it, I exploded. Kevin gagged at the force in the back of his throat, but he hung in there and started sucking me furiously. I almost fainted. I had never cum that hard in my life.

I looked up and saw Jeff coming toward me. He was standing next to me, with his mushroom-capped dick just inches away from my face. "I don't have to tell you what to do, do I?" said Jeff. I looked up to respond, but all I got was Jeff's dick crammed into my mouth. He turned my head to the side and went to town on my face. He had his hands holding my head and he was pulling my head back and forth on his dick. Talk about living a dream. Jeff grumbled something, pushed his dick all the way down my throat, and came. I was swallowing like crazy as Jeff just kept pumping away.

Jeff then pulled out of my mouth, turned around, and started to take a piss. I listened to Jeff's stream of piss. It was a beer piss. I reached over, grabbed his hips, and spun him around. Before he knew what was going on, I was getting pissed on. Jeff didn't move away. Actually, he moved closer and sprayed me from head to toe. As I closed my eyes, I noticed Kevin and Halsey untying Todd. I felt the warm liquid run off my shoulders and down my body. I felt

Jeff's stream getting weaker and opened my eyes to see Kevin, Halsey, and Todd standing over me. Their dicks were aimed at me. It was like walking into a waterfall. They all started pissing at the same time. I was loving this, as my body was thoroughly soaked with all my friends' piss. It was feeling like it had been hours, when I felt the last few drops on my cheek. The five of us were spent. So we headed back to our beers and the flickering red glow of the embers.

A few more logs and our fire was back to roaring. We had left the house in such a hurry, we forgot food. We dug into two bags of chips someone remembered to bring. Staring at everyone around the fire, I was trying to figure out how my friends got into fooling around with guys. Did Kevin's love for dick start way before me? From what I saw him doing to Todd, I could only imagine that many asses in my hometown knew of Kevin's dick. And Jeff, that was confusing. His girlfriend and I were really close. Boy, if she ever knew I was blowing her boyfriend! Todd was the biggest surprise of all. When do you realize that getting objects and huge dicks stuffed up your ass excites you? The thoughts were making me dizzy. But the night was young and I had some ideas of my own.

Kevin and Halsey had decided to stay nude. Todd put his underwear back on. So did Jeff and I. We still had a lot of beer left and only Todd had drunk any of the Canadian Club. There was still almost a whole bottle left. I was starting to think that Todd's getting drunk might have been a little act. With so little liquor gone, I could only assume that he needed to feel drunk in order to open up his ass to his friends. Now, Todd stood up and proudly displayed his hard-on. His underwear was still wet and his dick was slowly stretching the fabric. His dick seemed to keep growing. "Who wants to blow me while Kevin and Halsey try to fuck me?" asked Todd.

Jeff volunteered faster than I did. Todd peeled his underwear off over his hard-on. Kevin and Halsey were already behind Todd. I stood there, taking it all in. Then Kevin motioned me over. "You're going to have to help us get both our dicks in Todd's ass." Looking at both their cocks, I shook my head with a little bit of disbelief.

There was no way that Todd's ass was going to take these two big dicks. Todd bent over and raised his ass up as high as he could. Jeff scooted underneath Todd's cock and balls. Staring from behind, I notice that Todd had a nice set of balls. They hung really low. Todd's balls seemed to cover Jeff's face like a tiny blanket.

Kevin started by informing me that after his dick was in all the way, I was to use two fingers and try to stretch Todd's assring open further for Halsey. Jeff had already begun by giving Todd a ball-bath with his tongue. I watched as Jeff sucked up both balls and gently tugged at Todd's sac. Todd was liking this action. I was glad Todd was smiling because after Kevin and Halsey were through, I knew his smile would be replaced with agony.

Kevin spat on his dick and I watched it grow. He slapped Todd's asshole several times. You could actually see Todd's asshole opening up after every slap. Kevin was obviously ready. He grabbed his dick and shoved about five inches into Todd's waiting hole. A gasp from Todd only made Kevin shove harder. Within seconds Kevin's entire dick was in all the way. Kevin's motions were much slower this time. His hips were going in circles, opening up Todd even more. Then he told me to carefully squeeze two of my fingers up Todd's asshole. Careful not to scrape Kevin's dick, I did as I was told.

Todd squirmed, but once my fingers entered his assring, Kevin returned to a frenzied fucking. Kevin motioned for Halsey to get ready with his dick. "Now, David, I want you to gently pull open Todd's ass when I tell you. Halsey, get ready," said Kevin. "Go ahead, pull." I pulled gently and watched Halsey push two inches of his dick into the opening I had created. Todd's knees buckled a little, but he was still standing. Cameras couldn't have done this picture justice. You had to be there witnessing this attack on poor Todd's asshole.

Kevin and Halsey, looking like Siamese twins, slowly started to hump at the same time. Todd was swaying and moaning, but standing on his own. He was moaning with every one of Halsey's and Kevin's thrusts. Todd opened his eyes and raised his head toward the moon. "I'm cumming, Jeff, stop blowing me."

Jeff let Todd's dick snap out of his mouth. Todd started groaning loudly as Jeff now grabbed his balls and tugged them like he was milking a cow. Todd came with such force that several streams shot out of his cock and landed in the middle of our fire. I stared at Todd's cum sizzling on the logs, then realized that Kevin and Halsey were panting pretty heavily.

Halsey never got more than two inches of his dick into Todd's asshole. He had pulled out and was jerking off. Meanwhile, Jeff had moved from Todd's balls to Kevin's ass. Jeff was ramming away at Kevin's ass. I knew that Kevin was getting ready to shoot his load up Todd's wide-open asshole. His eyes had this glaze that was accentuated by the fire's glow. Almost demonic, somewhat surreal. I could tell he was filling Todd up with his spunk. I stood in front of Todd, in case he fainted. Halsey was cumming all over the back of Todd's muscular legs. I looked down at Todd's cock and was surprised that it was still hard.

Jeff yelled from behind Kevin and I figured he was cumming, too. I grabbed Todd's balls as Kevin was giving him his last thrusts. I saw cum dripping down Todd's legs. His asshole was overflowing like a faucet that had been turned on. Jeff was the first to disengage from this wonderful sight. He sauntered over to the fire and sat down. Kevin was taking great pains to pull out of Todd's ass slowly. His last pull released his dick from Todd's worn-out asshole. Todd sucked in air and then finally collapsed. We covered him with his sleeping bag and let him go to sleep. We all went down to the water and splashed our bodies. On our way out of the cold water, we all grabbed another beer and headed for the fire.

The fire dried us off quickly. We sat around and talked for another hour or so. Jeff had gone for more firewood. Kevin was still nude and absentmindedly playing with his dick. Halsey had put on his shorts. I sat there nude, feeling the warm heat from the fire on my balls. Todd was still resting and looking pretty worn out. Jeff returned with a couple of big logs. This would keep the fire going until we fell asleep (so I thought). Kevin leaned over to me and said, "I'm still so fucking horny. Do you want to fuck?" I was about to say that a little rest was in order, but then I realized that I was the only one who hadn't cum that last session.

I had barely nodded my head, when Kevin stood up and shoved his monster cock in my face. I didn't even give it a second thought. His dick was down my throat and staying there. Kevin was pretty surprised that I wasn't gagging. I started slurping away and impressed myself when I felt Kevin's pubic hairs tickle my nose. Kevin started to fuck the back of my throat—little short jabs that enabled me to breathe every now and then. Kevin pulled his dick out of my mouth, grabbed it, and shook it in my face. The more he squeezed his dick, the bigger it seemed to get.

He started slapping my face with his dick. "I know you want this back in your mouth, don't you?" Kevin said. I replied with a very wimpy yes. "I think I want to fuck you first," Kevin said. Jeff and Halsey walked over and stood in front of me. Kevin was gracious; I actually heard him spit on his dick before I fainted.

When I woke up, my asshole felt like it was on fire. Getting my bearings, I realized that I had been moved away from the fire. I was tied to the same tree where we had had our way with Todd. I heard and felt Kevin behind me. Even without seeing, I knew that was his dick up my asshole. He was wildly fucking my ass. Now I felt his dick slide in and out of my numbed asshole. He was pulling his dick all the way out, then ramming it back in. I felt his balls hit my ass. He was cumming. His dick felt like it was in my throat. I could actually feel his spunk coating my insides. He continued to fuck me for a couple more minutes. He pulled out fast and I let out a gasp.

Before I could thank him, Halsey took Kevin's spot. I knew it was Halsey by the stupid chuckle he always let out when he got excited. He pushed his entire length up my asshole. At this point there was no pain, no pleasure, just a numbing sensation. Halsey came fast and hard. He gave my balls a squeeze and walked away.

Jeff appeared out of nowhere and proceeded to untie me. Kevin and Halsey grabbed my arms and lowered me to the ground. I tried to stand up, but my legs were like rubber. "How long was I passed out?" I asked the group. "About twenty minutes," said Kevin. "We figured you wouldn't mind being tied up," added Halsey. Jeff walked over to me, put his arm around my shoulder and said, "Kevin fucked you until you woke up." Now I knew why my ass was on fire. Kevin's huge dick up my ass for twenty minutes, humping away like crazy.

When I felt stronger I got up and we all walked over to the fire. Todd was up and rubbing his eyes. "What did I miss?" I told him, "Nothing. We were just sitting around the fire shooting the shit, watching you sleep." We shared a quiet smile among the four of us. Todd stood up with a huge hard-on. "I gotta piss bad, I'll be right back." Jeff told Todd to stop. Todd turned around and Jeff said, "I want you to piss up my ass."

That got everyone's attention. Jeff walked over to Todd, bent over, grabbed his ankles with his hands, and said, "Go ahead." Todd didn't even spit on his dick. With one really hard push, Todd's dick slid all the way in. We were all impressed that Jeff didn't pass out. Todd stood still for about ten seconds with his eyes closed. When he opened his eyes he was smiling. "I'm pissing, I'm pissing up Jeff's hole!" Todd remained in that position for what seemed like an eternity. Todd then pulled his dick out and Jeff walked over to the fire.

Jeff turned his ass toward the fire and said, "Watch this, you guys." All of a sudden, liquid erupted from his hole. He was expelling all of Todd's piss. The fire hissed as Jeff continued this highly erotic spectacle. We were all speechless. Jeff finished, straightened up, and said, "Where the fuck you guys think that piss was going to go?"

By now, we were all exhausted. We finished our beers, smoked another Lucky Strike, and crawled into our sleeping bags. The fire was still burning. The logs that Jeff had put out with Todd's piss had now started to burn again. I was content. I went to sleep feeling like a happy camper.

Sleep didn't last long. I was nudged awake by Kevin. He pointed over to Jeff and Halsey. Jeff had his legs wrapped around Halsey's waist and his hands around Halsey's neck. Halsey was holding Jeff's butt with his hands. Jeff had his head back and Halsey was bent over and chewing on Jeff's nipples. They were trying to be quiet, but their muffled groans and moans kept us watching.

Halsey started to pound Jeff's asshole with his dick. We watched Todd wake up. Once he realized that sex was happening again, he leaped from his sleeping bag and ran up behind Halsey. Now Kevin and I were sitting and watching the festivities. Todd was fingering Halsey's butt. That didn't last long as Todd replaced his finger with his dick and, once again, rammed it home. That made Halsey fuck Jeff harder. Todd's motions were making Halsey fuck Jeff the same way.

Nothing lasted too long with the three of them. Jeff told Halsey to move his head away from his nipples. As Halsey moved his head away, we watched Jeff squirt cum up to his face and chest. Halsey let out a cry and let his cum fly up Jeff's asshole. Todd pulled out of Halsey's ass, ran around to Jeff, and came all over Jeff's face. The scene was hot. I realized that I was jerking off and Kevin was doing the same. We both stood up, and while Halsey was still holding Jeff, both Kevin and I came all over Jeff's face. As drenched as I was with everyone's piss, Jeff's face was completely covered with our cum. It was in his nose, his ears, his hair, and all over his lips. With both hands, Kevin scooped all the cum into Jeff's mouth. One big swallow and Jeff was done. Halsey let him down.

Kevin went to the water and came back with more beers, and Todd brought up that we still hadn't really started drinking the Canadian Club. He was right. We passed the bottle around a few times. The liquor had a nice warming effect. Jeff put another log on the fire, and we nestled into our sleeping bags. Reliving all that happened, I jerked off and went to sleep.

By the time I got home, my parents were getting ready to go out to dinner with friends. It was late afternoon and I was exhausted. I was glad to have no plans for the evening. As my parents were leaving, I was on the sofa, staring out into space…. The house was quiet and I was thinking that my life had changed for the better. I lit my uncle's last Lucky Strike and savored every drag.

# *Fantasy*

We usually think of all porn as fantasy—and, like all fiction, it is—but there are many different ways in which fantasy functions in sexual writing. A straightforward, realistic narrative like John Preston's *The Arena* works as fantasy because we want to believe that it *might* really happen. "Blue Light," Aaron Travis's classic story of the erotic supernatural, works because it allows us to move into a realm we know could never happen. Lars Eighner's stories in *BMOC* entice us precisely because they have the shape and feel of realism. Fantasy is where we go when we want to get out of our ordinary, material lives.

Fantasy has always been important to a gay male sensibility—you can see it on the stage of the Broadway musical; the make-believe world of Hollywood; the impulse of *haute couture;* the extravagant writings and images of the British decadents—and sexual fantasy, in particular, is a vital part of gay male thinking and culture. But what draws us to fantasy is not only its ability to present us with alternative lives and scenarios, but our intuitive understanding that fantasies instill in us a kind of power: the power of the imagination, the power of control. In our sexual fantasies we can choose to be—and do, or have done to us—things we would never experience in the real world. Sexual fantasies are a celebration of our desires, but they are also a method of survival. The psychic and emotional power that we attain from simply *imagining* alternative lives, actions, and feelings is at the heart of how we are able to deal with, and often work to change, a world that is hostile to our sexualities. Each of the stories here charts a different sort of fantasy: Some are purely pleasurable, others border on darker territory, exploring the underside of our sexual desires.

Randy Boyd's "The King and His Virgin Boy" reads like a traditional fable or fairy tale, perhaps a tale from an African version of *The Arabian Nights*. From its beginning—"In a faraway land untouched by machines…"—we know that we have moved out of our contemporary, urban mindset and setting. Boyd sexualizes the traditional fairy-tale narrative, and in doing so he makes us think about a specific erotic fantasy—in this case about a relationship between an older and younger man, between experience and innocence—that is prevalent in much of literature. Reading Boyd's story, we are prompted to examine our own relationship to its fantasy. Does the exotic setting enhance the sexual fantasy, or is it protecting us from some harder truths about inequalities in relationships? The story is highly romantic, but isn't "romance" itself a fantasy that is often at odds with a more urgent sexual fantasy? As we read of the boy's sure, steady journey to a happy, sexually pleasing manhood, what are we projecting from our own pasts in which the journey may not have been so easy? Boyd's romance of a never-land of free and easy gay sexuality seduces us easily, but makes us meditate on the differences in our own lives between the lure of fantasy and the often harder reality of life.

"The Shoeshine," by James C. Johnstone, delineates how subliminal fantasy can work in our lives. The encounter between a man with new shoes and a sexually exciting shoeshine boy might have been nothing more than a quick-fuck-behind-the-counter story, but Johnstone knows that often sexual fantasy—and the power and the flash of the fetish—can be more exciting than sex itself. "The Shoeshine" is more concerned with the nature of sexual fantasy—how it feels, how we use it—than it is with the fantasy itself.

Michael Rowe's "Nightmare Boyfriends" is part *film noir*, part Jacobean revenge tragedy with a twist ending. Violent emotions are here juxtaposed with romantic feelings, and the ensuing confusion drives the story into overload. Fantasies—sexual or otherwise—are not always pretty or pleasing, and Rowe's story takes on a dark edge as things get out of hand. We often think of sexual fantasies as being a safe place where we can enjoy and relish pleasure; "Nightmare Boyfriends" moves us to a place where the pleasures of revenge are more enticing, more stimulating than the pleasures of romance or love.

Fantasy is a place that we usually choose to visit. But what would happen if we had little control over the when and the why of our fantasy? Tom Cole's "Freon" is a Southern Gothic tale with psychotic undertones: Flannery O'Connor meets William Burroughs. Simultaneously alluring and repellent, the erotic is omnipresent in the world of "Freon"; it is a welcome relief from the ordinariness of everyday life and an inexplicable, confusing bane. Cole's contortionist protagonist is plagued by visions of pink spiders and a childhood dominated by the Catholic church—you just know that things aren't going to go well—and the story is driven forward by the terror of unwelcome fantasies (delusions? visions? hallucinations?) and the comfort of chosen fantasy.

# The King and His Virgin Boy
*Randy Boyd*

In a faraway land untouched by machines, where camels and oxen labored through the sprawling village, where peasants bartered in teeming streets and slept in mud-baked huts, where the merciless sun baked the earth brown and crackling dry every day of every year, a king sat high on his throne in the palace, watching his little offspring frolic amongst the statues, discussing the state of his gold with the wise men of the kingdom, accepting the parade of gifts from neighboring leaders terrified of his army.

He was a handsome king, with long sinewy muscles and dark cocoa skin as shiny as the sun-drenched sea that bordered the kingdom and as smooth as the bushels of silk his explorers brought back to him from the East. From the day he was born prince, not one hair had ever emerged from his head, and men from lands near and far spun tales of the good fortune they encountered after seeing their reflection in the King's skull.

The King seemed ageless, but the elders of the palace knew him to be near the end of his fourth decade on earth; and this meant that one day very soon, when the sun was at its apex, the King would rise from his throne and lead a hand-picked procession of the wisest men into the village, searching.

The King would not pick the day. The day would pick the King. He would feel the passage of time as never before, and the ancestors of his heart would sing to him a song of passion, reverberating without end through the chasms of his soul. And he would know: The time had come. To do as his father had, as his father's father had, as had every king since the first ruler of the land, his great-grandfather eighteen times. It was the kingdom's oldest ritual, the King's most revered and respected right: that once he had tamed the world with his iron fist, he could explore the deepest, most forbidden desire of the land.

Thus, on the seventh day of a spell when the sun had all but set fire to the earth, the King declared he had heard the song in his soul and set out for the village.

In the glaring light of day, the streets were filled with merchants' chants and peasants shouting loudly, children and geese running wild, smoke from kettles coating the air. The village was so chaotic, at first no one noticed the King in his long robe of red with gold trimming, flanked on all sides by the twelve wise men with their solemn black robes and thinning white hair. But then, as the procession wandered deeper into the masses, the crowd began to part like the sea. Many bowed as they saw the King, although it wasn't the law. Others sought the sight of their reflection on the side of his head. But the King paid no attention to his fawning subjects. Instead he traveled purposefully through the streets, face emotionless, eyes steady, looking to the right, then the left, always down toward the legs of the adults.

By a large, steaming kettle, amidst a sea of taller bodies, a young boy was playing with a short stick that had a small ball attached by a string. He was a light-skinned boy, perhaps seven, with straight jet-black hair and haunting sky-blue eyes that were consumed in trying to land the ball atop the stick. Eagerly, the wise men looked to the King. Barely moving, the King shook his head and looked away.

On the other side of the street a dark-haired brown boy of ten was straddling a mammoth ox, whipping it with a tree branch, admonishing the stubborn beast to move, while his tiny sister pushed at the animal's ass from the ground. For a moment the King studied the boy, whose too-large shirt hung loosely on his narrow frame and whose exposed brown thighs were made meaty by their pressing against the oxen. Tempting, but the King glanced away and continued on.

Under one of the merchants' tents, five young Arabian brothers were hawking garments for their rotund father, who was busy bickering with an elderly woman just outside the tent. The King's eyes swept over all five boys, who seemed to be lined up from oldest to youngest. The oldest was around eleven, with a tall lanky body that moved with stilted self-consciousness. The next one had buckteeth and anxious black eyes. Then came two seven-year-old freckle-faced twins, each lazily resting an arm on the other's shoulders. The youngest was a sobbing four-year-old with chubby cheeks made even chubbier by his tears. The wise men eyed each other expectantly, thinking surely one of these might do. But the King made note of them all, then proceeded.

Underneath a tent flap blowing in the wind was a pure black boy who looked to be twelve. He was bony and, because he was shirtless, his ribs showed through his flat torso as he raised his arms high above his head, offering a freshly caught fish to the crowd. His hair was nappy and still wet from the sea, and sun-filled droplets of water speckled his smooth ebony shoulders like glistening pearls of sweat. Trying to be heard above the rumble of the village, he cried out loudly about the fish, his voice alternately high and coarse, the change from boy to man only just beginning. From a distance of ten paces, the King looked the boy over, his still hairless underarms, his skinny but toned legs lost in his baggy khaki shorts, which were still wet and clinging to his hiked-up butt. Seeing the King's prolonged glance, the wise men stepped toward the boy, but suddenly the King turned away. The village was full of young boys of many origins with sprouting bodies, healthy heads of hair, and golden auras, but legend dictated that only the boy who unquestionably harnessed the desire reverberating in the King's soul would live at the palace. The fisher boy was not the one.

Next to a bountiful vegetable cart, a weathered, dark-complected woman with graying hair was arguing with an equally weathered merchant about his prices. Behind her, tugging at her drab brown dress, was a wide-eyed boy of mixed origins, younger than the fisher boy by three, perhaps four, perhaps even five years. His skin seemed pale but for a deep, rich caramel coating the sun had permanently poured into his pores; his upper lip turned upward, suggesting a hunger for experience. His eyes were green and blue at once, and atop his head he possessed big, overgrown curls that collected the sun's rays like tiny little magnets and rendered his hair as blond as the desert sand beyond the village. Yet he was neither light like the tribes to the far north, nor dark like the people of the King's region. Nor was he the color of yolk, as if from the East. He was all of them and he was none of them. He was his own breed of boy.

As the King laid eyes on him, the boy stopped tugging at his mother and glanced upward, not at the King, who was twenty paces away, but at the boisterous bodies surrounding him, looking around as if to take in this daily sight of life in the village. Though he could see him only through a maze of bodies, the King became immediately drawn to the boy, the flawlessness of his caramel skin, the promise of life and energy in his lean, developing body, the purity of his eyes, vacant of malice but ripe with curiosity.

The King's head lifted ever so slightly and his eyes widened with barely detectable anticipation. And the wise men knew the search was over. The King turned away and began walking in the direction of the palace while the wise men slipped through the crowd toward the chosen boy. Catching the suddenly sober reflection in the merchant's eyes, the mother turned around just in time to see the twelve wise men standing over her son, who regarded them unassumingly. Then, in the distance, she saw the back of the King moving away, and instantly she knew what was expected of her.

The eldest of the wise men extended his hand in front of the boy, who looked up to his mother out of confusion. As an answer, she returned glassy, stoic eyes, saying nothing, but nodding once and offering encouragement with a forced, bittersweet smile. The boy then turned back around, contemplated the hand before him, and began walking, not understanding why, but realizing that these were the most important servants to the most important man of the land.

The wise men formed a colonnade on either side of the boy, who marched slowly and solemnly through the parting crowd, following the King, who marched alone fifty paces ahead. Several times the boy looked back to his mother, who fought back tears filled with pride that her son had been chosen, and sorrow that her boy was being taken away from her.

At the palace the boy was told he would be living with the King now and was shown his room by the wise men. It was a vast room— second only to the King's in size—with plush sofas made of the finest velvet and a huge canopied bed draped in silk and covered with gigantic pillows that loomed like small mountains. The bed alone was as big as the tent the boy used to call home, and upon his request it would be surrounded by servants to fan him when the palace became too hot.

*And every night, in his own bed, at the opposite end of the palace, the King would stroke his massive cock, swirling and writhing, hands roaming over his body for hours on end, drowning himself in a sea of sweat and cum, dreaming of the virgin boy he had chosen, the tenderness of his chiseled jawline, the rosiness of his sunbaked cheeks, the supple muscularity of the curves of his back, the petite, cuppable nature of his perfectly round, hairless butt. Everything about him was pure and untouched, captivating the King's senses every night for most of the night. His boy, his smooth, innocent, virgin boy, the King would think over and over, stroking, throbbing, pulsating, praying for the day when he was finally ready....*

The boy's daily schedule was exact. He was given the best teachers in the land, the best philosophers, the best athletes, the best warriors, the best thinkers. In the palace's hallowed halls of learning, he was taught arithmetic and the secrets of the galaxies. He boxed with champion fighters and hurled spears with the most renowned soldiers of the King's army. He learned how to scale the palace walls and conquer the swiftest of horses. He was taught the history of all lands and lifted sacks of gold twice his weight for strength.

From time to time, the King observed these lessons, not in the boy's presence, but from behind hidden holes in the stone walls, sitting in the darkness of the elaborate series of catacombs that ran though the palace and were forbidden to all but the King. And what he saw of the boy and his lessons rendered the King numb with desire.

At mealtimes the boy was given everything to eat that his growing body cried out for. Tray upon tray filled with the land's best meats, breads, vegetables, and desserts were placed before his eyes, which never failed to widen with awe and delight. Dinner was a great feast at the palace, conducted in a huge ceremonial hall draped with flags of every color and attended by fifty of the King's most privileged guests. At one end of the long dining table sat the boy, flanked on either side by his teachers. In the middle sat the King's wives and his many children, and at the other end was the King himself, surrounded by the twelve wise men and visiting dignitaries.

But neither the King nor the boy paid as much attention to the royal guests as they did to each other. The King couldn't help studying his virgin boy's roving, curious eyes as they surveyed the feast and his soft, full lips as they engulfed the fruits of the village; and because the highest man in the land kept casting his gaze on the boy, the boy found himself perpetually glancing at the solemn-faced King in the distance, mesmerized and mystified every time their stares locked. But stare was all either could do, at dinnertime or any other time, as legend dictated: For now, the King did not speak to the boy and the boy was not allowed to speak to the King.

As the seasons passed, the boy grew stronger and stronger. His thin, cablelike legs became thicker, his buttocks rounder and fuller. Where a flat chest once lay, hills and valleys began to take shape, and his shoulders strained to expand like wings. His hair began to straighten and brown, retaining its sheen with streaks of gold caused by the sun; but elsewhere on his body, he remained hairless and pure, his skin as smooth as the day he was born, his blue-green eyes still full of life and wonder.

When he was a little older, the elite of the land came dressed in their most regal attire and lined the courtyard ten deep to see the King's virgin boy match skills with the other boys of the village in the palace warrior games. Naked but for loincloths made of oxen skin, the boys wrestled, boxed, and clashed with spears twice their height; and in each and every one of his contests, the King's boy emerged triumphant, rising proudly over the defeated boy, basking in the glorious roar of the onlookers. And no one was prouder than the King, who sat upon his courtyard throne atop a velvet-covered stage, barely containing his grin. To think that his boy was succeeding in becoming the fiercest warrior of the land!

After each day of courtyard conquests, the virgin boy would collapse behind the silk draperies of his canopied bed and fall fast asleep amongst the mountains of pillows, as peaceful as a baby, with his cheek thrust against the pillow and his lips barely open, effortlessly omitting a small steady breath. And sitting quietly on the other side of the wall in one of the dark catacombs, the King would watch him, peering hypnotically through a small rectangular hole cut in the stone wall.

*And every night, in his own bed at the opposite end of the palace, the King would stroke his massive cock, swirling and writhing, hands roaming over his body for hours on end, drowning himself in a sea of sweat and cum, dreaming of the virgin boy he had chosen, replaying his unparalleled athletic feats, savoring the way his soft, miniature muscles moved as he leaped and soared and wrestled the other boys down to the dirt, the way his solid little thighs tensed as he lunged forward, the crease between his jutted-out shoulder blades as he raised his spear high above his head, the way his buttocks spread like two perfect melons when he got down on all fours, straddling his soon-to-be-defeated opponent, the way his hair moistened with sweat from the unrelenting heat of the desert sun, the way his eyes widened as he went in for the kill, then shyly glanced toward the*

*King after each conquest, anxious for approval that was only forthcoming by way of a slight nod and an even slighter grin.*

*The King dreamed of these things every night, brandishing his cock with both hands, tossing his head from side to side, arching his back until he was offering himself to the gods, moaning and writhing until his cock blasted the juice that bore his love for the virgin boy. And the King devoured the juice, imagining it to be the boy's, knowing that that day could not come soon enough ....*

With each season, the boy became bigger and more strapping, so much so that he burst from his britches often, sending the royal tailor into a frenzy trying to keep up with his growth. No other boy, older or younger, could beat him in the warrior games, and none of the beasts brought in from the wild for a ferocious challenge stood a chance against his mighty spear. He treasured the physical labor around the fields of the palace, sweating away days at a time under the sun, lifting boulders and felling trees, harnessing his boundless energy in a way that only made his limbs stronger. He was growing by leaps and bounds, his enthusiasm for the life he'd come to know unmatched by his teachers and the other boys brought into the palace to play with him.

So great was his thirst for life, he was never motionless. At night, when all others were asleep, he roamed the palace alone, searching for clues to the biggest mystery in his life: the King. A man with whom he had never exchanged words. Somehow he realized their destinies were intertwined. He knew not how or why, but he understood that his presence in the palace was due to His Majesty, and relished putting a smile on the King's face, whether it was at the warrior games or in the great dining hall, where the King reacted with amusement to the boy's swift and furious devouring of meals. The boy admired the King in ways he couldn't articulate and savored even the briefest chance to glimpse the most important man in the land holding court, receiving other royalty, or dispatching his army.

The boy became obsessed with the King, and one night, during his secret explorations of the palace, he stumbled upon the catacombs forbidden to all but His Majesty. Curiosity won out over fear. The boy snaked his way through the pitch black corridors and eventually found a faint light emanating from a small rectangular hole cut through the stone at his waist. As he bent over to peer through the opening, his heart leaped into his throat: He saw for the first time the King's candlelit bedroom. And in the canopied bed— a larger replica of the boy's own—the King was wide awake, seemingly wrestling with himself with the covers torn off.

The boy squatted down and watched in amazement at what he saw upon a more careful look. The King was handling his dick in a way the boy had never thought of, never imagined: grabbing onto it with both hands, pumping it into his fists. It was ten times the size of the boy's, or so it seemed, and the boy looked on with eyes as wide as the desert, his breath taken away, his senses reeling, unable to take his gaze off the King and his dick and the way the King was stroking it and the strange, almost pained, look on the King's face.

Outwardly the boy was frozen. Inwardly he was shaking from the magnitude of his discovery and the fear of being found. Then instinct forced him to look down. Underneath his white bloomers, his own dick had popped upward with such force it was aching and he thought it would fall off. It had hardened before, but never like this. In a panic he looked back through the hole, as if the King might suddenly spot him and his aching dick and erupt with anger. But in the next instant, he saw that the King's hands had stopped their motion and now His Majesty's dick was peeing, peeing milky white pee all over the King's face and bed and chest and hands. The boy almost fainted from shock, but instead stumbled backward, away from the hole. Then he hastily crawled down the corridor, and when he was a safe distance away he rose and sprinted all the way back to his own room, diving into his bed and burying his head underneath the mountain of pillows, his whole conception of life and the King suddenly cast chaotically into the wind.

Every night after that, the boy ventured back through the catacombs to watch the King perform his ritual; and when the

King's big dick peed the white milk, the boy ran back to his own bed and stayed up half the night, replaying what he had just witnessed. Not a spare moment went by that the boy didn't think of the King and what he did with his dick, and one night, in the moonlit darkness of his own room, he summoned up the courage to give in to his desire to try the King's ritual for himself.

He felt pleasure immediately, but was disappointed when his dick failed to pee the white milk as the King's had. Must be something only kings can do, he concluded, but he repeated the ritual night after night anyway, always eventually giving up the quest to produce his own milk and falling asleep with his dick in his hand. Many times while he stroked himself, he imagined he was the King, pleasing his royal dick by pumping it into his huge, manly fists. Other times he fantasized he was lying next to the King in the royal bed, both of them handling their dicks until they wanted to shout out loud.

So began the boy's own nightly ritual, watching the King and repeating the act, and after a few more seasons passed, milk finally erupted from within the boy. He was overjoyed to be just like the King, and from then on, he practiced the ritual as many times as he could during the course of the day, all the while thinking of the King.

The wise men, who periodically monitored the boy through their own private viewing holes, saw that he could now ejaculate, so, as legend dictated, they watched and waited for his cum to be lily white, thick, and plentiful every time without fail before informing the King. The suns and moons came and went, the boy practiced his favorite new activity over and over, and soon his orgasms became as potent as geysers. Thus, on a day when the King was on his throne holding court, the wise men whispered the news in his ear. Wordlessly, the King smiled, a gradually evolving grin that had been years in the making.

For the rest of the day, the King canceled all business and did nothing but bathe and sauna and tone his muscles. Then, at nightfall, he dressed in his finest shiny gold pantaloons and frilly white shirt, and all of the palace was dismissed into the village.

The boy was to be dressed by his teachers in white britches and nothing else, and told to wait at his bedside to meet His Majesty formally.

The boy knew not what to say to the King or how to act, and once his teachers left him alone and waiting, he trembled with thoughts of meeting the mythical figure whom his days and nights had come to revolve around. Visions of the King's nightly ritual and his own nightly reaction danced furiously in his head, and every piercing look the King had ever given him came flooding back in his memory. The boy had no inkling what to expect, but every part of his soul told him that tonight, their rituals would merge into one.

The King entered the room and walked deliberately toward the boy, who sat on the bed. Then, standing over him, the King extended his hand. Nervous, the boy looked up, eyes darting back and forth, not knowing what to do. "Be not shy, be not afraid," said the King in a soft but commanding voice, his first words ever uttered to the boy. With trepidation, the boy placed his hand in the King's, and even though he had grown and was still growing, his hand was much smaller than that of the man towering over him.

With a firm grip, the King drew the boy up from the bed, then gently scooped him up in his arms and carried him out of the bedroom, past the sky-high stone walls, past the statues and the great halls, up the long, sweeping staircase to the King's wing and the King's bedroom. At the royal bed, the King set the boy down on the floor and they stood a breath apart, the boy barely reaching the King's shoulders.

Soundlessly, the King peeled off the boy's white britches, leaving the boy naked with his cock reaching upward like a bowsprit. His was a long but skinny cock still budding, just like the boy himself, with a light-colored swirl of pubic hair forming a small wreath around the base. After pausing to drink in the sight of the tender flesh before him, the King also stripped nude, then placed two fingers into the mouth of the boy, who stood there agape, still trembling with uncertainty. With his other hand, the King took the boy's shaking hand and placed it on the King's chest. The boy felt it on his own, astonished at being able to touch a man's chest, so much bigger and harder than his.

Slipping his fingers out of the boy's mouth, the King ran his hands down either side of the boy's torso, so narrow and lean. Then, as the King's hands reached lower, the underside of his forearm brushed against the boy's cock and discovered a wetness. The boy had cum already, shooting a healthy load on his stomach just above his blossoming pubic hair. Immediately, the boy's face flushed red. The King smiled to put him at ease, then went down on his knees and kissed the boy's waning erection and licked his taut, bald stomach, lapping up his fresh white cream, as sweet as any delicacy in the kingdom. Then, with a full mouth, he stood up and kissed the boy, the taste of the warm juice lingering on both their tongues. The boy kissed him back, so hard their teeth collided, and when the King brought their bodies together, he found the boy's dick was stiff as stone once again. The kiss grew harder. Their arms wrapped around each other, holding each other prisoner. The boy began running his hands all over the King's arms and backside, as if finally he was able to explore a body, like his own in that it was a male's, but unlike his own in that the King was a man, and the man was the King.

The King's hands went to the boy's butt, caressing his firm yet soft cheeks, sliding his fingers into the crack, feeling warmth and dampness within. Their bodies swayed against each other, the King's cock lodged against the boy's stomach, the boy's breath becoming shorter and shorter. He was on the verge of cumming again.

The King drew back to stop him and set the boy on the bed, easing him down on his back and straddling his face, then guiding the boy's head upward as the boy's mouth opened, taking in the King's cock. At first the boy's lips remained motionless, simply satisfied to be encased around the King's swollen head. Then he started to swallow the King's cock, then retreat for air, then swallow some more, then retreat, then swallow, and soon he got the hang of going up and down with his soft pink lips and hot watery mouth, sucking till the King feared he himself would cum.

The King twisted around so that he was facing the opposite direction and, while the boy still sucked on his dick, he bent over and nuzzled his face in the boy's crotch, inhaling the fresh musk of the tiny patch of pubic hair, eyeing the boy's quivering dick, which rose above his nose like a small tree trunk, and would surely explode again at a touch. So instead of reaching for the narrow little tree trunk, the King played with the boy's balls and burrowed his nose toward his ass. Then, without warning, he scooped the boy up by the small of his back and turned the two of them over, putting the King on his back with the boy over him; and while the boy became more and more adept at devouring the King's dick, the King planted his face in the boy's butt, flattening his tongue and running up and down the length of the crack several times before stopping at the pinkest of pink holes. At first the King merely stared and admired it, its softness, its rosiness. Then he gently kissed the slightly puckered lips. Then, unable to contain himself any longer, he dove in, burying himself deep within the dark tunnel of the boy's butthole, caressing the whiskerless outer cheeks with his hands and massaging the silky smooth inner walls with his tongue till the smell and taste and quite literally the boy's ass became another layer of skin on his face.

As if the sensation he felt on his anus were completely unexpected, the boy arched up in ecstasy, squatting even further down on the King's face, moaning a moan that was somewhere between an exalted cry and a helpless whimper. The King plunged even deeper into the boy's ass, eating away as if it were his last act on earth, and the boy began gyrating in sync with the wondrous tingling swimming from his butthole to the rest of his entire body.

Helpless at the hysteria every nerve and muscle was experiencing, the boy bent down to eat the King, his cock, his balls, his ass, sliding over the King's lower body like a puppy frantically lapping up water. The boy's reaction only encouraged the King to make a meal of his ass that much more, and the two of them began grinding

--

their slippery torsos against one another, the King eating and fingering the boy's butt, the boy slurping on the King's balls and ass and jacking off the King's cock while humping his chest. They became one feverish mass of flesh and heat, skin rubbing on skin, sweat dripping on sweat, spit cascading in rivers, their bodies frenzied and frantic and pumping and gyrating till the King blasted his cum high in the air and, moments later, the boy drowned both of their torsos with his own white milk.

The two collapsed side by side, facing opposite directions, panting for their lives. When conscious thought returned to the King, he lay still and quiet, waiting for the boy to recover, knowing they'd do it again and again and he would show the boy a thousand more things they could do with each other, that night and every night for the rest of their lives. And the King would rule his kingdom; his wives would set protocol for the women of the palace; his oldest prince would be groomed someday to rule the world; his other children would vie for other prominent roles in the village; and the King would be forever young with his boy by his side.

# The Shoeshine

*James C. Johnstone*

It is one of those sunny, soon-to-be-beach-day Monday mornings that too often follow rainy Vancouver weekends. The Skytrain I board at New Westminster Station is packed, standing-room-only all the way downtown. It screeches and squeals its way up past the drab, stuccoed bungalows on the Eighth Street hill, then eases itself up onto the gray concrete high-rise-dominated flatlands of South Burnaby.

For most of the ride I just stare down at my shiny new black Rockports, bought on sale over the weekend for seventy-five dollars. There's not much else I can do really. The windows are fogged and I am wedged between two gum-chewing Surrey girls. Well, they seem like Surrey girls, with all their makeup and hair spray. What's worse, they're friends. They prattle and gab through me all the way downtown. By the time the stuffy, overcrowded train finally lurches into the Burrard Station, I am starting to gag.

The doors open and I run for the exit, gasping for fresh air. Outside, at the top of the escalator, I pause for a minute to take a couple of deep breaths. Revived, I rejoin the flow of bleary-eyed commuters that stream up and out of the station and into the Bentall Mall, ready to face my pile of RUSH and URGENT faxes from Japan. Well, not quite. First I stop by the espresso bar just across from the shoeshine stand and treat myself to a cappuccino and pastry to go.

I pay my money and am turning around—cinnamon-sprinkled cappuccino, packet of raw sugar, wooden stir stick, and pastry in hand—when I see him, this new guy working the shoeshine booth across the way. Usually there's this older fellow. He's nice enough, always does a great job on my shoes but, you know, he's no Colt model. But this guy almost makes me drop my coffee right there.

He has dark hair and a mustache, looks as if he might be in his late twenties or so. He wears a white-and-red-striped short-sleeved shirt with a black bow tie. He has black pleated trousers and wears a pair of Rockports exactly like mine! A straw boater hat with black band finishes his outfit.

What strikes me most about him are his arms, his forearms to be exact. This guy has the most beautiful pair of well-muscled, down-covered forearms. Must be all the work with the brushes or something. But I tell you, just one look at them gets my knees a-wobbling.

His forearms remind me of this farmer I used to work for as a boy. I would earn my spending money each summer picking strawberries on his farm in Richmond. This farmer's forearms were thick and knotted from years of hard work in the fields. I would stare at them as he weighed out my load of berries at the end of each day, entranced by their size and how wonderfully strong they looked. It was my first inkling that I was interested in men. Of course, I didn't understand it then. I was only twelve. But that boyhood fascination, awakened those summers by the farmer's forearms, grew stronger over the years, and this fetish impels me even now.

I check the clock in the espresso bar. It's almost nine. No time to linger. On the sixteenth floor, a punch clock waits for my timecard.

I steal one last look. Then, careful not to spill my coffee, I hurry down the hall and up the escalator and into the lobby of my office building.

A couple of women co-workers greet me cheerily as I get on the elevator. I don't talk to them, though. I'm too engrossed in a fantasy, imagining how it might feel to be held in those arms, what it would feel like pressed against his body, pressing eager lips to that gorgeous bushy mustache, opening his mouth and kissing him.

The elevator doors open. We all pile out and run for the punch clock. As I wait in line with the others, I think about how I might go back and get a closer look. I look down and wiggle my toes inside my shiny black Rockports. I know now what I gotta do.

There are no customers at the shoeshine booth when I return an hour and a half later. I am supposed to be up in the lunchroom on my coffee break. The shoeshine man stands alone, leaning against his chairs with those beautiful forearms folded across his chest. I can see he is watching people's shoes as they walk by.

I don't go directly to the booth. No, I first go into the card shop beside the espresso bar and peer at him from behind a pair of revolving card racks. From there I can see him clearly. This time, I can pay more attention to his face. I take in the big, bushy mustache, his full mouth, and square, clean-shaven jawline. But oh, his eyes! They are a most strikingly beautiful intense blue. My knees start to get wobbly all over again.

It's time to make my move. Reluctantly, I take my eyes off the shoeshine man and look down to my Rockports. I chuckle as I admire the scuff job I did earlier on my shoes. Yes, I definitely need a shoeshine. I need one real bad. "Well, Mr. Blue Eyes," I say to myself, "ready or not, here I come." I take a deep breath and saunter over, my sweaty hands thrust into my trouser pockets.

"Good morning, sir," he says, unfolding his arms and standing to face me.

"Sir!" I think, this is going to be great! "Hello," I say, trying hard to keep an even voice. It is all I can do to keep from grinning. He steps aside, pats a red vinyl upholstered chair and invites me to take a seat.

I climb up slowly and carefully into the proffered chair and

Blue Eyes eases my feet into the cast-iron footrests. I can feel his strong, thick fingers through the shoe leather. He then sets about rolling up my pants cuffs. A deliciously warm tingly feeling starts in my chest as he holds my feet and carefully fixes the laces inside the tops of my shoes so the polish won't get on them.

"That's quite a job you did on your new Rockports."

I am startled by his choice of words. I wonder if he had noticed the polish on my shoes earlier.

"Yeah," I mutter guiltily. "Too many clumsy people on the Skytrain."

He grins slightly. "That'll do it," he says, and he leans over and reaches for a big, heavy-looking brush from a box under my seat. He gives my shoes a light brushing to get the dust off. He then puts down the brush and grabs a tin of Dubbin with his right hand, pops it open with his thumb, and soundlessly eases the lid somewhere down below my feet. He starts working the ointment into my shoe leather. He uses only his fingers. It feels wonderful, delicious, as good as any foot massage, but more sensual. My mind drifts to images of his thick greasy fingers doing other things, put to work elsewhere. Does he do house calls?

"How's the weather outside?" His deep voice jolts me from my reverie.

"Oh, it's hot, real hot. Great day for the beach."

"Yeah? Figures, doesn't it?" He looks up for a second and flashes me a big smile. I almost lose it right there.

He levers the lid off the black shoe polish and lays it down at the base of the cast-iron footrests. He chooses a small red toothbrush and begins to work the shoe polish all over the softened leather of my shoes. First the left, then the right. Each pass of the brush draws the warm tingly feeling further down through my body.

I watch as he works, how the muscles of his forearms dance under the thick dark hair. The pungent smell of shoe polish and leather permeates the air around the booth. And through it all, almost imperceptible at first, there is the sweet musky scent of Blue Eyes bending over me, working on my feet.

I wonder what his name might be, whether he is gay or just beautiful breeding stock. I check his left hand to see if he has a ring. There is a flash of gold, but on his pinky, not his ring finger. Still, that doesn't necessarily mean anything. Lots of straight men wear pinky rings. Lots of them pierce their ears and other places on their bodies. Blue Eyes has his right ear pierced, but nothing in it just then. God! It's getting so difficult to tell these days! Our gay signals too soon appropriated and co-opted as straight fashion.

Blue Eyes selects another big black brush and begins to work on my left shoe.

"That feels good," I murmur.

I gulp. I hadn't meant to say it out loud. Blue Eyes flashes another smile. I'm sure I must be blushing. It feels awfully warm all of a sudden. I can feel sweat trickle down the small of my back. I reach up with my left hand and loosen my tie. Blue Eyes pauses, rubs the back of his ample forearm through his mustache, adjusts the tilt of his boater, then bends down to work on my right shoe.

I tilt my pelvis slightly, hoping it will ease the pinch from the growing fullness in my briefs, but man, that only gets me harder. I'm glad I wore my briefs and not my boxers, but I wonder what will happen when I have to stand up.

I check the clock across the way. He is almost done, but it's getting late. I have to get back to the office. I look down again. He is giving my shoes a final buff with a cloth. Thwap, thwap. Thwapa-thwap. Thwap, thwap. Then, "Finished!"

Blue Eyes steps back to give me a clear view of my shoes, which now sparkle. My feet feel tingly and warm inside from the friction of cloth on leather. I am flushed, my entire body deliciously sensitized. Of course, I still have a throbbing hard-on that's ready to burst my Stanfields.

If he notices anything, he doesn't let on. Blue Eyes adjusts my laces and rolls my pants cuffs back in place. He straightens up and stretches. God, he's beautiful, both arms up and biceps flexed like that. He is perspiring slightly. I take in a deep breath and revel in his heady scent one last time.

"That'll be three dollars, sir." There is that smile again!

I look him in the eye as I slowly stand up and thrust my right hand into my trouser pocket. I adjust my hard-on and pull out a five in one deft movement.

"Thanks. That was great. I mean—please keep the change," and I hand him a well-warmed, slightly moistened bill. "You're new at this station, aren't you?"

He wipes his hands carefully with a rag. I swallow. It is hard not to stare at his rippling, down-covered forearms.

"Yep. Just here for a coupla weeks while the regular guy's on holiday. The name's Sam," and he extends his big right hand.

"Mine's Daniel." I reach out and take the tendered hand, careful to get a proper grip. His hands are warm and softer than I expect, probably from all the Dubbin and shoe polish.

"Well, Daniel, I'm here for the next few weeks. Come down and see me anytime you need your, uh, shoes shined," and he winks as he pockets my five.

It is all I can do to keep from squealing out loud right there in the mall. I thank him again and hop down from the seat; then, careful to restrain myself from dancing down the hall, saunter back to work in my newly polished Rockports. When I get to the escalator, I turn back for one last look, but my fantasy man is already starting on his next lucky customer.

As I ride the elevator back to the sixteenth floor, I admire the job he has done, wriggling happy toes in my shiny black shoes. I can hardly wait for my lunch break so I can go out and scuff them up again.

# Nightmare Boyfriends
*Michael Rowe*

"I killed him for love," I said to the bulldog-faced cop in the rumpled blue suit. It made perfect sense to me, but the simpleton didn't quite seem to get it.

The light was very bright. He asked me the question again.

"I killed him for love," I replied. "One of us had to die. We couldn't both exist, not at the same time. Things had gone too far."

I looked down. The Formica table separating us had cigarette burns scarring its surface. I thought of the neat roundness of the bullet hole in Toby's forehead. The detective said nothing, merely drummed his fingers on the table. Somewhere, a clock ticked. The rhythmic music of the clock became my whole world. I closed my eyes. I felt tears gathering there, and I knew I had to leave.

The room grew dark, and heavy clouds obscured the brutal white light. The detective lunged across the table and grabbed the lapel of my jacket. He screamed at me to stay where I was, but I felt myself dissolving, becoming a boiling red mist, the color of Toby's blood before it dried. I laughed through my tears at the detective. He called me a murderer, shouting that I was escaping justice.

I shuddered deeply as my body became transparent and indistinct. The ticking of the clock became a deafening roar, eclipsing the bellowing of the detective.

The crimson fog which had been my body swept up toward the window and out into the freezing night. The last thing the detective saw was my face. Before it vanished completely, I leaned down and moved my mouth next to his ear.

"Toby had to die," I whispered. "He's always taken whatever was mine, and eventually there was nothing left for me. We couldn't both exist at the same time. When he took Jerrold away with him, away from me, I had to kill him. I loved Toby. He was my best friend."

The cold rain fell in the blackness of the night, and I remembered that this was the night of the long-promised hurricane, and I'd met Jerrold at Marty and Allan's cottage near Lake Simcoe on a rain-devastated night much like this one. I felt him watching me before I actually turned and looked into his eyes. Black Irish, I thought to myself as though it were a flavor. His eyes were the color of antifreeze, the bluest hot-blue eyes I had ever seen. His hair was the color of espresso. My last thought before I fell irrevocably in love was *He looks exactly like Toby.* The same wide shoulders, the same long, hipless legs. The denim of his blue jeans was thin and faded, and when he turned and walked across the living room to change the CD, I watched him move, I saw where the cheeks of his hard ass carved the denim fabric, the way the cotton caught in the cleft like something out of some wet dream I'd had of Toby when we were sixteen. He came back to where I was standing, smiled at me, and took a long pull on his beer. His lips on the beer, hot chapped skin against ice and glass.

"So who do you know here?" he asked me, looking around the room at the chattering queens in crew-neck sweaters and khakis. He was wearing faded 501s and a blue chambray work shirt over a salmon-colored T-shirt.

"What's your name?" I asked him, ignoring his question. It was suddenly very important that his name not be something ordinary. I couldn't abide it if he was just a John or a Bill.

"Jerrold."

"Not 'Jerry'?" I said hopefully.

"Never anything but Jerrold," he said. And then he spelled it for me, letter by letter. When he finished, he smiled again, and my whole world tilted and went white at the edges.

That night, after we'd made love, I watched him shower. He had the body of a nineteen-year-old track star. The soap in his hair ran down across his neck and shoulders. His muscular arms, carved with ropes of sinew, were folded across his chest. Water cascaded from the shower nozzle. Drops of it clung to the ends of his hair like dew. Rivers of it ran between his pectorals. It ran into his eyes, and he rubbed them as a child might. His skin was winter peach and white, thin and smooth as young men's skin so often is. As he closed his eyes and undulated beneath the hot spray, I marveled at the way the water followed the contours of his body, flowing downward from the broad shoulders to the narrow waist, to the high, full mounds of his ass, and into the shadow between the smooth-marble cheeks. I felt my cock stirring again.

"Let me," I said.

"Okay," he said. "I'd like that."

I stepped into the shower with him and pressed my hard cock against his body. I adjusted the shower head, and directed a stream of clear hot water into his dark curls.

"Lean your head back," I whispered. I licked a droplet of water off his earlobe, and it somehow, I thought, tasted like him. I massaged his scalp and cleansed the soap from his hair. He turned away from me, presenting his back and shoulders. I slipped my arms around his waist from behind, thrusting against him. I laid my face against the athletic smoothness of his shoulders and closed my eyes. He leaned backwards, and we stood under the hot spray for a very long time. I knelt behind him in the shower, and the water ran into my eyes. I closed them, and in the wet red darkness I felt the steam and the water on my face. I pressed my face against his ass. I heard him sigh as I traced my tongue along the inside of his cheeks. I smelled musk and soap. With my hands, I reached around him and found his cock spearing away from his body, hard and hot, and clearly aching for release.

I poured some shampoo into my palm and began massaging the stiff cockshaft. Jerrold groaned, and I felt his knees buckle. I thrust my tongue between his cheeks and found his freshly soaped asshole. I fucked him with my tongue from behind, and stroked his stiff prick with my slippery fingers from the front. With my eyes still closed, I felt his body shudder with my rhythm, and then tense as his knees buckled again. The warm water pounded against my face as I held his muscular thighs in my arms to keep him from falling, and he came in shuddering waves. I massaged the cum into my skin, and when I raised my face to the hot spray, I licked the salty taste of his sex from my lips. He sat down in the shower and collapsed against my body. I held him in my arms for a long time as the steam billowed around us, mingling the scents of soap and fuck sweat.

Downstairs, I heard the ticking of the grandfather clock in the front hallway of the house. I heard it as we made love again after the shower, and it wove itself through my sleep as we lay entwined beneath the down-filled comforter in the darkness of the guest bedroom. The music of the clock carried me up and away, and I faded again, healing sleep covering me like the comforter itself, making me warm like the fire crackling in the grate, but there was no grate in the guest room of the cottage; it was in my living room in the city. The warmth of Jerrold's body imprinted itself on mine, and then I was dressed and sitting up in my rocking chair, mine, in my apartment.

I looked up at the ticking clock on the mantle. I smelled the incense, the scent of musk and sandalwood. Toby loved the incense, and he must have lit some while I was in the kitchen getting a Diet Coke. I smiled at Toby, who sat in his favorite chair by the fire. The Diet Coke can was so cold it burned my hand, and I put on the coffee table.

"You're *not* in love again?" Toby shouted.

"How can you tell?"

"You're acting sort of moony and stupid, and you can't seem to stop grinning."

"Maybe I am, maybe I'm not."

"No. No doubt about it at all," Toby said. "Here we go again." He jumped out of his chair and came over to hug me.

"I only want what's best for you," Toby whispered into my ear as he held me. "You know that. So, are you in love or what?"

I inhaled deeply Toby's wonderful smell. A mixture of Fahrenheit, soap, and the incense that he had lit.

"Yes," I said smugly. "You don't know him, and he hasn't got the faintest idea who you are, thank God."

"Yet," said Toby, smiling.

"Toby!"

"What's his name?"

"Jerrold. Hands off, Toby!" I laughed, to make it a joke.

Toby lay back on the couch and flexed his powerful body to its full length. I looked away from him, my face hot. I could feel him smiling behind me.

"Just kidding," he said softly.

"I know," I whispered. "I know you are."

I turned around and looked at Toby. I watched his handsome face, saw his lips move, but no words came from them. I saw him form the words I wanted to have him say, reassuring words, but somehow all I could hear was the sound of the clock, the measured mechanical ticking of wood and metal coming from Toby's perfectly formed mouth.

Rising, I moved toward him. My legs were heavy as steel, and I looked down at them, moving as though I were wading through knee-high water. Toby kept talking, and the ticking was deafening. I knocked the coffee table with my knee, and my can of Diet Coke fell to the floor. The sweet brown fluid blossomed into a spreading stain that soaked into the carpet. I looked at the pool of dark liquid on the white shag, then back at Toby.

He kept talking. I reached for him, to kiss him full on the mouth, to stop the words I couldn't hear. Gently, he moved his face away from my mouth.

*No*, I saw his lips say. *Let me.*

And he tenderly kissed me on the mouth, a beautiful Judas kiss that burned my lips, scalding me and arousing me, turn by turn.

The heat from his mouth spread through my body and out into the air. I smelled the caramel scent of Toby's marvelous body. It mingled with the sandalwood incense and the fire, and once again the borders of the room became misty and indistinct.

I reached down through the coming mist with my left hand, and grasped Toby's hand in mine. He squeezed it reassuringly. I reached out with my other hand, searching. I stretched out my fingers through the approaching darkness, and closed my eyes, summoning my lover. I called out to Jerrold, and then I felt my hand become warm and full.

I kept my eyes closed, because there was no reason to shatter the perfect harmony of our triumvirate by opening them. I felt the rhythmic caress of the clock's ticking bearing us up, as though we were bodysurfing through time and space. But I was beginning to see again, even through my closed eyelids, and when the waiter came to take our order, I knew that if I didn't open my eyes, it would look as though I had fallen asleep. I would look like a fool in front of my lover and my best friend. With Toby, showing weakness was almost always a mistake.

"It's amazing how much we look alike," Jerrold said, raising a glass of Beaujolais to his lips. "Toby and I, I mean." Jerrold's blue eyes were glowing with heat and wine. He reached across the table and touched Toby's face lightly.

Toby smiled at Jerrold and said nothing.

"If we had kids," Jerrold said drunkenly to Toby, "I wonder which one of us they'd look like?"

"You, I hope," said Toby to Jerrold.

"They'd look like me," I said uneasily. "It's the least you could do, the two of you, since I'm the idiot who's slit his own throat by introducing you. Ha-ha-ha!"

"You're actually the first gay man I've ever met who even talks about having children," Toby said to Jerrold, ignoring me. "I thought I was the only one who wanted them."

"It's hard to adopt," I said uselessly.

"Oh, I think persistence pays off," Jerrold said to me, looking at Toby.

"Well, I don't want to adopt kids, so we'll just have to find Toby a turkey-baster and a willing lesbian. Ha-ha-ha!"

Neither of them said anything, then Jerrold looked at me as though he were seeing me for the first time.

"Well, I always wanted to have kids," Jerrold said. "Just because you don't want to doesn't mean that I'm just going along with it."

"We've been going out for six months and you never mentioned something as basic as kids? What other secrets are you keeping from me, Jerrold? Ha-ha-ha!"

"Let's not get into this right now, okay?" Jerrold said coolly. "Besides, it's not really about kids, is it? It's about you not listening sometimes." He reached over and lightly patted Toby's hands. "Toby doesn't want to hear this, do you, Toby?"

"I've known Toby for ten years," I said to my lover. "If there's something that Toby doesn't need to hear, I think that I'm better equipped to judge it than you are."

"Actually," Toby said, "sometimes you *don't* listen, Stephen. This is as good a time as any to listen to what Jerrold wants. I'll mediate if you like."

"This is getting way too heavy for me," said Jerrold. "I just want to eat. Where's that old queen with our drinks?"

He began to laugh then, and Toby joined in. I didn't laugh; I just watched them, but they didn't notice me watching because they only had eyes for each other.

I heard a cook in the kitchen whipping something in a bowl, the rhythmic clack of his fork against the side of the bowl coming in precise, time-measuring beats.

Their laughter merged with the sound from the kitchen, and even when they stopped laughing and began to tell each other the stories of their lives, the metallic ticking went on, and the wine I had drunk suddenly blossomed into a painless scarlet flower with a center of pure white light. I looked into the light, and the ticking of the fork against the bowl became a clock's sharp reproach from somewhere I couldn't see because everything was white, like the fluorescent light from the kitchen at Marty and Allan's townhouse.

"Shhh," Toby whispered. He looked very smart in his navy blue suit. Jerrold was naked, sitting at Marty's kitchen table. I asked him why he was naked when Toby and I were dressed, but he just smiled enigmatically and said nothing.

"Stop that clicking sound," Toby said, indicating the metal mixing bowl and the fork in my hands. He nodded toward the dining room, where the sounds of a lively dinner party issued through the swinging door. "They'll hear you."

"Toby and I have something to tell you," Jerrold said, rinsing the soap from his hair as the water gushed from the shower nozzle in the middle of the ceiling. Clouds of clean-smelling steam rose from his body. The steam fogged Marty's glass-fronted kitchen cabinets, and Jerrold began to draw a happy-face in the steam, then changed his mind and turned the corners of the mouth downward.

"Shall I tell him?" Toby said.

"No," Jerrold said. "Let me."

I looked down at the metal mixing bowl and the fork in my hands. The bowl was full of Diet Coke, and as I whipped it with the fork, it turned red and foamy.

"Tell me what?" I said, although I already knew. Red foam splashed over the side of the mixing bowl and stained my white pants like gouts of fresh blood.

When I looked up, Jerrold and Toby were entwined in each other's arms. Toby disengaged himself, and began to undress. He removed the white shirt, exposing his broad chest and powerful shoulders.

"Doesn't he have a beautiful body?" Jerrold crooned, running his hands across Toby's bronzed skin. "I always wished you'd work out and get a body like that. Oh, well." He licked his index finger and smiled.

"Steve, it just happened," Toby apologized. "You'd told me so much about him, I kind of fell for him before we even met."

Toby was nude, although I hadn't seen him remove his pants. His erection flexed lewdly, and Jerrold reached down with his hand and covered it. With his other hand, he wagged his finger at me and smiled like a whore. Then he knelt down and took Jerrold's hard prick into his mouth and began to suck on it. Jerrold groaned, and his knees buckled. He gathered Toby's ebony hair in his fingers and pulled his face hard against his groin. Jerrold turned sideways and I saw the striated muscles of his lean hips flex as he accommodated Toby's mouth and throat.

"Please don't take this the wrong way," Jerrold said wetly. "When I met Toby, well, I felt the earth move. Not to denigrate our relationship, Stephen, but I never felt that when I met you."

Toby licked his lips and stood up. Jerrold grimaced in frustration and began to caress his own shaft with languid strokes. From somewhere in the distance, I thought I heard muffled screams, but the sound was very far away. The mixing bowl was still in my hands. The red liquid inside frothed as I whipped it with the spoon.

"Stop that goddamn clicking, would you?" Toby snapped at me. "It's pissing me off." He jerked his thumb toward the dining room. "And they'll hear you!"

I looked down and saw the gun in my hands. It was warm and heavy, the way Jerrold's body had felt next to mine that night in Lake Simcoe. I didn't wonder where the gun had come from, it had always been there, in my hands.

*Toby, I love you so much. I've been in love with you longer than you've been my friend. Why do you hurt me so much? Isn't there anything that's just mine? Couldn't Jerrold have been just mine?*

"You already know the answer to that one, Steve-O," Toby said. We were alone in the kitchen. It was dark, except for the moonlight which flooded the kitchen like phosphorus. Toby was no longer naked. He wore faded 501s and a blue chambray work shirt over a salmon-colored T-shirt.

"Anything you can do, I can do better," he whispered. "And I always will. It's my nature."

My eyes were blurred with tears, but I saw the moonlight strike the barrel of the gun. I cocked it. Click-click-click.

"Do what you have to do, Steve. You're my best friend. I only want what's best for you, you know that."

And then I fired. The explosion rocked me backwards against the wall. The smoke burned my eyes. I smelled Fahrenheit, and sulfur, and gunpowder.

Toby lay in the center of the kitchen, a perfect hole carved into his forehead just above his eyes. Beaujolais gushed from the wound, spilling across the floor like a red halo.

I heard the handle of the door to the dining room rattle, and I thought, now I will be discovered. Murderer, that's what I am. Jealous and vengeful and spiteful. Couldn't compete with Toby, never could, because I was a coward and I deserved to lose everything to him.

The doorknob rattled again, and I looked across the room at the door, which began to swing open. The light that exploded through the doorway was cruel and brilliant and blinding, and I stared into it, inviting the searing blindness as an atonement. The ticking of the clock erupted like hoofbeats, and I struggled to a sitting position, kicking away the sheets and blankets, and when Jerrold turned on the light in the bedroom, I sat upright and shouted, *"Toby, where's Toby's body?"* knowing that I was lost, and Jerrold was merely the first to discover my crime. I opened my eyes and winced in the harsh light.

"How's your headache?" Jerrold asked. He crossed to my bedside and touched my forehead. "You're still running a bit of a fever, but your forehead's cooler." He picked up the alarm clock beside my bed and switched off the ringer. The clock ticked softly in his hand. "I thought I'd come in here and see how you were."

"Toby…," I whispered. The bed was soaked with my sweat, and

the pillow was damp and streaked with tears. Outside, the wind blew fistfuls of rain against the window of the bedroom.

"Toby called about fifteen minutes ago from Miami," Jerrold said. "They've closed the airport. Nobody in or out. The hurricane is pretty fierce there."

"Rain..."

"Look at these sheets," Jerrold said, bending over and picking up the blanket from the floor. "Did you do this? I thought you were just going to lie down." He laughed. "I didn't realize you were going to trash the place."

Jerrold reached out his hand, and I grasped it. He helped me to sit up.

"Did he say when he was coming?" I said.

"He said he'd call when the airport was opened again," Jerrold said, sitting down on the bed beside me. "It's too bad. I was really looking forward to meeting him tonight. Your oldest friend." He laughed. "A piece of your past! That's what he is, a piece of your past. I want to know *everything* about you."

"I'll tell you all by myself," I said. I pressed my hot face into the cool skin of my lover's chest, and closed my eyes. "Anything you want to know, ask me. Don't ask Toby."

"Why not?"

"Just...don't."

Jerrold pushed me away gently and looked at me, confused.

"You told me so much about him," he said. "I thought you wanted me to meet him so badly. Now you're acting like you're glad the airport's closed."

"I'm fine," I said, remembering other men, other nights, and wondering if friendship and love and betrayal would always just be different shadows cast by the same man. "Really, I'm fine," I said to Jerrold, listening to the clock ticking on the table, wondering if a hurricane could last forever.

# Freon
*Tom Cole*

From a very young age Terrance knew he had a double. Out there, somewhere, there was someone doing the same thing he was doing, to the same tempo, the same rhythm, perhaps even the same strokes, but each time doing it differently. It was in those quiet moments he knew it. When he sat alone in the dark closet reading *Dynamite* magazine and eating ice cream straight from the carton with his fingers. When everyone was gone and he was left alone to roam through his parents' belongings with the ease and time he needed. When the water drained from the tub. When he put both feet behind his head and squeezed his lanky body into the refrigerator that sat in his backyard. When he fit his body into a clothes hamper. But he was absolutely sure his double existed whenever he spotted the pink spider.

When the pink spider appeared to him, it would hover and spin in the middle of the ceiling like a fan. He would lie in the center of the room on the floor and stare at it for hours, thinking of Ferris wheels, carousels, spinning rooms with removable floors, whirling dervishes, Tasmanian devils, and windmills. After a while it felt as if the room itself were spinning, and the spider was standing still. And then it disappeared as quickly as it had appeared, the room coming to an abrupt halt, and he could resume his daily life. The spider appeared at the strangest times, at the strangest places. And when it appeared, he looked at nothing but it, his eyes locked into position for hours. He was compelled to look at the pink spider. It had him under its spell. And after it disappeared, he slept.

The pink spider looked real to Terrance. Its black hair swayed in the wind as its arms moved up and down like a finely tuned machine. At times it appeared like a miniature version of the large balloons Terrance saw on television on Thanksgiving day. He wondered if there were strings attached to it somewhere, keeping the pink spider from escaping its position and flying up, up, up into the stratosphere.

Once, Terrance saw a float at Mardi Gras that looked like his pink spider. He had been separated from his parents for hours. He chased after a tossed doubloon and got confused in the chaotic crowd. He looked up from his crouched position, and through the legs of strange tourists he saw it. It was a float adorned with begonias. Scores of people stood on it in matching spider suits waving at the crowd. They seemed to be wearing full-body panty hose with a weblike pattern. There was a stereo blasting the theme song from the TV show *Spider-Man*. One large man with eight long arms sprouting out of his back and a hairy chest was tossing coconuts into the crowd. Whenever a female spectator revealed her breast he would let the tropical treat fly, aiming for the flesh. People would hurdle over each other to catch the strange football. "Show me some tit!" he screamed. A ninth leg crawled out of his fly. "Spider-Man, Spider-Man, does whatever a spider can, spins a web, any size." At this point in the tune, with a sneer, he spun the leg that crawled out of his pants. "Catches thieves just like flies, look out, here comes the Spider-Man." Above the coconut man was a huge spider with undulating arms. "At the scene of the crime, in the still of the night, he arrives unannounced, just in time!" It seemed to be made of pink carnations, Terrance's mother's favorite flower. He looked in awe as the huge spider crawled by.

The spider first appeared to him as a child in his mother's bathroom when he was nine. He would sit on the commode backwards, playing with his toys on top of the tank. He sat for hours, distracting his mind from his body so his bowels would move. And then the spider would appear in the middle of the ceiling and he would lean further and further backwards toward the floor, his head leaning against the cool tile, his feet resting on top of the tank, knocking some of the tinker toys into the bowl. His toe accidentally flicked the lever causing the toilet to flush, the water spiraling inwards to the same rhythm of the spinning spider. The miniature plane and pilot plummeted into the plumbing. His eyes spun into his head as the spider spun faster and faster until he felt as if his soul were going to spin out of his body, the centrifugal force being too strong to maintain psychic equilibrium. He knew, right then and there, he had a double, and the spider was some sort of clue. Out there, somewhere, was a confidant, someone who thought only of him. The spider was a message, a window.

Terrance's old shotgun house was as long and skinny as his body and there was only one window on each side of the rectangular structure, right smack in the middle of each wall. There was a three-foot gap between each identical house in his neighborhood, as if they were rows and rows of some crook's badly spaced teeth. The roads in Marrero weren't paved yet and seemed to be only a thin layer consisting of shells and dust, as leathery as Huey P. Long's tongue. Terrance only saw real roads when his family visited New Orleans in the summer.

In his backyard there was an old refrigerator and bathtub. On top of the tub was a wire mesh of the type used for window screens, held down by a large rock. Within the tub were three baby alligators his brother had caught in the swamp. They moved their tails around like whips.

The bathtub had been used for special occasions in the past.

The crawfish for the yearly boil were cleaned in the old tub. Because of their muddy lives in the swamps, they would have to walk the plank. A wooden board would be put across the tub, and the crawfish would be forced to walk it like Wendy in *Peter Pan*. As they scurried across, a steady stream of water was projected onto them from a garden hose. The dead crawfish were exposed and discarded, the live ones caught by the tub below.

Terrance felt sorry for the doomed mud bugs until one of them caught his little toe in its clippers. He screamed for help as he kicked his foot in the air with the crawfish hanging onto his toe for dear life like a pit bull engaged in combat. His mother had come to the rescue, prying the clippers open and throwing the red devil into a large pot of heavily seasoned boiling water which rested on a gas burner in the back yard. "Bad crawdad," she said. "You get to eat that one, Terrance. You can even eat the insides of its claw."

Terrance cried and cried as his mother went into the house to fetch a popsicle. She split the cherry treat on the corner of the cement steps which led up to the back door. She always had a knack for splitting it right down the middle. Whenever Terrance tried to do it himself, it shattered into small pieces. She gave half of the popsicle to Terrance and then placed the other half on his swelling toe. The blood red cherry juice oozed over his toe into the gravel and grass below, attracting an army of ants. Terrance clung to his half of the popsicle like a pacifier. From then on, Terrance enjoyed watching the crawfish struggle to get out of the hot pot. He would knock the determined buggers back into it with a large wooden spoon. He pretended he was Captain Hook whenever the crawfish were on the plank. "Now I've got you, my little pretties," he exclaimed, as he ran in a wild circle around the tub filled with the miniature lobsters. His father, who was spraying them down with a hose, doused Terrance with the cold water. "I'm gonna put you in the tub with them if you don't calm down," he would say.

Terrance and his brother Josh used to play blackjack for hours in their den. The room had shag carpeting, brown faux leather couches, and wood paneling for walls. In the center of each wall hung a God's eye. Terrance had made them at school by twirling orange yarn around two perpendicular sticks. They looked like sagging square rugs. Terrance liked making them, hypnotized by the repetitive wrapping technique.

"God is always watching you," his mother would say. "From all sides. He knows if you sin, whether or not you confess it."

Terrance always made sure he executed his most dastardly deeds outside of the den. The spider never appeared to him there. He figured it was afraid of God.

Once, when Terrance was feeling exceptionally rebellious, he stood in the middle of the room with all of his might. He closed his eyes, clenched his fingers into fists, tensing up every muscle in his body, and right then and there took the Lord's name in vain.

"Goddammit," he said.

He imagined bolts of lightning would come storming out of the four eyes like wasps, stinging him all over, but nothing happened. He thought he would be quartered, one portion of his body being sucked into each God's eye. Nothing happened.

Terrance never really understood blackjack. He could barely add.

"You would have to be a human calculator to win," he would tell his brother.

They gambled for real money, and at the age of twelve Terrance owed his brother three million, five thousand, and fifty-two dollars. Just as he thought God was really watching him from within the yarn eyes, he thought he really owed his brother that money.

"I'll pay it back somehow."

"Maybe you should get a paper route," said Josh.

"Let's play another round. Double or nothing." A desperate plea.

Josh was a football player. He was strong and mean and no one could believe that he and Terrance came from the same family.

He took in a deep breath and said, "All right, double or nothing, but if you don't start paying up I'm gonna slam your ass."

Terrance broke out in a cold sweat. This could be it, he could be released from all of his debt in the same way his sins seemed to vanish whenever he went to confession.

"I'll deal," said Josh.

The usual happened. Terrance took one hit to many. His debt doubled like an unconfessed sin. He collapsed into a ball and cried.

"Don't be a wus." Josh flung Terrance onto his back.

*"Mom!"* yelled Terrance.

Before he could yell out again, Josh stuck his fist in Terrance's mouth. Terrance tried to beg for mercy, but his lips could barely move. He bit into the fist hard and kicked Josh in the crotch. Josh let out a high-pitched yelp and his face turned red. Now I've done it, thought Terrance. This is it.

Josh pinned Terrance to the shag, both hands held down. He sat on Terrance's stomach. Terrance tried to kick Josh, but his feet wouldn't reach. Josh moved his face closer to Terrance and said, "You little pussy. You fuckin' little stupid spaced-out pussy. You got no common sense."

He spat onto Terrance's face. Saliva dripped off of his chin. Terrance was crying now. Saliva was serious. Terrance stared at the ceiling, which had fanlike shapes scraped into the heavy paint. For the first time ever, the spider appeared to him in the den. From the corner of his eye he could see the God's eyes spinning as well, rotating at the same speed as the spider. His eyes glazed over as he felt his soul leave his body, stopping to hover just above his brother in order to get a better view of the spider. From here he couldn't feel Josh's saliva. He couldn't feel the blood building up in his arms as it tried to run through the veins in his wrists where his brother had him pinned. Somehow, Josh could sense this, and it made him even madder. Terrance could hear his brother spitting and talking.

"You little spaced-out pussy. You're gonna pay. You are going to owe me for the rest of your life. Are you listening to me? What are ya lookin' at, faggot? I bet you never shook that little lizard of yours, have ya? Did ya ever get a little leg, a little lip? Nahhhh, you're too much of a little faggot. I've seen the way you eat those popsicles, you little prick. Go off and play tickle dick with all your little friends. You probably couldn't even bone a cat if you wanted to."

The confessional reminded Terrance of the old Westinghouse. Like the refrigerator, it was cold and dark and the light blinked on and off to the rhythm of the flimsy plastic door as it opened and closed. Terrance felt safe in it. The hard part was waiting to enter. He sat in the pew in front of the strange boxes. Terrance thought it looked like three refrigerators all in a row. The middle one, a bit grander than the others, was adorned with a large cross, and was meant specifically for the priest. The two slightly smaller boxes were on either side of the priest's box, one acting as a sort of loading dock. As the priest was hearing confession from one churchgoer, the previously purged sinner would exit, leaving the box empty for the next sinner to enter, sit quietly in the dark space, and collect his thoughts, his sins, his prayers, his soul.

Terrance knelt patiently, his original sin hovering above him like the spider. It weighed on him like an anvil, the sins piling up in his brain like a long line of anxious children waiting to ride an amusement park ride, anxiously awaiting the thrills and chills of some twirling mechanical treat. He could feel them bouncing around in his brain, aching to get out, leaving more room for his soul to breathe. Sometimes Terrance thought his soul left his body because his sins, some of them mortal, had piled up so high there was nowhere for his soul to go but up, up, up.

He wriggled his knees around nervously, trying to alleviate some of the pressure they felt from his body.

Mary-Jane from across the street was currently in the confessional baring her soul. Andrew was in the loading dock. Mary-Jane was taking a long time. Did anyone actually tell their real sins, thought Terrance. He had never been able to tell any real ones himself. Only minor ones like, "I fought with my brother, I took the Lord's name in vain three times, I did not honor my mother and father because I said I would take out the trash but I didn't." Some of these sins were lies. Terrance's parents never asked him to take out the trash. It would pile up in the hallway like a snowdrift.

Terrance thought he could hear Mary-Jane talking from where he sat in the pew. He strained to hear her, but all he heard was mumbling. He wondered if today would be the day he would actually confess a real sin or two. They were piling up like mad. Sister Roberts from school had told him that every time you didn't confess a sin, you were committing another sin, and your debt to God would double, more days in Purgatory and perhaps even Hell. He figured that if he had a dollar for every sin he had committed, he could pay off his gambling debt to his brother.

He clasped his sweaty hands together in prayer and stared up at the ceiling of the church. Stucco. He wanted to become invisible and wander into the confessional to hear what Mary-Jane was saying.

He imagined that there had been a terrible flood. He would swim up to the top of the church, the water being so high he could touch the statue of Jesus that hung above the altar. Then he would realize that Father Jim, Mary-Jane, and Andrew were caught in the confessionals below. Jesus would look at him endearingly, encouraging him to swim down to save them. Diving down into the water, he would force himself further and further down, his ears popping, in danger of drowning himself. In an act of religious heroism, he would release them from their vaults like Houdini, allowing them to escape just in the nick of time. He would be crowned a saint. Saint Terrance, the Jacques Cousteau of the religious world. Ciboriums, hymnals, and bishop's miters would float in the holy water like seaweed.

Mary-Jane exited the confessional with her hands clasped. With real religious determination, she headed straight for the altar and knelt in front of it. Penance. Terrance wondered what she got. Probably just a handful of Hail Marys.

He walked toward the confessional like Frankenstein's monster, drawn into it by its real leather seat and cushy kneeler. He closed the door shut slowly. The light clicked off mysteriously. Terrance wondered how they did that. He liked to think it was God who had his hand on some hidden light switch. He leaned forward and knelt on the kneeler. He could hear Andrew confessing through the screened window into Father Jim's chamber.

"I haven't sinned, Father."

"We all sin, son. 'Fess up."

"I...I...I...," he said before he burst into tears.

"Don't be a pansy, *Andrew...*"

Oh, my, thought Terrance, Father Jim recognized Andrew's voice. Terrance realized he was committing another sin. He knew it was strictly forbidden to listen in on anyone else's confession, but he just couldn't resist. I can't even sit still without sinning, thought Terrance.

"I've seen ya stapled up to the blackboard in Sister Roberts' class. Whaddya do to deserve that?" said Father Jim.

Sister Roberts had a habit of stapling mischievous kids' hair to the bulletin board whenever they acted up. Once she had five kids, all in a row, stapled up to the wall in the front of the class. Then she would take chalk and put it on their noses. "Scarecrows," she would say, "you all look like scarecrows." They strained their heads forward, feeling the hair break and tug at the skin on their scalp. "Now the fun part is getting out," she said, as she chuckled to herself. It made Terrance think of Houdini.

Andrew whimpered. He was caught. "I didn't do anything."

"If you don't 'fess up I'm gonna come in there and womp you across the head, and your hair is going to go flyin' through the air like a water rat."

"I told Sarah that she didn't have a penis because ants had eaten it all up!" Andrew blurted out. "I told her that it was better to have a penis because it's better to be a priest than a nun and it's better to be the baby Jesus getting spanked than it is to be the Virgin Mary."

"Well, there's a grain of truth in that, sonny boy!" Father Jim laughed. Terrance heard him take a sip of something.

Andrew was on a roll now. "I walked into my mother's bedroom while she was asleep. I touched her boob. It felt like a jellyfish. Then I hid behind her bed and waited for her to wake up. She got up and didn't notice me so I slid under the bed. While I was down there, she got undressed and went in to take a shower. I watched her dry off and get dressed again. She had nice tits for a mother."

"Yeah, your mom's tits aren't bad. I'd take her tits any day. Your sins are absolved, ya little squirt. Go say some Our Fathers. It's better to say Our Fathers than it is to say Hail Marys. Whenever you get a boner for your old woman, just say the Our Father till it goes away. Works for me."

"Thank you, Father." Andrew scurried out.

Terrance sat in horror as the window slid open. He had never confessed his sins to Father Jim before. He stared into the square hole that led into Father Jim's cubicle. Out of nowhere, the pink spider appeared to him in the screen. A miniature version, as if the house of the Lord had made it shrink into a less powerful prototype. Have spider, will travel. It seemed to him that a television broadcasting the spider had been inserted into the window, one foot by one foot by one foot.

"Forgive me, Father, for I have sinned."

"How long has it been since your last confession?"

"Three weeks," Terrance said as he stared into the whirl of pink legs which hovered in between him and the priest.

"'Fess up."

As if hypnotized by the spider, Terrance spoke in a voice which did not seem to be his own. He felt as if his double were speaking through him, rearing his head, able to express himself through Terrance, and Terrance alone.

"For starters, I always like to bite down on the communion host. I like the way it feels on my teeth. I like to chew on it like a nipple, squeezing down on the unleavened flesh. I like to think about bonin' animals while I chew it. Anything to forget. I'll fuck anything in sight. Anything that wriggles. They told us it would bleed if it touched your teeth. The host, that is. Nothing doing. Out of pocket. Just doesn't happen. I chew and chew and nothing happens. That ain't hay. No, not that. Not hay. So one time I went in and got the host, you know, in my hand. Someone had dipped it into the wine, the blood, so it was all soggy like buttered popcorn or blood sausage. Instead of putting it in my mouth, I wrapped my fingers around it and put my hand into my pocket. I walked straight out of the church without even flinching. Without even doing the sign of the cross. That gesture, that gesture, again and again, it is driving me mad—everyone's hands just flailing around their heads like a dragonfly, like they're making a figure eight, like they are making a God's eye—it is just driving me mad, all of those hands just moving around, just moving around. So I walk out of the church with that bit of flesh all clenched up in my hand in my pocket and my palms are sweatin'. I'm real scared 'cause I think someone could have seen me do it, walkin' out of there with my hand in my pocket. Just keep walkin' and don't look back, I tell myself. Ain't nobody gonna catch ya. Just act like you are taking an ordinary stroll through the neighborhood. I walk out and go to sit in my brother's Trans Am. My brother, he's decided it's cool to go to church if you wear jeans. So he's sittin' in there in his jeans digesting his little bit of unleavened heaven and I'm sitting in his car lookin' at my smushed-up saggy piece lying around all blandlike in my palm. I turned on the radio. Molly Hatchet. Acid rock. Hell yeah!! Woooooowo!!! So with my other hand I unzip my pants and wriggle them down to my knees, my dick getting turned on just by the thought of it. All the possibilities. Would God strike me down? Will I go to hell, I ask myself. You gotta take risks. Ya gotta take calculated risks. So I start shakin' my lizard, just jerkin' that tube. I could see Jesus standin' there on the cross, his dick hangin' out. I came into the communion host. The second cumming of Christ. The shit just oozed all over it. I popped it into my mouth and in the gob it went with. I chewed hard. Nothing happened, Father. Nothing at all."

At this moment the spider disappeared and Terrance fell to the base of the confessional, his face resting up against the cool door. Sweat drifted off his forehead onto the kneeler. He could barely see

Father Jim in the confessional. Terrance assumed he had bent over his knee in order to tie his shoe. Terrance thought he better get on goin' get on goin' on gone while the goin' was good so he bolted out of the confessional and headed up to the front of the church as if he had been given penance. Instead of praying, he heard the same voice, the same phrase, just runnin' around, just runnin' around his brain.

Father Jim never got up and never left that confessional. They found him, the following Sunday, still bent over his knee, mid tie of the shoe. He died of a heart attack. Terrance decided he would keep his sins to himself from now on.

The old Westinghouse refrigerator which lived next to the bathtub in the back-yard had functioned as the family icebox for years. It died about the same time the spider began to appear to Terrance. The handle had already fallen off years before and the door had to be opened by grabbing the dirty edge itself. Like winter at the north pole, it had been nighttime twenty-four hours a day in that fridge for years. Once, when Terrance went to open up the produce drawer it flopped out of the refrigerator onto the floor. A puddle of brown opaque liquid at the bottom of the fridge was revealed.

When the old Westinghouse worked, it always had a sickly odor to it, like sweet pickles. It clanked so loud his father would wake up in the middle of the night specifically to kick it. The clanking subsided, and the sounds of dragonflies flew into the house. Until one day the clanking stopped for good and the Westinghouse passed away. Terrance was sad when it died. He imagined that when the electricity stopped pulsating though the rubber veins of the fridge, Freon from within the coils left the metal frame and rose up, up, up to the heavens like the Virgin Mary.

It took them three weeks to get the refrigerator out of the house, and then another four months to get the new Westinghouse, this time yellow. It could never replace the green one. Terrance was loyal.

Terrance spent hours in the old green Westinghouse once it

was moved into the backyard, figuring out new ways to squeeze his body into it. He felt safe in the fridge, away from the other kids and closer to his double. And when he was lucky, the pink spider would appear at the top of the fridge, spinning like a ventilation fan.

Terrance learned he was flexible at a very young age. He could kick both feet behind his head without using his hands. He claimed he learned his unusual tricks from the old green Westinghouse. He would give shows for money in their backyard in front of the refrigerator. On top of the green door he painted, "Terrance the Terrific, Terrible, Terrifying, Transformer." Informing the other kids how dangerous the acts he was about to perform were, he would scowl, "Don't try this at home!" Next he explained how he could contort his body into a ball small enough to fit into the refrigerator. He stripped down to his holey BVDs. This, he felt, accentuated his long limbs.

Thrusting out the produce drawer from the refrigerator, he explained the expensive life of a performer. The kids threw change into it as if it were a donation basket in church. Sometimes he put on a pair of his Mother's panty hose, the old pair she used to tie her boobs down with when she exercised. Then, suddenly, as if moved by some unseen force, he kicked one foot behind his head without using his hands. Smoking a cigarette with the toes of his other foot, he explained to his audience that he was "death-defying," and "the most flexible thing this side of the Mason-Dixon line."

After putting the cigarette out on the ground, he kicked the other foot behind his head and forced it halfway down his back. He had succeeded at this point if he saw the spectators dry-heaving. An odd sort of thumbs-up. Then he waddled up to the refrigerator and closed the door shut with his teeth. He could hear the kids gasping. The tricky part, he thought, was getting out.

The pink spider would appear, hovering, spinning. He felt close to his double. As the air in the refrigerator decreased, he felt his soul escaping from the Westinghouse, flying way above the fridge, the shotgun house, and the gravel road. He could see all the kids surrounding the refrigerator, wondering what to do next. He tried to holler down at them to open the door, that he was running out of oxygen, but he realized his soul had no lips. One day, when he was twelve, he even heard the kids talking.

"Should we open it?"

"I don't know, if he is *so* terrific, he should be able to get out on his own."

"Maybe he slipped out the back."

"*I* think it's all done with *mirrors*."

Terrance thought this must be the type of conversations people hear from within an open casket.

This time, the other kids didn't open the door. They were getting bored with the old routine. Instead, just as Terrance was running out of air and in danger of suffocation, his mother stormed out of the long house with a wrench. Moments earlier, she had reached into the yellow Westinghouse for some buttermilk. A spider crawled out of the cardboard carton. She had screamed and run over to the kitchen window in order to toss the spider out of the house when she saw the kids standing around the old fridge with their hands in their pockets. As she ran to the fridge which contained Terrance, she forgot about the spider and it climbed up her sleeve toward her underarm.

From the sky, Terrance's soul watched her apron billow in the air like the balloon top of a jellyfish as she ran across the backyard, wrench held up high. The other kids scattered. She pried open the refrigerator door, half expecting to find Terrance dead. He fell out, gasping for air, his face pained and green, his feet still behind his head. She looked at him, exasperated. He handed her the money he had collected. She put it in her apron pocket and, with a confused look on her face, headed back to the house.

Terrance lay on the ground and looked up to the heavens as the door of the fridge swayed in the humid wind. His joints ached. I have premature arthritis, he thought. One of the clouds looked like a spider. He wondered if his double, whomever he might be, wherever he might be, could see the same cloud. Meanwhile, inside, the live spider, still covered in buttermilk, climbed across his mother's breast, stopping to rest on her nipple, the eight legs clamping onto all sides.

Terrance could hear the phone ringing and ringing from inside the house. He couldn't figure out why his parents weren't answering the phone. Perhaps they were "catching spiders," he thought. This was the euphemism his parents used for sex. Sometimes his father got that look in his eyes when they were watching television together on a Saturday night. Turning to Terrance's mother with a seductive grin, he would say, "Wanna go catch some spider?" Blushing, she would look away. After a couple of awkward moments she would find some excuse to leave the room. "I'd better go do the dishes before they crust over." His father would scratch his knees with all ten fingers and say, "I'm beat. I'm gonna hit the hay." Terrance thought it odd his parents actually thought he didn't know what they were talking about.

He stumbled up to the house, still out of wind from his act, and picked up the heavy receiver. The woman on the other line didn't give him a chance to say hello.

"Do you realize it is against the law to have an unchained refrigerator in your backyard!? Yawl, yawl, this just ain't right. If that's a refrigerator, it's a refrigerator from hell. I'm feelin' cold right now. I feel cold. I feel so cold. I feel like I am in a really dark space! It's freezing. Someone's gonna die in that refrigerator. They have commercials on TV. I'm gonna call the cops. I'm gonna call the cops. They have commercials on TV. I feel cold. This just ain't right." And then she hung up. How odd, thought Terrance.

That night, Terrance couldn't sleep. He was pouring over biology books that described the differences between male and female organs. He stared at the scientific drawings for hours, thinking of okra and caramelized onion gems. He went to the bathroom to look for something to do. He thought if he hung out in there long enough, the pink spider might appear and lull him to sleep right then and there on the bathroom floor. He read his father's *Reader's Digest* magazine. No spider. No yawns. Then he drew a spiderweb on the mirror with toothpaste. Hell to pay tomorrow, he thought. He wanted to smash the mirror, with hopes that the spiderweb cracks might evoke the pink spider, but fears of bad luck kept him from it.

Rummaging through the cabinets beneath the sink he found some cigars. They were white and labeled "Tampax." When he pulled the string he expected the cigar to light on its own or explode like a party favor on New Year's Eve, but nothing happened. He still felt restless. He imagined that the bathtub was a moon landscape, the soap dish a space port, the bar of soap a futuristic spaceship. He lay facedown in the tub and looked down into the drain. Nothing going on down there.

Turning over onto his back, he looked up to the ceiling. He took off his clothes and threw them onto the floor. He began to fill up the tub. He decided to rehearse his act. He kicked his legs over his head, his back flat up against the bottom of the tub. His penis rested above his face, dangling. He thought of the scientific drawings in the biology book, and it grew, the head of it touching his upper lip. He edged his legs further and further back by moving his toes down the side of the tub. He got the first half of it into his mouth. He had never thought it could get this big.

Watching the pink spider twirl out of the corner of his eye, his hips shook back and forth and his brain felt as if it were about to explode. The spider spun faster and faster. Terrance's body quaked. As if he himself were spinning some odd sort of web, he came in his own mouth. Convulsing. He swallowed hard. It was like having the ocean in his mouth. His legs flopped forward and slammed against the side of the tub. The water was about to overflow and gallons of it sloshed onto the floor. He could see the spider clearly now. Spider hunting, he thought.

He could feel his own semen drifting down his throat. He felt as if his esophagus were rasping. Repelled, he staggered out of the tub. Without drying off or putting on his clothes, he walked from the cool tile toward the shag carpeting in the hallway, looking back toward the tub. The water was overflowing, causing a puddle to form in the middle of the bathroom. He could see the spider spinning and spinning, and its reflection in the water. He thought it looked like some queer windmill harnessing electricity for the house. He turned away from the spider, somehow able to break its hypnotic draw. He walked forward like a zombie, putting one foot in front of the other. His face, expressionless. His eyes, locked. Stumbling down the stairs and through the dark kitchen like a somnambulist, he began to dream. In his dream he saw a large football field filled with hundreds and hundreds of refrigerators, all opening and closing of their own volition, creating a symphony of light. He could almost hear them humming. It must be half time, he thought.

He stumbled into the backyard and walked toward the refrigerator like a diviner to water. His smooth wet body glistened in the moonlight and the refrigerator appeared to be a monolith. He was overtaken by the size of it. It seemed bigger somehow, and more rectangular, as if all the dents and crevices had been filled. He felt himself in relationship to it, as if it were another person. He opened the refrigerator door. The light in the Westinghouse went on for the first time in years. "Rising to the occasion?" he asked it. No reply.

With the skill and ease of a rehearsed performer he threw both feet behind his head and dragged himself into the fridge. The door slowly shut on its own. The airtight suction made his eardrums pop. He swallowed again, unable to forget the spiderweb in his throat.

He waited for the spider to catch up with him. It must still be in the bathroom, he thought. This time, as the air dissipated, his soul did not separate so easily from his body. He began to gasp for air. He clawed at the door, but the suction prevented it from opening. He began to yell for help hysterically, but no one could hear him. He cried out, "Oh spider, oh spider, why have you forsaken me!" Nothing happened. The refrigerator light shone bright and bold into his eyes. He could see himself dying in the reflection of the chrome. His throat made strange floppy noises. When the last breath was taken, Terrance's soul evaporated into the air like Freon, finding its way up, up, up into the stratosphere. Without looking back, he ascended.

At this very moment, a thousand of miles away in Myrtle Beach at a country fair, Cody the Contortionist was in the middle of his act. He had squeezed his body into a tiny glass box, one foot by one foot by one foot. It was sealed, and he was beginning to run out of air. Perspiration clung to the sides of the glass box. Like a pretzel, one leg climbed up his back while the other was wrapped around his stomach. He had learned how to slow down his heart rate and his breathing to accommodate the small box. Three hundred members of the audience gasped as they thought mostly of back problems and neck cricks, when suddenly, out of nowhere, Cody the Contortionist felt a chill run through his body, freezing his spinal cord, chilling his very soul. A loss had occurred. Something was missing. He felt an odd sensation in his throat, as if a lizard were running down it, gripping onto the sides of his esophagus.

Suddenly, he felt too large for his custom-made cage. His soul had grown, he thought. It slipped through the cracks of the glass box and flew up to the top of the large tent. From there, the glass box looked like an ice cube, or perhaps a crystal which had caught some unlucky bug. The sides of the tent moved up and down like the balloon top of a jellyfish. The audience squirmed in their seats like tentacles. The glass box with his body within sat steady like the eye of a tornado. He wanted to fly away from the tent and the show. The sight of himself repelling the audience disturbed him. A baby was crying. An old woman was puking. Three girls sitting in a row were pointing at him and looking away in disgust. He heard someone say, "Oh my God, what he is doing with his body, it's so gross, I can't even look at him. Oh my God, Oh My God! I think I am gonna throw up. *Revolting!* Imagine what his parents must think."

At this moment his body grew a bit, enough to shatter all four sides of the glass. His soul zoomed back into his body and he was looking at the world through the spiderweb cracks in his glass box.

Without waiting for the end of his act, he climbed out quickly in his leotard and loincloth. When the audience applauded, he didn't bow. They stared at him as he exited the large tent. Something was terribly wrong. He couldn't put his finger on it.

He headed straight for his favorite ride, the Spindly Spider. The Spindly Spider was a large pink metallic dinosaur of a ride which was composed of twelve branchlike extensions; at the end of each was a car for two people in the shape of a spider's foot. When the ride was in full gear, the arms moved up and down and around and around while the feet themselves twirled. Lining each arm was a row of lights.

Cody the Contortionist was so famous he was allowed to ride any of the rides as many times as he wished, a twelve-year-old's dream. For Cody, however, the excitement had long since worn off. Like a junkie, he rode the ride anyway, never getting scared, never getting high. Whenever he got off the ride he felt as if he had wasted his time, and was sick for hours. Today, he felt sure, would be different.

Bill, the sixty-five-year-old ride operator with one tooth and cracked fingernails, stopped the ride especially for Cody. He unlatched the door to one of the cars as it came to a halt one foot from the ground. Cody stepped up into the car. As Bill hoisted the claw into its locked position he said, "Have a nice ride." Cody got special treatment. Contortionism was a dying art form. He was breathing new life into it.

Bill walked back to his rickety booth made of wood. As he pressed the red "Go" button, he said, "Lighting strikes now!" through a megaphone. The ride began to clank and twirl and wind blew around the arena like a tornado. Leaves and paper tubes used for eating cotton candy flew into the air as if pushed there by some unseen force. Little girls screaming and flashes of cheap cameras filled the air. The lights which lined each arm of the Spindly Spider strobed.

Cody felt numb. He imagined the spider was actually standing still and the fair around him was twirling in the same way the planets rotate around the sun. As the foot he was riding in spun, he had a vision. In his vision he was standing in the middle of Stonehenge. Instead of large slabs of stone, the figures were made of large refrigerators. They spun around him like a roulette wheel. "No one knows how they got here," he heard someone whisper in the distance as the refrigerators slowly came to a halt. Carousel music wafted in from a distance. They were of all different colors, but they were the same model Westinghouse. He walked up to the green one and opened the door. The refrigerator light came on. Equinox. Inside stood Terrance. He looked like a midget in the huge fridge. He swung from the metal shelf as he spoke. This is what he said:

"It started as a child. I liked being smothered by the king-size pillows my mother had on her bed. I would wrap myself up in her sheets like a mummy and squeeze my body into a pillowcase. I tied my shoelaces to grates on the ground and poles in horrible knots until I was bound to them, unable to escape. When I was found by a teacher or my mother, I blamed it on the other kids and said they had done it and isn't that cruel. I like closets. I like hanging out in closets. Once, when I was nine, the other kids put me in the closet. Kathy Okon, the fattest girl in the class, sat in front of it so I couldn't escape. There were little air holes in the top of the closet and the kids jabbed down the end of a broomstick through the holes. I couldn't predict which hole the stick would come through. One of its plunges scratched me across the face. I guess it could have poked my eye out. It was like I was really living, because at any moment I could lose it. When I got home I told my mother I had tripped over a curb and scratched my face on a tree. She believed me. From then on I got in the closet without being prodded or forced. I liked being in it, thrilled by the incidental jab. I remember a slide at my preschool. It was made of tin and formed a hollow tube. Once we crammed thirteen of us into it. I was in the middle. I loved it. I used to take the cushions off the couch in my house and lay as thin as a wafer on the bare boards. Then I placed the cushions on top of my body and waited patiently, trying not to breathe, for someone to sit on it. I could fit in any cabinet in the house. Find me a crack and I'll slip through it. There is no box small enough. No corner acute enough. Be careful if you open a drawer in my house. You might just find me in it."

When the ride was over, Cody went back to his tent to get dressed in his street clothes. Mary, the bearded woman, looked at him and said, "It ain't right not to bow. That's what we're paid to do. Bow. You gotta bow and you gotta smile. An audience always wants a smile."

Cody left town the next day, never to put another foot behind his head. It just didn't feel right anymore. Until that day he had always enjoyed repelling people. Suddenly he felt like a freak. He didn't even like to sit down after that. He only touched his toes if he absolutely had to. You could often see him standing up straight as a board, or lying down flat as a rug. From then on, everyone described him as stiff.

When Terrance's mother woke up the next morning, she couldn't find him anywhere. When she saw the toothpaste on the mirror, she knew something was up. She ran out to the refrigerator in horror. When she opened it, Terrance flopped out with his feet behind his head. Green. Thick saliva oozed out of his mouth and down his chin, filling his dimple and overflowing onto his neck, splitting into a weblike pattern that covered most of his neck. An unlucky dragonfly was caught in the mucous pattern. She tried to straighten out his body. She couldn't.

They buried Terrance in that old green Westinghouse refrigerator. "Terrance would have wanted it that way," she told everyone. Six feet under, Terrance's bones are still squenched up in the old icebox, in between the produce drawer and the butter container. Spiders have invaded the space, wrapping Terrance's bones in webs.

# True Life Adventures

The line between fantasy, fiction, reality, and reporting is a thin one. Every fantasy has a basis in some form of reality and even the most hard-line reporting carries with it an element of a more subjective fiction. The late Boyd McDonald, in his series of *Straight to Hell* chapbooks and in the collected *Meat, Flesh, Sex, Lewd, Raunch,* et cetera, pioneered the contemporary genre of true-to-life sex adventures. While the more mainstream sexual writings of the glossy skin mags were intent on spinning out elaborate, if predictable, fantasies of the horny telephone repair man, Boyd McDonald discovered that everyday people recounting their everyday experiences blowing sailors in dirty bathrooms were far more exciting. The simple recounting of sex *vérité* might lack the glamour of complex fantasy, but it carries with it the power of hard truth.

We live in a world in which sex is omnipresent as a commodity: Sex sells cars, cigarettes, candy, bourbon, books, movies, munchies, and that ever elusive, always unobtainable, notion of "lifestyle." The idea of sex permeates our culture—yet honest, open, and truthful discussion of sex and sexuality is rare. What does it tell us about our culture when, after fifteen years of the AIDS epidemic, Times Square can be dominated by a billboard of a highly sexualized, mostly naked man dressed only in his Calvins (complete with a full-sized and unmistakable bulge), and few television stations— network or cable—will run advertisements, no matter how tasteful, for condoms. Speaking openly and honestly about our sexuality is both exhilarating and frightening, demanding and necessary. These stories, in varying forms and styles, attempt to report some of the truths about gay male lives and sexuality.

Don Shewey's "Adonis: A Personal History of the Porn Palace" is a simple, plainspoken account of the author's adventures in one of Manhattan's most famous, and popular, sex palaces. Shewey's forthright, conversational recounting of his encounters with men at the Adonis conveys a truthfulness and an honesty that is missing in so much fictional and even literary sexual writing. Shewey understands the often-ironic complexities of gay male cruising— he celebrates the eighth anniversary of being with his lover by cruising the Adonis for the afternoon; after finding little comfort in a bereavement group at Gay Men's Health Crisis, he rewards himself with "life affirmation" at the movie house—and is as apt to tell us about sexual partners he found unattractive as those he found exciting. The sheer ordinariness of Shewey's story—this is the life of many gay men—brings a vibrancy and truth to his writing that is rare.

"Baños Guadalupe," by Charley Shively, is a pastiche of genres: part travelogue, part sexual adventure, part semi-fictionalized autobiography. Shively captures both the emotional and sexual dislocation of being outside of one's culture, as well as the intimate, often inexplicable, connections that occur in anonymous sexual encounters. Although Shively uses a fictional persona, his adventures have the absolute ring of truth about them. Like Shewey's writing, Shively's relies on a first-person narrative driven simply by sexual details and an accurate description of concurrent emotional states. The combination of the two presents us with portraits of lives as they are lived.

Dik Staal's "What's in an Inch," told at fever pitch, is a story about jerking off, piss, sex, and pumps. Staal's style is the breathless confessional, non-stop speed-talking that takes us into the mind of the narrator by refusing ever to let us pause and think. Late eighteenth-century British writing sported a genre known as "sensationalism." This was not so much about lurid events—although the supernatural did play a large role in much of the writing—as it was about engaging the reader's non-intellectual emotions: sensations. Dik Staal's narrative is a form of modern sensationalism; what matters here is simply how prose on the page can translate into bodily feeling for the reader. Staal makes our hearts race with his non-stop verbiage and he convinces us—manipulates us—into getting the same sexual rush he does, by words alone.

# Adonis
## A Personal History of the Porn Palace
### *Don Shewey*

*Aphrodite saw Adonis when he was born and even then loved him and decided he should be hers. She carried him to Persephone to take charge of him for her, but Persephone loved him too and would not give him back to Aphrodite, not even when the goddess went down to the underworld to get him. Neither goddess would yield, and finally Zeus himself had to judge between them. He decided that Adonis should spend half the year with each, the autumn and winter with the Queen of the Dead; the spring and summer with the Goddess of Love and Beauty.*

*All the time he was with Aphrodite, she sought only to please him. He was keen for the chase, and often she would leave her swan-drawn car, in which she was used to glide at her ease through the air, and follow him along rough woodland ways dressed like a huntress....*

—Edith Hamilton, *Mythology*

## 1

The other night I went to the Adonis for the first time. It's a huge theater, an old-fashioned glamorous movie palace with an ornately plastered balcony and wallpapered lobby, now gone seedy from a decade or two of unreplaced light bulbs and neglected plumbing.

The floors feel permanently sticky. Besides the seats and the back of the balcony, fuck places include the bathrooms on the balcony, ground, and basement floors and two curtained alcoves on either side of the balcony lobby. Lots of looking and walking around, not much doing. I got unthrillingly sucked off in the john. Had one nice big dick in my mouth, though he didn't come. Movies for shit.

## 2

*My Porno Life*—I've been exploring the Adonis, the New David Cinema, the Fifty-fifth St. Playhouse, the Loading Zone, Show Palace, the Glory Hole, and the Bijou. My curiosity won't be sated until I've investigated each stop on this dirty-movie-house circuit. However, I may die of guilt beforehand. Words from my lover S. to the opposite effect are at once consoling and alarming: He sets me free to follow my lust, therefore it's all up to me. I'm addicted to this perverse quest and can't stop it. The sensation is so rewarding of having a fat, juicy cock filling up my mouth that I pursue it again and again. A dyed-in-the-wool cocksucker, that's me. Constantly turned on. I used to let people suck me off, but wouldn't want to reciprocate; somehow even kissing someone would constitute infidelity, while the sex act remained impersonally faithful. Now I only chase cock and save my own juices for my lover. Should I be doing this? What if I get caught? What if I catch the dread amoebiasis? I worry about it constantly....

## 3

Last night I went to see one act of a terrible play at the American Place Theater. Afterwards, I went to the Adonis and saw *Sextool*, that porn classic. It really is the precursor of *Taxi Zum Klo*. It has the gamut of gay life: drags, beatings, piss, tit-piercing (I couldn't watch). Fred Halsted is so gorgeous—a beefy Richard Gere. I watched the whole movie without moving.

The second feature, *Sex Garage*, was a bore. I wandered around and finally, up in the balcony, blew a once-attractive older guy with an unremarkable cock, and then another guy with a prize-winner who'd gotten hard watching. That was it, except later, in one of the curtained niches, there was a stand-up orgy centered on two tall guys with lovely meaty cocks, both of which I got a hand on for a little while. It was so cute—these two big lugs took off together....

## 4

Much extracurricular sexplay lately and, fortunately, no guilt. Being unemployed and freelancing is a bore, a constant anxiety. Beating the depression is half the work. The other day I was especially down from spending the morning in the bewildering atmosphere of Sidney Lumet's movie set, where you can't sit down without being yelled at, and where a five-minute chat about nothing with Paul Newman is called an interview. How do I cheer myself up? I take myself to the dirty movies to see the new Joe Gage movie *Heatstroke*, which I'd been saving until I was horny for it. But I was, as I say, depressed, and this cheered me up immensely. God even rewarded me by sending my way exactly what I wanted: a curly-haired man with intelligent green eyes, movie-star cheekbones, and an immense but deliciously suckable dick.

First I went in and upstairs and watched the movie. It was about halfway done so I watched it until it was over. The best scene was the first, a drive-in movie where a cowboy initiates our innocent narrator into sucking cock by pulling his head down on his giant boner. Then, between features, they started showing a bunch of dated shorts, so I prowled. I went over to my lucky spot in the balcony on the right in the top section. Before long, the aforementioned hunk trooped up the stairs, gave me the eye, then went and stood behind me by the fire exit. I wasted no time in depositing my chewing gum on the railing and approaching him. He was friendly. We groped each other. He was soft but obviously huge. I quickly unzipped him and went down on my knees and took his soft prick in my mouth. It got hard soon, and for the next ten minutes or so I adored it lovingly, licking it up and down, stroking it with my spitty hand, licking his balls at his request. He had a smooth, muscular, hairy stomach which I stroked. He moaned occasionally, and he didn't seem to be in a hurry.

The specimen in my mouth seemed like the kind of treasure you hunt for in antique stores for hours and stumble across under a pile of dusty baby bibs. I wanted to inspect it with my eyes. But I always hate to pull away from sucking a good dick for even a moment. I guess I'm afraid they'll think I've lost interest, or someone else will horn in on the action, or they'll panic or get bored and go away. So I only allowed myself a few chances to sneak a look at his dick. It was a beaut. At least ten fat inches long, but maybe more, hard and taut, pointed up, not straight out at forty-five degrees, but up in a curve. Finally I took it all the way down my throat as far as possible. He loved that. He said, "Hold it there," but I couldn't breathe. Every time I pulled back to breathe, I went back in a little deeper. Finally, with me just staying still, he came copiously. I choked and sputtered a little bit, but drank all of it down. It was seven flavors of spunky heaven. In a trance I continued stroking his big squishy meat after he put it back in his underpants, and then patted his ass. He had a nice ass, and he was wearing very thin, soft pants so you could feel every bit of his body through it. I had the feeling he was maybe straight, or from out of town, or in any case didn't do this often. It was so amazing I just sat in a daze for a while, thanking the goddess.

After he came and I stood up, I nuzzled his cheek, but gathered he didn't want to kiss, which was okay with me. But I wish I'd gotten his name. Just writing this makes me want to go back there in hopes of a second chance.

The rest of the evening was distinctly anticlimactic. A young black boy came and sat down next to me. I felt him up, and he seemed to have a big one so I took him over to my favorite corner and went down on it. It was very thick at the end, but not so thick at the base, oddly, so when you took it in your mouth you had a mouthful but you could easily close your lips around the base. It wasn't really fun or exciting. He took a little bit longer to come than

I was interested in. Then he wanted to suck me, so I let him. A blond boy came up to us and was eyeing me. I gestured to him, and he came over and got down and started sucking me at the same time as the black boy. He started to inch around as if to rim me but I wasn't into that. He started sucking and jerking me, and I came rather quickly—in his mouth, I think, but maybe just on the floor. Not very satisfying.

Then I watched the rest of the movie, the first half. I wanted to suck more cock, but there was more competition and less action at this point, and it was getting late. Suddenly I discovered a dark little room under the stairs I'd never seen before. I went in, and there was lots going on. I went down on this short white guy with a nice dick and sucked him for a while. He started fooling around with a black guy next to him, eventually pulled out of my mouth, and drifted away. The room was pitch dark. Nothing else developed.

Earlier, in one of the bathrooms, there was a black guy with a nice-sized hard dick pumping in his hand, and I had the choice between him and a tall white guy who walked in and took the vacant booth. I chose the latter, and it was a mistake: He wanted to suck. I figured he was tall, so he must be well-hung and want to get sucked. He started to unbutton my vest, and I split. Later, in the same bathroom, I spied a balding but curly redhead stroking a big wiener inside his pants. Hot men there, not all willing to leap into action, though.

I've had nice times at the Adonis. One time in my lucky section I sat down next to a guy and pulled out his nice fat honker and sucked him off there in the seat. He loved it and I loved it. Another time I stroked, hugged, and sucked a balding redhead for a long time, standing up on the opposite side of the theater. He looked on with an amused but distant grin, not interested in coming or anything, just letting it happen. Not stoned, either.

## 5

Yesterday was such a gorgeous preview of spring that I couldn't work, so I took myself to the Adonis to while away the afternoon in the expectation of cock. The movie was *Heatstroke*, which I'd seen before. The audience was mostly uglies, but in the upstairs bathroom a gorgeous, athletic black man with an immense erection was lying in wait, and I bit. I proceeded to spend fifteen or twenty minutes gulping his humongous thing. It was nice and fleshy rather than rock-hard, so I found I could take it all in, even though it was very thick. He had stripped off his pants so he was wearing just gym socks and a thin yellow T-shirt. He stood up, straddling the toilet, and I went down on him. After a while, the adjacent booth vacated, and he had me go in there and suck him through the glory hole—a little awkward because he was tall. We did that for a long time. He didn't come. Eventually I moved back to his stall, but then he said he needed a rest. It was the closest I've gotten to the proverbial "baby's arm holding an apple."

Later, in the balcony, I fiddled with and sucked another black guy, nice but scroungy-looking, named Tom. He didn't come, but he sucked me off, not very adeptly. Then I left.

### 6

I went to the Adonis at dinnertime to stimulate my waning sex drive, and was amply rewarded. I had a long, pleasant encounter with a sexy dark-haired boy in a T-shirt named Richard. Sitting downstairs at the very back by the door, I sucked him and played with his balls and eventually jerked him off. "There's nothing I like better than a good handjob," he said. I sucked off a chubby, not very sexy, Spanish guy in the john. Then later, ready to leave, I went into the john and decided to take the empty stall and eventually landed Tom, a cute redhead I'd been exchanging interested glances with all night. He'd been getting lots of action, I noticed. We sucked each other off, but with lots of nice play and kissing. He had a very good hairy body, and he was in a business suit and tie and had a briefcase. But he was basically a clone—mustache, short hair, balding, cute. If I were looking, I'd go out with him more than once.

## 7

I've just met the perfect dick, and it was attached to a man named Kevin Keller. I felt rotten all day, just horrible, hot, depressed— vacation's over, back to work like how. So I decided I needed a porno lift. I went to MOMA to see Genet's tiny little erotic fantasy *Chant d'amour*, and then ran six blocks in the rain to the Adonis, which was hopping, as I somehow knew it would be. Quite quickly, I got down on a lovely hard, hard dick in the balcony, belonging to a blond bespectacled blank-looking guy in shorts, which easily pulled aside to release his cock and large balls. Kevin Keller I discovered downstairs. In the dark he looked older, sort of fading, balding, maybe chubby, but with a nice face. When I sat down next to him, I quickly realized he was a total hunk—bearded, green eyes, hairy chest. He liked his nipples worked, and he had a lovely, not-too-long, but thick, beautiful tool with a perfect, delicious mushroom head. I worked on it for a long time, but he had a cock- ring on and never came. He gave me a handjob and I quickly came. He leaned over and took it in his mouth, but then spat it out. We sat for a while longer. I wanted to kiss and neck with him. He wasn't inclined to kiss, and eventually stood up to move along. The man that got away?

The last one was Greg, who beckoned in the bathroom with a beanpole in his trousers—long and hard, also wore a cockring, also never came. He gave good head, too, but I'd already come. He had nice firm tits and a wonderfully pliant ass.

## 8

I went to the Adonis yesterday. It was quite busy, good movie (*Games*, with Al Parker and Leo Ford). There was action, but I wasn't getting any. Finally, I took an empty stall in the first floor john. One guy stood across from me, staring through the crack. He didn't seem very attractive, so I ignored him at first. Then he started stroking himself through his pants, so I invited him in. He turned out to have a lovely muscular body and a nice hard cock, which he let me lick through his shorts but not suck. It was so gorgeous-looking, I was very frustrated, even annoyed, that he wouldn't let me suck him. At one point I almost kicked him out, but I got into it. It was the first time I've had such a phobic sex partner, who prohibited everything but j/o. I was sitting on the toilet, my T-shirt pulled up, baring my torso (nicely rippled), while he was beating his meat. I finally shot a huge load across my chest, and in a few seconds he came too, thick and juicy. It was a mess, though—no toilet paper to wipe it off my shirt and chest. I wanted to chat with him and see why he did that, but he rushed off. Maybe he was diseased and wanted to spare me. When I stood up to hug him and dress, I pointed to the semen on my T-shirt and said, "What am I gonna tell my mother?"

## 2

He felt horny, or perhaps in need of a little sexual esteem, so he went to the dirty movies, which was a mistake. It was a Tuesday, not the most lively day of the week (in fact, he sometimes thought Tuesdays were malevolent, secretly evil), and he went around 7:00, just past the businessman's rush. When he arrived, a movie he'd seen before and liked a lot was on but nearly over. It was about an athlete who gets injured on the way to the gay Olympics and ends up in the hospital, apparently comatose. He's tended by a very cute young doctor who has the hots for his patients. The movie shows him actually carrying on with the boy who shares the star's hospital room, who doesn't look very sick when the doctor comes in, throws off the sheet, and starts sucking his cock. One of the most pleasing images is the doctor on his stomach, his ass in the air, getting fucked while his face is buried in the pillow, an expression of ecstasy all over it. Later, the doctor fantasizes about getting it on with the star of the show.

He had missed the best parts of that movie when he arrived and circulated through the theater, but he quickly came upon a scene as good as one in any movie. In the front row of the upper balcony, one man had stripped naked and was sitting next to another man who was clothed and jerking off the naked man, who was very muscular and sexy in a conventional gay-porno way. Then the naked man crouched in front of the clothed man and went to work on his cock, expertly it seemed, from the careful rhythm of his bobbing head and the apparent pleasure of the clothed man. The naked man had a broad back and wide but muscular, not flabby, buttocks, and he wore work boots and wool gym socks which he rested his ass on while sucking.

Watching the two of them, he became very excited, as did others who gathered in a circle to watch. He kept his eye on another excited voyeur, a blocky blond in a denim jacket. They stood nearby, stroking themselves, while watching the two men in the front row carry on quite uninhibitedly. Finally, the naked man and the clothed man sat back and jerked themselves off. It was spectacular, just like in the movies, with great gobs of flying come. The naked man came several large gobs onto his knee and the floor; the clothed man directed his ejaculation toward the naked man's torso. They seemed very happy, and for the next hour continued to neck in the theater. He was so hot watching them— he'd tried to get involved, but was pushed away; no third parties allowed—that he pursued the denim jacket until they settled in a dark corner. When the denim jacket started sucking him, he came almost immediately. The denim jacket didn't want reciprocal satisfaction and walked away. He felt ridiculous to have released his pent-up sexual energy so soon.

By now, the movie had changed to a dreary cheap film set in a succession of undisguised hotel rooms. Though he spent nearly an hour trying to drum up some oral action in the theater, the crowd had thinned. He left feeling worse than he had when he arrived. He had made no connection, but had inhaled the rancid smell of the porno movie house, a stale stench of toilet disinfectant and amyl nitrate. He vowed that he would not succumb to this temptation again, a vow that would surely be broken in a month, or a year, on another afternoon when he felt horny or in need of sexual self-esteem.

## 10

It was a lovely afternoon, a tiny bit breezy. I walked to the Adonis. The movie's gone up to six dollars. The theater was relatively busy—business as normal, AIDS or no AIDS. I didn't witness much action, and when I thought about it, I realized that, for all the wolfish prowling, not an awful lot does go on at the Adonis most of the time. Except for me; I insist. I started off as usual, watching the movie from the balcony, but the second feature was on, *Malibu Days—Big Bear Nights*, one of those skinny-boys-with-big-dicks-fuck-each-other movies. So I got bored very quickly. I wanted to see the main feature, *Job Site*, because I assumed it was about construction workers, but it turned out to be a crude silly thing about a male brothel. Anyway, the aisles were full (not full—a trickle) of prowlers. A Hispanic-looking guy sat down next to me. We took our dicks out and played with them a little. He had a very loose foreskin (I had the feeling I'd encountered this dick at another moviehouse before), but he got up and left before long. A black-haired fellow smoking a cigarette sat down two seats away and finished his cigarette with stealthy glances at me. Finally he moved over. We felt each other up. His dick was pretty small, his hair was very sprayed, possibly a wig; he sort of turned me off, but I idly went along. He bent over to blow me, and he had such a silky smooth mouth that I was ready to come in about a minute. I made him stop, but my orgasm had already begun. Some leaked out, some I choked back. I lost my erection, but he gobbled my dick for another five minutes before I stopped him. He was very sweet, spoke with a foreign accent, and wore designer jeans.

Then I walked around, checked out the johns, and settled on an older guy, whom I followed around a bit. He didn't seem to pay any attention. When I saw how duddy *Job Site* was, I was ready to leave. I took a last spin, and I locked eyes with another older man, short, with a white-blond butch haircut. He came right over and stood next to me. I couldn't tell from his baggy shirt (in the dim light) whether he was a troll or a doll. As I watched four skinny legs and two skinny dicks flail against each other on the screen, I thought, "Should I go along with this, or should I just leave?" The impulse to leave was strong—my half-orgasm with the pompadour had almost entirely sapped my sex drive. On the other hand, I hadn't gotten what makes me happier than anything else in the world—a big hard dick in my mouth.

So I went for this guy's crotch, and he grabbed my hand, and we stood there holding hands like teenagers. I finally turned to him and croaked, "How ya doin'?" He said, "What?" The usual witty openers. He wanted to sit down, so we sat down and, as if at dinner, went to work. He felt my body all over: my stomach, chest, dick, balls. He had a muscular-going-to-pot body like S.'s, not bad, big nipples, nice-sized dick. He was very cuddly, so we nuzzled, kissing chastely, no tongues. I went to take his cock in my mouth, and he said, "Let's just use our hands." He told me he liked "hot talk," and I told him I wasn't very good at it. He said he'd love to be naked in bed with me (I wouldn't have minded), and he'd like to have me shoot all over his stomach. He also notified me that he didn't have very much time because he had to meet some people. So I told him I wanted to make him come—his dick got very hard as I jerked it, pinching his tits, biting his earlobe, and he came nicely before too long. He asked me if I wanted to come, and I said not really. We exchanged names—his is Phil. He was a bit coy about particulars; said he lives in the West Eighties. He asked if I wanted to meet again. I said I lived with someone; he also has a boyfriend. I figured if I run into him on the street, it's okay; if not, also okay. He seemed a bit crestfallen, but there we were. I left right after him.

## 11

Today is the eighth anniversary of my relationship with S. I celebrated by going to the Adonis for the first time in maybe two years. Very busy on a rainy Friday afternoon. In the balcony, the first thing I noticed was a bunch of people standing around a guy on his knees sucking someone off. I felt shocked and disturbed—don't they know what danger they're in? Still it was sort of exciting to be a part of this taboo scene. A pretty Spanish boy with a big dick came on to me. I played with him, he didn't get too hard. I did; he wanted to suck my cock, but I didn't feel comfortable letting him. I cruised around for a while, and a scruffy-looking guy kept cruising me and finally started groping me. He had a nice big dick and was sweet and tender. We sat down and eventually pulled our pants down and played with each other's dicks. He was very careful, he took my dick all the way in his mouth, but only for a second to get it wet. His dick was cut, but with a very loose skin. He got very hot and close to shooting very quickly. We took turns a couple of times, and then he pulled up his shirt while I jerked his cock till he shot all over his stomach. It was beautiful. But quickly after that I lost my erection, so I didn't come—partly because a fat, crazy queen sat down next to me and started touching me, which turned me off. And in general sitting there in the theater, site of many lovely exciting sexcapades in the past, I felt queasy, particularly observing guys sucking cock all over the theater—something I long to do indiscriminately, but firmly feel would be disastrous healthwise. I know that I'm not comfortable anymore having sex with total strangers— I feel on guard and incapable of the spontaneity of great sex.

## 12

I went to the Adonis Saturday afternoon—things were hopping. The theater was in serious decline: The movies had changed from projected films to projected video (terrible quality, practically devoid of color), the balcony had been closed off, and besides the safe sex sign at the door, there was a sign about the presence of policemen on hand to arrest people using or selling drugs. The weird thing about all this is that it has made the subtext of going to the Adonis (for sex) the text, since going to see movies was out of the question. Up and down the side aisles were dozens of men— black, white, and Hispanic—sitting in seats sucking each other off. The center section, more well-lit (though still dimly) from the screen, was deserted. I cased the joint once, then zeroed in on a dark-haired big-eyed fellow who looked like Eric Bogosian. We stood next to each other at the back of the theater. He groped my hardening cock. I played with his nice butt. I suggested we find a corner; he led me to a seat. He took out his dick—uncut with a nice loose skin—and with his hand on my neck, indicated he wanted me to suck it. I weighed that back and forth, licked his balls, talked some dirty talk with him, then went down on his cock. After three good gulps, he was ready to shoot—pulled his foreskin closed and held it, though he did halfway come (not in my mouth). After a while I resumed sucking his balls extensively, which he liked. A crowd gathered to watch. After a while, he stopped and said he had to pee. His name was Steve; we parted in a friendly manner.

I walked around. One studious but handsome guy trailed me a lot. I watched one lad very expressively fucking another guy's mouth down front; the sucker kept stopping to spit out huge gobs—he did it several times, so I assume it wasn't come. On a stroll I locked eyes with a handsome balding redhead and followed him upstairs. He made a phone call; I stared at him from outside the booth, and he took out his dick. When he got out of the booth, we gravitated to a corner. I played with his dick, he with mine, but he really wanted me to suck him. He was a little rude about it, and he had a smaller-than-average dick. But he had a nice muscular body, and I played with his tits. He pulled my pants down and played with my ass. He wanted to go somewhere and fuck—or have me "work on" his tool, his mighty mighty sword. But I had an hour to get home, change, and go out with S. His name was Ted, he said, and he lived on Thirty-sixth Street. He went off to check with his roommate that it was okay to go to their place. He said, "If I'm not back in five minutes, it's not okay." I took that to mean he didn't care one way or the other, and I calculated it would be a fifteen-minute fuck at best, so I just left the theater. I felt a little guilty, but I figured our stand-up flirtation was ultimately better fantasy material.

## 13

I went to the walk-in bereavement group at GMHC, mostly to get pointers on visiting the parents of someone who'd died. No one had anything helpful to say at all. Afterwards, to reward myself with life affirmation, I went to the Adonis, which was really hopping. I had to pee, so I immediately went to the john, where all the stalls were taken and a lot of commotion was taking place in one. After I peed, I went to look. In the far stall, a naked guy was on his knees being forcefully face-fucked by a guy in cutoffs who was wearing a rubber. Just in front of the stall, two guys watching had gotten so hot they started, too—the mustachioed one on his knees, sucking off a young guy in blue shorts with a nice, shapely, very hard dick. He was very interested in me, so I stood there playing with his tits and his butt while he was being blown. This went on for a while and got to be quite a scene, drawing a crowd. Eventually I realized I was violating my vow not to have sex in bathrooms, so I wandered away.

I fooled around some with several other people, watching a fairly good Al Parker video. But I never came, so I left horny. As I passed Lincoln Center, I locked eyes with a salt-and-pepper-bearded guy in T-shirt and running shorts. As he passed, he looked at me and very casually, almost imperceptibly, grabbed his crotch—a wonderful signal I'd never spotted before. Anyway, I saved it for S., and we had hot sex that night.

## 14

Horny these days, looking for good sex to make me alert, to ground me in the moment, to give me something to look forward to. No luck recently. Friday sundown spin through the park a bust; the gym no fun. Yesterday afternoon I went to the Adonis, which was crawling, but it was disgusting and dispiriting: hot, smelly, bad films, bad projection, ugly guys made uglier from desperation, lots of street people just trying to stay off the street.

## 15

I visited the new Adonis Theater for the first time yesterday. The old one is clearly scheduled for demolition; the whole block is boarded up. The new location is at Forty-fourth Street and Eighth

Avenue, in what used to be the Cameo. It's much smaller, but clean and neat and in good shape. It has a balcony, which I like, and the men's room is downstairs from the main floor. I went just at 5:00 P.M. on Friday, to see what the after-work crowd is like—as expected, lots of older men in raincoats, suits, and briefcases. Lots of blowjob action in the seats. Very soon after I settled down in the balcony, I got to playing with a cute, curly-haired, slightly dissipated Jewish accountant from the Bronx (he now lives in Queens) named Stuart. We played with each other's dicks, he sucked mine, but his was leaky so I didn't want it in my mouth. He wasted no time in pulling his pants down to his ankles and unbuttoning his shirt to the neck. He had a nice thick dick, average length, nice big balls. One of his nipples was divided so it's like there were two on one side. He mostly wanted to kiss, and clamped his open wet mouth over mine, but I didn't want to swap spit—he was a little too eager. Feeling his butt, I noticed he had a dry scabby section just above his coccyx— probably from doing sit-ups on a hard floor (S. sometimes gets this). He kept telling me how beautiful I was, and when I would respond with the obligatory reciprocal compliment, he would visibly glow as a result, relax, and get happy.

This went on for a little over an hour, which made me eventually bored and tense. I always like to see what else is going on and check out the movies. At first I didn't want to exchange life histories, but I'm glad we did. I figured he was an other-boroughs kind of guy with a non-gay lifestyle. He said something about problems, to the effect that, "Being gay is my only problem." I asked him why it was a problem for him. He said because it wasn't accepted in society, because relationships don't last, because of drug problems, etc. He admitted that straights have many of the same problems, but regretted that he couldn't walk down the street holding a boyfriend's hand. He said he was bad at picking boyfriends—one turned out to be a suicidal alcoholic, another a minister who was always too busy to see him.

Since we were sitting right on the aisle with our dicks out (I didn't take off anything), a lot of people stopped to watch—

unattractive lonely older guys. But I saw one guy, a graying bespectacled older black man, sucking off a rather big hunky cock in the front row of the balcony. I saw it all in silhouette. Funny, isn't it? Any blowjob in reality is more riveting to watch than any on the screen.

*One sad day Aphrodite happened not to be with Adonis and he tracked down a mighty boar. With his hunting dogs he brought the beast to bay. He hurled his spear at it, but he only wounded it, and before he could spring away, the boar, mad with pain, rushed at him and gored him with its great tusks. Aphrodite in her winged car high over the earth heard her lover's groan and flew to him. He was softly breathing his life away, the dark blood flowing down his skin of snow and his eyes growing heavy and dim. She kissed him, but Adonis knew not that she kissed him as he died. Cruel as his wound was, the wound in her heart was deeper. She spoke to him, although she knew he could not hear her: —*

> *"You die, O thrice desired,*
> *And my desire has flown like a dream.*
> *Gone with you is the girdle of my beauty,*
> *But I myself must live who am a goddess*
> *And may not follow you.*
> *Kiss me yet once again, the last, long kiss,*
> *Until I draw your soul within my lips*
> *And drink down all your love."*

> *The mountains all were calling and the oak trees answering,*
> *Oh, woe, woe for Adonis. He is dead.*
> *And Echo cried in answer, Oh, woe, woe for Adonis.*
> *And all the Loves wept for him and all the Muses too.*

*But down in the black underworld Adonis could not hear them, nor see the crimson flower that sprang up where each drop of his blood had stained the earth.*

# Baños Guadalupe
### Charley Shively

Sebastian arrived at the Basilica on the northern edge of Mexico
City, a place called Tepayac, after the hill where the Aztecs
worshipped Tonantzin/Cihuacóatl. This great mother snake lady
always dressed in white; she was a friend of Quetzcóatl, the plumed
serpent. On December 12, 1531, on Tepayac hill, the Virgin Mary
appeared to Juan Diego on his way to catechism class. She sent him
to Archbishop Zumárraga with orders to build a church on Tepayac
hill. The Archbishop ignored the Indian, but the next time Juan
was there, the Virgin appeared again asking about her building.
Juan explained his failure to get a new church. The Virgin told him
to fill his cloak with Spanish roses growing nearby and take them
to the Archbishop. Juan said he had to visit his dying uncle and the
Virgin said, Don't worry I'll fix him, you go to the Archbishop.
Juan went to the Archbishop, opened his cloak, and the roses
became a painting of the Virgin (the uncle meanwhile recovered
from his deathbed). The most miraculous part of Santa María's
work was in having Zumárraga in Mexico that year, since he was

then in Madrid, defending his mistreatment of the Indians.

Sebastian thought the site should be good for cruising. He visited the Basilica and saw Juan's robe: the faithful passed under the sacred garment on a movable walkway that ended at the relic gift shop—all part of the 1975 new Basilica, whose roof resembled a gigantic circus tent. Sebastian bought a postcard of the cloak and then climbed to the exact spot where Mary had accosted Juan. Over the centuries, the faithful had built numerous churches and statues along the hill paths. In the old Basilica (badly damaged by the 1985 earthquake), there were hundreds of drawings of miraculous new apparitions and, in the midst of it all, a recovered pre-Columbian statue of Tonantzin. Pope Juan Pablo II's statue resembled hers; he, too, appeared on the hill in a white dress. The national bank, Banamex, now owned, or at least maintained, the spot of apparition. Sebastian checked out the tea rooms under the sacred vault. All to no avail; he saw only some people with broken legs crawling toward the cloak with hopes of being cured. One woman's knees bled on the stone pavement.

Basilica signs prohibited shorts and balloons. Expecting no fun inside the sacred precinct, Sebastian explored the plaza. Opposite the Basilica, a giant calendar device ticked out the days, weeks, years, and millennia according to the Aztec calendar. Two series of thirteen and twenty days linked time and space. While Sebastian studied the directions for telling Aztec time, his eyes fell upon a group of young men playing soccer. Kicking the ball had developed the calves, asses, and thighs of the soccer players. The *futbolistas* enjoyed being watched; the captain took his shirt off; his tan skin shone in the sun as he kept his eye on the ball, but occasionally checked to notice Sebastian watching. Juan Diego returned to life. Sebastian thought: no wonder the Virgin kept coming back so many times to check him out. Then he noticed that the *futbolistas* corresponded to the calendar emblems for either xochitl (flower) or Xochiquetzal (plumed flower). They danced inside the Fifth Sun, children of the goddess, strewing the path with their soft skin petals.

The playing stopped. Sebastian explored the surrounding streets. In the market at the foot of the hill, he got a fish chowder; the fishmonger shortchanged him. There were thousands of vendors preying on the pilgrims, going and coming from the church. Sebastian looked for cruising. There were no movie houses, few bars, but three bath houses. Sebastian easily found the three smokestacks for heating water and making steam. The three chimneys carried painted signs: TEPAYAC, GUADALUPE and SANTA MARIA DE GUADALUPE. These bath houses formed a trinity of flower, plumed flower, and plumed serpent. Their smoke rose from the valley to envelop the hill.

## I.

By the subway and closest to the shrine, Baños Guadalupe seemed quiet. Nearby, a woman wailed wildly under the underpass by the entrance to the Basilica; at first Sebastian thought she was a pilgrim, but she and her family lived under the bridge; one of the children had fallen off the embankment onto the highway. Sebastian may have been the first to hear her screams, but he felt helpless and sighed with relief when a shoe store clerk rushed over and began shouting orders to the congregated bystanders. An ambulance arrived; the woman got in with the victim. Sebastian entered the Baños Guadalupe.

The dressing rooms were built from reinforced concrete, with steel doors on two tiers; a couple of gay men sat chatting with smoothly ironed white towels wrapped around their bodies; one man was markedly handsome; the other markedly friendly; Sebastian smiled and said hi; they smiled and responded. Sebastian went into the shower room; it led into the steam room, which opened into the sauna. The sauna room was empty; it had ledges for resting on one side and a corner shower stall without a shower near the door. The friendly man came in and pulled Sebastian into the stall, stuck his tongue in Sebastian's mouth, and began fucking him in the stomach and pinching his nipples. Sebastian got hot and another man came in and from the back started fucking him between his legs. Then another man came in and they all pulled away. The first man introduced himself as Humberto; he had to go to work in ten minutes; they agreed to meet the next day; he taught English.

After Humberto left, Sebastian sat down on the floor; the other man began doing exercises; they were alone in the sauna. He had quite dark, mahogany colored skin with the Baños Guadalupe towel tightly wrapped around his body. With a pumice stone, he smoothed his glistening skin. He began a series of strenuous exercises without once looking at Sebastian. As his sweat accumulated, he took off his towel and touched his knees with his hands and performed knee bends. He turned the heat higher; they both began to sweat more. Soon Sebastian realized the man's asshole had moved closer and closer to his face. Did the man want to get fucked? Sebastian was somewhat exhausted; fucking the man would be a lot of work; the asshole eventually touched his lips; Sebastian stuck his tongue in and began rimming the dark hole: *copa negra*, they called it in the Yucatan.

The man's body quivered; he spread his cheeks further as Sebastian's tongue went in deeper. Then Neza turned around and pulled Sebastian's head down on his throbbing hard cock. The foreskin came back and Sebastian ate the raw smegma and swallowed the aroused cock; he pulled out and ran his tongue around the balls, then he swallowed the cock and added both balls. The man grabbed Sebastian's hair and pulled the head back and forth, back and forth. The heat, the sweat, the smell, the ripeness inflamed them both; the man's seed burst into Sebastian.

Sebastian licked the last come from the head, kissed the man, and stuck the come-wet tongue into his mouth. Neza grabbed Sebastian's head again and they grated teeth against teeth; both went to the shower room and stood under the cold water for a long time. Sitting down on the floor, they introduced themselves; he asked Sebastian to buy him a soda. Taking turns sucking the cold cider pop, they agreed to meet two days later by the Basilica in the afternoon.

## II.

Sebastian showed up promptly at four o'clock and waited an hour without seeing Neza. As the pilgrims streamed by, heading for the shrine, he set out to explore the other two baths. Sebastian passed the Baños Tepayac; a tempting crowd of young indigenous men were entering; Sebastian walked to the corner and spotted a young man about fifteen, dressed in black pants, a black-and-white shirt; their eyes met; both stopped on opposite sides of the street. The boy turned and went back down the street toward the Delegation headquarters (Mexico City is divided into about twenty delegations); Sebastian followed; the boy went into the building; perhaps it contained a public restroom; Sebastian leaned against a tree; the boy returned and sat down in a small park in front of the Delegation building; Sebastian lay down nearby. The boy stretched out on the grass; obviously he wasn't hustling or contact would have been quicker and easier; he was interested, since he occasionally looked over, but he avoided eye contact. Some stray dogs approached; Sebastian petted them; one then attached itself to Sebastian. The boy moved to the bus stop; Sebastian followed; the dog went along; the bus came; the boy didn't get on; Sebastian sat down. There was an empty information kiosk; the boy stood on one side; Sebastian on the other; their eyes finally met through the glass window. Sebastian sat down; the boy left. The dog also left.

Sebastian returned to the Baños Tepayac and saw a handsome youth enter. After Sebastian had bought his general admission ticket, the youth went into the individual section. The Tepayac had a very local crowd. About twenty-five men in their forties mostly, who seemed very businesslike in their bathing and soaking. At first, Sebastian thought he'd only get some steam. Tepayac seemed straight, but he soon noticed that everyone was on the make.

The steam room had heavy steam: three sides of the room had a ledge-bench; the room extended about twenty feet on both sides. As the steam deepened, the men began playing with their cocks. Sebastian sat on the floor on the side without a bench. His eyes were exactly level with the crotches of the men on the opposite benches. Beside Sebastian sat a handsome man, about six feet tall, dark-skinned with a sad countenance. He played with his cock; Sebastian rubbed his elbow against Benito's; the man neither responded nor pulled away. Another man came and sat down on Sebastian's right side; he had to squeeze between Sebastian and a man in the corner on the bench. He began blowing the man on the bench; Sebastian stuck his finger up the man's ass; he turned and kissed Sebastian's nipple as Sebastian massaged the silver-dollar-sized hard glans. Suddenly the man came in great spurts. Meanwhile, Benito hardly moved more than to play with himself; Sebastian casually brushed his hand onto Benito's nipple; Benito gently moved the hand away. Sebastian kissed his hand and noticed the gold wedding band.

Sebastian went to take a cold shower; one of the attendants had a hard-on and was cruising another man; Sebastian went into the sauna room. The one man there left as soon as Sebastian entered. Two young indigenous men came in; both were well built in different ways. One had a thin supple body; the younger of the two, he sat down on the floor by the sauna heater with his head directly in front of the other's crotch. The standing youth was very muscular, talked less, was less articulate, but had a much more muscular body. They talked the whole time about their work as *vendedores* in the market. The standing man noticed Sebastian admiring his body and smiled, but Sebastian could see that the seated youth wanted the standing one, so he went out to the showers. Sebastian loved the high-pressure cold water after the hot sauna.

When the hunkier man came out of the sauna, Sebastian went in; he smiled and said hi to the other youth, who gave him a very mean look and dashed out, only to return. Sebastian and the youth were alone; he ignored Sebastian, but began an elaborate kick box, jumping, wild dance. The youth began screaming; Sebastian couldn't understand; perhaps it wasn't Spanish. Sebastian realized he was not being propositioned, but he was not sure whether the screams were from disappointment at not getting his man and/or curses heaped on Sebastian's head. As Sebastian became turned on by the boy's whirling, screaming body, the youth became ever more agitated. To leave, Sebastian thought, would be rude; perhaps by staying he could absorb some of the youth's pain; maybe they could even get it on together. Sebastian thought it might be fun if the youth began beating him: his feet and arms and face came close but never touched. The dance ended abruptly when Benito came in the door; without a word the youth stomped out.

Without saying anything, Benito sat down on the floor three feet away from Sebastian. Benito played with his cock; it got half-hard; Sebastian moved his hand over to touch Benito's foot, but Benito moved the hand away. Someone came into the sauna. Benito stood up and began soaping himself; once his whole body was covered with soap, he went out to the showers. The other man left; Benito returned and soaped himself up again. Sebastian joined him and offered to rub his back; he didn't answer, but he didn't resist, and Sebastian began working his hands from rib to rib until he reached the shoulders. When someone came in, he said *Gracias;* Sebastian said *de nada;* they both sat down. The man left; Sebastian began massaging Benito's cock; it got hard; someone came in; he covered himself.

Sebastian went to the steam room. A young beauty came in; he had just arrived because his body was dry, and he wore a well-ironed white breechcloth. Carlos had deep brown skin with well-formed arm and leg muscles. His buttocks had well-defined cleavages; his square face and black hair made him seem older than his eighteen years. He stood by the bench near an older man; Sebastian sat on the floor to one side. Someone turned the steam up; the youth covered his face with the breechcloth and stood in the corner; the man went down on him; two queens and Sebastian moved over; the door opened; Sebastian stood in front to provide cover for the action. The older man got so excited, he soon came and left. Another queen went down on Carlos; Sebastian continued to screen the scene from the innocent who entered, so that no one had to stop. Sebastian's behavior seemed abnormal since Tepayac was not very cooperative.

Eventually, Sebastian went down on the youth's cock; Carlos liked the deep throating and enjoyed having his asshole massaged, but didn't want any fingers inside. Sebastian put Carlos's hands on his head; Carlos moved Sebastian's head back and forth; he got even harder. Someone entered; they stopped. Someone else went down on Carlos, but he lost his hard-on when another person came in the door. Each time the cock went limp, Carlos came to Sebastian to get it up again. The steam soon overcame Sebastian and he had to go for a cold shower. One of the men pointed out to Sebastian that his left knee had begun to bleed from the tile floor. When he showered, he washed the blood away from the tender kneecap. He noticed that one of the attendants went off to the dressing room with another customer.

Sebastian returned to the steam room after a short rest. Carlos was standing in the other corner of the room. A man sat on the bench with a great hard-on covered with a condom; he looked British; he wouldn't let anyone but Carlos touch him. Sebastian worked on Carlos's cock for a while. The Brit tried to fuck Carlos, but they had no lubricant and Sebastian had trouble explaining to Carlos that the cock could go in easier if he bent over. The condom man came, removed his condom, threw it in a corner, and left. Sebastian then tried rimming Carlos; he moaned and got harder as another man sucked his cock. He asked Sebastian to fuck him if he had a condom; Sebastian went to his dressing room to get a condom and returned. The bath attendants were cleaning things up for closing; it was 8:30 and everyone was leaving. Sebastian went into the steam room, gave Carlos the condom, picked up the Brit's condom and put it in the trash can.

The attendant asked Sebastian if he wanted something to drink as he dressed to leave. Sebastian asked where he could get some *tepache*, an ancient brew, which he loved dearly. They roared with laughter and admiration and said you couldn't get *tepache* around the Basilica; Sebastian had an orange soda. Carlos was still in the steam room; maybe he was in training to be an attendant or knew one of the bath house owners. Sebastian left; night had fallen; he felt dehydrated from all the sweating and stopped to get another soda. The waiter gave him a 500 old peso coin for a 5000 coin; they looked alike; Sebastian argued; a crowd gathered and cheered for Sebastian.

A week later Sebastian returned to the Baños Tepayac; from his last visit he realized that the place peaked just before closing time. Every bath seemed to have its own rhythm: some peaked at the siesta/lunch break between two and four in the afternoon. Other places around closing. A bath house in Jalapa opened only between six and eight in the morning; Sebastian never could get there before it closed. Some only functioned when there was a great crowd; others worked when there were only three or four customers. Sebastian arrived at Tepayac at seven in the evening. There was a good crowd; but he recognized only Benito, who still wore a sad countenance and a wedding ring.

As soon as Sebastian entered the steam room, he caught the eye of Jesús. He came from Toluca, was twenty, had thick black hair and well-developed muscles; as Sebastian rubbed his body, it seemed to turn to silk. Jesús quickly stuck his cock into Sebastian's mouth; Sebastian grasped his buttocks and pulled him back and forth with the cock in his mouth; Jesús pulled Sebastian up and they kissed. He said, Just wait I'll be back. He returned with Tedros: an older man, much taller, very Spanish looking, and sporting a huge cock, about nine inches. Jesús played with Alonso's cock; it quickly got stiff; Jesús pushed Sebastian's head down on the cock; the whole room admired the deep-throating and gathered around to watch.

Alonso began to shoot, but pulled Sebastian away and held himself. Alonso suggested that they all go somewhere together; Sebastian agreed; he gave them his dressing room number. He waited some time with the dressing-room door open; several men went by and he smiled; the attendant joked about Sebastian's taste for *tepache*. Alonso and Jesús came out and went to their dressing rooms; Sebastian left and waved to them as he went out; they promised to meet outside. The bath house was closing up.

Sebastian was thirsty and starved; he got some melon slices at a vendor on the corner. Benito came out; he was wearing faded blue denim pants and matching shirt; he looked particularly handsome; they began chatting. Sebastian worried about his dates, but they weren't at hand, so he went with Benito. They chatted about the weather, the time, and other neutral topics. They walked several blocks to the subway, more or less waiting for some advance from the other. Sebastian's hotel didn't allow guests; it wasn't near; the man didn't say anything about his own living arrangements, but he probably couldn't invite Sebastian back. They shook hands and said good night; Sebastian entered the subway, but took another exit out.

As he walked toward the bathhouse, he met Alonso and Jesús. Sebastian said he wanted some *tepache*; maybe they could all go to the downtown historical district where he knew a good vendor; the drink was sold out of barrels without labels. Alonso wore very proper clothing: highly polished black dress shoes, knit pants and matching shirt. Jesús wore tight black pants and a turquoise short-sleeved shirt. He looked even more handsome with the clothing than without. Alonso felt somewhat uncomfortable; he had the sniffles; the pollution in the city made breathing difficult. Sebastian offered a cough drop after Alonso began coughing. They took the subway downtown; Alonso worked in the downtown historical district near the *tepache* stand. It had closed before they arrived.

Sebastian then suggested that they go to one of the gay bars; Vienna was nearby but it wasn't open on Sunday. So they went to the Club 33. Sebastian would never go there alone. The sign on the door warned: NO KNIVES OR GUNS. Soldiers often went to the Club 33. Alonso, Jesús, and Sebastian took seats in the back of the bar; Alonso got a Coke, and Sebastian and Jesús each had a beer. Jesús got drunk very quickly on three beers. Sebastian still couldn't quite figure out their relationship: Jesús lived outside the city; Alonso lived in the western part; when they had transferred trains at the notorious Hidalgo station, Jesús joked about *putos* (male hustlers), but neither of them seemed familiar with the scene there.

The 33 was not particularly a dancing bar, but the jukebox was very loud. A man and woman got up and danced; when they sat down, a man in drag and his date got up; when they sat down, the date took a man partner and they began dancing. Alonso looked happy that no one from the street could see him. When they sat down, Jesús grabbed Sebastian and they got up and danced. Jesús looked into Sebastian's blue eyes and said that he had the eyes of Jesus Christ. He was leading and Sebastian followed. When they sat down, the whole bar applauded. At ten o'clock the shift changed for the waiters; when they came with the check, Alonso insisted on paying. Jesús now had had three drinks and was plastered; Sebastian teased and called him *borracho* (drunk).

Alonso and Sebastian agreed that the time had come to leave; Jesús would have been glad to stay, but he was a very sweet drunk who liked to do what people wanted. They left and walked down the Central Boulevard that went from the north to the south of the city. Sebastian's hotel was about six blocks south of the bar; they liked the idea of walking him home, even though they wouldn't be able to visit. Sebastian suggested a nearby hotel that had rooms by the hour, but Alonso had to get up early in the morning. They enjoyed the walk. Sebastian left them in front of the subway stop just by his hotel. As they said good night, Jesús whispered (without letting Alonso hear), "Meet me at Insurgentes subway stop in an hour." Sebastian liked the idea, but as soon as he lay down in his bed, he passed out and didn't wake up until the next morning.

### III.

Sebastian returned to the Basilica the next day; perhaps he could see Alonso, Humberto, or Jesús. He checked both the Baños Guadalupe and Baños Tepayac; everything in the neighborhood seemed quiet. At the Baños Santa María de Guadalupe, Sebastian spotted a handsome man ostensibly waiting for a bus on the corner of Avenida Zumárraga. Sebastian waited on the other side of the street where no buses stopped. He cruised the man, who didn't take any of the buses.

Sebastian crossed the avenue and headed toward the hill; the man followed. Sebastian sat down and waited. There was the small Delegation Park nearby and Sebastian strolled through, but the man didn't follow. Sebastian returned to find another man cruising the trick and soon the two left together. Since he had first seen the man waiting in front of the Baños Santa María , Sebastian took that as a sign to enter.

Of the three baths, Santa María's was clearly the most upscale. It had a parking lot and fancy barber shop in the lobby, with a lot of chrome and a fair amount of toiletries for sale. Sebastian went into the general men's section with the usual dressing rooms, shower room, steam room, and sauna. The attendant wore gray sweat pants with matching pullover. He looked Sebastian squarely in the eye and offered a massage; Sebastian answered, "Perhaps later." Virtually deserted, the bath had only Sebastian and three other men.

Sebastian followed the three men into the steam room. One was about forty and had elaborate tattoos; they formed a scrollwork across his body, written in an iconography that was immediately erased from Sebastian's mind. Later, he tried to recollect them. Miss Effay suggested *Siempre Te Recordaré* (I will always remember you) with *Siempre* inscribed over one nipple; *Te* in between and *Recordaré* over the other nipple. Sebastian remembered Raymundo in Guatemala, who had Christ over one nipple and Our Lady of Guadalupe over his heart. Perhaps the tattoo was the stunning quetzál, a bird which Providence Rhode Island shops could imprint anywhere on the body, and formed the national currency of Guatemala. Maybe the tattoos included lions, scorpions, crown-of-thorns, panthers, bleeding hearts, sinking ships, Aztec gods, Chinese New Year's dragons. Whatever the inscriptions, they disappeared instantly once Sebastian left the steam room.

The tattoo man wore a severely tight towel around his crotch and turned the steam up so that it virtually peeled Sebastian's skin. The tattoo man did some kung fu exercises and displayed his well-proportioned body: very lean, dark skinned, with lots of body hair. Sebastian worried about his own flabby body. Did tattoo man find him a crime against some male warrior code? Or perhaps he could work Sebastian into a great athlete? The man's eyes seemed as incomprehensible as his body: hard, bony, dark wells that made no contact.

One of the group was a youth. Like Sebastian, the boy had some baby fat and, like Sebastian, he enjoyed neither the exercises nor the heat. Juan, as they called him, had soft curly light brown hair that held its curl in the steam room. Juan's eyelids blinked rapidly over his soft baby blue eyes, which Sebastian shyly avoided. Juan had no pubic hair at all, and his cock and balls seemed to have shrunk from the steam. The boy pouted slightly and curled up on the bench beside Sebastian and rubbed his leg against Sebastian's. At first, Sebastian got a hard-on; then he worried that the tattoo man might be the boy's father. Sebastian didn't move away, but he didn't move closer. With this uncertainty, his hard-on went down; he decided to go into the sauna room.

Tattoo man followed; the two were alone; the man turned up the heat and started doing some body rendering exercises. Sebastian began to get off by imagining the man twisting Sebastian's body to his will, making him into an object of his desire. Sebastian smiled and said hi; the man didn't smile back, nor did he speak, but he did acknowledge Sebastian with a nod of his head. Then he turned the heat up even higher. Sebastian couldn't breathe; he left for the shower room to cool off.

After resting a while, Sebastian returned to the steam room. Young Juan seemed even more bored and wilted; he had fallen asleep. The tattoo man now had Tony, the other youth, down on the floor going through exercises. Tony had a stunning figure. About sixteen, without body hair; he removed his towel and lay down flat on the floor. The watery air made his skin glisten. Late afternoon sun streamed through the frosted windows. The steam moved between the shafts of light, and the human bodies refracted and wove together the shafts of light. Sebastian, Juan, Tony, and the tattoo man floated inside a wet, fluid space.

Tony's exercising kept Sebastian's eyes riveted on him. The

youth lay with knees bent together, touching his chin and pulled up at a ninety-degree angle to the floor. Tony then spread his legs so that each knee went down on either side until his kneecaps touched the floor; the tattoo man forced each bent knee down whenever Tony's knees failed to reach the floor. Tony quickly loosened up and could do the exercise without help, but the effort strained his whole body and gave definition to every one of his muscles. He had a very large, eight-and-one-half-inch, seventy-percent-hard cock with smooth, sweating balls. Tony had some pubic hair, but none under his arms or on his body. A fine black line drew a mustache across his crotch. Tony's knees became butterfly wings. His body seemed to fly miraculously through the steam and light as Juan became a sleeping cherub or cupid. The tattoo man urged Tony on and on, faster and faster. Tony did twenty or thirty of these genuflections; the tattoo man was counting. Stunned, just watching the exercise, Sebastian lost track of the numbers and of the time. The sun had set; the room became twilight.

Confused about what he should do, Sebastian left after the duo stopped exercising, when more people came into the steam room and they turned on the lights. Sebastian went to his dressing room with hopes that one or all of the three might follow. The attendant, when he noticed Sebastian's arousal, followed and offered a massage. They closed the door, they kissed, they flipped into a sixty-nine position, and came together.

# What's in an Inch
*Dik Staal*

I'm dazed by my memories of last night's scene. It has saturated my vision this afternoon. I have been horny as hell remembering his magnificent swollen uncut dick. I do believe I have found a peer. He is a novice, but kinks on dicks, pumps like a master. What transpired is as follows.

I went into our back room. Next to an army-green massage table stands a metal box which houses my pump and cylinders. I stripped down to the skin, my dick and balls expectant, eager for the tubes. I donned my camouflage jacket. It shows off my tattoos fantastically and emphasizes my big tattooed tool and low-hanging balls. I stepped into my rough black rubber boots. They make me hot as hell. Then I reached out for my pot of grease.

I take a great dollop of the stuff and massage my dick steadily, watching myself in my full-length mirror. I put *Hi Tech* on the video and sniff heavy and deep into the poppers. I slide my dick into its loving cylinder, tighten the clamp, and attach the pump.

Pull one...pull two...pull three...stop.

My dickhead runs surging away from its root, drawn from my body, pushing deep into the tube. The force and suction is such, I fear the stump will be torn right off. I watch magnetized, as my gleaming, greasy tattooed dick thickens and tightens up. I fill the tube, ease the clamp ever so slightly, and then again: pull one...pull two...pull three. The suction is great tonight, I am beginning to make headway.

My slave enters the back room expectantly. He's a quiet guy, Dutch; his eyes are mesmerized by my huge swelling dick. I tantalize him with my cool but urgent pumping. Pumping till it hurts and then *air*. And again I begin the relentless sucking of my dick, sucking and straining down and out into the tube. High on poppers, I slowly ease and slide the tube, yeah, ever so slowly slide it off my fucking dick, a big fat stump of a dick hanging down between my legs. My slave waits to suck, his eyes riveted on the juicy thing, dripping with precum and grease.

"I want to piss, get on your fucking knees and swallow it whole. All the way down your throat! Don't suck and don't bloody move!" Like a gunshot he is gobbling all the way to its root, deep, thick, and swollen. "Not a sound," I bark. "You're just a bloody pisshole." My piss gushes and floods his body, gurgling deep down into him, my swollen half-rampant tool crammed into his pisshole of a head, and I grab hold of it and shake it into his mouth just as I do in any public urinal.

"Right now, pump my dick and balls. I want those fuckers banging down my leg when I go cruising in my leathers tonight. Twenty minutes or so and then I'll have a break, so do your stuff."

I grease my shaved nuts and swollen dick and ease them into my second cylinder. My whole packet is enclosed like some piece of randy meat, ready and waiting for that all-too-familiar click as the pump is attached. I now lie down, my legs spread-eagled. My slave is in between, eager with the pump. He wants to really work at it, pump it up, make it massive. I place a mask over my eyes and fill my head with poppers.

"Okay, fuckhead, just take it, go for it." He takes the first three pulls at the pump. "Steady…steady I tell you, go real slow. I don't want to hear you and I don't want to hear the pump. Right. Pump now." The suction takes up again. I feel my balls beginning to grind, to harden up, to work down the tube. They are being stretched down to my dickhead. My whole bloody crotch is on fire, expanding in every direction at the same time. My dick holds fast and is jammed in the tube, pressing hard against the swelling balls. They are sucked forward, out, away from my body. The head of my tool traps my nuts.

The pumping continues, the poppers heavy; my packet feels as if it will explode. All around me is silence, apart from the *Hi Tech* soundtrack running its course. Even that seems to go further and further away as my mind goes deeper and deeper into my lust-crazed, swollen, greasy, horny packet.

The time is running, the pumping relentless, the pleasure almost unbelievable; I am obsessed.

My hardened, swollen balls draw deep now into the tube. "*Air,* right.*" There is a long hiss as the air rushes into the tube, breaking the pressure of the vacuum. I am lucky with this slave, such a dick-slave. He releases the valve and slowly removes the tube. My pumped, stretched, and glistening tattooed dick and balls drip and ooze a mixture of thick precum and sleazy oil.

I stand and perve on my swollen packet, my new possessions, one big massive tool and gigantic gleaming balls. My slave is totally gripped by its now truly colossal and swollen state. Saliva drips from his mouth. He knows what is to come next, but first another piss out of this fucking dick of mine.

"Get down and drink, you fucking shit." I stand, my tool thrusts out as I watch the piss gush from my enormous dickhead into his eager, greedy, wide-open mouth. A steady stream and not one drop spilt. My toilet-slave, well trained, on his knees now, sucks and slurps. Reflected in the mirror, we are now four guys in action.

"Time to work it, mate," I say, my voice heavy with the lust that comes from pumping. I plow into the deepest recesses of ultimate lust. I tremble like a racehorse with the expectancy of the frenzied shooting of my thick, creamy white load. I take a last look into the mirror, "*Yeah…*hung *like a* fucking *stallion.*"

I look down at my quivering slave. "Right, you're going to work it over good tonight, boy, good and bloody proper. You know just what I mean by that, don't you, you fucking piece of shit." The tension of the night was as sharp as a razor. "Okay, get the grease, slave." As my slave reached out for the grease, the doorbell rang unexpectedly.

Framed in the door was Gerrit, a real humpy bugger if ever you saw one. I had forgotten that I had invited him over for a pumping session and work over by my shithead of a piss-drinking slave. There he stood: six feet tall, just my height, very torn jeans, leather jacket, and boots. Man, what a nice basket in those fucking jeans. They were torn everywhere except on his packet and, by the bulge, recently pumped.

We had a couple of beers and a few smokes while I let him become familiar with the setup of the back room. My massive, still greasy, tool throbbed hard as I sat across from him in position to have a good perve on his filthy jeans. I narrowed my eyes at his thrusting dick and balls and pierced and pumped-up tits. He returned the compliment, burying his eyeballs deep between my legs, a visual rape, and an enormous pleasure. We sat drinking our beers and perving our heads off on each other. The first time we met was at a little leather shop. We talked about a pumping fetish 'zine and went out for beers. We told each other our histories and tossed around our pumping experiences. Now he was here, oozing raunch from every pore, radiating sleazy masculinity.

I glanced up at the clock, 10:45, a good time to get going again, but this time pumping with a new mate. Gerrit took my lead, removed his boots, and eased his way out of his jeans. His lumpy packet surged and flopped out into the smoke-filled room. It was one massive lump of a cock and enormous turgid balls. He replaced his boots, pent-up, ready to pump. So there we now stood, totally naked, except for our boots, looking like two fucking stud animals. Yeah, the night was hot; our thick rampant dicks both throbbed, eager to get into the action, eager for the fucking tubes.

"Okay, mate, let's get going with this scene, give my grease a try and see what you think of it."

The cylinders lay like four primitive virgins on the massage table, waiting to be stuffed by two huge expanded dicks and yearning swollen balls. We both took great dollops of the stuff and started to grease up each other's packets, shaven and totally hairless. He had discovered that a naked dick and balls was easier to pump. It was a bloody great experience to be man-handled while man-handling. Working the grease into and around every fold of skin, the two tools were being worked out, lovingly massaged, prepared for the pumps.

"Come here, slave, take hold of his dick and balls, slowly feed them into his pump, and take fucking care."

Gerrit had never had his packet fed into his cylinder by a slave before, and you could see by his face that the experience was a very hot and horny one indeed. Expertly, my slave eased in the dickhead and then one ball and then the other. Gerrit closed the valve, attached the pump with that sudden click, and made the first slow pull on the handle. I had been attending to my own tube as I watched my slave servicing Gerrit's cock and balls. We were both pulling in unison, that long, slow, sensual pull, that first pull of the scene that is so full of expectancy. We could see each other's dicks surge forward. We knew exactly what the other felt as the tightness of the cylinders began to take hold. They were tight and firm and dragged the balls slowly down to the dickheads. The beginning sensations were a hot tingling—sort of chewing and nipping at the same time. Yeah, the pumping was under way.

Two fat dicks were slowly growing fatter, pressing hard, firm against the tightly confined balls. We had both been pumping earlier, so the scene would truly be great. The head of my slave was now dick-height as he knelt between our legs, our encased equipment thrusting straight out in an almost threatening manner, had they not been so encased. As the pumping continued to increase the vacuum, he watched with horny hunger on his face. The first drips of precum were drawn out. He begged for all that oozing liquid he loved to suck up so bloody much.

Fifteen minutes had passed by.

*Click. Click.*

The two pumps were released from their cylinders, two men stood, naked, booted, their bodies taut and beginning to show signs of sweat. They stood face-to-face, an act of camaraderie. The two tubes seemed to be packed full of dick and nuts.

"No more ball-sucking for you tonight, slave." Two stuffed cylinders, thrusting out, standing rigid and rampant from our crotches, waiting for release from the tubes, and together we both gave a turn on the valve.

*H-i-s-s-s-s...*

Tonight that sound grabbed me doubly in the guts. The two packets readjusted themselves and slowly pulled back. We eased ourselves free from the tubes and watched each other's dripping, greasy dicks as they flopped out, now swollen even more. Our great turgid balls sort of tumbled and fell banging between our legs, so hot, so sensitive, and so bloody horny.

"Okay, slave, get the grease on those two dicks, and go easy."

With two dollops, he carefully massaged the two cocks, making them ready for the dick-tubes. Gerrit was almost beside himself with lust. There was not very much difference between the sizes of our tools. We were well matched. Freshly greased up, we gently eased our precious dicks into their cylinders. The pumps we attached; the suction this time was different as we started to pull on the pumps, and the dickheads roared forward. The pumping continued slowly, easy, no, there is no need for haste, not at all, the night is just beginning. We pumped and perved, we took it slow and rested. Another sniff. These poppers were powerful stuff. "Here, mate, take a hit of this. I'll take your pump and you can pump on mine, and you, you fucking slave, just keep your distance and do your perving in silence, just stay there kneeling on the floor between us and be ready."

Gerrit, now hot on the poppers, drew on the handle of my pump as I did his. We pumped together, we pumped each other together. "Slower, Gerrit," I said. He was not used to such high quality of poppers. They rushed to his head and his enthusiasm almost got the better of him. We both kept at it, our lust-ridden eyes daring the other to stop. With our eyes, we searched into each other, wanting to climb into the other's ball sac. We each were full of untold hunger and lustful yearnings of going further. Just how far could we go with this brief experience? "Okay, mate, that's good, very bloody good, that was just about the best fifteen minutes of my whole fucking life, mate." Gerrit knew instinctively it was now time to take a short break.

*Click. Click.* The two pumps were released from their cylinders. Slowly we both turned the valves.

*H-i-s-s-s.* How I loved that hissing sound.

"Right, slave, draw those two fucking tubes from our dicks and suck on some really juicy pieces of meat." Slowly, the two great cocks were freed from the confinement of the cylinders. Gerrit's dick, a very dark pulsating pink tool, contrasted vividly with mine, a somber greasy stump of tattooed skin. Both of our tools hung like two fucking stud pricks in a stable. They were both so thick, so pumped out of proportion, greasy and dripping, that the eyes of my slave bulged from their sockets: two huge pieces of man meat right before him and neither one of them could he possibly get into his bloody eager, wanting to suck, pisshole of a mouth.

"You can't suck the fuckers, shithead, so just lick up those fucking fuck-stumps." He took both dripping greasy tools in his hands and was able to slurp and slide his greedy tongue from ball sac to ball sac. Backward and forward that greedy mouth traveled, sucking and licking the two dickheads at the same time. He moved along the two rampant dicks. They were one great fucking shaft, stretching out from crotch to crotch, one huge fucking piece of man-meat joining our two bodies together, the dickheads merging, Gerrit's puffed-up foreskin rolled completely over my tool's knobhead, two dickheads seeming to gobble at each other, their piss-slits kissing. The sliding, slurping, sucking, hungry mouth continued to gobble, mouthing its way along the tools until they were both completely dry, yeah, dry now, ready for another greasing, ready once more for their respective cylinders.

"Okay, that's enough of this fucking sucking shit. Grease these two packets up and then get yourself off to the night-shop and get us some more beer." As an afterthought, I said, "And don't hurry back." So now there we stood, both as horny as hell. Two great swollen packets, slave-greased, ready once again for the pump. Together we watched each other as we slid first our dickheads and then one ball, two balls, and we were in. Gently now, even more gently, we pushed on the tubes, pushed to the hilt. Our great naked and shaven packets were enclosed again, a tightening of the valves. Our packets surged forward, straining to get to the end of the tube. They instantly filled the shafts of the cylinders this time. The great fucking nuts strained to bypass the dickheads, but held back as the knobs fattened, smoothing out, now losing their natural shape, great swelling mushroom heads.

*Sniff…sniff…*and *sniff* again as we both inhaled the poppers. Two great bloody rigid tubes sticking, thrusting, out from our crotches, jam-packed full of our precious equipment. Now began a throbbing in the dick.

"Make your cock throb, mate, make it throb and pulsate, just push on it and throb it and throb it." As I watched, I saw the first few tentative twitches in Gerrit's cock. There we stood, our two packets encased, trapped in their tubes, the two dicks throbbing hard now, and even harder as they were being drawn and sucked down deeper into the tubes. We stood before the mirror, perving on ourselves and each other. We took hold of each other's cocks and started to rub the knobs and along the cockshafts, rubbing the dripping liquid into them, adding more grease for the smaller, tighter tubes, feeling that throbbing, swollen dick in my hand, rolling that bloated foreskin over its now very sensitive knob, back and forth relentlessly while Gerrit manhandled my tool, massaging the thing, hotter now, yeah so fucking hot.

*Throb…throb…throb.* The feeling was almost audible, and I could not hold myself back from kissing this guy, urgently thrusting my tongue down his throat. He sucked on it as though it were my tool, we were eating each other and our tools were getting hotter and even more ready. Gasping and grabbing some breath, I said, "Shit, man, do you want to shoot already? I think we can go a hell of a long way yet. Ease it up, mate, there's stacks of time. Okay, man?"

So there we sat, two hot and horny guys ready with our big, fat packets greasy and sweaty, just simply taking a break.

We were all heartbeat and sweat. We breathed in the scent of our sex. We lay at the ebb of our endurance, and when we were ready, we stood once again, applying heavy dollops of grease. Our dicks were great swollen things, the two huge greasy poles protruding from our crotches. They had their own personalities, and were eager to be back inside the tubes. Now they had to be gently squeezed into the tight confines of the cylinders. We attached the pumps. With each pull of the pump, the balls gripped tighter. Our tightening ball sacs showed off huge, impressive nuts, enhancing the two huge trapped and encased dicks. Gerrit's grew redder. His was a great big horsemeat of a thing, looking as though it might burst into flames. His foreskin looked as though it were at the point of boiling, his dickhead mushrooming. Indeed, if I didn't know it beforehand, I would have said that his dick was cut. Mine was darker than it had ever been, the tattooed skin even more stretched, gleaming in its plastic case, smoothing out into just one big bloody stump.

Keys could be heard turning in the front door lock; it opened and closed.

"Yes, who is it?" I said into the surrounding darkness. It turned out to be the two guys that I lived with, two fucking faggots, two fucking brilliant cocksuckers, two bloody slaves-to-dick. Gerrit looked at me with apprehension, our dicks entrapped in this way, stretched in the cylinders, hot and very bloody fat now. We were both in the process of going for the extreme limits of our respective tubes, and now this intrusion, this violation of our privacy, of our unique camaraderie, pumping our dicks together, the poppers making our heads spin. And I had to think fast, or else I could lose this fucking humpy, horny bugger, and that was not my meaning, no, not at all.

"Bring some fresh beers in here. Come see what we have got for you two guys to work on." We slowly opened up the valves, and a long hissing followed. Our two great fucking tools were released into the air. They came flopping out with a kind of expectancy, ready to be worked, just as the door to the back room opened up. In walked my two faggoty slaves, my two dicksuckers, neither of whom could get enough. Their hungry eyes bulged when they saw what lay before them.

"Okay, you buggers, get down and do your stuff, start sucking those dicks. Wrap your fucking tongues around those dickheads and suck out the juices of those great fuckin' tools. Get that man-meat down deep into your throats and don't bloody bite the fuckers, just suck and suck deeply. We're going to fill you to the brim with our man-juices."

Instantly the two faggoty slaves were on their knees sucking and slurping away at our great pumped and swollen dickheads. Slowly we both eased our dickshafts deep into those two hungry throats. We watched each other being sucked and worked on, now slowly we began to thrust those great fucking, heavy, horny, fat, and bulging tools, the tempo increasing steadily with the ramming. We began to pace each other with our dicks, now pumping into those two eager, hungry, sucking mouths, yeah, pumping harder and harder, our balls banging harder and now slapping at our own assholes as we swung heavier into the action. Two pairs of huge nuts banging away between our legs. We increased our head-fucking. Harder and harder we rammed and pushed our tools. I took hold of Gerrit's head and drove my tongue down his throat. He responded, working his tongue with mine; we were now tongue-fucking each other's heads as our dicks were ramming deeper and deeper. Sucking, fucking tongues. The urgency was increasing. I could feel the boiling hot spunk building in my pulsating, heaving packet. I was quite sure that the same was happening to Gerrit. Our gut-level groaning building harder, the room was full of animal lust.

When the noise reached a crescendo, we would bury our sex screams into each other's heads and kiss harder and harder, as only two men can when they are having their heavy pumped and swollen cocks sucked and swallowed deep to their hilts. We were rocking and swaying with the heavy fucking action, pushing and ramming in unison as we sucked deep into each other's throats, kissing and eating each other's mouths, building our spunk-slime together. The slaves were now fucking our dicks with their heads, going for more of that precious meat, desperately sucking as there might be no tomorrow. The stench of male sex in action was rising as though it were a solid state. We were all dripping sweat, and the pulsating, throbbing urgency increased. And still we fucked, kissed, and swallowed, gobbling while being gobbled. The two great fucking dicks now throbbed hard like two red-hot steel rods, pumping yet again into those faggoty heads like two great fucking pistons driving a steam engine. The ball sacs filled and heaved tighter now. The urgency was beginning to drive us crazy with our lustful kissing. Our sex-crazed bodies craved climax.

My tool was burning hot. The more I rammed it, the more it was sucked, and the hotter it seemed to get. My balls were on fire, yeah, now all I wanted to do was to shoot my fucking nut load, shoot it out of my balls. I was totally carried away by this ultimate perversity. We two guys having our dicks sucked and worked and the heavy kissing, the mouth-fucking, our tongues fucking each other's heads, our dicks ramming harder and deeper into the fucking slaves' throats was fucking heavy and even more heavy. I rammed it deeper and was close to shooting my load. Shit, did I want to shoot! I sucked and ate at Gerrit's mouth, in and out, sucking his body through his mouth as we were both being sucked on and he was sucking deep into me. We were two fucking animals, we had found our match. Gerrit was indeed my peer.

"Are you ready, mate?" I gasped, as I was on the verge of shooting my fucking load.

*"Yeah, oh fucking yeah,"* he answered, "I'm screaming ready to shoot with you, yeah, together!" Our bloody balls boiled, heavy with the shoot loads, boiled like one massive packet. We were now completely in tune with each other. Then it happened. The roaring, driving sensation of the heavy churning, deep in our guts, tearing through our bodies. The screaming lust of shooting began. Deep down inside my dick, the sensitivity grew, the pulsating throb as my dick hardened, the slow beginnings of the rush of my shooting. Now the even more urgent sucking by the slave on my tool. He knew I was about to shoot my load of slime; shoot and shoot I would until he had swallowed every last drop of my spunk. So was it with Gerrit. His dick also throbbed harder and expanded. Thrust deeper into the face of his slave. Expanding down that eager throat. Our two tools were gobbled and suckled with such urgency that we knew we would be drained of our liquid manpower, our juices, our slime spunk. Our ball sacs would be sucked dry and we would not be satisfied until they were.

I thrust my tongue even deeper into Gerrit's mouth. I wanted to eat the bugger's heart out his throat. He was thrusting down my throat. He could take me, too. Fucking each other's mouths, senselessly drawn to the basest, most primal level of lust need. Our dicks were being devoured by two of the best-trained hungry slave mouths. Our dicks were raped, fucked, and sucked to the hilt. We were on fire, ready and burning with fucking lust. Our pumped-up dicks were ready to fire like fucking Napoleonic cannons. They were weapons, senseless, fevered, raging; ready to shoot their cannonball loads.

"I'm going to shoot, you fucking bastards!" I drove my tongue deeper into Gerrit and knew he was ready to shoot his load as well. We would shoot together. Our nasty spunk would drown our slaves in our sex.

The screaming roar in my head began. It tore my guts, my groin, and snapped my back into a full arch. My slave, relentless, tireless, matched me in his rhythm. Gerrit lost his place in my mind as an individual and became simply something to suck. He matched my fervor and pulled me to him.

We were both in male spasms of shooting. The noises accelerated as we shot into our slaves' heads, choking them with our manhood. Gerrit and I fed on each other, our tongues entwined. Drowning our slaves in ejaculation, we rammed deeper and harder, stuffing those slave holes with our power.

# *Enlightenment*

It would be foolish to claim that porn—sexual writing—does nothing more than simply turn us on. All writing is, to some degree, pedagogic: We learn about new sexual acts, we learn protocols of sexual etiquette, we learn how other men feel about their own sexuality and activity. Even the most fantastical sexual story has the potential to teach us something about how we think and conduct ourselves sexually.

For many gay men, reading porn is the way that they learn what it means to be gay: that glimmer of truth that burns brightly, hotly, often hidden behind bad prose and even worse plotting. Sex is frequently portrayed in our culture as a mystery, something hidden, slightly dangerous, and possibly unsolvable. We talk about "discovering" our sexuality, about "finding" our sexual identities, about "uncovering" sexual feelings: terms that are descriptive, yet do not really do justice to the incredibly complicated process in which we become cognizant, enlightened—in the classical, eighteenth-century sense of the word—about our sexuality. This process remains unnecessarily complicated because the truth about homosexuality—its goodness, its nurturance, its pleasures and powers—are considered unspeakable in our culture. On a basic level, sexual writing, by breaking the taboo of explicitly speaking about physical sexuality, contributes to a process of personal, psychic, and sexual enlightenment.

The characters in the following stories find different paths to "enlightenment": pleasure, sex, fear, trust, relationships, fantasies—each of them a different route, each with varying consequences.

The storyteller in William John Mann's "Learning the Secrets," following the advice of an older, more adventurously lascivious friend, discovers the joys of broadening his "type." Mann's story—with its clear sexual moral—is refreshing in a literature that so often depends upon all kinds of "types" (physical, sexual, situational) as easy shortcuts to formula writing. The "secrets" of Mann's title refer as much to sexual satisfaction as they do to the tricks of successful cruising.

David Laurents's "Burning Bridges" is about the passion of sex and anger. A cross between a sexualized *Firestarter* and Freudian dream analysis, "Burning Bridges" moves its narrator through the confusing labyrinth of feelings that surface when relationships change. Through dreams, fantasies, sex, and even some scary—possibly supernatural?—occurrences, Laurents's protagonist comes to a better understanding of what is happening in his life.

A great deal of sexual writing concerns itself with a young person's journey into sexuality, and as such it is a cross between self-help literature and "how-to" manuals. "Game Nights" by Edmund Miller relies on the high-school-coming-of-age genre—locker rooms, long group showers, basketball games, liquor, and cars parked on dark streets. The staples of suburban U.S. secondary-school homoeroticism all come together here to move the story's protagonist to a better understanding of his sexual desires. Miller's use of these archetypal icons places "Game Night" in a solid American tradition of sexual storytelling.

"Chilies and Chocolate" by Stan Leventhal charts the growth

of a gay male relationship. As Kitt and Antony learn about one another—sexually, as well as in their individual tastes in food and music—they begin to grow. If Edmund Miller is concerned with the blooming of sexuality, Leventhal is focused on how sexuality informs interpersonal relationships. Leventhal, who died January 15, 1995, of complications from AIDS, was a perceptive writer on urban gay male lives. His novels *Mountain Climbing in Sheridan Square* and *Skydiving on Christopher Street* are astute records of New York gay life in the 1980s.

# Learning the Secrets
*William John Mann*

Once, I was a naive young boy. I'd seen the cars, of course, every time I drove past the rest stop, but I never *knew*. And why would I? Such things were not a part of my world.

Besides, I was always in a hurry, my windows down, my radio blaring, anxious to be up the Cape and into Provincetown in time for tea dance. I used to pride myself on not stopping the whole trip, not once between New Haven and Provincetown, not even to take a leak. "You're young," my friend Joachim, who is older than I, told me. "Your bladder will hold."

Then, about a year ago, I was no longer as young as I was once. My bladder didn't hold. Passing by the rest stop, I had to pee.

Not so young, but still naive. I was twenty-eight. I noticed the number of cars parked alongside the trees and I wondered why they were empty. A rustle of movement off in the bushes caught my eye. There was someone back there, someone behind the fence. It was a man: older than I, gray hair, a beard. Why had he gone all the way back there to take a pee, I wondered. Surely these bushes right here were privacy enough.

As I hauled out my dick and let my water flow, feeling the rush of relief settle all through my body, I spotted another man, and another, this time coming out of the bushes and heading for their cars. Now, and only now, I began to suspect. Had it just been peeing they were doing in the woods?

"Silly child," Joachim told me later, sitting on the deck at his house in Provincetown. "Every rest stop in the world is a gay cruising spot. If you weren't so focused on tea dances and which boots were popular this year, you might have discovered that a long time ago."

Joachim was about fifteen years older than I, a man of the world. He'd been, as they say, around. Rest stops were just one part of his expertise.

"You know all the secrets, don't you?" I asked, smiling.

"Most. Not all. I'm not through learning," he said. "You'll learn them, too, one at a time. If you're open to learning them."

Secrets, I thought. Gay life is filled with secrets. Well, I didn't want secrets. No sex in the bushes for me. I was better than that. I was out, loud, and proud. I wasn't sure I wanted to learn all the secrets of which Joachim spoke. "Have you done that one?" I asked, referring to the rest stop on the way to the Cape.

"Sure, lots of times," he smiled. "It's a very hot place. Very popular."

I shook my head. How could anyone find that hot? "No offense," I said. "But those guys—well, they're—"

"What?" Joachim asked, arching an eyebrow. "Too old?"

"Well, there aren't many guys my age—"

"How do you know?"

"They all seem so—sleazy—"

"Sometimes they are," Joachim smiled. "Only when you're lucky."

I laughed. Whatever floated one's boat—that was my philosophy. It just wasn't my thing. I checked my hair in the mirror before heading off to the bar. Joachim could have the rest stops, and the dunes, and the bath houses, and the back alleys. It just wasn't my scene. I laced up my boots and headed out to find a trick—someone who would look, I realized then, with a growing sense of discomfort —exactly like me.

So maybe now I should give you a quick description of my appearance. I've got dirty blond hair, blue eyes, and dimples. I'm about average height, five ten, with a slim, swimmer's build. I work out regularly, and I'm pretty proud of the sharp definition I've achieved for my chest, my arms, my tight, flat stomach, and my firm, round butt. My nipples are perky, I'm completely smooth, and in the summer I make sure I get a nice all-over even golden tan. I don't have any trouble getting guys. On the dance floor, my buddies and I take off our shirts and sweat a lot. We pick up guys who do the same thing and refuse to dance with anyone older than we.

I'm not proud of that.

In fact, this last summer, I actually said yes a couple of times and danced with guys probably in their fifties. My buddies couldn't figure it out. I said, hey, we're all getting older. I can't even hold my piss all the way up to the Cape anymore.

Which brings me back to the rest stop. I don't know why exactly, but Joachim's description of it—"a very hot place"—stuck in my head. On my way back to New Haven, I slowed down as I passed the rest stop, and counted the cars. Three, and a fourth pulling in. One guy was in the second car, his window rolled down, his elbow resting on the door. The other two cars were empty. The new car pulled up alongside the guy with the open window. And then I was past them, wondering what they said to each other.

"There aren't many guys my age—"

"How do you know?" Joachim had responded. How did I know?

All week I was horny. And busy. I work for an insurance company. It was hell week. All I did was process claims from eight A.M. to six P.M. I was excited about the overtime, but by the time I got home I was too tired even to jerk off. So I got hornier. And hornier.

And one afternoon—I think it was Wednesday, halfway through

the week—I was sitting outside, enjoying the sun for a half hour while I ate my lunch, and this guy walks by. I don't know why I noticed him. I mean, he wasn't my type. He didn't look *anything* like me. He was older, probably at least forty-five, with lots of gray in his black hair, and a mustache. I didn't normally like mustaches. Too much like those pictures of those guys in the seventies. But I remembered something else, sitting there, eating my ham-and-cheese sandwich: a video I'd seen, vintage 1977, of these two guys, rough and hairy, with big mustaches, and boy, were they ever getting into it. None of that fake talk and prissy preening that goes on in today's videos. Like 'Ryan Idol.' *Please.*

Suddenly I was struck with a sense that I didn't know a thing—that I really *was* just this naive kid who thought the sex he'd been having all these years was the hottest it was ever going to get. I raised my eyes over to the man with the mustache, who was leaning against the wall now, his face turned up to the sun. He was tall, probably six feet, and his skin was rough, lined not only with age but with—experience, I realized, and I felt my dick stir in my Calvin Kleins.

"Christ," I said to myself, looking away. What's going on with me? That man over there—I would never have looked at him before today. I'm just so fucking horny, I guess. But I looked back at him, and now he had turned his eyes to me. Deep brown eyes. I shivered. He inhaled the clean summer air, pushing his broad shoulders back and lifting his chin. I noticed his Adam's apple over his red-and-blue tie, knotted tightly at his throat. His gray suit seemed the color of the highlights in his hair, and much too small to contain the powerful physique I now imagined waited beneath it.

He didn't linger, but he stayed in my head. Each day after that I'd look for him, wondering which part of this huge company he worked for. It was no use. I'd just have to wait until we ran into each other again.

And then what? I didn't even know if he was gay. And even if he was, what would I say? And even more troubling: Would I be able to get him, even if I did manage to work up the courage to talk to him?

For the first time since coming out, I felt inadequate, as if I might not measure up, as if all my attributes might not be relevant in this scenario. Might even be obstacles. The smooth, clean-shaven look might work for tea dance, but with this guy? I doubted very much he cared which boots were in style this season. I imagined on the weekends he'd trade in his shiny wingtips for a pair of work boots, the kind that held together for decades, the kind he'd been wearing since—well, since 1977.

And, thinking that, I got hornier. Hornier than I'd ever been before.

Maybe that's why I pulled off at the rest stop that late Friday afternoon, heading back up to Provincetown for the weekend. Or maybe it was just that I had to pee, again. All I knew was that I was going to stop. There was no way to avoid it.

There were two cars there. One was empty. The other had someone in the driver's seat, his window rolled down. It was a bright day, very warm, and the air smelled clean and clear, despite the proximity of the highway. I pulled up behind the empty car, and turned off my engine. I could see the guy in the first car look into his rearview mirror, but I had no sense of what he might look like. Some fat old troll, I thought to myself—yet it was a hollow thought, as if I didn't mean it. As if fat old trolls might have something to offer, too, something I'd always rejected out of hand, and thus never knew.

But I can't deny that I hoped it would be some hot young thing, wearing the right boots, suitably muscled, with a big dick. I could hear Joachim's voice: "Expand your horizons." Yeah, yeah, I thought. If only that guy I'd seen at lunch was here—well, maybe *then* I'd consider expanding my horizons.

The man in the first car was opening his door. I squinted my eyes to get a better look. And I felt weak, light-headed, all of a sudden. It was the guy from lunch, in a T-shirt and jeans. And work boots.

Okay. So maybe it wasn't him. But from this distance, it could have been. He was tall, had dark hair peppered with gray, and a mustache. He looked back at me just once, and then locked his car door and headed up the dusty path into the woods.

I swallowed. What the hell was I supposed to do?

Another car had pulled in behind me. I looked into my rearview mirror this time. The guy was probably a teacher: fortyish, with round glasses. Small, thin face. Nothing remarkable. Yet the thought that he was here, sitting there in his car, as horny as I was, his dick mine for the taking, and mine his—I had to catch my breath, literally, by closing my mouth and looking away.

In the bars, on the dance floor, there's this elaborate dance—a mating dance, if you will. It's hot and exciting in its own way. You ask the required questions: "What do you do?" "Where are you from?" "Come here a lot?" You buy each other drinks. You pretend you are not at all interested in sex, that you are just meeting casually, that there is no ulterior motive. Until that final question, which still ignores the truth: "Want to come back to my room?" When, in reality, what is going on is that you are sizing each other up, and what you want to be saying is: "I want to suck your dick" or "I want to fuck you up the ass."

Suddenly the honesty of this place—this rest stop on the side of the highway, and all the places like it—hit me. I didn't care what the man's name was in the car behind me. I just wanted him to suck my dick. And maybe to suck his. I didn't want to have to buy him a beer. I didn't care what he did, or if he came here often. I just wanted his sex. Here. Now.

I got out of my car.

I was arrogant enough to know he'd follow. I knew my ass looked good in these jeans, I knew my arms and chest showed well through my tank top. I stumbled through the brush into the bushes, and could feel my dick getting heavier.

Behind me, I heard a car door close. I didn't look back. I knew that man with the mustache was in here somewhere. Part of me was too terrified to find him. And besides, I had my schoolteacher rapidly gaining on me. I walked briskly along the path, and the realization that it had been forged and matted down by thousands of feet belonging to men as horny as I was thrilled me. I was in the enchanted forest, the forest of sex, and from every corner it pulsated with energy.

How many loads had been shot here? I contemplated that question briefly, as I came to a curve in the path by three tall trees. That's what made these woods so alive, so energized, I thought—the decades of cum that have fallen to the ground here, revitalizing the earth, fertilizing the trees.

"Hi," the schoolteacher said behind me, in a barely audible whisper.

I turned, stopping by the trees. He continued on past me, and I was perplexed for a moment, until he turned and looked over his shoulder, once, quick.

Now I was the one who followed. What was wrong with the spot I'd chosen? I wasn't sure, but I followed anyway. For a moment, I was fearful he might be a cop, but I was too horny to stop now. He was dressed in loose-fitting beige chinos and a white polo shirt. He wore blue-and-white running shoes that did not match the rest of his outfit. But somehow he was the picture of sex, and I wanted his lips around my cock.

He stopped abruptly, changing direction. And then I saw why. The man with the mustache was leaning against a tree, and another man (a fat old troll, as I might have called him once) was on his knees in front of him, working his dick with his mouth. The man with the mustache had his arms crossed over his chest, and his forearms looked huge. His eyes were locked on me. Damn, I thought. Somebody else got him. Yet from the evident pleasure he was receiving, I didn't imagine he was disappointed.

And the man on his knees seemed to be giving a better blowjob than a lot of the pretty boys I was used to picking up in the bars.

Finally the schoolteacher stopped, partially obscured behind a large bush. I stopped too, not a foot away from him.

This was it: the moment of truth. I was going to do it. All of Joachim's stories came back to me at once, of hot sex behind the docks, in public restrooms, in the woods, in the dunes. When the man's hand reached out and gripped my crotch, I let out the kind of sigh I usually made only after long, long foreplay, when I was getting close to orgasm.

The schoolteacher wasted no time. He got down on his knees and awkwardly began unfastening my belt buckle. I had to help. Then he popped open my jeans, and stuck his face into my open fly. I looked down at the top of his head: thinning hair, like my father's. It was an odd thought, and what was even odder was that it made my dick get harder. That's when the schoolteacher pulled down my white briefs and fumbled my erection into his mouth.

I leaned back against a tree and looked skyward into the lacy network of limbs that crosshatched against the bright blue sky. The man's mouth was warm and slippery. He moved up and down my shaft in record time, and I could feel my cock swell and fill his mouth. He licked the underside and then rolled his tongue around the head, pushing at my peehole, and then took it all again, all the way, into his mouth. I have a good seven inches, sometimes more, and he seemed to have no trouble sucking it. Experience, I thought to myself. *Experience.*

His hands inched up under my tank top to feel my pecs. I instinctively flexed. This was hot. I suddenly had an image of myself: this hot young stud, flexing his chest, having his dick sucked and being worshipped by an aging, nerdy schoolteacher, who wished with all his life he was as young and attractive as I was. He pinched my nipples, which drives me wild. I began thrusting jauntily into his mouth, fucking his face.

"Taste good?" I heard myself ask, and he nodded, my dick still lodged down his throat. "Suck it," I said. "Take it all." I laughed to myself. I sounded like a porn star.

In and out of his mouth my dick moved, and I could feel the back of his throat each time I gave a thrust. I was getting ready to shoot, disappointed that I could not bear to contain it much longer, wanting this worship to go on for hours. I was planning to pull out of his mouth and shoot into the bushes—while, I was sure, he would watch in awe—when I noticed the man with the mustache approaching.

A three-way? I asked myself. I felt a moment of panic, and slowed down my thrusting. My dick softened just a bit, the cum inside of me retreating back up my shaft. I suddenly became conscious of my breath, how fast I was inhaling and exhaling.

The man with the mustache now stood in front of us. The schoolteacher, oblivious, seemed to think it was his fault that my dick had softened, and he was sucking with renewed vigor.

I looked at the newcomer. I was frightened to make eye contact with him, yet I was too intimidated to look away. He had short black-and-gray hair, with a large mustache over thick, full lips. He might have been the man from lunch; he might have been someone else. It didn't matter. He *was* the man I'd been looking for. He filled out his jeans well, with strong, round thighs and a basket that seemed unreal. I didn't wear my jeans that tight—it was considered out-of-style—but I was sure glad he did. There was a slight paunch to his belly, but very slight, where his tight T-shirt tucked into his jeans. His large, round pecs pushed out from the thin fabric, and his broad shoulders stretched it across his upper torso. Big biceps—and I mean *big*, not the "defined" muscles for which I prided myself—emerged from his sleeves, and a tuft of black hair rose from his neckline. His brown eyes had fixed on mine—and I knew then that my time as object of worship was over.

The schoolteacher stood up, checked out the new man, and went back to his knees, hands reaching up to unbutton another pair of jeans. So we'd both get serviced by the schoolteacher, I figured, feeling vaguely unworthy of being given equal status with this man.

"No," the man said, still looking at me, "not yet." The schoolteacher, confused, stood up again. The man with the mustache reached over and placed his large hand on my shoulder, and pressed down. He wanted me to suck him. Yes, I thought, yes, *yes*—and I gladly obliged, falling to my knees. I'll be your boy, I thought. I'll suck your cock.

But he took the top of my head in his hand and pushed me away from his enticing basket, and instead into the flat beige crotch of the schoolteacher. I started to recoil, but his hand was firm. And then, as a new flood of desire washed over me, I thought: yes, yes—this *is* what I want.

I pulled down the zipper of the schoolteacher's fly, and smelled something clean. Like soap. His blue underwear—tacky, I would have called them yesterday—were wet with precum, so aroused had he gotten sucking my dick. Now I would suck him: the young buck having the tables turned, down on his knees worshipping the man who had worshipped him. I took his cock into my mouth.

It was thin, but surprisingly long, and I gagged almost immediately. But I persevered: I wanted to give this man pleasure, this man I never would have looked at before today, whose dick would never have been in my mouth except for here, in these woods, alongside this highway. It was an egalitarian place, a place of leveling out the leagues that divide us. That's what I thought about, as I struggled to fit his long cock all the way down my esophagus, struggled to give this man as much pleasure as I could.

"That's a good boy," I heard above me, and I knew it wasn't the schoolteacher talking, but my dream man, who was teaching me this lesson. I sucked on the schoolteacher's dick even harder when I heard his voice, and I tasted the salty release of new precum. I pulled off his dick and looked up. The schoolteacher's body tightened, his face contorted, and he drew in his breath—just before cumming in thick, forceful spurts, all over my face and hair.

"Yeah," the man with the mustache moaned, now stroking his own massive tool, sticking straight out of his jeans.

The schoolteacher did not make eye contact with either of us again. He hastily zipped up his pants and walked off, hurrying back to his car. In only a few moments, there was no sight or sound of him, and, still on my knees, I turned to face the next cock I would suck.

"You want this?" the man asked, rubbing his big dick with its big head all over my cheeks, my nose, my eyes.

I nodded, desperately.

"You're a pretty boy," he said, and I couldn't tell if he said it in derision or appreciation.

I moved in, opening my mouth for his cock.

"No," he whispered, putting his large hands under my armpits and lifting me up. "First things first."

He peeled off my tank top, tossing it behind him. He ran his hands—hard and rough—up against my smooth, soft skin, grabbing my pecs and my shoulders, which suddenly felt small and undeveloped in his hands. Then he pulled his T-shirt up over his head, tossing it behind him in the same careless way he had my tank top. His pecs were huge, big and round, with nipples the size of quarters. Thick black hair grew from the cleavage between his pecs, and down in a gently thinning line over his stomach and into his pants. He lifted one arm up, bending it behind his head, revealing a deep, dark pit. With his other hand, he took hold of the back of my head and pushed my face, not roughly, but firmly, into his armpit. "Lick," he ordered, and I obeyed.

It smelled dank and musty, but not unpleasant. I thought suddenly of my buddies on the dance floor, who, after they had worked up a sweat, always had to shower before sex. I lapped my tongue as hard as I could, burrowing it into his skin, amid the mat of tangled hair and the pungent taste and aroma of mansweat. If my friends could see me now...

Then he moved my head to his chest. I licked all the way down, seeing and smelling nothing but his tough, textured skin. I found his right nipple and sucked it into my mouth. I bit gently, then more firmly, then rolled it around my tongue. I did the same for his left nipple, and his hands, wrapped around my head, pushed me into his chest, leaving me momentarily unable to breathe. Slowly I moved my lips down his torso, licking and kissing his stomach, falling to my knees again, not caring that my jeans would bear the muddy marks of my humility.

This time he let me suck. He opened up his jeans and revealed no underwear beneath, just a thick, long dick—nine inches, at least. It stuck straight out from his body, and I took it all with one gulp.

There was no way to breathe except through my nose now, and all thoughts were banished from my head. His dick tasted so different from any other dick I'd ever sucked—not unclean, but not clean either, not like the schoolteacher's, not like the boys' I tricked with at the bars. It tasted, I imagined, the way a cock was supposed to taste.

He thrust his tool in and out of my mouth ten, maybe twenty, times. My neck was craned back as far as I could manage, giving him the easiest access down my throat. I was vaguely conscious that a couple of newcomers had gathered at the edge of the path, watching us. Let them, I thought. *Let them* see me sucking his cock.

He lifted me again, but my eyes stayed glued to his tool, shiny from my saliva. He hastily undid my jeans, the belt buckle still dangling by my side. He roughly pulled down my pants and underwear in one forceful yank, and turned me around, so that my back was to him. Jesus, I thought—he's going to fuck me. Maybe this had gone too far. I wasn't sure I wanted to be—

*And a condom*, I thought. My condoms are in the car.

It was as if he'd read my mind. "Don't worry," he whispered, and I heard the tear of cellophane. Peeking over my shoulder, I saw him unroll the latex over his throbbing cock, and it looked so huge that I was sure I wouldn't be able to bear it. I glanced over at the two men watching us, both of whom were now frantically masturbating themselves, their eyes glued to his cock and my ass.

I braced myself, thrusting my ass out to him. He cupped my cheeks in his hands and gently coaxed me toward the tree. I put out my hands to steady myself against it. I don't know if he had lube, too, but it seemed as if his cock slid into me relatively easily. Maybe I was just so turned on. But then the pain came. All at once it was as if I were being split in two. I tensed, letting out a cry, a weak little-boy kind of cry that embarrassed me, and he stopped pushing. He had one hand on my back and with the other he reached around to play with my nipples. My dick responded, my sphincter opened, and I relaxed. He slid all the way in.

With his right arm he lifted me from under my rib cage into him. The tips of my feet barely scraped the ground. I still tried to steady myself against the tree, but now he was holding me, he was in control, and he was thrusting in and out of me at his own pace, irrespective of my desire. I couldn't breathe. His dick filled every space in my body, it seemed—my whole being felt in sync with his heartbeat, with his rhythmic pumping. With each of his increasingly hard thrusts, my breath was expelled, and I closed my eyes, no longer comprehending where I was, or who I was with. His huge tool each time pressed harder against my prostate, making me feel as if I might piss, bringing me pleasure as nothing had ever done before. He might have fucked me for hours, as the saying goes, but it was probably only about five minutes. I couldn't tell. All I knew was that this incredible man, this incredible, hot, sexy, hairy, gray-haired, mustached, older man in work boots, was fucking me in a way I'd never thought possible.

And when he pulled out, I felt as if the life were drained out of me. He set me down, pushing me back to my knees. His cock suddenly in front of me, he tore off the condom and shot huge, streaming loads of white cum all over my neck and hair and bare chest. I gripped my own cock, and just the mere touch of my own hand brought me to climax, and I came in long, streaking white lines in the dusty earth below me.

I was suddenly aware that the cum of two men now covered me. The two guys watching were shooting now, too, and I reeled back and forth on my knees, trying to stop my head from spinning.

"Here," the man with the mustache said, handing me my tank top. He had retrieved it for me. It made me almost—love—him.

He pulled on his T-shirt. "See ya around," he whispered. "That was hot." He winked at me.

"Yeah," I said, watching him go.

I waited until no one was around before I went back to my car. There I sat for a while, watching the sun go down. Suddenly, getting to Provincetown in time for tea dance seemed totally irrelevant. I wondered if it would ever be relevant again.

And when I sat on Joachim's deck that night, watching the moon rise over the bay and telling him the story, he said: "Welcome to the world of secrets." I smiled, open for more.

# Burning Bridges
*David Laurents*

The bed was on fire! I jumped up, pulling the blankets with me. Reflex made my fingers shy away from the heat. By force of will, I grabbed the burning linens, flipped them over, and smothered the fire.

My heart was racing as I sat naked on the floor amid the smoldering bedding. The smoke detector still cried overhead. I forced myself to stand and reset it. I looked at the bare mattress and burnt sheets and stumbled into the living room, where I flopped down on the couch. I winced as I landed on my stomach; I still had a hard-on from my dream and had bent it in my landing. I wondered what I had been dreaming as I rolled onto my back and tried to fall asleep. In the early-morning light, I could see smoke still drifting from the bedroom.

I have a spark, a tiny flame inside my mind, like the spots that dance before your eyes after you've looked at the sun. Sometimes it gets loose.

I closed the lid of the toilet and sat. The ceramic brought goose bumps to my skin as I leaned against the tank, pressing up against it to absorb the cold into my shoulder blades, the small of my back. October and it was still as hot as August or July, the sun blazing during a drought. They promised me it never got this hot when I was thinking about moving to San Francisco from New York City. But then, a lot of promises had turned up empty, I reflected, as I stood and turned on the tap. I dipped a washcloth into the sink, soaking up the cool liquid. Elliott... I held the cloth up to my lips, letting it drip against my neck and chest, cold. Elliott...

I hadn't seen him in months. I had given up all that was familiar so I wouldn't see him at our favorite haunts in San Francisco. I know I didn't get very far (Oakland), but I couldn't bear the thought of being away from him. I was still madly in love. He had my new address and phone number, I knew, but I hadn't heard from Elliott since the night I walked out on him, when I found him in bed with another man.

I ran the towel under the tap again, and pressed it against the back of my neck, reveling in the feel of the cold, wet cloth.

My rage knew no bounds that night. It welled up inside me, a searing pain in my gut, burning as though I was on fire. And suddenly my anger burst free, setting fire to items at random as I ran from the apartment. The thought of someone else making love to Elliott, other hands running across his body...

I leaned forward and stuck my head under the tap, but the image of Elliott's body stayed before my eyes. I imagined they were my hands pressed against his flesh again and opened my mouth to nuzzle one of his large, dark nipples. I bit down on my shoulder, running the cold cloth down my body, between my legs. I cupped my balls, remembering the feel of his mouth on my cock, our bodies pressed together in ecstasy.

I grabbed the bar of soap from its dish and pressed it to my groin, rubbing it back and forth along the length of my cock until it produced a lather. I remembered when Elliott and I had showered together the first night we slept together. He was in New York on a business trip. Was it two years ago, already? I remembered every detail: our first lovemaking, deliciously awkward as we explored each other's bodies, uncertain of everything but our desire for each other. I let the soap slip between my fingers into the basin and reached for my swollen, lathered cock instead. I remembered the taste of Elliott's skin, the salt of his sweat under his armpits, his balls, the sweet flesh of his cock. I remembered the feeling of being inside him, the half-closed look on his face as he lay below me, his hands on my hips, pulling me toward him.

I could not hold back any longer and sat down, hard, on the toilet as I began to cum, shooting pale white arcs against my chest and stomach, legs. Beside me, the roll of toilet paper burst into flames. I ignored it, stroking my cock as it spasmed with pleasure.

*I am lying in the top bunk. They are the bunk beds I had as a child. I look about me and find that I am in my room at home, except everything looks odd. I step on the ladder to climb down, when the rung snaps under my weight. I fall, snapping each of the rungs as my legs push toward the floor. Am I grown so big since last I slept here? I catch my breath, then lean down to pick up one of the broken ladder pieces. They are candy canes. I lick one to prove by its peppermint taste that I am right. This is what is odd: Everything is made of candy.*

*I walk into the hall and hear noises downstairs, follow them into the kitchen. My mother is cooking. She is dressed all in black and has a big wart on her nose. On her head she is wearing a large black witch's hat. "Good morning, dear," she says. "I'm making myself some breakfast." She points to the corner near the stove. "Would you like some?"*

*Elliott is chained to the refrigerator. He is naked, gagged, his hands and legs cuffed. I cannot help thinking he looks like he's ready for a B&D session, even as I open my mouth to protest. "You can't eat him," I say.*

*"What's the matter?" my mother asks, cackling as I have never heard her do before. "Don't you want to share with your mother? His flesh is sweet enough for you to eat, isn't it?" She crosses to where Elliott is bound. He tries to shy away from her, but the chains prevent him. She turns to look at me and grabs him by the balls. I know it hurts, because Elliott stiffens, his back suddenly hunched. "You eat his meat, don't you?" She shakes his flaccid penis for emphasis, violently tugging it. "You eat his meat all the time."*

*Suddenly, my mother throws open the door of the oven. It is enormous, like a huge, gaping maw. Inside, the coils are so hot that flames leap up from their orange filaments. I rush forward to stop her, but she throws Elliott into the oven and shuts the door. I try to open the door, but it will not budge. The light is on inside, and I press my face against the glass, desperate at least to see him one last time before he burns. Behind me my mother cackles on and on, her voice as high and nasal as a smoke detector.*

I was choking, and bolting upright, coughing. A blanket of smoke covered the room. My spark must have gotten lose again, during the dream. Frantically, I looked about the room, wondering what was burning, and for how long; was I too late?

The smoke detector cried angrily overhead and I felt I just had to get out of there. I struggled into a pair of jeans, thinking as I did that this was no time for modesty, and ran down the stairs. Fire raged up and down the street. I cringed from the heat, awed and overpowered by the strength of my anger. What a dream of Elliott I had been having! Everything was on fire, from my block all the way to the hills!

I felt my insides suddenly wrench with guilt. I had to make sure everyone got to safety. It was my fault if they died!

I heard shouts for help to my left. The neighbor's house was on fire, the roof crumbling in. I rushed into the building without hesitating, following the shouts. The heat was incredible, like standing in an open furnace. My jealousy-induced pyrokinesis was no help in protecting me from fire. All it did was cause damage, cause harm.

Even with Elliott. Elliott was afraid of my anger's spark. Afraid of me. That's why he hadn't called. He was too afraid to face what it meant, my love for him.

The shouting woke me from my memories. I rushed upstairs and into a bedroom filled with smoke. "Over here!" a voice shouted. "Help me! Over here!" I stumbled toward him. He was trapped beneath a fallen beam. I struggled to push it off his legs. Come on, I berated myself, *lift!* You caused this fire! Adrenaline surged within me and I managed to lift the beam, holding it on my shoulder as he scrambled out from underneath. I reached out with one hand to help pull him free.

"Get your hands off me, faggot," he shouted, swinging a fist at me.

I dropped the beam, ducking the blow. I felt a chill in my bones, as the adrenaline burning along my muscles froze.

"You're disgusting. Take advantage of a man trapped in a fire." He stumbled toward the door, turned, and spat. "Pervert," then he slammed the door behind him.

I was in shock. Why had I bothered? I had saved his life, and all I got in return was hatred. I wished for a moment that I had left him trapped beneath the beam.

No. This was all my fault! As full of hate as he was, I wasn't ready to kill him, wasn't prepared to be responsible for his death.

His, and how many others?

I saw Elliott's face before me, inside the oven. I tried to reach him, but the glass was in the way. I banged against it with my fists, but it would not budge. I cast about me blindly, looking for something, anything, to break the glass. My fingers closed on a pipe, and I swung it desperately at the oven, hoping I wasn't too late.

I choked suddenly, as I gulped in huge lungfuls of smoke. I stared blankly at the wooden door in front of me.

Elliott? Where had Elliott gone?

I was in the burning house. Elliott wasn't there. He hadn't been there at all, but was safe from the fire, miles away.

But I still heard his voice, calling for me.

"I'm coming!" I shouted, my voice tearing my throat. Panic surged through me; I had to get to him, save him from the fire. My spark burst forth, incinerating the door. I could feel the intense heat as I ran through the now-open frame, but I didn't care. I had to find Elliott, I had to save him. I ran down the stairs, out into the street.

Where was he? I heard shouting to my left, turned toward my own apartment. I saw the man I had saved, ignored him. I could still hear Elliott calling my name; where the hell was he?

Suddenly, the door to my building flew open and Elliott was

there, shouting for me. I rushed to him, practically threw myself at him. He held me in his arms, arms that were so comforting and familiar I couldn't help but believe he was real.

"You're safe," he said, hugging me so tightly my chest hurt. "I'm so glad you're safe."

I began to cry, an overflow of fear and frustration and happiness, and then passed out.

I could feel the flames licking at my skin. I was on fire, burning up, but I had to go on—I had to save them—this was all my fault—I had to find Elliott—I had to save Elliott!

And suddenly he was there with me, holding me, cradling me in his arms, shielding me from the flames. His hands were deliciously cool, draining away the heat.

"But we have to save them," I said, trying to push him away. "This is all my fault!"

"Shhhh," Elliott crooned. "You're safe now. Nothing is your fault. It was an electrical fire. Up in the hills. You had nothing to do with it. Because of the drought, it got out of control."

I stopped struggling. Electrical fire? Not my spark. Not my fault at all. I wanted to laugh with relief! I thought of the neighbor I had saved. Did I regret it? Risking myself for the sake of preserving his hatred?

No, I realized. I didn't.

I opened my eyes and looked at Elliott. His concern was obvious as he stared down at me, as he held me against him. I never wanted it to end, wanted to remain frozen in that moment, forever the object of his full attention. I was afraid that if I looked away, even for a second, everything would fall apart and I would suddenly wake up from a smoke-induced hallucination and find that I was still trapped in a burning building.

I could feel cloth beneath me, and finally I tore my eyes away from him to look at my surroundings. I was in Elliott's bed. In our old bed. Everything was as I remembered it. He hadn't changed a bit. I even pressed myself up onto my elbows to peer into the corner by the closet and laughed when I saw his dirty socks and underwear in a pile.

I lay back against the pillow again and closed my eyes for a moment, simply for the pleasure of opening them again to find Elliott before me. He really was there, holding me, running his cool hands along my body, draining the heat away. We were both naked. I wondered what had happened between the fire and waking up here, wondered if perhaps the last few miserable months had been nothing more than a nightmare. But then I coughed, my throat still raw from the smoke, and I knew that Elliott had found me in the fire, had brought me home and nursed me until now. I knew that he still loved me.

Tentatively, I reached out with one hand and pressed it against his chest, over his heart. His skin was as cold as marble, or perhaps I was burning up. I let my hand drift, luxuriating in the cool feel of his body as I explored its familiar planes, in the feel of his hands along my body, my chest, arms, thighs, draining away the heat. It was as if he were absorbing my spark, all my built-up anger and frustration. I surrendered to the sensation.

I sat up, pulling him toward me. My tongue was stone-dry as it entered his mouth, but he didn't care and, after a moment of kissing, it was soon wet. My hands ran up and down along his chest, which felt like a Grecian pillar, solid and safe; I clung to him. He pulled away for breath, and I kissed my way down his smooth neck and chest to his nipples, those large, dark nipples that had haunted my dreams. I ran my tongue around them, moving from one to the other in figure eights. Small tufts of hair grew in rings at their edges, the only hair on his smooth chest. I let my hands fall into his lap to his cock, swollen with desire and anticipation. His hands ran through my hair and down my back. I licked the strong muscles of his abdomen, working my way toward the sweet flesh of his cock. I felt his mouth wrap around my own cock, moist and tight. I wanted to consume him with my passion, to devour every last piece of him.

Unbidden, my mother's voice from my nightmare echoed in my

mind as my tongue was about to touch his cock: *His flesh is sweet enough for you to eat, isn't it? Don't you want to share with your mother?*

I shook my head, trying to clear the voice from inside my skull. Elliott sat up, concerned. "Are you okay? Did I hurt you?"

I looked into his face, at his loving concern, and felt there could be nothing wrong with the world. I pulled his head toward me, kissed him deeply, my tongue pressing far into his mouth. "I love you," I said, grinning from happiness like a baby.

He smiled back at me and winked. "Likewise."

I laughed out loud. He hadn't changed one bit!

I turned and eagerly buried my head in his crotch, licking my way down his shaft to his balls. My tongue thrilled at the familiar taste of his skin. I could hear Elliott's catch of surprise as I took one testicle into my mouth, which turned into an almost-purr in his chest as I began to suck on it gently. I let it drop from my mouth and rubbed my face back and forth along the length of his wet cock, letting it slide against my cheeks, eyes, chin, neck. With one hand I reached for his nipples, teased them with pinches and twirls. With my other hand I lifted his cock to my lips. Even his swollen, throbbing cock felt cool, inciting my own desire as the heat of my spark drained away.

I felt Elliott's mouth on my own cock, pumping up and down its length, his lips tightly clamped. It felt as though he was going to suck the fire from me! We fell into a rhythm, in unison in sex, life, everything. I tried to hold back, to make the moment go on forever, but I crested over into orgasm, crying out in pleasure. A moment later, Elliott came, too, cum shooting up at me; I bent my face to catch his warm seed on my nose, eyelids, chin. He shuddered, and I felt an intense fulfillment that was soured by only one thing.

I looked about me nervously, wondering what my spark had set on fire. But nothing in the room was burning. I smiled, turned around toward Elliott, and kissed and held him tightly.

We walked down to the Embarcadero and stood together at the water's edge. The Oakland hills were glowing like the coals after a barbecue.

I kicked off a shoe, let it drop, splashing water onto the reflected image of the flame. I stepped from Elliott's embrace and dipped a toe into the water, to prove to myself how cool it is, how wet it is, orange and red from the fire and the lights. I had to prove to myself that I had escaped the flames as I had finally escaped my anger at Elliott.

I thought of my life on the other side of the Bay, in Oakland. I was perfectly happy to step back into the life I had left behind when I ran away instead of staying to talk. Life seemed so perfect right now, I never wanted it to end. It didn't have to, I thought. All I needed to do was forgive Elliott. He had proven himself when he came searching for me in the middle of the blaze. And he had forgiven me, for leaving him, for my anger, for my dangerous spark.

To my left, three people conversed in French, leaning against the rail and smoking. Ash drifted before me, dropping to the water. One of the tourists laughed loudly and I began to shake.

Elliott put his arm around me and turned my face toward him. "Likewise," he said, and kissed me deeply.

When we came up for air, I focused on the tip of the tourist's cigarette, and let go of my anger, forever.

Our arms around each other, Elliott and I turned our backs and walked home.

# Game Nights
*Edmund Miller*

Back when I was in high school, a lot of talk about dating went on around me and over my head for years without ever meaning anything to me. Dating was some sort of social activity that other people seemed to enjoy. But girls were like basketball: something some of the other boys liked but nothing to get excited about.

Then all at once one day something hit me. I had no idea what could be happening. I had never even heard about guys with other guys before, but there it was.

And suddenly just to look at him was a venial sin. He overwhelmed me with an irresistible force. When I thought about him I knew what the other boys meant when they talked about girls. Here was a white-hot passion, an obsession; here at last was something to whack off over at night under the covers. At last everything made sense.

His real name was Robert Biron. Although he used Bob as a sort of semi-public nickname, his real surname had been distorted into Byron in childhood. Those who knew him always called him by that nickname, and he almost lived up to it. It was not his face so much, although he did have a cleft chin and blue eyes and dirty blond hair. But on the whole he only had what you call an interesting face, meaning first of all that it really was not handsome, whatever else it was. But he had bold irregular features with an engaging openness. And he was attractive to everybody, a magnet.

And his body was another story. It was hard all over and all square lines. He had very wide shoulders and very narrow hips— although we all had narrow hips back then. And his waist was a little low in proportion to his body, a surprising thing in a basketball player, but I have been a sucker for low-waisted guys ever since. When he wore a short-sleeved shirt, there was a discernable biceps muscle bursting out of his upper arm and hiding away in the sleeve. I had never seen anything like it. My upper arms were just serviceable tubes. He had, on the whole, a muscular frame, another odd thing in a basketball player, now that I think about it.

But he was the captain of the basketball team. He was also the captain of the football team and the baseball team, and I suppose those teams did all right, but basketball was king at our school, and we had the team to beat in those days.

Byron was not the best player, but then he was not the tallest player by three. He did, however, clearly deserve his place in the starting lineup. And he probably deserved the captaincy too: People wanted to see him in the spotlight.

Our basketball team did not lose a single game in my last three years of high school. We had the best team on the Island. Just before the start of basketball season during our senior year, Byron asked me to be team manager. I had never really been interested in sports even as a spectator, but of course I did not say "no" to a request coming from such a source. At the time I was not quite sure why he had asked me. What the job involved mostly was making little charts of baskets attempted during practices and games, and marking where the players were shooting from by noting their numbers in the approximate places. The numbers were circled for successful baskets.

Another of my duties as manager was to fetch and carry equipment, like the balls for practice. During away games I held the players' valuables. And I distributed uniforms and towels on game nights and made sure they were sent off to be cleaned afterwards. In those days basketball players wore skimpy little shorts cut off at the crotch with kick pleats in the sides. A lot of the eroticism has gone out of the game with those ridiculous droopy monstrosities players wear nowadays.

And as another one of my duties I was actually allowed—required—to go around the locker room collecting those dirty uniforms and towels while players were showering and getting dressed after games; I was required to collect them and touch them and sniff them after they were all sweated up. Well, I was not actually required to sniff them, but it was easy enough to do. Some of the guys tossed their uniforms to me as they ran off to the showers discreetly wrapped in towels. Some of them just left the uniforms on the bench as they took a slow buttocks-heaving saunter to the showers, their towels casually hanging over their shoulders.

But Byron always waited for me to come by for his stuff. Sometimes he said he was sore and needed help getting his things off. Sometimes he played with me, snapping his jockstrap in my face or dropping his shorts over my head and then tickling me to boot. I always pretended to be offended and so after a while had to tell him to stop and let me get on with my work. I did not want the other guys to start teasing me in the same way, and I certainly did not want them to start teasing me about these little encounters. As I look back on it now, it seems strange to me that they never did, but I was Byron's choice for the job, and he was their elected captain, so I guess they must have liked the way things were going, too.

He and I had never had gym class together, so I had never seen him naked before. I was already half in love with the manner and the shoulders and the way he moved, but the actual naked body was even better than I had imagined, and I had imagined something pretty wonderful. First of all, he was white all over. Nowadays I can appreciate the eroticism of a tan line, but in those days there was something marvelous about his overall whiteness. And it was not so much the lack of a tan line as the fact that there were no dark secret places in his body. His crotch and his armpits and his ass and his cock and balls were just blazing with brazen white reality. I thought of my own body as having dirty parts I had to hide from the world. But he was completely at ease with his naked body.

And it was some body. He had square-cut sharp definition in his chest. I guess it was all natural too, since this is long before body-building got hot. I could even see little lines between his abdominal muscles. His ass was firm, with a sharply defined bottom line.

And his cock. It was a large tubular thing (yes, like my arm) with a thick foreskin. At first I thought he was half-erect all the time, but then I realized that this was just his regular size—right out of the jockstrap. His balls were large, too, and suspended in a big, loose, free-swinging bag. He had just a little pubic hair, and it was all back away from the gleaming white organ. And it was blonder than the hair on his head. He was something to behold as his stuff bounced up and down when we walked off to the showers. The back view was great too. And he always took his time.

In addition to the regular games of the basketball season, there was an invitational tournament sponsored by our school every year just afterwards during the Christmas vacation. My father dropped me off at the school every night for this as for other games, but Byron volunteered to bring me home. He had a car, of course, and a license; I had neither.

The first night of the tournament everybody was in high spirits. We had not been beaten in years and were top seeded, so we played one of the weakest teams in the area. In fact, we fielded our second string for most of the game. The biggest excitement was an argument among the referees about the length of the cheerleaders' skirts (cheerleaders were all girls in those days). It was a technical foul for small-school teams like ours in the B League to field cheerleaders with skirts that did not at least come down to the middle of their knees. Some of the cheerleaders had slightly shorter skirts, but these girls were with an A team, and it turned out there was a leeway of two more inches at the larger schools.

Since we were the first seed, we had an easy time of it opening night. Byron hardly worked up a sweat. So there was not going to be anything much special to sniff when I picked up his uniform. I had saved him for last, however, as I usually tried to do. But when I came round to his locker, he was still dressed in his uniform. He had only just taken his sneakers off. "Oh, are you here already?" he asked, in a low key I seldom associated with his doings.

He seemed preoccupied, so I said, "I can come back later if you'd like," and started to move away.

"No, don't go," he said, gripping me firmly, almost painfully, by the upper arm. With his other hand he reached under his top and pulled it up over his head in one clean movement. Only then did he let go. I rubbed my arm where I could still feel the indentation of his fingers. I didn't complain. It hurt, but somehow it felt right to have his mark on me. I kept running my finger through the indentation as it began to disappear. At the same time, he ran his hand over his chest, outlining the underside of his pectorals and the wonderful abs. Then he pushed his hand into the waistband of the shorts and shoved them down without unzipping them or undoing the little buckle thing at the top. He was half naked in a second, but then the shorts got all tangled up and he suddenly fell over on the bench. We both started laughing. Then he grabbed me to steady himself and said, "Hey, help me out here!"

Without even thinking about what I was doing, I started to help disentangle him, and then as I realized I was touching his thighs, I almost fainted. I reeled back a little and let go. The shorts slid down his legs. He kicked them into the air and then twirled them around on his finger. "I think this is what you're looking for," he said with the old twinkle in his eye. He tossed the shorts to me, but I was in a daze, and they just hit me in the chest and fell to the floor.

I snapped out of it and bent down to pick them up. As I started to straighten up, I saw that he had turned around suddenly and was bending over with his ass practically in my face as he removed his jockstrap by reaching all the way down to the floor to pick it up around his feet without raising them. While he had not been playing very hard, there was enough of his musky odor in the air to make me feel faint again. I almost reached to steady myself by resting my hand on his ass. Just as I pulled back and fell against the lockers, he pulled up and swung around, grabbing his towel in the process, and snapping it at me: "Gotcha!" he sang out.

Then he noticed that something was the matter and jumped over the bench, pulling me down to sit on it. Still holding me by the shoulder, he put his leg up on the bench next to me and asked if I was all right. He put the back of his hand on my forehead and pushed away my hair, I guess to see whether I was sweaty or feverish. His big beautiful white cock was staring me in the face. I could see a big vein down the side and a big circle of the head peeking out from under the foreskin. But I was even more conscious of his foot pressed up against my thigh on the bench. I did not want him to take it away. Ever. But he did. With both hands he turned me around and pushed me down to lie on the bench and said, "You're all sweated up. Rest here while I go shower; I'll be right back."

Some of the other guys were on their way back from the showers already, and they started to ask what the matter was. "Leave him alone, and let him rest for a minute," Byron shouted out as he went off to the showers: "He's just a little dizzy."

"Just what I always thought," Billy R. said. But Billy J. poked him in the ribs and shoved him along, and they all left me alone for a few minutes. After a while it quieted down as people started to leave.

Except for Byron, the last one to go was Tom, the one who wanted to be a minister. As he left, he said, "1 Samuel 14:43."

I could hear the water running; after a while it stopped. I kept my eyes closed, and perhaps I dozed off for a bit. Then I sat up suddenly and found my head was clear. A moment later, Byron came round the corner. "I put the balls away for you," he said; "Here're your keys." He tossed them to me, but I just let them hit me in my chest since my first impulse was not to catch them but to feel for my pocket, wondering how he had managed to get them out without my noticing. "Are you all right now?" Since I felt fine, I told him so.

And we went off to his car together. We got in without saying anything. He took off at an easy pace: he was not a reckless driver. And we did not say anything until he turned onto Old Willet's Path, about halfway to my house. A short way along that road, he turned into the woods along a little path so overgrown you could not even tell it was there from the road. This had at one time been a shortcut to my place, but it was so washed out it could not be used any more, and I told him as much. But he was already stopping the car. "I know," he said; "I just thought you'd like to talk a little and maybe get a grip on yourself before you go home." With that he lurched up in the seat and bent over to get something from the back. I almost fainted again with his ass right there in my face. I turned away.

He was getting a beer bottle from the back seat. He took a swig. Not bothering to offer me any because he knew I hated the taste of the stuff, he put the bottle down and started to unbutton his shirt. "What are you doing?" I blurted out.

"That should be pretty obvious," he said smoothly, as he continued, removing his shirt entirely. "I'm taking my shirt off."

"Why are you doing that?" I asked. I was not really thinking these questions through. Everything seemed to be happening too fast.

"So that you can admire my chest," he said, running his thumbs slowly along the underside of his pectoral muscles. He heaved his chest up a little, too.

"What makes you think I want to look at your chest?" I asked.

"Well," he said, flexing his biceps a little and doing one of those fingers-together isometric moves with his hands across his chest, "it seems to me we have kind of gotten beyond that question, haven't we? You are admiring my chest." He ran a finger through the definition in his abdominal muscles, smiled, and took another sip of beer.

I looked away. Then I looked back. He was still smiling, but he was not sneering. I tried to look away again but could not. "What are you fighting?" I thought.

"What are you fighting?" he asked. "Look, I don't mind. Why should you? Feel free to touch."

"Oh, I don't think I…"

"If you'd rather, I can always put my shirt back on," he said, but he made no move to do so.

I knew I should probably tell him to, but I did not. We sat there for a while, me staring, him with his hands clasped behind his head when he was not taking an occasional swig of beer.

Finally I made a tentative comment on the scene: "You do seem to have everything nicely in proportion."

He laughed. "Yeah, you could say that. Come on: Get the feel of things." He reached over as if to grab my hand. I pulled back—just a little but enough to make the point of my reluctance. I assumed he would pull me over and make me touch him. But he did not. He just put his hands back behind his head.

Then I laughed. "You're not making this very easy for me," I said. And then we both laughed.

"I think I'm being about as easy as can be," he said as I reached over and touched a finger tentatively to the areola of his nipple. "Now that's more like it." I ran first one hand and then both over the span of his chest, drinking in the hard, glossy surface. I was fascinated by the little valleys in his abdomen—mine was all just flat. He nipped my finger with a muscle contraction, and I jumped back. "Yes, it's alive," he said.

I reached around him and held him in my arms, my head cradled at his breast. I licked off a dab of sweat.

"There's more under the arms," he said. I slipped back a bit, loosening my embrace and scratching his back as I let go. I looked into his armpit. I sniffed at it experimentally. It had a faint musky locker-room smell. It was wonderful. I nestled into his armpit as he pulled his arm down and wrapped it around me.

I passed out again.

"Okay, enough for one night, I guess," he said. "I'd better get you home." He tossed his shirt on and tucked it in front but did not button it up. He gently straightened me up in my seat, but he did not stop me from running my hand back and forth across his chest and tweaking his nipples. He backed the car out and resumed the drive home. He did not say anything, but when we got back out on the main road again, he pushed my hand down to his abs so it would be out of view of any passing motorist. I played along by sitting back in my seat, staring straight ahead with a solemn look on my face while continuing to play across his abs with the fingers of my left hand.

When we got to my place, he pulled into the driveway and stopped. Looking straight ahead the whole time, he leaned back with his hands behind his head again and closed his eyes, but it was not the same. He opened his eyes and turned to me. "Tomorrow night," he said, pointing at me with his index finger and winking.

Reluctantly, I got out of the car. I could not think of anything to say. I turned back just before I went inside. He was still in the driveway. He was looking down at his chest, cupping his pectorals in his hands.

A few minutes later, from upstairs in my room, I heard his car pull out. "Tomorrow night," I thought.

The second night of the tournament, we again won our game and thus moved on to the championship final. Several of the other guys asked if I was okay because of the fainting incident the previous night. But I stayed away from him in the locker room. I wanted to keep control of myself.

Once I turned a corner too fast and came upon Billy R. fiddling with himself somehow inside his jockstrap. I was embarrassed and slammed back against the lockers and looked away. But he just laughed. "Hey, it's okay. I just got kind of all constricted in here," he said. I started to move away, but he grabbed me by the arm. "No, wait take this," he said, handing me a bundle of his dirty stuff. "Cheer up," he said, giving me a little pat on the chin. While I was watching his tight little butt move off toward the showers, Byron came up beside me.

"Hey, you're not avoiding me, are you?"

"No. Yes. No," I explained. Then we both laughed and knew it was okay.

"I'm still driving you home tonight, aren't I?" he asked. "I just thought maybe Billy there…"

"No. No! No, of course not."

"Yeah, I know: He means nothing to you," he said, as he very annoyingly snapped his towel against me and went off to the showers. He was certainly something to see in motion.

He took me home. When we got to the little overgrown path in the woods, he again turned off the road. He took off his shirt. He flexed a little. I reached over to touch him, but as I did so, he unsnapped the button on his pants. To my ears, it sounded like an explosion. I pulled back and looked out the window. The zipper going down was pretty loud, too. I turned back to him as he was pulling his pants off and tossing them into the backseat. "What do you think you're…?" I began.

"Are we gonna go through all that again?" he asked. "I just thought you might enjoy looking at the goodies up close. You spend enough time sneaking peeks."

I opened my mouth to complain about this as an unfair characterization of my completely disinterested service as team manager, and then I suddenly realized it was perfectly true. I laughed.

"That's the spirit," he said. "Here's your chance for a really first-hand examination." And with that he pulled his briefs down below his knees and let them drop to the floor so that he could step out of them. He picked them up and tossed them to me. I closed my eyes and took a good whiff, but I could not keep my eyes away from his cock for long. "It's a beauty, isn't it?" he said, hefting it in his hand and slapping it against his palm with a pronounced smack. It seemed to get bigger.

"Don't do that! You'll hurt yourself!" I said, involuntarily reaching forward.

He pulled away and looked at me coyly. "Are you sure you want to do this?"

"Do what?" And then suddenly I realized what was happening, and blushed—and pulled back.

"Hey, come on: I was only joking. There's nothing wrong with a little admiration. Here, look at this." And with that he pulled his foreskin down over the head of his cock, revealing about two inches of skin. He stuck all his fingers inside and stretched the foreskin out as wide as his open hand.

I do not have a foreskin, so this lavish display fascinated me. I could not keep my eyes—or my hands—off, and, before I quite knew what I was doing, I had my hand in there alongside his. Now his cock really was growing, no question about it. I hefted it in two hands, and it lurched out past the hand on top. I could barely reach around. "Move the foreskin," he said. I touched it gingerly, then pushed it back tentatively. Suddenly the head popped out. It looked about three times as big as anything I had seen before. My mouth dropped open, but I held on tight.

He stuck a finger in my mouth and I suddenly realized I was gaping. I closed my mouth and tried to push his hand away, but he started playing with his finger in my mouth, pulling it back a bit but not removing it, and then thrusting it forward again. It started to be fun. I reached up and cupped his hand with both my hands, but he gently pried my right hand free and put it back down on his cock.

Then a funny new idea occurred to me. I realized I could suck his cock, put it in my mouth. The concept had just never occurred to me before: This was a long time ago, remember. People did not talk about sex all the time in those days. Nobody had even thought of using rubbers in a situation like this; I had never even seen a rubber.

I pushed his finger out of my mouth and looked him in the face. He closed his eyes. I looked at his cock. It moved, and I started back in surprise. Then I grasped it firmly again and bent over to bring my face down into his lap. Just then, he pulled the seat adjustment switch, the seat sprang backwards, and I fell forward, open-mouthed, right onto his cock.

I gagged about six or seven inches down and grabbed hold of the base to steady myself. I pulled back to get the feel of the controls and found that if I held my windpipe in a certain way I could get more in. I started slicking him up. At first I took long slow runs, but as I got more used to the action I speeded up. The foreskin sliding back and forth was an even more interesting phenomenon from this perspective. After about five minutes of pretty steady work, my jaw was aching. I pulled off—reluctantly, to be sure.

Byron moaned, and I remembered he was there, too. I continued to play with the foreskin with my hands. I licked his cock around the edges like an ice pop that was getting ahead of me on a hot day. When my jaw was once more a little relaxed, I went down on him again and found that the little practice workout I had just been through had taught me how to go all the way down. I did this again and again and again, each time staying down until I could no longer breathe and coming up for the shortest time possible. I cupped his balls in my right hand as I was doing this—or at least I tried to. He had an enormous ball sac, and I just could not get the whole thing in one hand.

Suddenly, his balls contracted in my hand and a few seconds later he exploded in my mouth. I could not quite imagine what was happening at first and started to pull back. Byron placed a hand on my head—ever so gently, but the gesture was enough to reassure me that everything was as it should be. Of course, I quickly figured out what was happening, and then I started thinking how amazing it was that it was going on so long. It seemed like hours, but of course it was only a minute or too. I could not help thinking how this usually takes only a few seconds. And it was like Alice in Wonderland's "Eat Me" drug—warm and icy cold at the same time, a little like a turkey dinner and a little like a raspberry tart, both together.

Finally I got to thinking that it was a good time for me to pass out again. But Byron brought the episode to a neat close by lifting my head off his lap and putting me upright in my seat to heave and catch my breath. He pulled some paper towels from somewhere, and after tidying himself up, helped me. I kissed his hand as he was wiping my mouth. He did not laugh, but he smiled and tousled my hair.

Somehow he got dressed—I really do not remember his doing so. I noticed that afterwards even his shirt was all buttoned up that night as he looked over his shoulder to back out of the path in the woods. He took me home, again without saying anything.

In my driveway, he leaned over and tweaked my nose with his index finger. Again the only thing he said was, "Tomorrow night."

At the championship game that next night, Byron excelled. Since he was not especially tall, he never had the most points, but he bested his personal record that night by scoring thirty points in the game, and it was, after all, a championship playoff. But the best thing about the way he played that night was that he broke the school record for assists. He was not just doing well himself; he was helping the team.

Of course, we won. The coach brought champagne into the locker room and then made a quick retreat. The stuff was not to drink, although of course you could drink legally at eighteen in those days. It was for horsing around. And like the players, I was sopping with the stuff before everybody was through horsing around. Unfortunately, unlike them, I was not wearing a nice uniform I could doff and toss to the team manager before heading for the showers. But I tidied myself up as best I could, even taking my shirt off and rinsing it out in the sink. I was ogled a couple of times while doing this, but it meant nothing in particular, especially since one of the oglers was Tom, the intended divinity student.

The sink did give me a good view of what was going on in the showers. They were taking a lot longer than usual in there because of all the high spirits. But most of the guys were actually soaping and rinsing, although they were soaping and rinsing again and again. But Byron was just rubbing his hands over his body. I did not see a hint of soap. And while the others always turned toward the spray of water and away from their teammates—and me—when it came time to do cock and balls, Byron deliberately turned toward the others—and me—for this little ritual. He kept at it till he had plumped up to something that was pretty obscene, although not actually a hard-on. I must have stopped fiddling with my shirt under the blow dryer and must have just been standing there open-mouthed when the players started to come out.

Billy R. said, "Nice chest," and reached as if to squeeze a nipple, but I squirmed out of the way. Tom said only, "I did but taste a little honey with the end of the rod that was in mine hand, 1 Samuel 14:43," and passed by. I had a sudden paranoid flash that Byron had told them all. But then I realized that, if they knew, they did not seem to be particularly upset.

When he came out of the shower, he grabbed me around the waist as if it were all just part of the fun. I could feel his cock poking against my ass. "Hey, cut that out! You'll get me all wet," I said, but of course I meant something entirely different.

He raised his hands and said, "Oh, excuse me," all innocence, but I noticed that he winked at me before he turned to get dressed.

Later, after we parked on the path, he got out of the car and said, "Come on: Let's get in the backseat."

He got undressed almost as he was getting back into the car. Luckily it was a warm January that year. It did seem quite a bit roomier in the back seat: Cars were built on a bigger scale in those days. He had a hard-on before I quite knew what was happening, and I took it in my hands to admire it before getting down to business. It was quite a pole. He reached down to the floor and pulled up a bottle of champagne he had managed to come away with. It was only about a quarter full. He took a swig and offered me some. I took a tentative sip. It was certainly a lot better tasting than beer. I took a little more, then he poured a little out on his cock. I took the cock in my mouth, and it was a whole different experience from the night before: The cock seemed bigger. And of course everything was a lot messier and wilder. I went down on him, and he started to pulsate in my mouth. I was having trouble going all the way down because he seemed to be getting wider. And then he came just a few minutes after I started. I swallowed as fast as I could, but he was faster, and there was a lovely mess to clean up. I was glad I had not gotten any on my shirt. The champagne was going to be hard enough to explain to my mother.

Then abruptly he swung over in the seat and up on his knees facing away from me. And there they were: two basketballs in heat. I did not even stop to think but leaned over and kissed him— gently—first on one flank, then the other. And then I did so again and again. He took a swig from the champagne bottle and scraped away at the label. And then he did the same thing again. I put my hands up and felt the hard indentations at the sides of his hips. I ran my hands over the smooth hairless globes. And I did this again and again. "Kiss me," he said. "Kiss me!" I thought that was what I was doing. I kissed him again, a big wet one. He reached around and pulled the globes of his ass apart. I saw his little pink rosette pulsating, panting for me. In a flash, I knew what he meant. I pulled back a little, and my jaw dropped, but I held on. He took another swig from the champagne bottle and scraped away at the label some more. It fell away from the bottle, which was naked then. He put the bottle down.

His rosette was still pulsating. I touched it gently and then pulled back quickly as if my finger had been singed when it grabbed back at me. I leaned forward slowly and licked the sweat off the area. I was drinking up some exotic, otherworldly nectar. I licked all around. He was pulsating faster and faster. I went for it, and he let go of some pent-up tension inside him, and in an instant everything was calm and cool, not hot and intense at all anymore. He began moaning softly. His upper body fell forward, limp. But I discovered his cock was still rock-hard—and so were his nipples. I licked and licked and licked away. I must have kept it up for fifteen minutes. I found that I could get my tongue right inside. There was a whole cosmos in there. It was as if I became part of him. I brought my hand up to help spread him wider and get a better vantage, and he opened up like the rabbit hole in Wonderland and we fell into another dimension, lips and fingers and all.

He shot off all over the seat cushions and the hump between the seats in back. He was going to have a nice mess to clean up the next day. "Fuck me," he said, so quietly at first that I was not quite sure I had heard him. "Fuck me! Fuck me!" Instinctively I knew what he meant, although this was something else I had not really ever thought about. "Fuck me! Fuck me!" I sat up on my knees and undid my belt—with some difficulty because I was fully erect and all tangled up in my clothes. My cock popped up and banged against his butt, pulling me forward. He reached down under the seat and pulled out something that looked like a tube of toothpaste. He unscrewed it somehow from his awkward position—I was rubbing my cock up against him the whole time now—and squirted a gob of the stuff out into his hand. It was a clear, watery substance. He smeared some of it back on his butt and plunged two fingers into his asshole right up to the base of his hand. "Fuck me! Fuck me!" It was a soft moan by this time. I knew what I had to do. I leaned forward and fell into him, into his marvelous squishy softness. But he was still all hard on the outside, as I reassured myself by slapping him on the side, feeling up those beautiful hipside dimples again. I thrust into him and pulled back to the very brink. Then I thrust again. Three times. Four times. And then I exploded into him.

I fell over him, reaching around to feel up his beautiful hard pecs while I did so. I thought I might pass out again. I was floating in Wonderland on another plane of reality.

I heard a sort of murmuring. I realized he was saying something. "Fuck me! Fuck me!" he was saying again. I tried to oblige. I was still inside him, but there was nothing left of me to fuck with. I tried to pull back to thrust again, but I just fell out. I was still swollen out of shape, but there was no firmness to me. It was over.

"Fuck me! Fuck me!" It was a sad, plaintive call now. I looked around for inspiration and saw the champagne bottle. I picked it up and then almost dropped it as it started to slip through my hands, slick with Byron's manliness and the goo he had prepared himself with. There seemed to be only one thing to do. I put the rim of the bottle up to his rosette, throbbing again now with his need. He pulled his asscheeks apart in anticipation. Then I noticed there was still a little champagne left in the bottle. I pulled it back, stuck my finger in the neck of the bottle, and gave it a good shake. Then I quickly thrust the top of the bottle into him. It slipped in for a good two inches without any pressure at all, and then he started foaming over. I licked at the champagne, and he became a victory celebration all by himself. Then he grabbed the bottle from me and turned over on his back, holding it still inside himself. He started to work it back and forth. At first I thought he was going to hurt himself, but then I saw he had a roaring hard-on again. He got a good section of the wide part of the bottle into himself, and then he started pulling it back and forth slowly. Back and forth. I went down on him, and he shot me full of his champagne almost instantly. We both lay there exhausted. I scarcely had strength to run my tongue around his still swollen cock.

Finally we had to pull ourselves together and get home. He said nothing as he drove me home, but he did squeeze and pat my thigh at all the lights and before I got out of the car in the driveway, so I knew everything was okay.

And that is the story of how I learned all the important things in life during the basketball tournament in my senior year of high school. All the later times have had to measure up against that first experience, so it has been a hard, fast game with lots of extra time periods. But well worth the effort.

# Chilies and Chocolate
*Stan Leventhal*

"First I like to admire the color, the sensuality of the curves, the tiny hills and valleys. Then, on the palate, the hard, smooth texture of the skin, the juicy heat of the pulp and seeds. I feel warmth spreading to my extremities. My forehead and the back of my neck become moist with perspiration. When the endorphins are released into my cerebral cortex, I'm in Habañero Heaven."

Kitt grasped a stem between his long fingers, brought the chili pepper to his lips, sighed as he bit into it, juice running down his chin. As his eyes reddened, and tears trailed down in two paths on either side of his nose, a beatific smile overtook his face. Drying his cheeks with a linen napkin, he pushed the small dish of chilies across to the other side of the table.

Without speaking, keeping his eyes riveted on Kitt's, Antony chose a small dark green chili and did his best to imitate the routine he'd just witnessed.

"Not so fast," said Kitt "Savor it. No one's going to steal it away from you. Enjoy."

Within moments after biting the meat from the stem, Antony gagged, coughed, almost toppled his chair as he moved like a bullet to the sink, where he bent, twisted his neck, and drank cold water directly from the faucet.

Kitt, watching Antony's efforts, chuckled. "Water won't help. It will just make it worse, actually. Lactose, milk, is the antidote. Sour cream is the best as far as I'm concerned. But maybe we should start you off with something milder. Like jalapeño. And if that's too hot, Scotch Bonnet. After all, this is your first time. We'll take it slowly. There's no rush. Ah, but what a rush! It takes time to learn to appreciate it."

Kitt waited for Antony to respond to his pun, but Antony barely paid attention to Kitt's words as he dried the water from his mouth and asked himself if getting involved with Kitt had been a wise move. Not that they were living together, yet, or even calling each other lover, yet. But there were aspects of this young man's personality that Antony found threatening, dangerous. Perhaps this is what made it all seem so thrilling.

"You got any sour cream?"

"For you, anything," said Kitt as he made a solemn ceremony of fetching a teaspoon and the stout container from the fridge, scooping out a small white mound, and laying the spoon on Antony's tongue and lifting it ever so slightly, like the actress moms on baby food commercials. "Better?"

As Antony moved the cool, smooth stuff around the insides of his mouth, Kitt grabbed him, pulling him close, pushed his tongue between Antony's lips, shared what was left of the disappearing cream, then led him into the bedroom, turned out the light, and closed the door.

Kitt had been trying to goad Antony into sampling some of his hotter creations. Claiming he couldn't handle anything spicier than a slice of pizza, Antony had resisted. But the gentle teasing, the artful taunting I-dare-you attitude, meted out in tiny doses at just the right moments, had, finally, softened Antony's resolve. The result of this, though, was that a sort of competition—a kind and easy competition—began to develop, with Antony's challenges emanating from his vast sphere of knowledge about music.

Melody, harmony, and rhythm were things to which Kitt had never paid much attention. While growing up, his main interests were swimming and soap operas. A feeble attempt at piano lessons at the age of twelve quickly convinced him that he did not possess the talent that his sister so dexterously showed off, confirmed by an embarrassing moment in ninth grade choir practice when his voice had changed from a trebly squeak to a deep sigh, hitting several non-existent notes in the Western scale on its way. The role of swim team captain and the unfolding melodrama of the sexy vampire Quentin on *Dark Shadows* were enough to keep him busy until he'd left home for college, leaving behind the sensible bland meat-and-potatoes menus his mom worked so hard on, and discovered things like Tabasco sauce, sliced pork with black bean sauce, and his ultimate find, jalapeños. After tasting his first chili-laden nacho, then jalapeños relleños, followed by poblano with mole sauce, he never again ate burgers and fries, meatloaf and mashed potatoes, or steaks with baked spuds. Eventually he found curries and mustards and his fate became sealed, like garbanzos in an air-tight can.

Antony had come from a family which was exposed to a wider variety of victuals, broccoli and asparagus, for example, foods which Kitt's family never experienced. But like most people, food was not something he thought a great deal about, unless he became hungry, in which case anything that could fill him and quell the rumblings would be fine. But when it came to music, Antony had an interest that often distracted him from his responsibilities and got him into trouble.

Several of his relations had worked in various areas of the entertainment industry, and, as a child, Antony had been given many promotional copies of records. For birthdays, at Christmas, for no reason at all. A box would arrive at the house, his mother would call to him from the kitchen, and with great excitement, he'd help her open it, then stare in rapt wonder at the colorful glossy sleeves that held the miraculous vinyl discs.

Antony's parents were not interested in music, beyond their fondness for Sinatra. When his mother would lift the albums from the box, a look of bewilderment or disdain emerged briefly, as she'd flip through baroque harpsichord concertos, avant-garde freebop, long-haired rockers from England, and sad-eyed Cassandras from Greenwich Village. Antony, noting her displeasure, became all the more eager to steal away to his room with his new treasure, close and securely lock the door, listen as attentively as he could. Whether the sounds caused his parents' dismay, or the illustrations on the covers, Antony could not say, nor did he think about it much. But it seemed the more something disgusted them the more he liked it. It was like a surefire formula. The less they liked anything, the more it appealed to him.

Kitt met Antony during the Clinton versus Bush presidential campaign. At the bar where they'd tentatively introduced themselves and cautiously navigated each other's minefields, they discovered soon enough that they both planned to vote for the Bill and Hill Show, and this seemed like a sensible basis for the beginnings of some kind of relationship.

A not very clean, not too well lighted place, the bar where they met on the Lower East Side had become the meeting place of choice for the downtown chic crowd and others in the know. The Subway, with its dark atmosphere and connotations of decadent underground life, attracted the punkier members of the queer culture, the defiant ACT UP boys, the performance artists and conceptual painters, leatherdykes, smokers, drinkers, drug-users, and back room frequenters. After deciding that becoming a piss-elegant Upper East Side queen was not as exciting as it had looked from afar, Kitt had moved downtown, cut his hair so that it stood up all around in shiny black spikes, gotten rid of the cashmere sweaters, and stocked his wardrobe with black jeans and shirts. There were several bars which had recently opened in his new neighborhood and he'd begun to investigate them all, checking out how the crowds differed depending on the night of the week and the lateness of the hour.

On a Friday night, just after midnight, Kitt sauntered in, smiled to the bartender, ordered a draft, and sat on a stool, watching the pool players move the colored spheres on the green felt surface, move their bodies around the six-pocketed table. An older man, rather rotund, in polyester with a Sansabelt waistline, easily defeated his younger adversary, a slim black boy with a Lambda sign shaved from the back of his scalp. Kitt contemplated joining the tournament, but just as he decided against it, because he would rather play the loser than the winner—the older man arousing no interest, the younger seemingly packed with potential—he turned to look at the young man who'd just punched up the jukebox. As loud drum beats began to pervade The Subway, the player swayed his hips and continued to scan the selections and press the buttons. When he turned from the jukebox and made his way to the bar, Kitt took note of his face, the mustache, his build, his gait, his hair, his clothing. The guy appealed to Kitt immediately. He didn't dress too obviously down or up, but comfortably, like Kitt. His hair didn't look too fastidiously styled, nor wildly disarrayed, another plus. The flat torso and slender hips were offset by very firm and curvy buns, tightly bound in almost white jeans. And the stride, no trace of feminine delicacy, nor over-compensating swagger, caused Kitt to consider the possibility that this individual might be worth his time.

After ordering a light beer and tentatively sipping it, Antony turned to face and evaluate the other patrons. He'd had a very rough week at his job—the recession had given his already cruel and greedy boss the green light to pile more work upon fewer employees —and lately, he'd been too tired to go out after a full day's labor. But life being short and unpredictable, and Friday and Saturday the most crucial nights for New Yorkers seeking to pleasure their bodies in a frenzy of sexual interaction, Antony raced home at the end of the week, napped through the early evening, and awoke just in time to shower, shave, dress, and get to a bar by midnight.

Ordinarily, he frequented the bars of the West Village, most of which were only a few blocks from his apartment. But lately, he'd occasionally begun to visit the places on the East Side, as the center of queer activity had imperceptibly shifted from West to East. Although the West Village had for years been the mecca where most queer boys worshipped, over a decade of changes in health, fashion, politics, and art had resulted in a lessening of acolytes and intensity at the West Side places, and increased attendance, renewed spirit, and more abundant social possibilities in the East.

As Kitt approached Antony that night, he formulated the perfect opening line in his mind. Having witnessed this guy play the jukebox, he smiled, said, "Hi, my name's Kitt. What's yours?"

"Antony."

"Tell me, Anthony, what's the name of this song and who is it? I know I've heard it before and I recognize the voice, but I just can't remember the name or title."

Kitt had learned early on that a quick way of ingratiating oneself with strangers was to ask a lot of questions about something that interests them.

"It's Antony. I dropped the "h" when I moved here. Kitt? What kind of a name is that?"

"Short for Kittredge. I know. It sounds so pretentious. But, hey, neither Mom nor Dad consulted me about this. You don't get to choose your own name any more than who your parents are, where you were born, if you have fabulous hair or not."

The first thing Antony noticed about Kitt, after the bone structure of his face, the spikes of his thick and luminous dark hair, were the body contours beneath the fabric of his clothing. It was obvious that Kitt worked out, but unlike other gym dandies, he did not show off the results of his efforts with quite the same ostentation or flamboyance.

"'Losing My Religion' by R.E.M." said Antony.

"REM Speedwagon? I've heard of them."

"You're thinking of REO Speedwagon. This is R.E.M. Stands for Rapid Eye Movement."

"Like when you're dreaming."

"Right. Where do you live?" Antony asked.

"A few blocks from here. You?"

"West Village."

They spoke briefly about the presidential campaigning and impending election. Then Kitt asked, "You want to flee this dive, come over to my place for a while? I've got some cold beer and a few other things."

On Kitt's sofa, Antony sat casually, leaning forward, waiting for his host to emerge from the bathroom. He'd been surprised at the decor. Kitt's clothing and hair had suggested a somewhat punky, new-wave lifestyle, and Antony expected his apartment to be disorderly, odoriferous, and full of mangy cats. But as he sprawled and waited, he was surprised to note the newness of all the furnishings, the sweet scent that seemed to hang in the air, the tasteful prints and objects, like the quaint old French mustard container on the mantle above the brick fireplace, and a lone peacock feather rising from a simple terra cotta vase.

It became clear to Antony immediately that Kitt was somewhat passive, and that he'd have to initiate everything. Some guys were all over you as soon as the apartment door was closed, but Kitt, wanting not only to have sex, also assumed that part of the deal included playing the perfect host. Anyone invited to his apartment was welcome to spend the night, would get a clean towel, a glass of orange juice, a croissant, and a cup of coffee in the morning, the wages of this generosity were simply listening to him chatter about the office politics where he worked, his favorite movies, favorite restaurants, and accepting his fussiness over what they'd like to drink, is it too bright, is it too cold, can I get you anything else?

Antony accepted a beer, after being offered wine, tequila, orange juice, vodka, coffee, or tea. Then he endured several minutes of Kitt's monologue about a woman he worked with—Dora, the accounting department supervisor—something about how she won the lottery and took everyone at the office out to lunch at a very swanky restaurant in the financial district. Realizing that it might be a while before anything happened, and not being particularly interested in Dora's largesse, Antony moved closer to Kitt on the sofa, wrapped an arm around his shoulder, slipped his tongue into

Kitt's lips—the top thin, the bottom thick—and forcefully rubbed the warm mound beneath the fabric of Kitt's jeans.

Interrupted mid-sentence, at first Kitt was a little shocked at such aggressive behavior on his turf, but Antony moved his tongue around so artfully in Kitt's mouth, so craftily, that he immediately forgot about the office, wrapped an arm around Antony, and proceeded to rub his crotch in return. They kissed for a long time, both very pleased to have found someone else who did it so well and appreciated it so much.

As they'd begun, Antony had thought briefly about safe sex, how far he would go with this guy, would they use rubbers? But eventually he lost himself in the sensuality of the moment and forgot about practical considerations. Toward the end of the kissing part, before they removed their clothing, Antony's mustache began to irritate Kitt's lips, and just prior to concluding this phase of the evening, he, too, thought briefly about what was to come, and who would be the first to bring up the subject of safety in bed.

Kitt realized Antony had taken a big risk by so boldly initiating the kissing phase, so he felt it his responsibility to begin whatever was to follow. In so many aspects of his life, Kitt was expected to be in control, to make decisions, to chart the course toward progress. At his job with the Children's Book Council, even his boss would delay normal processes and routines, to consult first with Kitt, before making any irrevocable moves. Consequently, Kitt was delighted to pass the compass and tiller of responsibility to another during his leisure time, and temporarily forget the cumulative stress of his job, his family, and surviving as a queer in New York City during the final whimper of the twentieth century.

With a mischievous smile on his face, he stared dreamily into Antony's soft brown eyes and began unbuttoning his shirt. As the two panels of blue cotton were released and separated, Kitt noted the fine hair of Antony's chest, the way it narrowed from a reservoir to a tributary and, like the shaft of an inverted arrow, became thinner, pointing to whatever secrets lay behind the leather belt and metal zipper securing Antony's jeans to his waist.

As soon as Kitt had begun to undo Antony's shirt, Antony reciprocated, holding Kitt's stare with his own, trying very hard not to laugh because sometimes moments like these could cross the line from solemn to silly with no provocation whatsoever. Once their shirts were removed and they'd studied each other's torsos—Kitt's muscled and shaved, Antony's slender and flat—the host lowered his face to his guest's crotch, undid the belt buckle, and pulled down the zipper; then, digging his hand beneath the tight blue fabric of Antony's bikini briefs, pulled the stiffening penis from its hiding place of confinement. He licked it, sucked it, caressed it with his lips and tongue, did everything he could to communicate without words that he wanted this penis to get hard, stay that way, and penetrate to the core of his being with intensity and power.

Antony did not need a user's guide or Rosetta Stone to translate Kitt's actions into ideas. At the thought of ass-fucking this punky new-waver, Antony's penis became rock-hard, and remained so while Kitt backed away, slid down his pants and Jockeys, and, waving his flaccid penis like a lariat, beckoned Antony to follow him into the bedroom.

As they stripped themselves of their remaining clothing, Antony casually studied Kitt's inner sanctum. Like a holy shrine, the contents of the room seemed arranged to focus all attention on several prints on the far wall, the entire room dimly lit by votive candles in small glass cups scattered randomly on almost every horizontal surface. The dancing flames flung moving shadows on the posters, which depicted colorful photos of chili peppers and old mustard pots. As his eyes adjusted to the flickering light, Antony glanced around for a radio, a television, a stereo, a VCR, a tape deck, anything that could provide a little music to enhance the mood. But there had been no such appliances in the living room, and there were none in here; Antony remained silent although he wanted to ask how anyone could exist with no music, no news, no movies.

But he didn't really miss the music as Kitt led him to the cool sheets, fluffy pillows, and paisley satin comforter upon which they cuddled and writhed for hours, after fiddling with a tricky condom that the host had casually produced and toying with some greasy lube fetched from beneath the platform bed. Much later, after Antony's penis had fucked Kitt's ass until both were sensitive and sore, as they fell asleep entangled on the tousled bedding, Antony wished for some mellow sounds to help obscure the street noise, the perfect finale to an event that had turned out to be much more satisfying than he'd anticipated from his experiences in the past and his projections based on everything he could guess about Kitt's personality. Entering Kitt's apartment, he'd been apprehensive and pessimistic about this latest conquest. When he left in the morning, rushing to get to work—it was too late for a repeat performance— he requested Kitt's phone number, something he rarely did.

And he actually called a few days later. Although he hadn't missed the music while they were exploring one another's sexual inclinations, the silence of the aftermath, no melodies or news to focus on while waking up and getting ready to leave, created a small itch that he needed to scratch. So he invited Kitt to attend a concert with him, hoping to find out why this person had such an aversion to radios and music machines, also desirous of another night of bed-play.

When he phoned Kitt and made the date he hadn't as yet decided exactly what kind of music would best suit the occasion, and since Kitt had no records or CDs or cassettes lying about, had not mentioned enjoying anything in particular from the musical spectrum, did not inquire as to what he was getting himself into when he consented to Antony's query, the question remained unanswered for several days. Fortunately Antony had a week to decide if an intimate chamber recital would be best, or a rowdy rock concert, or perhaps some mellow jazz—or would Kitt respond best to some unpredictable avant-garde experimentation? Kitt's appearance suggested that he might appreciate something unconventional, yet his sexual proclivities indicated that he could possibly be rather conservative and traditional in his tastes.

Anxious over his final decision, Antony obtained two tickets for the k.d. lang performance at Radio City Music Hall, sold out by this time, of course. But Antony knew the publicist, and had written favorably about many of her clients, so last-minute house seats were not a problem. He figured since k.d. lang was queer, and he and Kitt were queer, and most of the audience would most likely be queer, it was the safest of the choices at hand.

The night of the concert they met at a bar downtown, then took a taxi up Sixth Avenue. Antony, who strove to appear as though nothing had changed, took in Kitt's hair, which was now parted, combed, and quite presentable, and his clothing, the khaki slacks, navy sports jacket and Weejuns placing the wearer in a category diametrically opposed to the image he'd previously conveyed. In worn jeans, sneaks, and a black sweatshirt, Antony felt good that Kitt had so drastically changed his appearance, and this feeling grew stronger because together they looked completely different. He had once been a part of a cute couple and had come to hate the attitude this seemed to induce in too many people. They'd whimper and sigh and talk baby language whenever he and Marty were in their presence. And he had developed a particular antipathy, with no apparent justification, to those couples—gay or straight—who dressed the same, like pathetic twins forever doomed to follow Mama and Papa's strict rules of sartorial display.

Most of the audience, wearing everything from tuxedos and ballgowns to flannel shirts and Doc Martens unlaced, consisted of women, largely lesbian, with a scattering of gay men and cool straight people. With wild enthusiasm, much applause and whistling, rising en masse at certain moments, the audience, like a pack of intoxicated bacchantes, received the sounds and presence of the star as though granted a miracle by some fabulous deity. Although Antony adored k.d. lang, he concentrated more on Kitt's receptivity and responses than anything that happened on stage. Unlike the rest of the attendees, Kitt sat there, immobile, politely clapping a few times at the end of each song, with a placid blank face that, to Antony, screamed utter boredom.

In actuality, Kitt enjoyed himself immensely that evening. It simply wasn't detectable by observing his behavior. And when the concert had ended and they'd finally flagged a cab to go back downtown, since Kitt had nothing to say about the show, conversations about music not being a part of his everyday routine, Antony assumed that he'd been disappointed and began to feel guilty for having subjected him to it. He fully expected that the evening would end as soon as they'd arrived at their destination and disembarked from the vehicle.

But somewhere between Twenty-third Street and Fourteenth Street, Kitt moved his hand firmly over the expanse of Antony's thigh, kissed him on the cheek, and whispered, "Thank you. That was wonderful. I'd heard about her, of course, but never heard her sing before. Amazing voice. And I liked a lot of the songs, too."

Antony would have liked to ask Kitt why he never listened to or watched anything at home, but the surprising touch and words told him to remain silent on this subject, for now, in the hope that he might be invited to spend the night. As Antony responded, saying, "It's totally my pleasure, I'm so glad you enjoyed it. I couldn't tell while we were sitting there. You're not very demonstrative. I thought you were hating it," he rubbed Kitt's thigh.

"Would you like to come up for, um, a cup of coffee, or something?" Kitt purred after they'd maneuvered themselves out of the cramped backseat of the ancient cab.

On the sofa, Kitt, like the first time, began kissing and unbuttoning, pushing and pulling Antony toward the bedroom, in which they re-enacted, almost exactly, the scenario of their initial encounter. This did not bother Antony, who enjoyed himself just as much the second time around. But Kitt, midway through the routine, began to feel a sense of déjà vu, that this rerun was not as thrilling as their first night together. And afterwards, while Antony slept peacefully by his side, he stayed awake long into the night, thinking of ways to add some spice to what he now considered his new relationship.

Kitt's history of boyfriends, like an illustration in a social studies text, looked like an undulating sine wave, with victories and defeats, times of prosperity and periods of famine all duly indicated by the peaks and valleys of a fluctuating, uninterrupted line. Early on, he'd learned that successful relationships require work, planning, effort, and compromise; that in these turbulent times, with changes happening so quickly and in-your-face sexual imagery on every screen and magazine cover, that those who pursued their affairs casually were the ones most likely to wind up losers.

In an effort to win, and to determine the course of this new alliance, Kitt decided to be the initiator, the inviter the next time they got together and planned an evening around some of his favorite recipes. He hoped that if he were in charge the next time, as Antony had been, he could steer the sexual play into other directions.

But the meal did not go as smoothly as he'd planned. It started out well, it seemed. Antony enjoyed the cheese, crudités, and pâté Kitt had arranged and served so charmingly. When it came time to sample raw chilies, however, Antony's palate couldn't handle it, and they wound up in the bedroom much earlier than Kitt had anticipated, the pasta never cooked, the sauce dehydrated, dessert still sitting in the fridge, the cool white wine warming up on the table.

If Antony had been shocked by the searing taste of the chili, there are no words to describe how he felt when Kitt forced him onto his stomach, straddled him, pulled down the waistband of his briefs, slapped his tender buttcheeks, and said, "Let's play rodeo. You'll be the bucking bronco, I'll be the cowboy...and I intend to ride you for as long as I can."

Antony trusted Kitt enough to know that this fantasizing was harmless and would not lead to anything really dangerous, but he did twist his neck to look back and make sure that a condom was properly in place before the initial probing had begun. Stunned at first by the boldness of one who had seemed so passive, he eased into the idea in his mind, as his muscles relaxed to accommodate Kitt's delivery, pleased, actually that this was happening.

In Antony's experience, many of his lovers had been exclusively tops or bottoms, and it was his versatility, his appreciation of both roles, that allowed these relationships to thrive. But almost always, at some point he'd become bored, crave the part of the other. The one time he'd dared to articulate this thought and asked his lover Walter if they could switch for a change, the response had been so hostile and negative, he'd never requested this ever again. He would simply endure the times when he wasn't enjoying himself.

He'd never met anyone like Kitt before, someone who could give it and take it, equally, without sarcasm, regret, or vengeance. Although Kitt had decided they were having a relationship the night they saw k.d. lang, it was not until a week later, after Kitt's joyride, when he felt completely spent and contented, that Antony came to the same conclusion.

It could have been the introduction of music and food into their sexual arena that began the struggles they survived, or it could be looked at from just the opposite view, that sex had begun to undermine their other interests, but in either case, the honeymoon did not last very long.

The next day at work, both young men experienced pangs of anxiety, wondering if their activities of the night before had been a slight detour until they could get back to the main thoroughfare, or if this new path would be the one to follow for some duration. Since Kitt had arranged the last meeting, it came time for Antony to reciprocate.

He found himself in an inexplicable state of duress. Unaware of exactly what bothered him, he sulked about Video Village as though he'd sunk into the Marianas Trench of despair, with no hope of ever rising to the air and sun ever again. Listlessly, he checked cassettes in and out, shelved, reserved, canceled, verified credit cards, endured the sluggish pace of the computer like a martyr, fixed the cash register when it jammed and wouldn't open. To the customers, the slightly aloof, obviously bored man who suffered their demands with stoic efficiency must be having a bad day, everyone does, and they ignored his rudeness the way most New Yorkers learn to do. His fellow workers, however, did not excuse his lapses in cheeriness, especially when his lassitude dragged on for several days. Uncertain how to plan an evening with Kitt, Antony avoided making any decisions for as long as he could.

When Kitt finally got a phone call from Antony, it ended a string of excruciating days during which he had careened from the twin poles of thinking he'd been abandoned, would never hear from Antony again, to the fear that Antony had been angered and would create some kind of embarrassing situation. With a great feeling of relief, he listened as Antony calmly and quietly, with a slightly seductive edge to his voice, invited him to attend a piano recital—Debussy, Beethoven, an up-and-coming pianist from Ukraine. And his co-workers, the handful of men and women with whom he interacted for forty hours a week at the Children's Book Council, were equally relieved when he turned up one morning having apparently shaken whatever demon had been bugging him.

The concert, though beautifully executed and a delight to all who paid attention, might never have happened as far as Kitt and Antony were concerned; so nervous were they about what would transpire later, they never relaxed enough to be able to concentrate on the sonorous beauty of the acoustics, the finesse of the player, the genius of the composers.

To make matters worse, afterwards, as they awkwardly donned their jackets, Antony suggested that they return to his apartment instead of Kitt's. His reason for doing this—he wanted to see what it would be like to fuck with music in the background rather than the street noise of the Lower East Side—might have been appreciated by Kitt if Antony had bothered to explain. But fearful that saying anything might upset the delicate balance they'd been maintaining, he assumed that a bit of mystery, an invitation without an explanation might be appealing. This, however, only increased Kitt's anxiety as they got closer to the apartment on West Tenth Street, to which he'd never been before. Antony, as well, nervously anticipated Kitt's response to his smaller, less clean, less organized clutter of books, cassettes, disks, his wall of hardware.

As some light jazz coated Antony's studio like something warm, blue, and sweet, Kitt removed his jacket, took in the mountains of stuff stacked everywhere. He found this dwelling to be cozy, comfortable, friendly, and beckoning in an almost womblike way.

"This is very nice," he said. "It's got a helluva lot of character. There's a warmth here, a lived-in comfy feeling."

Relieved that Kitt had spoken these words, although not entirely convinced that he'd really meant them, Antony offered Kitt something to drink, then worried what the next move should be. They sat on opposite ends of the worn couch, the only sittable surface not taken up with collectibles.

"I realize it's not as aesthetically pleasing at it could be," said Antony. "But it is very practical. I'm always doing little projects that require constant referral to certain books, music, and films, and I've created my own library so everything is always close at hand."

"What kinds of projects?"

"Basically, I like to trace influences. Try to determine the exact ways that Bach influenced Beethoven, for example, Hemingway's influence on Raymond Carver, the effect that forties film noir had on French filmmaking. That is, when I'm not serving time at Video Village."

"That sounds very interesting," said Kitt, and not knowing what to say next, added, "I really enjoyed the recital tonight. Thank you. I've never been to one before."

"I gather music doesn't interest you very much."

"Not exactly. I really like it. But I have no talent for it and it's something that I don't think about too often. But when it's there, I generally like it. Except for heavy metal, rap, and country. This is nice, what's this?"

"Red Garland, recorded soon after he joined Miles Davis's band. It's very interesting because it demonstrates that Davis got the inspiration for many of the standards he recorded from his sidemen. Particularly, the piano players."

"Oh, really? I keep meaning to pick up a radio or cassette player or something, but I never do. I guess it's just not one of my main priorities."

A few moments later, when the gap in their conversation widened to the breaking point, Antony took one last sip of beer and, with the taste still strong on his lips, scuttled closer to Kitt, drew him in, and kissed him long and hard. After a brief duel of tongues, they nervously disrobed. As Antony converted the couch into a bed, Kitt stood there, his bare feet on the soft area rug, his arms crossed over his chest, waiting. Then they sat side by side on the bed, both wondering what would happen next.

Had they been able to overcome the silence sooner, their dialogue might have been less halting, more confident, not at all unsettling. But when the void was suddenly broken by Antony clearing his throat, Kitt started at the sound, thought he was going to be asked a question, and said, "What?"

"Nothing, just a cough."

"Are you all right?"

"Just clearing a frog."

A pause ensued, during which the tension between them became so great, Kitt began to tremble. "Is it a little cold in here or is it me?" he asked.

Antony, grateful for the opportunity to do something, closed the window which had only been open about an inch or so. He wished he had candles so he could use them as an excuse to turn out the light. Unlike Kitt's boudoir, Antony's studio had not been designed with seduction as a priority. To him it did not seem romantic at all, particularly because of the brightness of his lighting and the unadorned white walls. "Is that any better?" he asked, returning to the convertible.

Kitt said, "Thank you," not at all sharing Antony's attitude. On the contrary, because he'd never been to Antony's before, and had fantasized what it would be like, the novelty of actually being there and seeing it made him curious about everything, and therefore highly receptive and eager to please.

Nervous to begin with, especially with the bright lights illuminating their vulnerable nakedness, Antony froze when Kitt began to kiss him. Although he attempted to flow along and try to get into it, after a while he felt as though he really wasn't there, wrapped up in Kitt's lovemaking, but had risen from his body to look down upon the two of them. Pretending that nothing was amiss, he followed Kitt's lead as though reading from a script. But when the crucial moment came, and Kitt interpreted Antony's passivity as a sign that he should continue to lead, when he'd sheathed and lubed himself and attempted to penetrate, Antony had not relaxed sufficiently to receive Kitt with pleasure. The pain made him wince and cry out as he retreated, maneuvering away from Kitt, lying on his back staring at the cold chipped ceiling. Turning his head to face Kitt, he said, "I'm sorry. But I'm just not into it tonight. I don't know what's wrong. This has never happened before."

"It's okay," said Kitt. "Happens to all of us eventually," although his placid tone hid the disappointment resulting from his taking this failure as evidence that Antony did not like to be fucked.

This misunderstanding repeated itself, in reverse, at their next meeting, at Kitt's place with the candlelight and street noise. Assuming that Antony would be on top, Kitt faked the hugging and kissing, the light foreplay, patiently waiting for the real action to begin, for Antony to take control.

But still embarrassed from their previous encounter, when he'd been unable to perform, Antony had promised himself that if given another chance, Kitt would fuck him and he'd relax into it and really enjoy himself, as would Kitt.

When Kitt's lips became sore from the attentions of Antony's mustache, he considered that excuse enough to draw away and indicate that the next phase should begin. Antony waited for Kitt to do something. Kitt waited for Antony.

Finally, Kitt stood up, said, "Let's try something new tonight. I have an idea. Wait here a second." A moment later he returned to the bedroom with a green chili in hand. "I've been meaning to try this for some time. But I wanted to do it with someone special."

There is no way Antony could have anticipated what happened next, and he did his best to suppress his surprise as Kitt indicated that he wanted to have the chili pressed up against his anal pore just prior to the entry of Antony's penis.

"Why?"

"Remember how hot it tasted on your tongue?"

"And how," said Antony, shuddering.

"I want to show you just how hot these little suckers can be. Here, just touch it, and then bring your finger to your tongue."

Antony did as he was told, and found that the mere touch of the chili left a hot but pleasing mintlike aftertaste.

"Cool, huh?" said Kitt as he positioned himself on his back with his knees pulled up to his chest. "Go for it," he commanded, and when Antony had gingerly rubbed the hard green chili across the rim of Kitt's upturned ass, he stiffened, then sighed, and whispered, "Rubberize, lubricate, and dive in."

What had begun so awkwardly, with the potential for chaos to break through at any moment, became smooth, harmonious. Like the silken luster of a fine string section, as satisfying as a perfectly prepared soufflé, they moved through the night, complementing one another, an exquisite *pas de deux* after a good meal and a fine concert. As the candles flickered on the walls and ceiling, and the sound of shrieking tires invaded the apartment, Kitt and Antony lounged on the bed, euphoric in the afterglow, touching, talking softly—about the subject where their interests overlapped—the post-Columbian history of the Atlantic, when chili and chocolate as well as silver and gold made their way from the Americas to Europe, while musical seeds as well as slaves traveled from Africa to the colonies. This period of contentment and smooth travel would not last forever, of course. In several months the relationship would be over, each eventually finding another person to journey with for a while. But that night everything clicked into place so easily, nobody could have predicted that this good thing would not last forever.

A while later, Kitt went to the kitchen and returned with another chili and a flat brick wrapped in gold foil. "Hungry?"

"Sure. But not for chilies."

"Try some of this."

As Kitt chewed off the pointy end of the chili, Antony carefully pulled away the thin layer of foil and gasped with delight as he broke off a brown square and popped it into his mouth. "I adore chocolate. Never met a chocolate I didn't like," he said, munching with satisfaction.

"Chilies for me, chocolate for you—to each his own."

"Just one thing, Kitt."

"What's that?"

"Would you mind if I picked up a radio and brought it over, and could we keep it in here and sometimes listen to music?"

Kitt smiled. "Anything, lover," then pulled Antony down, rolled on top of him, and licked his lips with the still-hot tip of his peppery tongue.

# Violence

The use of violence in sexual writing is quite common. The connections between violence and sexuality are deep and the taboos against discussing them are strong. Because physical violence and brutality have always been used by those in power to keep gay people, women, and people of color "in their place," many readers are troubled by depictions of even consensual violence. Often mainstream culture has promoted images of eroticized violence—brutality—to enhance, excuse, or promote oppressive actions against those people who do not fit into the dominant culture.

Jean Genet, in his 1976 essay, "Violence and Brutality" makes an important distinction: "violence" for him is any strenuous life-affirming activity which must fight to assert itself. "Violence and life are virtually synonymous. The grain of wheat whose germination breaks the frozen ground, the beak of the hatching chick which cracks the shell...the birth of a child—are all implicated in violence." Genet sees all of life—including sex—as a series of violent acts; it is the way that life and history move on. But he is careful to separate violence from "brutality," which he defines as "that gesture which would destroy all free will." Brutality is the power of the state against the individual; the power used by one person against another without consent and spurred on by hatred. For Genet, violence is a form of physically strenuous activity, and we can see consensual sexual violence—beating a partner with a belt, struggling against restraints, play-acting violent, even brutal, scenarios—as a form of this. And if we believe that all sexuality is good, it is pleasure that can be taken by violent, strenuous, sexual activity. The writers in this section explore the connections between violence and sexuality and uncover the myriad ways in which the two are connected.

R. S. Thomas's "Broken and Entered" details the sexual assault by a burglar on a sleeping victim. The action is taut and brutal; sexuality here becomes a tool for hurt and humiliation. But as the story progresses it's clear that Thomas is interested in looking at what the conditions and emotions connected to humiliation actually mean. The sexual fantasy here—knives, bondage, huge cocks, verbal and physical assault—moves the story along, but it also makes us question what these objects and actions mean to us. "Broken and Entered" shocks us, sometimes in unpleasant ways, by taking us places that feel at once comfortable and highly unsafe.

The violence in "Breaking in Baby Face" by Aaron Travis entices and charms us. Travis is famous for using brutality and violence in his sexual fictions. While his novel *Slaves of the Empire* explicates— and relishes—sexuality and violence in a historical context, his highly praised short story, "Blue Light" examines contemporary sexual violence in a supernatural and psychological context. Both *Slaves* and "Blue Light" (as well as much of Travis's other fictions) have serious underpinnings; "Breaking in Baby Face" is something of a departure for Travis. Its tone is lighter—although its content is as sexy as anything he has written—and while it uses sexualized force as its driving plot motivation, it is essentially a comedy of violent manners.

Matthew Walker is quickly becoming one of the most noted

writers of homoerotic sexual fiction today. His stories, appearing in such publications as *Drummer* and *Manifest Reader*, have startled and shocked readers while never failing to excite them sexually. Walker's use of violence—here in the genres of science fiction and sexual submission—is purposeful and calculated. The sexual thrill here comes not so much from the energy of the violent rage, but the cool, planned, methodical strategy. "A Tame Animal" takes place on another planet in a future time, but you will easily recognize the sexual drives and manias that fuel the story. Beautifully crafted and resonant, "A Tame Animal" will give you a sinking feeling in your stomach as quickly as it instigates a burning in your groin.

"Confessions of a Peter Gabriel Fan" by Wickie Stamps is a short, concise, and deeply disturbing story of a self-loathing/closet case/queer basher. But Stamps's story is more than simple slice-and-dice fiction; she has managed to get to the heart of what happens when sexual desire is repressed and thwarted, and becomes brutality. If Thomas, Travis, and Walker explore the ways in which we can play with, and be turned on by, the concept of violence, Wickie Stamps proves Genet's point by showing us the true nature of brutality.

# Broken and Entered
*R. S. Thomas*

"You know I'm gonna fuck you, punk. You can't wait."

It was just a statement—something obvious. But of course he meant it as a threat. Hearing it made my muscles tense and my head spin.

The clock tower in the church across the street struck eleven.

I heard him laughing as he stood over me. "That's right. I can see your little pussy ass clenching when you think about it. Well, think about it good and hard, punk. Think about getting fucked, 'cause you're gonna get fucked, all right."

He knelt over me and put his hand on my ass. He squeezed my asscheeks tightly, bending close so I could feel his hot, wet breath on my ear as he growled: "And this is where I'm gonna fuck you. Right here."

He squeezed my ass tighter and jammed his fingers into the crack. I squirmed and pulled against my bonds, tried to make some kind of noise—to shout for help, even though I knew no one would hear me. I lived upstairs from an accountant's office and they would be long gone for the day. Besides, I couldn't make a sound—this bastard had gagged me with several of my own dirty socks. And I most certainly couldn't move.

People always said that surprising a burglar in your house was the best way to get yourself killed—or worse. But I never thought it would happen to me, or that the guy would let me get undressed first while he watched from under the bed. Or that a guy would be able to overpower me like this.

I had put up a fight—that was for sure. My shitty little apartment was in a shambles and there was a cut above my right eye and dried blood on my face. I had put up a fight—but he had subdued me. He had held me down and tied my hands, ripped off my bathrobe and cut the remaining rags off with a knife. Now he had me on my side on the rug, naked except for my Jockey shorts. My ankles and wrists were tied together in front of me. I was doubled over, which meant that my ass was exposed.

He went around the apartment, emptying out drawers and looking for valuables. He didn't find much, but he made a real show of trashing my apartment.

He got my wallet and looked through it.

"Not much money, Jacob. Or do you get called 'Jake'? Well, Jake it is. Jake. You're a poor boy. Not too much to sell. I'll have to take something else that you got. I think it'll do just fine."

He kept going through my drawers. I felt my stomach turning as he opened the drawer which held my photos. He pulled out the brown envelopes and looked through them one by one, chuckling.

"That your girlfriend, Jake?" He whistled, as if in awe. "Man, she really can strut it. She likes to do things for the camera and make pretty pictures. Looks like she does chicks, too, but maybe that's only if you're watching. Well, one cock up your ass ain't gonna make her too jealous." He rummaged some more. "Yeah! Lube. That's what we need, and lots of it. Your straight ass is probably pretty fucking tight. But that's the way I like them...oh, more pictures! Mmmm...she likes it in the ass, too. You ever taken it up the ass, straight boy? Nah, I didn't think so. You fucking arty types are all chicken shit. How'd you get a dildo that big up her ass, anyway?"

I flushed red and hot.

"Well, now I know what your girlfriend can take, pal. But it's you I'm interested in. I want to see how much you can take. I'm pretty horny, and I need a good cum. I think I'll put it inside your ass." He bent close to me.

"You and me are gonna get a little more *acquainted*, punk."

He roughly pulled down my Jockey shorts, exposing my ass, and wedged his hand in between my asscheeks. I squirmed and choked as I felt his finger going into me.

"That's right," he growled. "You're gonna get a good ass-fucking tonight, Jakey-wakey. You thought you were real tough, putting up a fight and all. But you're just a punk. And I'm gonna punk you real good tonight, straight boy."

He worked his finger in and out of my ass, chuckling with evil glee the whole time. I whimpered and shivered as he finger-fucked my dry ass.

"What the fuck do you care?" he said. "You like chicks who take it up the ass, from the looks of the pictures in that drawer. Take it up the ass from real big cocks. It'll be just like that, only you'll be the one getting it."

He jammed two fingers up my ass, squeezing my cheeks tight as he worked me up. He kept rubbing his prick through his jeans with his free hand, getting himself ready to fuck me. He wore a tight pair of work jeans and he filled them pretty well.

He backed off, grinning, and disappeared for a second. He came back with a coil of rope in one hand and a switchblade in the other.

"Come on, honey, let's go to bed. It's our honeymoon suite! I'm gonna pop your cherry, you fuckin' blushing bride!" He laughed as though he thought that was the funniest thing in the world.

He slipped the switchblade into his pocket and hung the rope from his belt so that he could use both hands on me. He pulled me up by my hair and my wrists, throwing me onto the bed. It smelled of sweat and sex. He got me onto my belly and used his knife to slash the ropes that tied my wrists.

"Don't fight, now, or I might have to hurt you! I did it once, I'll do it again, fucker!"

He wrestled me down, holding tight. He had me good. He got one wrist tied to the bedpost and I managed to get the other free, twisting away from him. I got to my knees and tried to pull the rope free.

He bellowed in rage and brought his knee between my legs to connect with my balls. The wind rushed out of me and pain shot through my body. I collapsed onto the bed. He crawled back on top of me.

"See? All it takes is a knee in the balls and you're real, real obedient. Don't try that again, punk, or it'll be your face next time."

He got my other wrist tied and checked the first one again. I started to struggle a bit, just a bit, as he moved down to my ankles.

*"What did I tell you!"* He reached down between my legs. He got hold of my balls and my whole body spasmed in pain. I quieted down right away. He squeezed harder, and I howled through the gag.

"Keep still, now. Don't want to damage you for your fucking horny girlfriend. She'd never forgive me."

He tied both my ankles. I was careful to keep real, real still. He walked around to the side of the bed, inspecting me.

"Not bad," he said. "I think your ass can probably get me off."

He slipped off his clothes slowly, taking his time. As he got out of his Jockeys, I saw that his cock was fucking huge. He was a monster. I'd never seen a cock that big. I breathed hard.

"Like what you see?" he said. "It's gonna feel real, real good getting into you."

He used the knife to cut away my Jockey shorts. Then he settled down on top of me, letting his naked cock sink into the cleft of my ass. His hairy arms curved around me.

He clicked open the switchblade, and took care of my gag. He held the knife close to my face.

"Way I figure it, asshole, by the time you could make enough noise for anyone at all to hear, I could make you very, very sorry that you did. Plus, this apartment is pretty damn far from anything. I think you could scream all you want and all you'd get is a real, real bad cut, maybe as bad as they get. Isn't that what you think? *isn't it?*"

I nodded quickly, desperately. He was right. There was no way out.

He slipped the knife down, away from my face. He wedged his hand under my body and got hold of my balls, squeezing them hard so that my eyes watered. He wrestled me onto my side, just a little, so that he could get hold of my balls good. He squeezed until I didn't think I could take the pain. Then I felt the knife. He was stroking me with the edge of the blade, right at the tender underside of my balls. Teasing me with the feel of the knife's edge. Telling me what was going to happen if I put up a fight or wouldn't do what he wanted.

He was talking real low, in an almost gentle growl. "I knew you'd understand. I'm gonna punk you real good, put it right up your ass and fuck you till I cum in your chute. And if you don't go along with it, I'm gonna take your balls with me in my pocket. Doesn't matter to me. Your straight ass is tight, just the way I like it, whether or not you got balls on that puny cock of yours."

He rubbed the knife more firmly over my balls, shaving off some of the hair. I whimpered a little and squirmed against him. He pressed harder, the tip of the knife against the soft nut sac. I held still. Slowly, he eased the knife up my body, letting me feel it sliding against my flesh. He held it up against my face, pressing the edge to my lips. He began to stroke my face with the edge of the knife, almost tenderly. Tears formed in my eyes.

"But I got a funny kink about straight guys. I like to hear 'em beg. Can you beg for me, Jacob?"

I choked back a sob.

"Do it, Jacob. It gets me so fucking hard. It'll make it so much better for me when I fuck your ass—if I can just hear you beg for it first. It'll make me happy. And when I'm not happy…"

He moved the knife again, getting it up against my balls.

"All right, I wasn't making myself clear. I want to hear you say something, punk. Just once, I want to hear you say, 'Fuck me up the ass.' And you better say it with feeling. Can you say that for me or do I have to make your girlfriend buy you a strap-on dildo?"

I panicked. My heart raced.

"Fuck me up the ass," I whimpered.

"You asshole. You can't get away with saying it like that. I guess your bitch gets fucked by a rubber dick from now on. 'Cause yours ain't gonna be doing much." He stroked my nuts with the edge of the blade.

"Fuck me up the ass!" I said it louder, harder, desperate with fear.

"Not quite good enough." He ran the tip of the blade slowly up my cock.

"*Fuck me up the ass—!*" And he made me say it again and again, thirty or forty times, chuckling every time he heard it, and threatening me. Finally I sobbed and panted and moaned it, "Fuck me up the ass!" Like all the women in the porn movies I'd seen. And then he was finally satisfied. He leaned back on his haunches and picked up the lube.

"Sure thing, loverboy. I guess you must want it pretty bad."

The ice-cold lube landed in my crack, and he began to work it in. I felt two fingers going into me. I gritted my teeth. He worked me up to three. I held my breath.

"Mmmm….not as tight as I thought. Maybe she's the one with the strap-on?"

He lowered himself on top of me, and his long cock slid into my crack. He took hold of my hair and sank his teeth into the back of my neck, hard. He knew right where to put his cock; my asshole had been opened by his fingers. I groaned as I felt the head pushing its way in.

"Real easy, punk. Just take it and it'll feel a lot better. You're gonna love it."

He pushed in, and my ass clenched tight. He didn't give way but forced it deeper, stretching my ass open and pushing his cock home. He got it into my ass, just an inch or two, and I felt as though I was going to explode. Just to hurt me, just to torment me, he held it there right at the entrance.

The edge of the knife touched my cheek.

"Say it again, punk. Just once. For me?"

Gasping, aching, straining: "Fuck me up the ass!"

"Oh, that's good. You say it like you mean it."

With that, he sank in another few inches, slowly, then gave it to me all the way. I squirmed against him as I took it. His balls slapped between my legs.

I felt invaded, dominated, humiliated. I had been entered, and my will was broken. Every tiny bit I moved made my ass ache and clench tighter. I tried to relax and just let him fuck me. I lay there, limp, as he did me good, opening me up, taking what he wanted out of my yielding, unresistant body.

"Good boy," he said. "Now just lay there while I do you. I never take too long. I'm not one of those tender, loving types. I do it fast. I'll try to make it real fast for you, since I know you can't wait for my cum."

He pulled out a little, then shoved it back in hard so that I gasped. He took his time, first going fast, then real slow, letting me feel every inch of it. He laughed as he took his time. He knew that every second I was being fucked was humiliation and agony for me. But I lay there and took his cock up my ass. Accepted it. Submitted to it. Sweat dripped down my back.

"That's right, that's right," he growled into my ear. He brought his hand down my side, stroking my flesh. His sweat dribbled onto the back of my head. He shoved his hands under me and took hold of my hips, giving himself leverage as he went on fucking me. He seemed to enjoy every second of it.

I tried to give up my asshole to him. I gave myself over to his cock. It seemed to relax, and his lubed cock slid in and out much easier. But I could feel every inch of his flesh as he reamed me

It started to feel better as he fucked me. But it stretched on, minute after minute, until I lost count of the thrusts. I couldn't believe his control. I could never be in a pussy that long without shooting my load. I realized that he was holding back, just to see me endure the ass-fucking as long as possible. The sweat burned into my eyes. The bells in the church outside struck midnight, then one. My ass was open wide, fucked open until it was nothing but a sheath for his cock. It was beginning to hurt like hell, my bowels filled with lube and shit and agony.

Finally, he growled into my ear: "You just don't get it, do you? You gotta beg for me to cum. Say it."

It took me a long time and a few slaps across the face and a couple of strokes of the knife across my balls before I could croak desperately: "Cum in my asshole!"

Then he told me it wasn't good enough, he was going to have to...finally, after I'd said it thirty times or more, he laughed and started pounding into my ass. I gasped in agony. He was finally going to do it.

"Oh yeah," he grunted as his cock shot long, thick streams of cum into me. I could feel it squirting in and dripping out my asshole. He took a long time to cum, and my ass felt like I'd just gotten a hot enema.

"That's good," he said. "Real good. Now I've got a few things to do before I finish up."

After he put his clothes on, he went into the other room and came back with several large brown envelopes: the photos from my drawer. Nude photos. He tucked them into one of my gym bags, along with my few valuables: a watch, a gold picture frame, one of her bracelets, a couple of other things. He zipped up the bag and got on top of me again.

"Now, I don't think you're in any condition to struggle," he told me. "But in case you are: don't. That offer still goes, if you want to try life as a girl."

He cut the ropes on my wrists and ankles, still holding me down. The long ass-fucking had left me helpless. I didn't even squirm as he dragged me onto the floor and tied me on my side with my wrists and ankles together in front of me. I could feel his cum smeared across my cheeks, dribbling down my thighs and onto the carpet. He gagged me with rope this time.

"Way I figure it," he said, "you can get out of those things in about fifteen minutes. That's enough time for me to vanish like the wind. Now, I didn't take anything worth much, so if I were you I wouldn't think about calling the police once you get loose. Or I might have to come back with a couple of my buddies, some time when you're not alone. Got it?"

I nodded, and he smiled, patting my slick ass.

"Just remember, Jake. I can always come back. Your ass is mine, any time I want. Keep it open wide for me, okay? And do yourself a favor and get that bitch to use that dildo on you sometime."

The door slammed. He left it unlocked.

It took me ten minutes, not fifteen. I crouched on the floor among the remains of the ropes, found a pack of matches and my smokes. I lit a cigarette. I finished the first and smoked four or five more, until I felt vaguely sick.

The door opened again, and Micky came in. The gym bag was gone. He grinned.

"Jacob! Don't you make a fetching sight," he said, coming over to me. He bent down and kissed me, sliding his hand down my bare, sticky chest. "How was work?"

I cracked, and started to sob, and Micky picked me up and carried me to the bed, holding me, asking me many, many times what was wrong. He thought the scene had gone sour.

But it wasn't sour: I just had to cry, to close the scene, to complete the exercise and follow the night to its conclusion....

Like the other, it was just an act. It wasn't long before I stopped sobbing and started moaning, and Micky soothed me with tender violence.

"What did you do with the pictures?"

"I burned them in the alley," he said.

I took a drag from my cigarette, dabbing cum from my lips onto the butt.

"Nice touch."
"I thought so."
"And the bracelet?"
"In the river."
"Like a true artist."
The clock in the church struck three.

# Breaking in Baby Face
*Aaron Travis*

"So this is the new kid?" Larry McMasters raises one eyebrow and flicks his gold-plated Bic, igniting the fat cigar wedged in his mouth. He puffs, filling the air with blue smoke, then leans back in his swivel chair.

McMasters is impeccably dressed: gold cuff links, silk tie, a dark blue polyester suit specially tailored to fit his enormous shoulders and chest. McMasters is impeccably groomed: His black hair is sheared off in a severe flattop, his manicured fingernails are buffed to a high gloss, oddly out of place with his big strangler's hands. Some people call him handsome. Others are put off by the stony set of his jaw and the predatory glint in his eyes.

His office is plushly carpeted, paneled with fine dark wood. Daylight has faded beyond the skinny blinds. The only illumination comes from the silent bank of video screens set into one wall. Each of the screens plays a continuous loop of videotape; all twelve screens show a wrestling match in progress. Larry McMasters, a millionaire at the age of thirty-eight, is the Bossman, head honcho of the Worldwide Pro Wrestling Confederation. The Bossman can afford expensive toys.

Toys like Mongo Monahan, who stands smiling and smug on the other side of McMasters's desk. Like the Bossman, Mongo is larger than life—six foot two, two hundred fifty pounds of rock-solid muscle poured into a black tank top so tight that his shaved nipples peek out on either side of the straps, and a pair of skintight blue jeans that show off a bulge the size of a grapefruit at his crotch.

Despite the dim lighting, Mongo wears his trademark mirror shades, along with the trademark smirk of disgust beloved by wrestling fans around the world. Greasy kid stuff keeps his jet black hair swept back from his brutally handsome face.

Mongo reaches over and squeezes the shoulder of the tall young blond standing next to him. His voice is deep, gruff, and stupid. "Yeah, Boss, this is the one. The kid I told you about." His grip bites into the blonde's flesh like metal pincers. The kid tries to smile, but only manages a crooked wince.

"So, kid—Mongo here tells me you're interested in trying out for a spot on the show. Says you got ambitions to be a pro wrestler."

The kid shuffles his feet, clears his throat. "That's right, sir." His blond hair is cut boyishly long, curling down onto his shoulders, a golden frame for a sweetly angelic face—bright blue eyes, spunky upturned nose, soft red lips. His smooth cheeks are deeply tanned, with a faint blush shining through. A baby face. Mongo's already told McMasters the kid's age: nineteen. But with a face like that, they'll be carding him at bars until he's thirty.

Below the neck, the kid is hardly a baby. From the rib cage down, his white T-shirt hangs loose above his tight, flat stomach, but from the chest up the shirt seems to be two sizes too small. The kid is top-heavy with muscle—big square shoulders, a massive column of a neck, huge biceps that threaten to pop his sleeves. His pecs are enormous. The shirt is stretched thin across his chest, barely able to accommodate the bulging slabs of muscle. Set at the tip of each sweeping curve is a nipple the size of a half-dollar, softly swollen and protruding against the thin white cotton.

Inside his faded blue jeans is a pair of big, muscular legs—the denim is frayed thin above the knees from rubbing against his bulging thighs. The kid doesn't show much basket, especially compared to the hamlike bulge that pushes from Mongo Monahan's crotch. But he bulges very nicely from the rear, where the hard muscles of his ass seem ready to split the seam of his pants.

McMasters puffs on his cigar and looks the kid up and down. He likes the innocent, slightly blushing face. He likes the way the boy's plump nipples show through his white T-shirt. He especially likes the little bead of sweat that clings to the kid's upturned nose, and the way he stands there with his arms at his sides, fidgeting, too nervous to look him in the eye.

"You wrestled before?"

"In high school, sir. All-state three years in a row. And gymnastics. Swimming. Track. Football. Weight lifting…"

"Yeah," Mongo says, "that's how I met the kid. Working out down at Sharky's gym. Always hanging around when me and Matt Matthews were pumping the weights. Turns out the kid's got a thing about pro wrestlers." Mongo sniggers. "I mean, about pro *wrestling*."

McMasters nods through a wreath of cigar smoke. "So, kid, just how much do you know about pro wrestling? It's not much like the wrestling you did in high school—if you know what I mean."

Mongo gives the kid's shoulder a punch and answers for him. "He knows the score. I been giving him some private training. Teaching him the ropes. Hell, like the kid said, he's a fucking gymnast. He can fake a tumble."

"Been training him, huh?" McMasters raises an eyebrow.

Mongo smirks. "Not the way you mean. Not yet." He steps back, out of the kid's eyeshot, and reaches down to grope himself. He and McMasters exchange a knowing grin.

"All right then." McMasters settles back in his chair. "Show me what you got, boy."

The kid bats his eyelashes, confused.

"Come on, kid," Mongo sneers. "Take off your shirt. The Bossman wants a look at your bod."

The kid blushes and bites his lip, then reaches up and peels the T-shirt over his head. Larry McMasters is used to being surrounded and serviced by some of the finest physiques in the world, but even the Bossman of the WPWC can't suppress a low grunt of approval. The symmetry is breathtaking—massive shoulders and chest, flaring lats, a hard flat belly corrugated with muscle. Skin like satin, burnished with a deep golden tan.

"You shave your chest, kid?"

The kid seems shocked. "Why, no, sir."

McMasters nods. Naturally hairless. Smooth as a baby. Probably not a hair on his legs, either. "Okay. Take off your pants."

The kid hesitates, then unbuttons his jeans and slides them down to his sneakers, unties his sneakers, and kicks his feet free. Now he's dressed only in cotton socks and a pair of skimpy briefs, white as snow against his honey-colored flesh. Just as McMasters expected—the boy's legs are virtually hairless, long and sleek, superbly muscled. McMasters purses his lips and sucks in his breath.

"What did I tell you?" Mongo says. "The kid's built like a goddamn Greek statue. Yeah, like a fucking statue."

"A *fucking* statue, huh? My favorite kind." McMasters smiles. "You might do, kid. You just might. Turn around."

McMasters squeezes his crotch. Mongo grins and does the same. Both of them run their eyes over the kid's backside, from the long golden hair that brushes against his broad shoulders, down the tapering V of his back to the silky depression at the base of his spine, to the big muscular ass still hidden inside his briefs. On down to the broad thighs, and the kid's unusually developed calves, thick ankles, and big flat feet.

"Interesting," McMasters says. "Let's see the rest."

The kid looks over his shoulder. His voice quavers. "The rest, sir?"

"Yeah, the rest," Mongo smirks. "Don't act stupid, kid."

The Bossman waves his cigar. "You see, kid, I hand-pick every man who enters the ring. We've got pretty high standards in the

WPWC—damned high. I've got some of the finest bodybuilders and pro athletes in the world working under me. My viewers expect the very best. If I'm gonna take you on, I've gotta see exactly what I've got to work with. Exactly what you've got to offer. Pull down your shorts."

The kid darts another quick, blushing glance over his shoulder. Turns his face away. Grabs the waistband of his briefs and peels them down over his thighs. Bends deep to step out of them, thrusting his naked, flexing ass directly under Mongo's smoldering stare. Mongo licks his lips.

The kid stands, straightens his back, squares his shoulders. Naked except for his white cotton socks.

McMasters and Mongo exchange a leering grin. The kid's ass is phenomenal. Two bronzed globes of rock-solid muscle, revealing the skimpiest tan line McMasters has ever seen—just a tiny strip of snow white flesh like twin arcs across the top of his buns. The remainder of his ass is as honey gold as the rest of him—shiny brown buttocks, hard and round with muscle, melting down into his sturdy thighs without a crease. Smooth as silk, gently dimpled, perfectly molded to fit a man's hands.

McMasters puffs on his cigar. "Okay, blondie. Turn around."

The kid reaches for his underwear. Mongo is too quick for him. He catches the briefs under the toe of his boot and drags them out of the boy's reach. "The Bossman didn't say nothing about you putting your panties back on."

The kid freezes, bent over with his ass in the air. He twists his neck and looks up at Mongo. The big wrestler stands with his hands on his hips, sneering down at him, the bulge at his crotch straining against the fly of his jeans like a clenched fist. The kid bites his lip, looks away, then slowly stands straight.

"Go ahead, kid." McMasters flicks the ashes from his cigar. "Turn around."

He starts to turn, then stops. Starts again, and makes it halfway. Then finally turns to face McMasters.

The kid hangs his head, blushing furiously. Big veins stand out on either side of his neck. Even his big pecs begin to blush, turning apple red and shiny in the lurid light. His hands fidget at his sides, as if he'd like to cover himself—but doesn't want to draw attention to the stiff erection springing up from his hips.

McMasters smiles. The kid's cock is a definite disappointment—or would be, if McMasters had any interest in his dick. The important thing is that it's hard—hard as a rock. So hard it looks almost painful, poking up red and swollen from his tidy little bush of golden pubic hair. A short, stubby cock, like a tiny handle sticking up from his groin, ludicrously out of proportion with the big muscles popping out all over the rest of his body.

McMasters makes a point of staring at the boy's puny hard-on and shaking his head in sympathy, as if the kid had just shown him an embarrassing handicap, like a club foot or an ugly birthmark. "Well," he says, "at least you've got the *body* to make it in the WPWC."

The kid stutters a grateful, "Thank you, sir."

"Don't mention it." McMasters bolts from his chair, walks up to the kid, and slowly circles him, puffing on his cigar, raking his eyes up and down his naked nineteen-year-old body. The kid is blushing all over, lighting up his golden tan with an inner glow. His muscles glisten under a thin sheen of nervous sweat. His cock stays hard as a rock.

"Well, now that we've seen the raw material, let's see what we can do to dress it up."

The kid sighs with relief at the idea of getting into some clothes. "I brought some wrestling togs. Blue and green—"

"No. Uh-uh. I don't think so." McMasters shakes his head. "You don't seem to understand, kid. We don't just put you in some wrestling trunks and send you out into the ring. You gotta have a package, a concept. An idea to build on. We could start with your name."

"My name? It's—"

"Forget it, kid. Not the name your momma gave you. The name *I'm* gonna give you." McMasters steps closer, reaches out, and cups the kid's chin. Skin so baby soft and smooth McMasters wonders if he's ever had to shave it. The kid flinches at the contact.

McMasters tilts his head back, purses his lips. "Baby Face," he announces. "That's it. The whole world is gonna know you as Baby Face. Yeah—Baby Face Billy. Or Bobby. Or maybe…"

"Bruce!" Mongo grunts.

"You're a fucking genius, Mongo. That's it—Baby Face Bruce from Billings, Montana!"

The kid chews his lip and stares at the carpet. His shoulders slump. Even his hard-on goes down a little. But he makes no objection. McMasters is the Bossman, after all.

"Now we got the concept. Now we're rolling!" McMasters walks to a big mahogany bureau against one wall and rummages through a drawer, tossing out slinky wrestling thongs and mail-order panties, leather straps, and shiny dog collars.

Mongo watches and sniggers, wondering what the Bossman will come up with. Panties are McMasters's favorite fetish, slinky see-through handfuls of nothing purchased from trashy mail-order catalogues—Mongo knows, from personal experience. Once upon a time, under similar circumstances, Mongo himself was pressed into modeling a frilly pink pair for the Bossman's amusement—and ended up bent over the Bossman's desk, the panties pulled down to his knees, squealing and grunting while McMasters plowed his foot-long cock in and out of Mongo's ass. Of course, that was a long time ago—back when Mongo was still a nobody named Joe Smolinksy, just a fresh young kid with muscles and a dream, ready to do anything to break into the pro wrestling circuit. Like Baby Face, standing obediently in the middle of the room, nude and erect and blushing, waiting for the Bossman to dress him up.

McMasters finally finds what he wants. He steps behind the kid. "Raise your arms, Baby Face."

McMasters wraps something around his hips, draws it up between his thighs, pulls it tight. Steps back to take a look.

"What do you think, Mongo?"

"Damn, Boss! It's perfect! What a fucking imagination you got. I don't think it's ever been done before."

The kid looks down, and feels a sinking sensation in the pit of his stomach. McMasters has put him in a diaper!

"Gee, sir, I don't know if—"

"For chrissakes, kid, stop whining." Mongo rolls his eyes in disgust. "The man is a professional."

"But I feel—ridiculous." The kid blushes deep red from head to toe.

"Don't sweat it, kid." McMasters circles him, staring down at the diaper, adjusting the big metal pins with pink plastic heads. It's a skimpy fit, like a tiny white loincloth—slung low beneath the kid's navel, poking out in front to show the outline of his hard-on. In back it rides up the crack of his ass, showing off his smooth tanned buttocks.

"The long hair may be a problem," Mongo says. "All the babies I ever seen are bald. Maybe we oughta shave it."

The kid turns ghostly pale and makes a funny noise in his throat, like he's about to be sick.

McMasters laughs. "Nah, that can wait. Maybe we'll save it for a grudge match, Mongo, one of these days when we need to pump up the ratings. Let you shave him bald right there in the ring, so all the rednecks can watch."

The kid sighs with relief, but his legs feel wobbly.

McMasters rubs his chin. "There's still something missing. I know what it is!" He reaches into his desk and pulls out a big plastic bottle with a pink label. He pitches it to the kid.

The kid tries to catch it and fumbles—the slippery bottle pops right out of his hands and lands on the carpet with a thud.

"Baby oil," explains McMasters as the kid stoops to pick it up. "Baby oil for Baby Face. Slick yourself up, kid."

Baby Face squirts the stuff into the palm of his hand, smoothes it over his big shoulders and down his biceps. McMasters watches, smiling like a shark. "Come on, Brucie boy, pour it on. Like you're basting a chicken. That's it, squirt it all over your tits. And rub it in good."

The kid looks like he's feeling himself up—playing with his big fleshy pecs, cupping the smooth slabs of muscles in his hands, rubbing and squeezing, making his big nipples pop out between his fingers.

"Your legs, too." McMasters steps behind to watch as the kid bends deep, slicking his hands down his thighs, stretching to oil up his calves and ankles.

"Good enough. Hand me the bottle. I'll do your back."

Baby Face stands. McMasters squirts a stream of oil across his broad shoulders and roughly massages the big muscles, probing the resilient flesh under his gliding fingertips, trailing his hands down the kid's spine until his thumbs come to rest in the hard little dimples just above his ass.

"Bend over, Baby Face."

The kid goes stiff.

"Come on, Brucie boy. Grab your ankles. We gotta oil up your bottom."

"But—I could oil it up myself, sir."

Mongo snorts and rolls his eyes. "Sheeze, kid, you're embarrassing me. Come on. Do what the man tells you."

Baby Face hesitates, straining to get a glimpse of McMasters over his shoulder, then takes a deep breath and bends over, keeping his legs straight, grabbing his ankles. The diaper digs into his crack, baring his buttocks completely. His cheeks blush golden red as they rear up and make contact with the Bossman's waiting fingertips.

McMasters lets out a sigh of pure lust. The kid's ass feels even better than it looks—taut as a drumhead, smooth as marble. He takes his time oiling it up. Feeling it up. Running his greasy palms all over the hard round globes. Giving Baby Face a nice greasy butt that glistens in the colored light from the TV screens.

He loops his finger under the little flap that runs up the crack of the kid's ass and pulls it aside. The sight of the boy's hole hits him like a fist in the gut. Bent over, with his cheeks stretched wide open, the little hole is completely exposed and slightly protruding, like pouting lips. A trickle of oil runs down the boy's crack and nestles in the wrinkled folds, making the rosebud shimmer.

Virgin ass. Larry McMasters knows it when he sees it. The kid has never been dicked. Virgin boypussy, sweet and tight. Ripe to be split wide open by the Bossman's cock. He imagines his hard dick poised at the opening, nudging up against it. He closes his eyes and can almost feel the tightly clamped ring of flesh nipping at his cockhead as it shoves relentlessly forward and then pops inside—can almost hear the kid squeal and feel him squirm, the way they always do. Virgins squeal loudest of all....

But not yet. McMasters opens his eyes and lets out a sigh of anticipation. He snaps his middle finger against the tiny hole—watches it snap open and shut, hears Baby Face gasp in surprise. Then he steps back, slapping the kid's greasy ass—a friendly swat, just hard enough to leave a glowing red handprint.

"Okay, Baby Dick—I mean, Baby Face. Time for you to strut that ass for me out in the ring...."

Baby Face hits the boards flat on his back and lets out a grunt. Damn! Mongo was never this rough in their practice sessions. For the last thirty minutes he's been tossing him around the ring like a rag doll. Slamming him into the turnbuckles, back-flipping him onto the boards, spinning him into the ropes.

And hitting him. Hard. Punches in the gut, chops across the shoulders, even a few stinging slaps across his face. It's almost as if he's really trying to hurt the kid.

Baby Face can't understand it. He knows the rules, the illusion behind the brutal facade of pro wrestling. He and Mongo are supposed to work together, fake the falls, put on a good show. But it seems like Mongo is trying to kill him. And that scares him. Because when it comes right down to it, Mongo outweighs him by at least fifty pounds and packs a lot more experience and muscle. Baby Face is like putty in his hands—it's all he can to do just to keep Mongo from breaking him in two.

McMasters watches it all from a folding chair in the corner of the ring. He sits with his arms crossed, legs sticking straight out. The kid occasionally looks to him in confusion, thinking he'll put a stop to Mongo's rampage. But it's obvious from the smirk on his face that this show is just what the Bossman had in mind.

The auditorium is empty except for the three of them, silent except for the kid's gasping and grunting and the echoing crack of flesh against flesh. Dark except for the cone of blinding light illuminating the ring. A spooky place, strangely unreal without a hoard of screaming rednecks to give it life.

The auditorium is just a short distance from McMasters's office, across a wide expanse of empty parking lot. They could have driven, but McMasters insisted that they walk—and insisted that Baby Face take the trip in costume. "You might as well get used to your diaper, kid. Twenty million raving American rednecks are gonna see you in it every Saturday night...."

So they strolled to the auditorium, Baby Face blushing and barefoot, glad the parking lot was empty so that no one would see his hard-on poking against the front of his diaper like a tent peg.

On the way, McMasters explained a few things. "You may think that the world of pro wrestling is split between good guys and bad guys. It ain't so. The split comes between what I call Tops and Bottoms. A Top may be a good guy or a villain, an angel or an asshole, but whatever, he's got that certain something that makes the crowd wanna see him come out on top—like Mongo here. They love to see him mop the floor with some guy. Same thing with a Bottom. Good guy, bad guy, doesn't matter. He's got that certain something that makes the crowd go wild when they see him get the shit knocked out of him.

"Take you, for example. Good-looking kid, clean-cut, all-American. Definitely a hero type. But my viewers aren't gonna like you one bit. They're hard-working, beer-belching, American rednecks, and to them you're just another pampered pretty boy who's got it made on his looks. They're gonna love it when a goon like Mongo throws you down and stamps on you, drags you up by your hair and backhands you across the face. I know my audience, Baby Face. They want to see a kid like you humiliated out in that ring. See you suffer and squirm. They want to see the look on your pretty face when Mongo pins you down and the ref counts three, and the pretty boy loses out to the neighborhood bully. You understand what I'm saying, Baby Face? You were born to be a Bottom in the world of pro wrestling."

McMasters kept his face hard and stony all through his little speech—then suddenly smiled as he took a sidelong glance down at the kid's greasy buttocks, popping out of his diaper and jiggling with each step that brought him closer to the ring....

Baby Face lands flat on his back again. He just can't take any more. He aches all over, his muscles are like jelly, he can hardly breathe. If Mongo would only let up for a second. Just give him one second to catch his breath. At least his hard-on has disappeared.

He stares up, blinded by the lights. Mongo looms over him, his sweat-drenched tank top molded to his muscular torso, his eyes hidden behind the mirror shades, his jaw clenched in a taunting smirk. The bulge at his crotch is bigger than ever. He cups his hand and curls his fingers back, gesturing for Baby Face to get up.

"Come on, Baby Dick. On your feet. I haven't even started working you over yet. Come on, you a pussy or something? The man's watching."

Baby Face struggles to his knees, stumbling forward. For just an instant his nose brushes against Mongo's crotch. The odor has a weird effect on him, making his head go light, making him tingle between his legs. He rises to his feet—and immediately Mongo's big meaty fist slugs him square in the belly. The kid doubles over and tries to back away, but Mongo's other hand clutches the back of his neck, holding him in place while he slams the kid's washboard stomach over and over, knocking more breath out of him with each blow until the kid is as limp as a leaky punching bag.

From somewhere far away, the kid hears McMasters laughing. The room spins as Mongo grabs him by the hair and waltzes him toward the ropes, whirling him around, lifting his helpless arms and tangling them in the ropes, putting him into a crucified pose.

"Come on, kid!" McMasters sounds angry. "Put some emotion into it. Ninety-nine percent of this game is acting. Just look at

Mongo. A pussycat—but he can sure play one mean son-of-a-bitch, can't he? So let's see some feeling. Show me some *real* suffering!"

Baby Face manages to lift his head. Lips pouting and swollen, eyebrows drawn together, cheeks hollow. Not acting at all.

"Nah, that's not it. Help him out, Mongo."

Mongo grabs him by the hair, wrenches his head back and slaps his face back and forth. The kid is helpless, unable to move, his arms trapped in the ropes. The slaps are real, hard and meaty, making his eyes tear up, making his cheeks sting and burn hotter than the blush spreading across his face—because Baby Face is starting to get a hard-on again.

Mongo notices. So does McMasters. It's time to speed up the audition. Time for Baby Face to learn what it really means to be a Bottom in the world of Larry McMasters.

Mongo slaps him a final time, then yanks the boy's head up, turning his face toward McMasters for the Bossman's approval. The kid's dick pokes as stiff as a broom handle against his diaper. He stares back at McMasters through bleary eyes, then opens his mouth and grunts as Mongo punches him in the belly. "Yeah," McMasters croons, "that's better. Now *that* looks like genuine suffering."

Mongo untangles the boy's arms, grabs him by the hair and walks him toward McMasters. The kid stumbles, held up by the fist in his hair. His hard-on bounces up and down inside his diaper. Mongo spins him around. The kid stands on his own two feet, but just barely, and not for long. Mongo pokes his chest. Baby Face tumbles backward, trips over McMasters's outstretched foot, and lands flat on his ass.

McMasters laughs. "Get up, Baby Face."

The kid struggles to his knees, but that's as far as he can manage. He takes a deep, rattling breath and finally finds enough air to eke out a whisper, "Please, sir. Please, I don't think I can take any more."

McMasters raises an eyebrow. "But you haven't taken anything—yet." He blatantly squeezes the enormous ridge of flesh running down his pants leg. The kid shakes his head to clear it, catches sight of the thing in McMasters's pants, and blinks in disbelief.

"You look real good, Baby Face. Damn good." The Bossman's voice is low and crooning. "All smooth and muscular and innocent in your little white diaper. Taking your punishment from big ol' Mongo. Oh yeah, you've got what it takes, Baby Face. The fans are gonna eat you up."

Baby Face just nods, fascinated by the impossible bulge at the crotch of McMasters's pants.

"Just one more thing, kid. One more test. I gotta see you crawl. That's very important, crawling. You'll be doing a lot of it in the ring. Crawling on your hands and knees for big mean studs like Mongo, and Lanny Boy Jones, and Leo Logan and Brick Lewde, while twenty million American rednecks get an eyeful of that big shiny butt of yours. I gotta make sure you got the right look. Gotta make sure you know how to crawl like a genuine Bottom Boy. So do it for me. Crawl for the Bossman, Baby Face."

For a long moment, the kid can't tear his eyes from the swollen ridge running down McMasters's pants leg—the thing reaches almost to his knee! Then he slowly drops onto all fours and heads toward the opposite corner, keeping his limbs pulled in tight, his chest grazing the floor, raising his ass high in the air, crawling like a baby. Behind him he hears McMasters suck in his breath, and then another sound, a zipper being unzipped.

The kid blushes furiously. His cock throbs between his legs. He crawls all the way to the opposite corner. Then he turns—and stares, unable to believe his eyes.

McMasters's legs are spread wide open, his hands on his knees, his pants undone. His huge cock juts up nude and erect from his open fly—impossibly big, incredibly thick. This is it—the King of Cocks. The heart and soul of the WPWC. The throbbing engine at the core of the pro wrestling world. The key to Larry McMasters's spectacular success, the big stick he uses to keep all his boys in line.

Baby Face stares at it, mesmerized, and then begins to crawl toward it.

Suddenly Mongo blocks his way. The big man plants the tips of his boots on the boy's outstretched fingers, pinning them against the boards. Baby Face gasps and rolls his eyes up, but he can't see Mongo's face—his view is blocked by the eight solid inches of meat sticking out of Mongo's fly.

Mongo has a big, clublike cock, hefty and thick—but just a piker compared to the monster between McMasters's legs. He tears open a foil packet and smears a handful of glistening jelly over his hard-on. Baby Face groans. His asshole begins to twitch.

Mongo pulls his greasy cock to one side and smirks down at him. "Your first time, Baby Dick?"

Baby Face stares up at the hard, lubed cock. He feels a strange warmth in his gut. His asshole itches and tingles. He nods his head.

A mean, nasty grin spreads across Mongo's face. He steps off the kid's crushed fingers and circles around behind him.

Now Baby Face can see McMasters again. His mouth waters. His dick throbs between his legs. Everything goes dark, except for the shiny bars of light reflecting off the huge, spit-slicked truncheon of meat waiting for him across the ring.

He completely forgets about Mongo—until he feels the diaper being unpinned from his hips and ripped away. Mongo kicks his feet apart, forcing him to spread his thighs wide open. Baby Face is naked on his hands and knees, about to be fucked for the very first time.

The air feels cool and moist against the sweaty crack of his ass. Then he feels a sudden sharp twinge at the lips of his asshole. Something blunt and hard presses relentlessly inward against his hole. He instinctively tries to resist, but Mongo's cock is hard as steel, driven forward by the full strength of the man's powerful hips. The clenched hole suddenly snaps and gives way.

Baby Face drops his jaw in a silent howl. His body bucks in a spastic convulsion, then goes rigid as Mongo spears his cock all the way to the hilt. Baby Face is no longer a virgin. Baby Face is impaled on Mongo's cock. The shock is electric. Mongo's cock is like a lightning rod inserted up the boy's ass, sucking up all his energy from the inside, sapping his will.

"That's it, Mongo." From somewhere far away he hears McMasters laughing. "Ride him over here."

The big cock spears his guts—pulls back with a slurp and spears him again. Baby Face jerks forward. Mongo coils a lock of blond hair around his fist and pumps his cock, riding him like a pony until they reach the Bossman, then reining him in with a sharp tug at his hair. The kid's head snaps up, right in front of McMasters's rampant dick.

The Bossman waves his cock, watching the kid's eyes bob back and forth. "Hungry for your bottle, Baby Dick? Or maybe you're feeling a little too stuffed already."

The kid blushes furiously, staring cross-eyed at McMasters's huge cock.

McMasters chuckles. "You like playing pony, Baby Dick? Yeah, Mongo'll get your insides good and loosened up, all soft and squishy and ready for the Bossman's big toy. Hey—you look like you're about to start crying, Baby Face. Whassa matter, kiddo—you need a pacifier, huh? Something big and warm to suck on?"

The kid grunts, licks his lips—then lets out a little squeal as Mongo delivers a deep jab to his prostate. He squints and stares slack-jawed at the Bossman's meat. The thick shaft stands straight up from the man's lap, spitting and drooling a steady stream of creamy white slag. McMasters tilts the shaft downward and traces the tip of his tool over the boy's wide-open mouth, glossing his smooth pink lips with a coating of shiny semen. He holds his cock poised an inch from the gaping mouth, feeling the boy's warm, moist breath on his cock. "Is Baby Face hungry?"

Baby Face whimpers. McMasters teases him with it, drawing it out of range and batting his cheeks, laughing at the boy's slack-jawed, cross-eyed confusion. Baby Face suddenly goes crazy, opening his mouth wide and sticking out his tongue, lapping frantically at empty air.

McMasters rudely shoves his head away, rises to his feet and kicks the chair aside. The big man peels off his jacket and slings it over the ropes. He undoes his tie and takes off his starched cotton shirt. His undershirt shows off the massive concentration of muscles in his upper body. Larry McMasters is a rugged giant of a man, his body every bit a match for the overgrown truncheon of flesh that pokes like a hairless forearm from his open fly.

Baby Face crouches on the floor—nude, erect, impaled on Mongo's big dick, staring up dazed and hungry. McMasters swaggers toward him, gently slapping the underside of his big dick, making it quiver and drool. "You passed the audition, Baby Face. You're hired. Now it's time for your first job—your first *blow*job."

Mongo settles back on his haunches, holding the boy's naked, trembling body impaled on his lap. Baby Face squeals and clutches Mongo's hips for balance, keeping his mouth wide open. McMasters has never seen a boy hungrier for it.

McMasters steps forward. Tilts his cock slightly down. Takes aim—and then heaves forward with his hips.

His massive cockhead pops into the boy's mouth, straining his lips to the limit. McMasters pauses for only an instant, savoring the look of shock in Baby Face's eyes, and then drives home, drilling his cock all the way down the boy's neck. Baby Face is skewered at both ends, his throat impaled on the Bossman's throbbing mallet, his ass split open by Mongo's thick eight inches. His body goes rigid from the shock, his holes convulse—and suddenly both men are coming inside him, both monster dicks pulsing and spitting, setting up a shuddering vibration that turns him to jelly....

Eventually...after the stamping and sighing...the throes of ecstasy...the shudders...McMasters slowly extracts his glistening cock from the kid's bruised and battered throat. At the same time, Mongo pulls out of his ass. Baby Face crumples exhausted and empty to the floor, belching and farting and seeping juice from both ends.

"Good job," the Bossman mutters, staring down at the boy's gleaming, oil-slicked ass. He gently strokes himself—hard as steel, despite the orgasm that emptied his balls only moments before. "Now it's time to play pony again. Only this time it's gonna be me in the saddle, Baby Face. The Bossman is gonna teach you how to canter and prance and gallop like a good little pony. You get good enough at it, I might even take you outside to show you off—take turns with Mongo, ride you across the parking lot all the way back to my office. Up on your hands and knees, boy—and get ready to whinny...."

Two weeks later, Larry McMasters introduces a new star in the world of pro wrestling. The auditorium is packed with screaming rednecks. Mongo enters first, to a chorus of hisses and boos. Then the challenger: Baby Face Bruce from Billings, Montana. Necks crane, flashbulbs pop—everybody wants a look at the new kid.

The crowd isn't quite sure what to make of him—scattered applause, along with more than a little laughter. Baby Face blushes a bit, but he's gotten used to his diaper. It's all that McMasters has allowed him to wear for the last two weeks. Of course, the crowd can't see the extra-thick buttplug the Bossman makes him wear up his ass or the electrical tape strapping his cock against his leg— Baby Face never could stop throwing a hard-on during practice.

Life as a pro wrestler is harder than he ever expected. But the rewards are substantial, and the guys, once you get to know them, are all very friendly. Tonight, Baby Face is going to do his best, because after the match, if he's done a good job, McMasters has promised to throw a little welcome party for him. All the guys will be there. McMasters says they'll each have a present for him, a big surprise package, and they'll all gather around to watch as he unwraps them one by one. And the Bossman says he won't have to wear his diaper. In fact, he won't have to wear anything at all....

# A Tame Animal
*Matthew Walker*

Mickey and I vowed partnership on my twenty-third birthday. For our honeymoon, we requested four weeks of shore leave—the full allowance for partnership celebrations. Instead of going to one of the Terran colonies closer to the station, we came here, to Habilay. We didn't want to share our happy occasion with the bustle of the New Century Festivals.

Our hotel suite in Sarie was lavish, and the legendary Habilayan hospitality we received exceeded our inflated expectations. Even so, we didn't spend much time in the room. The mountains and coastline are fabled for their beauty, and the Habilayans have taken great care of their world. Between our rented hoverjet and Sarie's excellent public transportation system, we saw plenty of the surrounding sights.

On the west end of the city are the public gardens. High walls of smooth bluestone screen out the noise of the city. Constant breezes from Mount Kiyamor keep the gardens cool and pleasant even on the hottest days. Among the vast triangular beds of broken roses, the sweeping curved patches of open faces, and the sparkling blue-water fountains, we felt we were in the garden of an ancient king.

Rising against the foot of the mountain at the far end of the gardens is a kind of zoo or museum of natural history (the Habilayan word for it includes a sense of each). Mick and I stumbled upon it by accident in the third week of our visit.

The museum is housed in a jumble of square, faceless, black buildings in the style Habilayans seem always to have preferred. In small climate-controlled cages at the front there are all sorts of strange beasts from Habilay itself: a creature with the body of a gorilla but the teeth and claws of a lion, an amphibious fish with poisonous barbed fins, a broad-backed invertebrate that dissolves the flesh and bone of its prey.

After a few minutes, I noticed that the animals had in common their great savagery. We saw nothing, in fact, that could be considered cuddly, or cute, or endearing: only predators with snaggle teeth and sharp claws seemed to interest the gentle Habilayans.

Past the first building, we came to the exhibits of animals from other worlds. Many were on loan from their home worlds. Others were captured by intrepid Habilayan hunters.

Holographic imaging gave visitors an idea of every animal's natural habitat. More importantly, to the dumb animal the holographic world was infinite, giving it the illusion of freedom.

Near the end of our wanderings, Mickey and I saw a sign that made us break into cold sweat: THE HOMO SAPIENS BUILDING, it said. Inside, in cages no bigger than those given to the Arcturan orangutans, men were exhibited in pairs.

My pocket translator helped me with the placards underneath the exhibit windows: CELLMATES, one said. COWBOY AND INDIAN, said another. GREEK PHILOSOPHER AND STUDENT. PRIEST AND ALTAR BOY. PIRATE CAPTAIN AND CABIN BOY.

Mouths open, Mick and I watched the cellies. They were accoutered as modern-day convicts, wearing nothing but shackles.

Thin metal restraints glittered like jewelry around their wrists, ankles, and necks. Their bodies were completely hairless from head to toe.

The cell was authentic, if I could trust what I saw on the daily news broadcasts. The ceiling was high, the walls smooth and bare. The edges of the door were invisible, flush with the surface of the wall. On the left, the lower bunk was open. Only the small blue button that opened it marked where the upper rack would be.

Smoking a clovestick, the "stud" sat on the bunk with his back against the wall. His "bitch" knelt on the floor, sucking the stud's cock. The cables running from the back of the bitch's collar to his bracelets had been shortened so that his hands were drawn high up his back.

The stud was an inch or so above average height—six eight, six nine at most—but his build was considerably better than normal. His shoulders were broad, his belly rippled with muscle, his thighs heavy enough to crush stone. His cock, too, was above average: at eleven inches or so, it was a good match for his frame. In its straining, throbbing hardness, it was a deep shade of purple.

The bitch was only about six feet, making it clear how he'd become the bitch. His body was slim and lean, and without hair he seemed boyish. His cock—shorter than the stud's by half—was circumcised, an unusual feature almost certainly associated with his bitch status.

Finishing his stick, the stud leaned forward and put it out on the bitch's ass. There were hundreds of burns where he'd done the same thing before. The bitch knew better than to protest.

Standing, the stud motioned for the bitch to climb onto the bunk. Without question or hesitation, the bitch obeyed. Touching a button at the back of the bitch's collar, the stud shortened his cellie's cabling even more, drawing the smaller man's arms and legs into a painful-looking knot.

The stud flipped his cellie over. The bitch's body arched steeply over his own arms and legs; his hard cock rose like a tower above his bare crotch.

Extending his own cabling to its limit, the stud wrapped it around his bitch's genitals. Even at its full span, the length of the cable did not allow much creativity, but two or three turns were all he needed. The bitch's cock flushed a shade darker.

With his victim's cock and balls trapped, the stud slapped, poked, beat, and jabbed at them. Always the stiff pole came back for more. The bitch moaned.

Dancing like an ancient boxer in a primitive arena, the stud pulled his bitch's goods this way and that. The thin cable sawed mercilessly at the base of the moaning slave's cock and balls. The stud jabbed hard at the bitch's tight, glistening ball sac. Helpless to avoid the blows, the bitch groaned and shook. His cock never wavered in its hardness.

The stud unwrapped his bitch's balls. The cable slipped away, revealing a thin, ragged cut alongside the slave's cock.

Just then, Mickey pulled me from the window. I'd been so busy watching the cellmates and rubbing my own crotch that I hadn't noticed that he'd wandered away.

"You have to see this," he said, breathless. His hand was sweaty and warm on my bare forearm as he led me toward the back of the building.

He'd found one of the masterpieces of the whole museum. Open to view on three sides, the exhibit depicted a town square in the infamous Folsom Colony, a Terran colony in the Dionysian system where, for the last half of the twenty-third century, sexual slavery was legal.

Fifty-eight short years it lasted, before it was destroyed. Terrans were scandalized. Heteros briefly took to calling their partnerships "marriages." Politicos made speeches on the Council floor begging for a return to "simpler times." A few small provinces in Africa and Southwest Asia tried to set precedents by passing local forced reproduction ordinances.

But all of that had passed by the time Mick and I were born. During our separate childhoods—his on the moon, mine in East California—we read everything we could about the colony's history.

It was a dream come true. It was Eden.

At the Academy, our mutual interest in the colony brought us together. We bought each other books about it and spent free weekends living out the fantasies we'd built around it. We grew wistful as we spoke of the freedom it represented, sullen as we thought of its demise.

The colony's photographic records had been destroyed, but by some miracle the Habilayans had prepared an exhibit that exactly matched my mental picture of the place.

Across the front stood a dozen pillories. Rough-hewn from goldenwood trees, they glistened in Dionysus's powerful light. Each pillory held a naked slave sentenced to public punishment. Welts and bruises over most of their tan bodies bore witness to the severity of their ordeal, but none were being punished at the moment.

Behind them, the dusty square buzzed with activity. Men in jerkins and boots of black leather led their naked, collared, shackled slaves on the day's business. Merchants in adobe huts specialized in the equipment of torture and bondage; many of the Masters were having their slaves fitted for chastity devices, anal inserts, gags, and restraints. Nearly a hundred men were involved in the exhibit, all of them mouth-watering examples of the male form.

We didn't have long to wait to see more urgent action. A Master and slave approached the pillory on the end nearest Mickey and me. The slave in the pillory was hairless, no doubt having been shaved as part of his punishment. His slim, muscular body was deeply tanned. The head of his stiff cock bore the angry blush of sunburn. As the men's shadows fell over him, the pilloried slave grew still, then began shivering with either fear or desire.

The Master's slave could not have been more than sixteen. His young body was fully—almost ridiculously—packed with bulging muscle that dwarfed both his cock and his face. His Master had allowed him to keep the hair on his head, but his crotch and chest and limbs were bare.

The Master pushed his slave to his knees. Needing no further direction, the Master's slave knelt on the base of the pillory and buried his face in the older slave's ass, feasting on the hairless hole. The Master, drawing a strap from his belt, began whipping both his slave's ass and the pilloried slave's back.

In a nervous rush of New English, the pilloried slave thanked the Master for each stroke: "Un, Mas, tank, Mas. Toe, Mas, tank, Mas. Tary, Mas, tank, Mas..."

Beyond them, another Master had found his slave fondling another slave. Exploding in anger, the Master drew a cat-o'-nine-tails from his belt and ordered both slaves onto the ground. Trembling, the slaves obeyed. A crowd gathered instantly.

Almost in unison, the slaves begged for mercy: "Mas, us dint min...Pulse, Mas, us dint...Dunt, pulse, Mas, dunt."

Unmoved, the Master brought the whip down on their asses. The knotted strands of the cat drew blood from the first stroke, cruelly tearing the skin on the slaves' backs, asses, and legs. Still, among their gasps, groans, and screams, we heard their breathless cries of "Pulse, Mas, pulse, dunt, Mas, pulse."

Some of the Masters in the crowd made their own slaves watch the punishment as an object lesson. Others were too aroused for that; they unbuttoned their codpieces and forcibly took their slaves' mouths.

Mickey and I have trouble controlling our urges under the most stifling of situations; as we watched this sudden orgy, we were swept away with lust. Falling to my knees, I fought with his trousers and pulled his hard piece through the open fly.

His throbbing pole slipped easily down my gullet. It knew the way very well. Mick held my ears and bucked hard against my face. The smell and taste of him filled my head until all I could think of was getting his hot juice down my throat. While he drilled my mouth, I slicked him with my tongue.

With an angry shout he pushed hard into me one last time. Dumping into me, he held me against him. He pressed his booted foot into my crotch, trying like hell to hurt me. He did, but not nearly enough.

With some embarrassment, we noticed that we weren't alone. As Mick hastily buttoned up, a Habilayan approached from the corner where it had been watching. The iridescent skin across her —its—chest and belly glittered in stripes of blue and dark green, an unusual combination.

Reaching for my translator, I grasped for the Habilayan for "sorry" or "excuse me." The open display of sex or genitalia is universally supposed to be a major social gaffe on Habilay.

To my relief, the Habilayan spoke the Terran Common Language perfectly: "I hope you enjoyed yourselves," it said. Its face beamed with cordiality.

Mickey smiled. "Yes, yes, we did. This is quite an exhibit, isn't it?"

"Thank you," the Habilayan said, "I designed it. I'm the Homo Sapiens Curator."

"I have to ask," I said, wiping Mick's scum off my chin. "These aren't really *people*, are they?"

"No, no, of course not. These are mechanical representations of Terrans programmed with very complex artificial intelligence routines."

Mick nodded; AI was his field. They talked shop while I pretended to be interested. The Habilayan bragged that the "mechanical representations" never duplicated routines.

"I'm a little ashamed to admit it," it said, "but we find your sexual habits extremely fascinating. This is the most popular building in the—zoo, is it? museum?—and our guests would be very disappointed if they saw the same show each time."

The curator walked us out. I noticed as we passed the cellmates that the cuts around the bitch's cock and balls had disappeared. He lay on the floor, his arms and legs spread, while the stud repeatedly kicked his crotch. The bitch gasped and moaned but did not protest or call out.

"There are also male-female and female-female exhibits," the Habilayan said at the door to the Homo Sapiens Building. "You must come back and see them."

Mick thanked the curator and promised we'd be back.

Squinting in the brilliant sun, Mick and I took our time and walked back to the hotel. Midday in the streets of Sarie can be a beautiful sight—thousands of Habilayans take to the streets, and their jeweled skins glitter in the sun's pure white light—but it is also disorienting.

It's impossible for a person of specific sex to understand—*really* understand—the Habilayan's sexlessness. Whatever reproductive organs they have are internal, eliminating the need for modesty and, for most, clothing. But their entire reproductive system is a mystery; they will privilege no one outside their species with knowledge of it.

I could not help thinking of the Habilayans as being female, since they are nearly a foot shorter than Terran men on average, their features are delicate, and their voices are mostly in the alto range. It was a constant battle to remember that they were neither male nor female.

Terrans automatically look to facial features as the symbol of individuality and a means of recognition, but Habilayans' facial features are not distinctive. Instead, they recognize each other by the unique patterns of jeweled skin across their bellies, chests, and backs. The jeweled skin is mostly inelastic and tough—squamous, really— and it apparently serves to protect the tender internal organs.

The curator had admitted to the Habilayans' fascination with our sexual habits, which did nothing to help me keep their sexlessness in mind. As a child on Terra, I'd heard tales of the Habilayans, the strange creatures who were exceedingly kind to humans, but railed at the mention of our bestial sexual habits.

Why, then, if they were so offended by our sexuality, did they build a monument to it?

I discovered that I'd been thinking aloud when Mick answered my question with a question: "Why are Terrans so fascinated with the repressive culture of the early twenty-first century? It's partly a sick feeling of pleasure you get from looking at something and knowing that nature must have taken leave of her senses that day, but it's mostly plain old curiosity.

"We wonder how someone could live with constant intrusion on private life, the denial of basic medical procedures, the rhetoric about who should and shouldn't have rights. We hope we'll figure out how it could happen just from looking at it long enough."

I nodded; he was right, as usual. I made a mental note to reward him when we got back to the hotel.

On the eve of our last day, Mickey and I went back to the museum. In our shock and excitement, we'd missed most of the Terran exhibits the first time. Now we wanted to see the rest.

Through some misunderstanding of the Habilayan clock, we arrived just before closing. We had barely enough time to begin drooling over the Cowboy and Indian before the Habilayan curator came around to usher us to the exit. She—it—recognized us.

"Good evening," it said. "I expected you much sooner than this."

Smiling, Mickey said, "Your city has so much to offer. We couldn't spare the time until now."

The curator allowed a small grin. "The zoo is about to close, but there is a new exhibit under development. If you'd like to see it, I'll show it to you in a few minutes."

We nodded, rubbing our crotches.

"Wait here," the curator said with a broad smile. It hurried away.

While we watched, the exhibits went dark. The carefully constructed holographic worlds disappeared without ceremony. Rough hands pulled the mechanical actors from their cages. The building grew still.

The curator returned on silent feet, startling us as it drew near. "This way, please," it said.

Following the Habilayan, we ducked through a low doorway and into a narrow room. The walls were bare, revealing the building's dull gray bones. In the distance I could see two of the Folsom Colony figures being carried away. The curator led us in the opposite direction.

Along the wall to our right were the doors into the holographic cages. Small square placards above them bore Habilayan inscriptions to match the spiky script of the exhibit placards. I guessed from my visits on the other side of the wall that we passed the Cowboy and Indian, the Priest and Altar boy, and the Twin Brothers. I pulled out my translator, but we were moving too quickly; I couldn't type in the characters quickly enough.

The curator stopped at a door that resembled all the others and pressed a button to open it. I pocketed the translator and dropped my jacket to the floor. My hand in Mickey's and my heart in my throat, I stepped through…

…and the compartment was steamy with our breath and the heat of our bodies as we fell together. His mouth was on my mouth, taking me. He fucked me roughly with his rough tongue. His hands found my ass, his fingers gripped and squeezed me, sizing me up. In the moist heat of my skivvies—all I was wearing—my asshole clenched, ready for him, hungry for him.

But he had something else in mind first. He stepped away from me and crouched in front of the duffel bag he'd brought with him. Without the support of his body, I grew dizzy from the rolling of the ship.

Sneering at me over his shoulder, he said, "Something wrong, Private?"

"N-no, Sir." But something *was* wrong. I vaguely felt that I'd forgotten something, something very important. I looked around the compartment. Thinking slowly and calmly, I reminded myself that I was aboard the *Corcoran*. That the Lieutenant had brought me here, to the weight room, on some flimsy excuse—I couldn't remember it now. And that I'd known all along what he really wanted.

So here we were, alone together in the weight room. My cock was hard and tenting my skivvies. The Lieutenant's ass was round and firm and made my mouth water. The bulge in his trousers proved that his cock was as ready as mine.

All was as it should be, yet something was missing. A door—what the fuck was it about a door?

The Lieutenant turned; he'd been rigging a couple of lead

fishing weights to a loop of cord. They dangled from his spread hand, twisting in the air.

"Are jarheads tough, Private?"

"Aye aye, Sir. Jarheads are the toughest fuckin' men on the planet, Sir."

He frowned, as if he'd expected a different answer, but he said, "Knew you'd say that. Drop 'em soldier."

I hastily obeyed. I stripped off my skivvies and tossed them onto the pile in the corner with the rest of my uniform—or meant to, at least, until I saw that there was no such pile.

The Lieutenant squatted in front of me. He grabbed my balls, none too gently, and slipped the loop of cord around them. My piece, spoiling for a fight, smacked him in the chin. My balls tentatively took the weight.

He stooped over the pile of my clothing in the corner and picked up my boots. He tossed them to me, and when I leant to catch them, the weights pulled hard on my 'nads.

"Hold these, Private. Arms out."

"Aye aye, Sir." I obeyed, stretching my arms to the sides in a classic planton.

He was behind me. He kicked my feet apart. "Spread 'em nice and wide. That's it."

Wait. Back up. I stared at the heap of olive drab in the corner. Hadn't I looked there a minute ago? Hadn't the corner been bare?

"I'm waiting, Private," he said.

"Sir, I'm sorry, Sir. I didn't hear you."

He moved closer and spoke directly into my ear. "Swing the weights, asswipe. *Now*."

"Aye aye, Sir." I wagged my ass for him, letting the weights pull my nuts in a wide back-to-front arc. Almost immediately I felt the stretch and pull deep in my belly.

My arms were already growing weak. "Keep those arms up." His belt sang as he yanked it out of the loops.

"Aye aye, Sir."

The first stroke fell across both asscheeks and stung like hell.

Without thinking, I cried out and stopped swinging the weights. The second stroke made the first seem like a caress.

"Don't think about the belt. Think about the weights and the boots. I won't tell you again."

"Aye aye, Sir."

He whipped my back and ass and legs without mercy. The belt seemed to fall harder each time. My balls ached to the roots, and my arms quivered on the verge of dropping. Vaguely, I heard myself begging for him to stop. I swore I'd do anything.

"I'll stop," he said. "Do you want me to stop?"

"Yes, Sir, please, Sir, yes, Sir, please, Sir."

"I'll stop if you tell me what a jarhead pussy you are."

"Aye aye, Sir," I said, blubbering. "I'm a jarhead pussy, good for nothing but fuckin' up the ass, Sir. I'm a fuckin' jarhead pussy asshole, Sir."

"And tell me why you have a mouth, Private."

"I have a mouth so I can suck cock, Sir. So I can make real men happy, Sir. So I can give pleasure to the real men who would never let a cock in their mouths, Sir."

He was still beating me, but his voice was smooth. "And why should I feed my healthy, clean, straight babymaker to the filthy queer likes of you?"

"Because I live for cock in my mouth, Sir, and I'll give it every ounce of strength I've got, Sir."

"Good enough." He gave me one more, a real killer that rattled my bones. "Suck me, soldier, but don't you dare drop those boots."

"Aye aye, Sir."

I turned to face him. His cock poked from the front of his dungarees. It was a real monster, a handful longer than my own. The thick round knob was already slick with precome. I sank to my knees, careful not to let my arms fall. The weights did not reach the floor and relieve my balls of their burden.

Smacking my lips, I snaked my tongue into the folds of foreskin around the shiny pink head of his tool. He was clean, which surprised and disappointed me: I'd been hoping for a salty lick of cheese. Slowly, I worked him inside of me. He fit neatly into the back of my throat, and I swallowed him with pleasure.

He groaned and, lacing his fingers together at the back of my head, he took over. Endlessly and savagely he bucked into me, until my head spun with the pleasure of his thrusts and, without regret, I dropped the boots. He did not seem to mind, and when I put my hands on his round ass to whet his ferocity he did not accuse me of insubordination.

At last he shuddered against me and slammed home one last time. I braced myself, waiting for a deluge of squid juice, but none came. Panting, grimacing, grunting, he resumed his humpery. He fucked so hard that I choked on him, but still no spunk....

From nowhere—from everywhere—a soft alto voice: "That's enough."

The Lieutenant let go of my head. There, where there had once been an ordinary bulkhead, was the door.

"Oh, *that* door," I thought, and the world disappeared—the mysterious uniform piled in the corner, the rolling of the ship, the weight on my balls—all replaced by the clear glass of the cage and the dark exhibit hall beyond.

"They'll do nicely," said the curator. "Take them."

Two Habilayans—the burliest I'd yet seen and the first I thought of as male—yanked us from the cage and dropped us at their feet. While Mick and I lay drained and helpless on the floor, the curator dressed them down. He—it—spoke in the Terran Common Language, presumably for our benefit.

"More gas next time. I want this exhibit to be marked by great brutality. And change the routines. The bigger one"—Mick— "should be the jarhead. It"—the curator smiled cruelly, mocking us—"has the better body. Besides, who will believe a *sailor* could be forceful enough to handle a Marine like that?" Another mockery, no doubt; Mick and I were only sailors of a sort, but we were certainly not Marines.

The curator said something else in Habilayan, speaking bitterly and with great wrath. I understood one often-repeated word, "farh," meaning clothing, and guessed that the curator was not happy about the missing pile of jarhead uniform.

My jacket lay where I'd dropped it, easily within my reach. At the mention of clothing, I clutched at it. I hoped against all reason that I'd brought along some kind of weapon. I believed I'd found one when my fingers brushed a smooth plastic surface in the left pocket, but it was only the translator. Making sure the curator and his goons didn't see me, I palmed it.

Abashed by their superior's angry words, the curator's brawny assistants lifted us roughly over their shoulders. They punched and spanked our limp bodies while they carried us to a large holding cell. We've been here since, fucking all day for public entertainment in the Jarhead and Squid exhibit, sleeping and eating at night with the other meat puppets in the cell.

Later that night, we learned what the curator meant by "more gas." They pump it into the cages to increase sexual potency and speed the body's healing processes. It's also hallucinogenic, making the virtual world of the cage seem all the more real. When the gas wore off, our balls felt as though they were being smashed to bits with a mallet.

For most of us the gas wipes out big stretches of memory at random. I'm one of the unlucky ones. I can remember everything. I have to look into my partner's eyes every day and see that he has no idea who I am. And worse, I know that, to him, I'm just some pussy squid who needs a good fucking to put him right.

Once, while Mick was trying to fuck some sense into my worthless squid butt, one of the bulkheads faded slightly, and I suddenly found myself straddling the two worlds: twentieth-century Terra aboard the *Corcoran* and twenty-fifth-century Habilay inside the zoo.

In the darkened exhibit hall two Habilayans moved swiftly, binding a Terran—the young, muscled slave we'd seen in the Folsom Colony pillory on that first day—to a kind of slab suspended between two slender columns. The slab pivoted on its supports; the Habilayans raised him so that he was nearly vertical.

The Terran slave tested the leather cuffs that held him spread-eagle. As he settled into the helplessness of his bondage, his cock throbbed to its fullest length and girth.

Mick's sweat drenched me as his thick pole split my ass. Seeing the young Folsom slave in front of me freshened my desire; I snuggled my ass against Mick's belly, urging him deeper.

As if obeying my sense of curiosity, the bulkhead faded further. One of the Habilayans was the curator, I saw now. Its companion was younger—judging by the splendor of its jeweled skin—and much larger. Their colors shone as if lit from deep inside their bodies. Glints of orange and red and blue dazzled me.

Leaning over my back, Mick crooned obscenities into my ear. He was approaching his climax with grim zeal, forgetting that it was hopelessly blocked by the gas, that he would not have his release.

The curator's companion wheeled a small cart alongside the slab. The Terran, staring at the cart, panicked. He struggled against his bonds, to no avail.

Mick slammed into me one last time, bellowing in rage. I slumped underneath him, broken. I missed feeling his sweet liquid flood my ass, missed the passion and tenderness in his touch that was meant for *me* and not some cherry sailor boy he barely knew.

Mick tangled his fingers in my hair, pulling it like reins as he mindlessly fucked me, forcing me to face the action in the exhibit hall.

The curator brandished a knife with a very thin blade—a scalpel. He—it—let the light glint off its shining surface, blinding me. I knew then that the bulkhead had not disappeared because of a malfunction, or because of the force of my will, or for any other reason but this: The curator wanted me to see what happened next. Knowing by now that I had kept my memory, it had prepared this as some kind of warning to me.

With great care, the curator lifted the slave's balls away from his body. Though the boy trembled and sweltered under the weight of his naked terror, his cock only grew harder.

The curator made a single long cut from one side of the scrotum to the other. At first I thought the cut had missed its mark somehow, or that the scalpel was dull, or that the curator had faked the cut to confuse me. But then a film of blood washed the slave's legs—the flow matching the pulse of the slave's softening cock—and the testes dangled in the curator's hand.

The Terran slave passed out, and the Habilayans paid him no further attention. He would bleed to death, but he would go peacefully.

The curator neatly severed the cords and tubes and muscles that held the testes in place. In its small hand the naked, blood-slicked orbs appeared freakishly large.

Mickey grabbed my nipples, twisting them sharply while he rammed me. I barely felt him.

Dropping the scalpel, the curator beckoned its companion, who came as called and then knelt. The curator dropped the larger of the slave's testicles into the younger Habilayan's mouth. Closing its eyes, it chewed slowly. A small grimace passed over its face, but then it smiled and rose to its feet.

The curator ate the other testicle, licking the blood off it for my benefit, rolling it around on its tongue, savoring every bite of it.

Facing each other, the two Habilayans linked hands. While I watched them in profile, the smooth, blank skin in the forks of their legs began to swell and pulse. Soon I realized what was happening: They were growing penises. The two members rose, bumped heads, and crossed.

Bare of foreskin, showing no veins, lacking a clearly defined glans, the columns were formidably long and thick, but rather more plain-looking than their Terran equivalents. Instead of hair at the base, the jeweled skins cowled in a kind of wrinkled cushion. Sacs of tight, smooth skin drawn close to their bodies apparently held their balls or some equivalent organ.

At last—now that I could not possibly care—I knew the secret of the Habilayans' reproductive system. It was the simplest and most commonly offered explanation: They were not sexless at all. Each was potentially male or female, and developed genitals appropriate to the role it was about to take. The infusion of hormones from the Folsom slave's gonads rapidly caused these two to become males.

And, when they were both fully and impressively male, they set out to mock me with their sport-fucking. Surprisingly, the curator was not the dominant partner. He knelt before his companion and opened his mouth wide to accept the younger man's broad member.

He licked the underside sweetly and gently, in a way that made me hungry for the old familiar tenderness between Mickey and me. The younger man allowed the gentleness for only a moment, then slammed home in a single smooth stroke.

As if following their lead, Mick rammed his cock soundly up my bunghole and held it there—pretending, perhaps, that he was coming. My bawling allowed him to boast of his own prowess.

The curator's companion had little patience for fellatio. He soon arranged the curator on his belly and, searching with his blunt pole for the tiny hidden anus, rammed home. Their fucking was animal, as savage as the feeding of the tigers and bears on exhibit in the zoo. They scratched and howled and bit. They shook and roared and fought.

They came and came and came.

It took me several days of reprogramming and several weeks of typing, but I've stored this text on my pocket translator's microchip. I only have a little more space left. If you've found the chip and broken the code, you are probably Terran. Please forward it to the Terran diplomatic liaison.

I am almost certainly dead by now. No one is coming to rescue me, I know, and even if someone were, this is the last place anyone would look. Escape is even less likely, and after more than a month of daily exposure to the gas, it's not even a good idea. A tame animal isn't capable of surviving outside of captivity.

# Confessions of a Peter Gabriel Fan
*Wickie Stamps*

I started the night as I always do with a trip to the video store. The place up by Castro, on Seventeenth. I fucking love walking up Castro, taking my time, letting all the boys check me out. I figure it gives them a thrill. So that's what I did. Walked up Castro, then right onto Seventeenth and into Superstar Video.

First I checked out the suspense section. I always do. But I never check out the boys. Never. Like I said, I don't go that way. But I got that look that they like. Hard. And scary. The look they like.

I didn't see anything I liked in the suspense section, so I cruised into the back where they keep the porn. I took my time. I guess it was around 6:30 when I left the store. I don't wear a watch, so I'm guessing.

Sure I'd done a line or two of crystal by then. Jesus, man! It's fucking San Francisco! Sure, I'd probably smoked a joint by then. Comes with the territory, if you know what I mean.

I walked home the way I came. Through the Castro, down

Eighteenth, into the Mission. I got a room in a hotel on Van Ness. More like a fucking rat hole. Jesus. Anyway, the first thing I did when I got back to my place was slip Gabriel into my boom box. Peter. Peter Gabriel. The fucking musician man! Fucking cool bastard. I swear he can read my thoughts.

So, I'm in my room. Next, I pour myself a glass of booze. Bourbon. That's my drink. Bourbon. Then I pull out my crystal from under my mattress and do up a line. I probably lit up a another joint, too. I usually do. With the booze. Weed and booze. Yeah, that's what I did. Lit a joint. Then I did what I do. I went over and sat down in the chair by my window and started checking out the bar. The fucking neon flashes right into my space. Jesus.

*Looking out the window I see the red dusk clear. High upon the red rock stands the shadow with the spear. The land here is strong, strong beneath my feet. It feeds on the blood, it feeds on the heat.*

She always shows up around eight. Usually she's all decked out in a dress, with heels, a wig. The whole nine yards. A fucking freak, man. A motherfucking freak, I'm telling you. Maybe the first time I saw her, I thought she was a real lady. I mean she's good. Real good. But, you can tell, you know what I mean. You can tell. Anyway, I can tell. So, anyway. Yes, I knew he was a guy. But Jesus, he sure looked like a lady.

*The rhythm is below me. The rhythm of the heat. The rhythm is around me. The rhythm has control.*

I cranked up Gabriel and started getting ready.

*Drawn across the plain lands to the place that is higher. Drawn into the circle that dances round the fire.*

I remember that before I left I washed my hands.

*We spit into our hands and breathe across the palms.*

By the time I walked into the bar I was fucking cooking, man. I was fucking cooking.

*The spirit enters into me and I submit to trust.*

No, I'd never been in the place before. Never. I told you. I don't go that way. I just don't fucking go that way.

*Coyote calling. It has begun.*

The first thing I did was walk over to the bar and order myself some of their top-shelf shit. Then I paid for my drink and went over to a table that was in a corner. Before I sat down I turned my chair so as I'd have a good view of the place. I always do that. Cover my back. Keep the spaces open. Then I tipped back in my chair. I could feel my dick stirring. Getting hard. Getting ready. It does that, you know. Like it's talking to me or something.

*Something moving in. I tasted it in my heart and in my mouth. It feels like dying.*

She was sitting at the bar all dressed up like a fucking woman. Jesus, it wasn't weird. The whole thing was fucking weird.

She made the first move. Not me. Walked right over to my table. Bold as brass. I'm telling you. It was like she knew I was coming or something.

"Hay Baby." That's the first thing she said to me. "Hay, Baby." Like it was normal to call a guy like me "Baby." Then she slipped into the chair next to me, crossed her legs, leaned forward, and asked me to light her cigarette. I remember because I saw her tits. Did you think they were real??

"Got a light, Sugar?" That what she said. "Got a light, Sugar?" *They feed you scraps and they feed you lies.*

At first I just sat there. I mean she scared the shit out of me. *They put you in a box and you can't get out...*

But she kept on. Pressed her thigh against my leg. Wrapped those long fingers around my arm. Jesus. I didn't know what to do. *The light is the strength that pulls me through the fear.*

So, I reached into my jacket pocket, pulled out my lighter, and lit her cigarette. *I hold the light.*

I remember the flame. And the red sequins on her dress. I remember staring at her. Sure, I was scared. Jesus, who wouldn't have been?

That's when she put her hand on my dick. Dug those nails in.

"What the fuck is the matter with you?" I said. Real loud. So's no one in that place would get the wrong idea about me. Jesus. She scared me. I wasn't expecting the bitch to be so pushy.

I remember she grinned at me. Like I was some kind of fool or something. Or like it was all a big joke. My being there. I remember she turned and looked at the bartender who was wiping off the bar. The two of them smiled. Like they had some kind of secret or something.

Sure, she pissed me off. Wouldn't she have you? Like I was a fool. I remember she leaned back in her chair, took a drag of her fucking sissy cigarette and just stared at me. Like she was trying to figure something out.

*Hold the line. Hold the line.*

That's when she said it. "Mama will take good care of you if you let her." Just like that. Jesus.

*The pushing of people. Such a mass emotion. Do not know where it goes.*

I told her right out that she wasn't my fucking mother. But she kept on. Teasing me. Making fun. Rubbing my dick. Saying that mother shit.

It was her idea to go out into the back alley. Not mine.

*All those introductions. I never miss a cue.*

No, I don't know what time it was. I told you I don't wear a watch. All I remember is the sound of her heels and that red dress. And the smell of her perfume.

Sure, I thought about grabbing the bitch by the hair and...but I didn't. I kept it together.

*They tell you how to behave. They take you to your limits. For all that they are doing there is no way to respond.*

We did it in the back alley behind the bar. Yes. Up her ass. *Up her fucking ass!!!* Is that loud enough!!! Jesus, can't you hear me. I blew my wad so fucking hard, so deep that I swear it came out her mouth.

Yes, that's when I slit her throat.

*Suffocated by mirrors. Stained by dreams. My hand moves out. And I have the touch.*

I didn't mean to cut her so deep. Jesus. No, I'm not saying I didn't mean to cut her. But, Jesus. I cut her so deep that her head almost fell off her shoulders. Jesus.

*Wanting contact.*

Oh Jesus. I swear I didn't mean to cut her so deep. Afterwards, though, I made sure I held her close. I made sure I held her so her head wouldn't rip off.

*Stroke my hair.*

I made sure her wig didn't come off either. And I didn't let her dress get messed up either. Do you hear me? I knew she wouldn't like getting dirty or nothing. Did I tell you she was pretty? I mean in her own kind of way.

No. No. I didn't run or nothing. Some boys who were passing on the street saw us. They said what? That I was rocking her in my arms? And crying? Well, sure. I probably was. "Sobbing," they said? Hmm…sure, they are probably right.

*And the tears flow down my swollen cheeks.*

I remember telling her I was sorry. And trying to put her wig back on. Did I tell you that? And trying to make sure her head didn't come off.

"Crying like a baby," they said.

Jesus. I didn't mean to cut her so deep. Did I tell you that already?

# Obsession and Devotion

Obsession has always been at the heart of sexual writing. Traditional psychoanalytic writings have tended to view sexual obsession as a negative experience—as a problem, an emotional regression, or lack of sexual development. But obsession can also be viewed as much more: a celebration of sexuality, a way of discovering alternative modes of sexual expression, an attempt at breaking away from culturally enforced sexual repression, even as a way to worship a higher, idealized form—be that God or an unobtainable love object.

Gay people are constantly told to deny, repress, and disown their sexual desires. When we do not, we are often told that we are "obsessed" with them. When we vocalize them, we are told that we are "flaunting" them. When we defend them, we are told that we are making too much of an issue. Basically you can't win. The very concept of "obsession" is part of a system of thinking that would deny gay people their sexuality.

One of the gifts of obsession is that it gives us the time and the ability to ruminate over our sexuality. Jean-Paul Sartre, in his introduction to Jean Genet's *Our Lady of the Flowers*, describes the book as an obsessional, masturbatory fantasy: "a controlled waking dream" in which the author mediates his elaborate sexual fantasies with the very act of writing and producing them. "The emotional pattern begets the image, and Genet, like an analyst, discovers the emotional pattern. His thought crystallizes before his eyes; he reads it, then completes and clarifies it. Whereupon reflection is achieved, in its translucent purity, as *knowledge* and as *activity*." Simply put: Obsessional thought and writing is a form of sexual meditation that grants us both insight and power. The two pieces in this section examine "obsessions" in both conventional and unconventional contexts. They celebrate the obsessional urge, but at the same time attempt to delineate the shape, form, and parameters that drive and fuel it.

Samuel R. Delany has been one of our most noted speculative writers for more than three decades. His novels, *Dhalgren* and *The Bridge of Lost Desire*, as well as the multi-volume Neveryon series, have transformed how we write and read science fiction. *The Mad Man*—with its contemporary urban setting and its insistence on detailing contemporary issues of sexuality and identity—is something of a departure for Delany. John Marr, its African-American narrator, is an academic in search of the secret life of Timothy Hasler, a Korean philosopher who died a decade earlier. As Marr uncovers more and more details about Hasler's life he finds himself drawn into relationships, activities, racial and sexual obsessions he never imagined. This excerpt from *The Mad Man* recounts one of Marr's adventures. The extreme physicality and graphic descriptions of Marr's sexual exploits are, for Delany, a way to examine not so much the limits of human erotica and experience but the very nature of them. As Marr's sexual encounter with white homeless men careers into the most transgressive of territories—shit, piss, racialized language, public sex—it is clear that the author is taking on more then simply detailing a sexual activity. *The Mad Man* is a critique and an indictment of how we live today.

It is about social and personal boundaries, sexual repression, conflicts between the private and the public, and a profound examination of what it means to have, and maintain, an identity in a world that increasingly demands conformity.

Walta Borawski's "The J Poems" are an eight-month record of a sexual and romantic obsession. Like Dante's poems to Beatrice, "The J Poems" detail the poet's desires and hopes, his fears, regrets, and longings. As the poet roams through the streets hoping to "run into" the object of his love, as he leaves him messages and notes, even attends early morning Mass to glimpse his *inamorato*, the search becomes more than simply about tricking, or sex, or even love. If Dante's poems were written with the great plague of the Black Death as their background, so are Borawski's. As a person living with AIDS, Borawski's obsession takes on new meaning. Is this going to be his last great love? Can intense sexual desire mitigate, even for a little while, his feeling of imminent mortality? Is this obsession—bordering on unstinting and unrequited devotion —a sublime plea for physical or even rational transcendence; an escape from the all-too-palpable realities of AIDS? Is the very act of writing the poems—transforming the object of desire into an object of art—an attempt to leave a lasting, permanent record of his desire and his life after his death? "The J Poems" are a record of sexual obsession, but they are also a testament to the desire to live and the desire to create, the need for love and the need to transform one's life, emotions, and sexuality in the face of death. Walta Borawski died of AIDS-related causes on February 9, 1995.

# from *The Mad Man*
## *Samuel R. Delany*

It was that first week toward the end of June '90 when, as I looked out the living-room window, I could see, down on Amsterdam, that finally New Yorkers had relaxed into their shorts and short sleeves, deciding spring really had settled into summer. I had watched myself turn twenty-nine—the age of Hasler at his death—then thirty, when I was a year beyond Hasler. Only last month, I'd turned thirty-one: two years older than Hasler had ever been. Surely I was beyond whatever had been so dangerous as to bring about his destruction.

"Phel," I said, "I'm probably going to take a little walk. And maybe I'll drop in to see you, later this afternoon."

"All right," he said, at the other end of the phone. "I'll probably be here."

Earlier, the weather report had been something about possible showers, but then I stepped out on the stoop, looked up at pale, lucid blue—and just laughed. The air above and between apartment buildings was drenched in sunlight.

In a way, it started like something out of a Mack Sennett comedy. As I was crossing Broadway, from the Burger King's glass door, I saw this guy in his maroon uniform something between shove and throw this kid, who was wearing neither shirt nor shoes: "Now get the fuck out of here—!"

The kid—that is to say, he looked about twenty—hit the sidewalk staggering, stumbled into the wire trash basket on the corner. Both he and the basket went over into the street.

For a moment, twisting around, he half sat on it; then, as it rolled, he slid down. That would have hurt anyone's back, and the kid went: "*Arrhhhh!*"

Right behind the uniformed guy who had given him the toss stood a man in a dress shirt with a maroon tie that had the Burger King insignia on it—the manager—who called now, upset: "You're a fucking pervert, is what you are! We've got women in here. And kids, man! Get the hell out. And don't come back in here—I'm serious, now! You keep away from this place!" He rubbed a finger nervously under his nose; then, with a hand on the uniformed worker's shoulder, he went inside.

The kid slipped down all the way, so he was sitting in the street—as the basket rolled away from behind him, I heard his head go back against the wire. Then he went over, to lie on his side.

His big hands were very dirty. So were his feet.

He was white. (Both the uniformed guy at the Burger King and the manager weren't.) His hair was curly and brown, on the stringy side, and getting on toward neck length.

I saw, up on the curb, a couple of people passing look down at him. But nobody stopped.

The basket reversed its direction and rolled back up against him—spilling trash all the way; one end swung around his head and clunked against the curb.

Through reflex, I grabbed up the metal rim and yanked the trash basket upright. The kid turned over now. Across pimples and freckles on his back, a red lattice from where he'd rolled down the metal marked his shoulder and flank with crossed diagonals.

Lifting the trash basket had been automatic. With the kid, though, it wasn't. About to step over his outstretched arm, I looked down: he had big, heavy feet and hands; and, as I looked, his broad fingers curled up. Short and dirt dark, of a length beyond the quick exactly that of the thickness a medium-point felt-tipped pen would make, pressed to the paper, had it marked the forward rims of his nickel- and dime-sized nails, those nails were neither long nor short. His street life would with time, I suspected, take them down farther. I walked seven, eight, nine steps along the curb and beyond him.

Then I thought, What the fuck is *wrong* with you?

I turned around—and didn't go back to him.

I stood, looking, while he kind of rocked in the gutter and, after a moment, drew up one knee. He was wearing a pair of dark blue pants (not jeans), dirty to the point where I wondered if they weren't really black; and too big. He straightened his leg again.

Another clutch of people walked by—six guys in different-colored shorts, talking together, who didn't even glance down.

Thinking about going over to help him, while the sunlight clutched the back of my neck like warm fingers, I actually felt scared: that coldness at the throat's base when you're about to do something no one else is doing, or wants to do, or would approve of if you did: the feeling before swiping something or starting to sing in the street or going over to help some homeless guy tossed out on the sidewalk.

I *hate* that feeling more than anything.

I walked back to the corner, stepped off the curb over black water trickling in the gutter, and squatted. "You okay?"

The kid got his head up, to feel around on the tarmac with one palm. "I hit my back...on that fuckin'...." He pushed himself further up, and grimaced.

One middle tooth was broken halfway off, unevenly.

"On the trash basket," I said. "Does it hurt?"

Then the guy in the maroon uniform, lurking inside Burger King's glass door, opened it again and leaned out. "Don't *help* that guy, man! He's a fuckin' pervert!"

"Well," I said, loudly over my shoulder, "so am I. I suck a lot of dick, myself."

The guy in the uniform didn't look put out so much as confused. Frowning, shaking his head in his yellow cap, he stepped back inside and let the door swing closed.

I shook my head, too.

The kid moved his shoulder. "I don't think I broke it." He was trying to grin: I realized that was supposed to be a joke. His gray-green eyes were set within dark lashes. Against his spring sunburn, his eyes looked a little startled, and a little crazy. The face around them was one of those weasely white-guy faces, though he was fairly muscular in a lean and stretched-out way.

He got one knee up, swung the other around underneath, and with one hand clawed down at his crotch.

"What were you doing inside that got them so twisted out of shape?" I asked.

"I wasn't doin' nothing man." He kept rubbing. "I was scratchin' my dick, that's all!"

"Can you get up?" I asked.

"Yeah." He put his other hand on my shoulder. "I think so."

With an arm around his waist, I helped him stand, getting him back to the curb.

"Yeah," he repeated. "I'm okay." But he didn't let go of my shoulder.

"You go in there for something to eat?" I asked.

"Sure," he said. "But I couldn't get nothin'—I was just sitting there, waiting for somebody to finish."

I'd seen the Burger King gambit: a homeless person goes in, sits in the corner, and when a few people leave without busing their places, he or she quickly circuits the tables, picking up any half-eaten Whoppers, burgers, or red cardboard holders of french fries—to leave moments later and stand on the corner, where we stood now, shoving the food in her or his mouth, chewing doggedly. Sometimes you'd see the idea get to one of them, who'd suddenly turn and throw the rest into the trash basket (the wire one the kid had knocked over), and scuttle off. Sometimes, yes, it was because they'd eaten enough. But sometimes you could see them realize they were standing on a corner, eating junk-food that kids and their mothers and off-duty policemen and old men with pensions had half-chewed—and they couldn't put any more in their mouths. I said: "You want some cold cuts, man? Some fruit, maybe a piece of cake or something? I'll get you something from the Red Apple over there."

"Yeah?" He had a kind of smell, like the inside of a closet where leather coats and old shoes had been stored. "That'd be real nice of you, man." He was still holding onto my shoulder and leaning close. "'Course, what'd be even nicer is if you got us a couple of bottles of beer—the big bottles, you know? Forty ounces? That's the cheapest way to get it."

I looked at him a moment. He was about half a head shorter than I was. His expression was confused and hopeful and cocky and scared—even as he held on to me. I said: "Okay—beer. And…what? Bologna? Salami?"

"Bologna, man! That's my fuckin' favorite!"

"You got it. Come on, wait for me outside the store over there."

"Oh, man!" As we started across the street, he released me. "You really gonna get us some eats and some beer? Man, that's real nice of you. That's real nice."

"Don't worry," I told him, as we stepped up the far corner. "I'll take it out in trade."

He barked a laugh, reached over and squeezed my shoulder again: "You got it!"

"You wait here," I said. "I'll be out in five minutes."

At the gate-covered door, I glanced back.

He'd gotten down on the sidewalk beside the building, big fingers splayed on hot pavement. With people walking around him on the sunny avenue, he was doing push-ups!

Inside, the air conditioning was knife cold. I got a yellow plastic package of bologna from a row of packaged cold cuts hanging on a white wall, and two hard rolls from a clear plastic bin behind the checkout counters, a couple of nectarines from beside a slope of summer citrus, and two Bud tallboy six-packs—substantially more than in a pair of forty-ounce bottles.

Behind a ratty little black guy returning two red-white-and-blue plastic shopping bags full of cans, I paid the sixteen dollars it came to for them at the checkout line (and realized I'd expected it to be about two dollars less; but that was Red Apple; fortunately I'd just come from my bank's ATM machine), and after the sullen, overweight cashier in the scarlet uniform and the big gold (plastic) earrings loaded them into a paper bag for me, I carried them through an aisle whose walls and floor were shaled with fliers and trampled sale newspapers. The electric door was still not working when I shouldered back out into summer.

Leaning against the plate-glass window backed with red-and-white "sale" signs, the kid had his outer arm down between his legs, moving it up and down as though he were scratching his flank with his elbow. Blinking in the shadow of the supermarket's marquee, he stood up: "Shit"—he looked at the bag—"you got a fuckin' *week's* worth of groceries!"

"Lunch," I said. "That's all. Let's go over to the park—where we can stretch out and get comfortable.

"Oh, yeah." He fell in beside me, hooking his hand over my shoulder again. "Want me to carry?"

We turned the corner, heading toward Riverside. "Sure." I handed the him the bag. "Here you go."

He took it, looking in the top. "Hey, you really got some beer!" He looked up at me, surprised.

"That's what you asked for."

"Yeah," he said. "But I wasn't sure you were really gonna do it." Holding the bag against his naked chest with both arms, he moved up beside me till his arm was pressed against mine, hotter than the sunlight. "Were you serious about takin' it out in trade—that thing you told the guy, about suckin' dick?"

"Never more serious in my life."

"God *damn!*" He hefted the grocery sack once more. "I guess I fuckin' lucked out today!" Now the sack went to his far arm, and for the third time, with the near hand, he grasped my shoulder. "Thing is, I'll tell you now, I don't usually go with most cocksuckers," he explained. "Not that I got anything against it, man. I mean, I love to get my dick sucked—more'n just about anything! But most cocksuckers, man, they suck you once, maybe twice if you're lucky. Then it's 'So long,'"—his hand left my shoulder to flip on ahead— "'See ya!'" It came back. "And that just drives me crazy, man! I need it three, four—" He scowled and shook his head—"maybe even five, six times. Or I just can't take it. I go a little crazy, you know what I mean? I mean, you ain't like that, are you? You bought all this food and beer. You wanna hang out together for a while, do me a few fuckin' times, huh? Right? Otherwise, you wouldn't've bought all this shit! Just once, man, and it makes me feel goddamned awful. I mean, it makes me feel like I'm sick—I shouldn't have even got started, you know what I mean?" We neared the corner of West End Avenue, as usual all but deserted. "I mean, I got a big dick. Cocksuckers are always tellin' me what a great dick I got. Got me some big balls, too." As we reached the sunny corner, he looked up and down the street. "Here—lemme show you!" Again his hand dropped from my shoulder; with thick, dirt-dark fingers, he pulled down the brass tab on his zipper, and, with a slight bend of the knees stuck his hand inside his fly, to haul out a…fucking sausage— uncut. A pair of nuts tumbled out beneath, bigger—I'm not kidding —than the two nectarines in my bag. (And the nectarines weren't small.) His cock—soft—was too long to stash in one of the sixteen-ounce beer cans, nor would there have been much leeway in the diameter, getting it in. He held up his meat by the middle for me to see. "How you like that?" He let it all flop down, still out of his pants, and gripped my shoulder again—my heart had started to thud, real loud, in my chest, from the surprise. "Cocksucker told me a long time ago, man, if you wanna impress a faggot, just take it out and show what you got. It don't matter where—come on. We got the light."

I had to glance back—and there *were* people passing behind us.

But, true, no one was crossing toward us from the opposite corner. We walked out into the street.

At the end of the next block, though, somebody *was* coming up: a middle-aged woman pushed a flabbily frail-looking man in a wheelchair.

"That's…impressive," I said. "But don't you think you'd better put it away for now?"

"Why?" He leaned closer: "Reach down and grab hold of it! You wanna put it away for me, you can—or you can play with it till we get to the park."

I reached down and took it—really, I was going to shove it back into his pants. But two things stopped me: one, it was incredibly warm—warmer than the sunlight around us. And two, it felt like twice the size I knew it was. But that's probably because I just hadn't spent a whole lot of time walking down the street holding some homeless kid's ten-inch-plus wanger.

"Oh, yeah, man…that feels real good. It's nice to have somebody playin' with your dick, just walkin' out in the street like this."

In my hand, I felt it growing, thickening, lifting—one of those whose natural curve was down instead of up. As we walked, his balls moved under my knuckles.

"That's a dick-and-a-half, ain't it, now?"

"Shit!" I said, hefting him in my hand: "Your cock is so heavy!" It sounded inane; but it felt as weighty as something rubber, filled with hot water.

We reached the far corner.

"Yeah, I know."

In front of us, the wheelchair was still three-quarters down the block. I glanced up. The sun shone full on us, a plate of silver polished too bright to look at. Really, I *started* to push it back in, but the kid leaned over to whisper: "Don't put it away yet, cocksucker. This is a really beautiful day, man. And it feels so good out today—"

"—you think you'll leave it out today," I finished for him.

We'd started down the next block before the park. "That's about where it's at," he said to me. "Hold the fucker for me, man. They ain't gonna see it, I swear!" It was pushing my fingers apart, still getting bigger. But by now, I was afraid to look down at it because I thought I might direct the attention of the woman and the man in the wheelchair toward it—who were about thirty feet in front of us now—if I glanced.

My hand tingled up and down both my sides. I couldn't tell you if I was breathing or not.

And the kid wasn't talking anymore, just holding the bag of beer with one hand and my shoulder with the other.

My hand on his cock began to feel as if it wasn't there—I mean I could feel *him*, like the humongous trunk of some baby elephant. But I couldn't feel my hand on it.

And, like that, I watched this guy with a few blades of gray hair combed across his freckled scalp, wearing thick tortoiseshell glasses, and a black yarmulke on the back of his head, roll up to us in his wheelchair, pushed by this woman in a gray sweater held corner to corner by one of those little pearl chains with a jeweled dog on one side, till they were not three feet away from us on the sidewalk—while somebody thumped rhythmically below my Adam's apple with a forefinger.

Then, without anyone's pointing, or screaming, or sputtering, or even widening their eyes—really, they hadn't looked at *all!*—they were behind us.

I breathed: "…fucking baseball players!"

Moving my hand down his rigid shaft—feeling poured back into my fingers—I fingered the glans inside a foreskin that slid as loosely over the head as parachute cloth might over a golfball; I managed to say, "What the fuck were you *doing* in that Burger King anyway, that got you kicked out?"

"I told you." Again he leaned over to whisper. "Just scratchin' my dick."

"Was it inside your pants or outside"—I sneezed, but it was the sun and nervousness—"when you were scratching it?"

"Started off inside," he told me. "But pretty soon, I guess I pulled it on out—I was beatin' off, where I was sitting, with it under the table in the corner there. Two little girls across from me was watchin' me—and like to bust out gigglin'. One of 'em had her hand down between her legs. I thought she was maybe doin' it, too."

"Would that have turned you on?" I asked.

"Shit," he said. "Anybody doin' it turns me on. An' women can do it a lot easier, too—some of them can just do it by pressing their legs together. Did you know that?"

"No," I said. "Actually, I didn't."

"When I was in the hospital, some girl told me she could do it that way. But in the Burger King back there, this one woman was just starin' and starin'! When I took it out, under the table, and started shuckin' on it, I thought she was really gettin' into it. I think she *was*, too. 'Cause she just watched me, about three whole minutes—*before* she went up to the counter and told the manager. That's when they threw me out."

I laughed. "I think the guy who threw you out of there had to be one jealous motherfucker."

"Yeah, I know," he said. "People've been tellin' me that for years. Even one of the doctors, he told me that. It was suppose to be a joke the way he said it. But I don't think it's a joke, man. I think it's serious. I mean, all my life, *everybody* wants to look at my dick—they always asking me to see it. Because I got such a big one—kids and people, they're always askin' me to take a look at how big it is. This one wants to know how fat my balls are. That one wants to see how far I can shoot any load. The other one wants to know if I use one hand or two hands to beat off—*I* like to use three! Or maybe two and a cocksucker's mouth—that's best!" He grinned over at me. "And I *like* people to see my dick—I *love* playin' with my dick, man. I'm crazy about playin' with my dick. 1 play with my dick all fuckin' day long—or maybe have somebody else play with it, like you—"

Just then, these three guys came around the far corner—three black kids in baseball caps and baggy jeans. And I lost it. I pulled his cock up (which, since the wheelchair guy had passed, was half-soft again), jabbed it back into his fly, and snatched my hand away.

He just chuckled and went on. "I used to play with my dick so much, they put me in the crazy hospital—twice! That's where the doctor told me other guys were jealous of it, which was half the reason it was always gettin' me in trouble, but they don't got to be jealous of it! All they got to do is fall down on their knees and suck it! Then we'll *all* be happy, see?"

"Where was this hospital?" I asked.

"Up near Hyde Park. But my mom lives out in Brooklyn—that's where I'm from."

"I never would have guessed." But his "th's" were closer to "d's" and his "r" had the flatness of those raised on the other side of the river. (The "oil" for "I" exchange, of course, these days you only hear in old movies: probably it has something to do with the homogenization of language by television.)

"Least she used to live out there. I ain't seen her in the longest time. First time they put me away, I was fourteen. I thought they was punishin' me—at first. Then I realized I could sit around my room and beat off all I wanted, all day long. I figured I had it pretty good. By that time, I knew some guys liked to suck on it. Back when I was a kid, I thought it was just *old* guys! Really, I thought that was what old guys was for. *That* was pretty stupid, huh? But I learned quick, no matter what I did, the *doctors* didn't seem to mind—so I'd go in to see a new one with my hand already in my pants, playin' with it. I'd be in the office there playin' with it, and some doctor would ask me, 'Does that feel good?' I'd say, 'Yeah!' Another one wanted to know what would happen to me if I stopped playin' with it. I said, 'I dunno. But I don't plan to find out anytime soon.' Another one said if I didn't stop playin' with it, I couldn't come back and talk to her no more. I said, 'That's all right.' I mean, what would *you* rather do—beat off or talk to some fat old woman with glasses and a purple birthmark all up her jaw? I got this one real old doctor, and I asked him if he would suck it for me. He asked me why. And I told him, 'Cause it *feels* good, motherfucker!'"

One of the three guys coming toward us suddenly kind of stared—then laughed and started pointing. Then they pretty much all started looking and laughing. As they passed, one of them gave us a thumbs-up sign.

The kid was just grinning. I was wondering what that was all about, when I looked down at his pants:

"Oh, Jesus—"

Though I'd put his cock back in his pants, his nuts were still protruding out his fly (the curve of his dick like a third ball on top of the lower two) in their cloud of bronze brown hair.

"—will you put those things away!"

"Whatever turns you on!" He dropped his hand from my shoulder, hooked his thumb in his fly, and flipped his balls back in. Then his hand was up again—though he *still* hadn't zipped his pants. "One of the doctors, he told me: 'You ask everyone you meet to suck your dick. Why do you do that?' I told him, "Cause I really like to get it sucked. Besides, a whole lot of people say yes!' He says to me, 'Don't you realize that's very hostile?' I told him, 'Man, that ain't hostile, that's hopeful!'"

I laughed now. "Well, you didn't ask *me*."

"I didn't *have* to ask you," he said. "It was the first thing you said you was gonna do. Plus you got us some beer and some bologna. Man, I figured I lucked out. You know—" As we reached the corner, he lowered his tone, "—a lot of you stoned cocksuckers, the kind that come and just say right out, I wanna suck your dick, man, they like it if you a take a piss in their mouths. I mean, I've had guys who like to drink the piss right out my fuckin' spout!"

As we walked across the street together, I asked, "Do guys who just come up and say, 'Hey, will you suck my dick?'—do *they* like to piss in a guy's mouth?"

He grinned at me. "*I* sure as fuck do!"

"Well, I don't think that's going to be a problem with you and me," I said. "I'll drink your piss like it was going out of style."

"Oh, man!" He reached between his legs like he was adjusting himself—only, through his pants, he grabbed himself and pulled on it; and pulled on it two, three, four more times. "I was pretty sure you was my kind of cocksucker. And I noticed I didn't have to argue you into gettin' no beer—that's always a good sign."

Stepping between some cars, we started toward the curb. (And he kept pulling.) "Oh, shit!" Looking down, he stopped. "I don't think I can make this." A windshield must have shattered here because the mounded asphalt on the curb was thick with the pea-sized nuggets shatterproof glass makes when it shatters.

I looked at the kid's bare feet. "Come on. Let's go around a little further."

He was still tugging at his pants as we backed from between the cars. We walked around a pair of Dodges and a Chrysler before we turned in to try for the sidewalk again.

"The first time I was in, they turned me out the hospital right at New Year's—that was the year before last," he told me. We stepped between cars again: a handful of years back, the city had torn up all the little six-sided paving stones from the walkway beside the park and replaced them with a Lobby concoction of macadam and gravel spread unevenly up to—and sometimes slopped on top of—the cobblestones still squaring the trees and lining the benches' stanchions. "I had me a coat—but I don't think I had me no shirt under it. I don't usually wear no shirt"—on the sidewalk now, we turned toward Seventy-ninth Street—"but I got me a bottle of beer. I'd panhandled me up a couple of bucks. I was down on Times Square, you know, where all the people hang out. And after I finished my beer, I stood around in the middle of that crowd, with everybody pressin' up against me—and I pissed in my pants! You ever do that—piss on yourself in a crowd?"

"No." Lots of broken glass lay over the sidewalk's graphite-colored mounds. I watched the kid lengthen one step or shorten another, to avoid curved shards. "No, I never did that."

"It feels pretty good, man." He was still pulling at the shape in his crotch. "I had hot piss in both sneakers, man. It was really nice—"

"Until it began to cool off?"

"No, it was still nice! It feels sexy, you know? But then I got me another bottle and took it into one of them dirty movies—on Eighth Avenue?"

"Now, that I've done," I told him.

He hefted the grocery bag higher on his chest. "I went and sat on the side, opened my coat—under one of the lights, so people walkin' by could see I didn't have no shirt on under it: you wanna get your dick sucked, you gotta show some skin. So I drank me some more beer, then I closed my eyes and put my head against the wall and pretended to be asleep. Pretty soon someone sits down next to me, and there's this hand feelin' around between my legs. But soon as he feels my pants are all wet, he gets up and scoots. Two more of 'em come by, felt me up and run off. I don't even open my eyes. But finally somebody sits down and puts his hand there, and don't take it away. He's feelin' my big dick and rubbin' my fat old nuts, and don't seem to care about the piss at all.

"So I open my eyes and look over at him.

"It's this white-haired old nigger—scrawny little black guy in a navy pea jacket, about a hundred years old. Well, maybe sixty, sixty-five. So I lean over and whisper to him, 'I sure hope you wanna suck my fuckin' dick!' He grins and nods at me—this little old black guy. But he has these big, rough hands. I told him, 'I'm afraid I pissed all over myself. Hope you don't mind.' He shakes his head, still grinning. So I say, 'I just might do it again, too—while you're suckin' on it!' And he asks me, 'You want me to take ma teeth out? And I tell him, 'Gee, Pops—would ya'? 'Cause you can't get a better blowjob than from some old guy with all his teeth out! So Pops flips them pink-and-white suckers out his black old mouth and sticks 'em in his pocket. And he goes down on my dick like a trooper. Man, he sucked my cock till they put us out at six o'clock the next morning. I really like that, see? A cocksucker what'll let me stash my dick in his face and leave it there till it really gets to feelin' at home. He got down on the floor between my legs, with his head in my lap. I sat there, drank my beer, and watched the movie—with that black bastard's come all over my sneakers. A couple of times I took me a good long piss in his mouth—he really liked that, too. The first time he swallowed everything—didn't miss a drop. An' I bent over and told him, 'You don't have to swallow it all, man! Gotta let some of it spill around my balls, ya know what I mean?' And he did too cause the next time I had the warmest, wettest balls in New York City! That nigger's mouth was hot, man! I swear, I must've come ten, twelve times—"

"Hey, come *on*—" (He stopped near the waist-high wall.) "You don't have to bullshit me, now," I told him. "I like you fine just the way you are—"

The kid put the grocery bag down on the broad stone. "I ain't bullshittin' you, man! I swear, that's the way I like to do it; ten or twelve loads in a cocksucker what'll stick on my dick for a few hours—maybe seven or eight. That ain't nothin'!" He parked his butt on the wall's edge and swung around to put one big, dirty foot up there with him. "Once, man, I had my hands down on his head and was humpin' that old man's face, only I guess he must a' gone to sleep, if you can imagine that; 'cause when I came, he started coughin' and stuff, and cum run all out his fuckin' nose, all over me. But he *still* wouldn't turn loose my dick! I guess he just woke up, that's all. The next time"—the kid had his hand in his lap, working again—when he said he was tired, I took my dick out of his mouth and jerked off all over his face for that one—that's cool, too." I glanced down: his dick was out of his pants *again!* He sat there, lifting his fist up his towering prong—dropping it again, lifting it again; sitting on the wall, grinning at me. Hunched over the way he was, it went well over halfway up his chest!

I looked left and right. Yes, there *were* people walking toward us and away in both directions—I hoped to hell they were *confirmed* baseball players! I was about to tell him to put it away again—

"I was about ready to marry that old nigger—I swear, man! I was hopin' he was gonna ask me to come home with him in the worst way. But once they turned on the lights to clean out the movie theater and got us up out of there, he cut me loose—I guess nobody wants some crazy snaggletoothed fucker who plays with himself all the time and stinks like dried piss, I don't care *how* big his dick is!" He grinned at me, broken-toothed.

"Well," I said, angling around to the side, to get in the way of whatever the people coming up might see, "maybe he was just a little scared of you, I mean, he's some old black guy. And you're this white kid—"

"Man"—still rubbing his dick, he narrowed his eyes up at me with his head to the side—"how the fuck you suppose to know I'm white? That's fuckin' presumptuous! There're black people as light as I am—don't you know that?"

I frowned at him. But this kid looked *so* white...

"I mean"—and he looked down at himself, dropping his fist into his hair, to waggle himself side to side—"does this look like some white guy's dick to you?"

"Yeah," I said. "More or less—"

"What's that joke they say, man? What's twelve inches long, two inches across, and white?"

"What?"

"Not a fuckin' *thing*, man! You know that. Well, this here is eleven inches when it's soft. Some guy told me it was fifteen and a half hard. He measured it—in fact, a couple of other people took a ruler to it. How could I be white and have a dick like *this*?"

People were coming up by the park wall in the other direction, too—

"I figure that's about half Polack and about half nigger—with maybe some Italian or Scottish or something thrown in." He gave it a few vigorous rubs. "I heard they got some big cocks on 'em, sometimes."

—but they were a little farther away.

"Look," I said, "it's certainly a *big* white dick—it's a Johnny Wadd dick. It's a Moby Dick dick. But it still looks like a *white* dick to me."

He laughed; and took my shoulder once more with his free hand. "Come on," he said. Then he lifted his other foot up on the wall, turned himself around, releasing me, and moved to the back, to put his legs over—and, cock out like a flagpole—pushed off, to drop out of sight. I heard him crash in leaves below.

The grocery bag sat on the stones.

A moment later, his soiled hands—both of them—reached up above the stone wall. (He was too far down for me to see his head.) One hand snapped its fingers. "Gimme the beer," I heard him. "Then get your black ass on over here, sucker!"

I lifted the bag up and handed it to him, then sat on the wall, brought my sneakers up on the stone, and turned to the trees and foliage that was the park. I moved forward to the wall's edge, put one shoe down, glanced down. Inside, six or seven feet below, the leaf-strewn ground at the wall's bottom was actually the top of a thickly wooded slope that dropped away into the park and toward the river—only, more than fifteen feet off, nothing was visible through the trees.

Down behind the wall, the kid was dragging over this big piece of cardboard—like a large air-conditioner carton come open—with the grocery bag sitting on one end of it. Now he grinned up at me.

I pushed off, landed on the cardboard, went down to my knees—lost my balance, and went over on my seat, flailing.

The kid stood, grinning down. The top button on his pants already opened, he pushed the waist down to his thighs, to his knees, then got one leg out completely. "Pretty neat, huh?" He gestured around the woods, backed by seven feet of black stone running off left and right.

On the street, it had been hot. Here, under the trees, it was just warm. I could smell leaves and dust and stuff, which wasn't so bad, here on New York's edge.

His cock was in his hand again, and he pulled on it, overhand and down. "My mother was Scottish—or Irish, or somethin' like that. I think. But I don't know who the fuck my dad was. He *could've* been some black guy, though—I don't know," which kind of came out of the blue, till I realized he was finishing up our conversation from above.

The grocery bag still lay on the cardboard's corner.

"He was probably just one of these little guys who are all dick," I said, from where I was sitting. "You just inherited it—in spades!"

"Yeah." His other foot kicked free; the pants fell to the cardboard. "Man, I just don't like wearin' no fuckin' clothes if I don't fuckin' have to—you know what I mean?"

In a pile there next to his big, dirt-grayed right foot, his pants looked even filthier than they had when he'd worn them. But that's because you just don't usually see people wearing clothes that dirty, and I'd been cleaning them up a little in my mind. He planted his grimed, oversized heels apart, and stood in front of me, grinning down and pulling at his cock. "Nice, huh? You like it?"

I smiled; I nodded.

Suddenly he turned away. "Wanna see a shitty ass, man?" He bent over and the paper bag scrunched and chattered as he rummaged for a beer. "Take a look at mine. Go on—spread it open and take a sniff."

I got up on my knees on the cardboard.

With one hand now, he reached back to tug aside one buttock, reddened with half a dozen pimples. Disembodied like that, pawing at his scrawny butt, his fingers looked immense; I was struck all over again how large his hands, and feet, and (though I couldn't see it that moment) dick—really were.

I said, "Jesus—"

Within the crevice's length was a brown-black crust, matted to his hair either side and cracked across and up and down, like some dried mud reed. I couldn't even *see* his asshole!

"Something huh? You can sniff it, but keep your tongue out of that shit trough, okay? I keep it like that for a friend of mine."

"Don't you ever wipe yourself—"

"Not no more—" Now he stood, turned back around—and the head of his dick, curving down, hit my cheek. "He said I don't have to ever use no more toilet paper—" (Yes, he said "terlit," and that one always gets me) "—as long as he's around. I kind of like that." He took it in his great fingers and began to massage it inside its generous skin. In his other hand he had a beer can. "Here—open that for me?"

Reaching up, I pulled the tab on the can. A little spray cooled my left cheek. "I hope he pays you a lot of money."

"Naw," the kid said. "This is another homeless guy—like me. I wouldn't take no money, anyway—not no more than a penny. And he just likes to eat shit—that's all. I sleep up here, usually, and he comes around, every night—pulls down my pants, and laps out my shit-hole till it's clean as can be." He raised his can and took a drink, while his large, soiled knuckles, working on his cockhead, brushed my cheek. "Dirty as it is when I go to sleep, every morning I wake up with the cleanest asshole you ever seen. That's real nice, man, havin' someone come up at night and eat out your ass. Sometimes, when he wakes me up doin' it, I jerk off a couple of times while he's down there lickin' it out. So we got an agreement— I don't wipe my ass no more when I take me a shit. I don't even go in the shitter now—it's like pissin' on myself. It feels sexy. I just go and sit somewhere, on a bench or something, and pull my pants down and take me a shit. I like to sit in it, and wriggle around a little—and beat off a few times, you know? I do that in the morning, before anybody gets up. Then, at night, this guy comes around and cleans it up. Pretty cool, huh?"

"If it's your thing," I told him.

"He don't suck no dick, though. That's the only thing wrong with him. But—hey, now I got you, I don't have to worry about that. Come on," he said, looking down at me. "Give my big old dick a kiss."

So I did. Very gently, on its heavily veined side.

Immediately he squatted in front of me, still pulling at himself. "Now, why don't we have some of that there bologna and drink some beer together; then we can really have some fun." He took another swig from his tallboy. "It's better, though, if I just beat off the first time—you can watch, I don't care—just to get some of the pressure off, you know? Then you can have everything else that comes out of this all-day sucker, man. I mean, once I get rid of that first load, it's all yours." Now he dropped to sit—right in front of me. His foot went right into my jeans crotch. While he reached over for the grocery bag, through my jeans he kneaded my hard cock with his toes.

He dragged the bag back and came out with a roll. "Here, you want this?" He handed it to me, pulled out the other one. Now he put his beer can down on the cardboard; and, holding the bag rim with one hand, he went in with the other.

He came out with the yellow plastic bologna package, already ripping it apart. He fingered out a slice, which collapsed into a bologna-colored flower that he shoved into his mouth, pulled out a second slice—his balls, out of their hairy cloud, in front of him on the cardboard, were the color of the lunch meat—and shoved that in with the first, then tore off a bite of roll. Chewing, he looked at me again, and asked, through crumbs: "You want some?"

"Sure," I peeled a round slice off the pile from under the transparent plastic cylinder he'd ripped apart. "When's the last time you ate, anyway?"

He shrugged, grinned—"I dunno"—and chewed. "Yesterday, sometime. Out here on the street, you can't pay too much attention to when you eat or not. Otherwise, you get pretty unhappy. Know what I mean?"

"Yeah." I nodded. "I guess so."

"But I could tell you everywhere I jerked off—in the park and out of it, in the last three days!" He turned to swipe up his beer can again. The bologna package was lying beside his knee. His roll, a third of it eaten, was on the other side of him. His leg was still jackknifed up between us. "About three o'clock in the morning, I did it sitting out on the bench on the island in the middle of Broadway. Right in front of the Burger King, where we was before. Two people come by while I was doin' it, but there weren't no policemen. So they just looked for a little bit and didn't say nothing." His toes were still moving through my pants. He took another swallow—and I reached forward to brush crumbs off his chin; then a few others off his chest.

"Go on—that's right." He grinned his broken-toothed grin. "You can touch me. Anywhere you want—that's okay. Put your hand under my balls and tickle 'em."

I eased forward a little more and slid my hand beneath his heavy testicles, which were too big for my palm, so the one on the right kept rolling out between my thumb and forefinger, and I would thumb it back; my hands aren't particularly small, either.

He drank some more beer—we were close enough that I had to lean back to let him raise the can between us.

His other hand was down on the thick shaft of him, a knot of knuckles and fingers and nails and rough, soiled callus, rising on his long, long cock, and falling again; and rising again; and falling.

"You wanna suck my dick, doncha?"

I nodded.

"You wanna suck it so bad you can already taste my fuckin' cheese, right?" His voiced dropped to a tone like troubled gravel. "It tastes salty, man. That's the kind of dick taste you like, don't ya', cocksucker?"

I nodded again.

"You're a fuckin' scummy-mouthed cocksucker, ain't you?" His fist moved faster. "Ain't you?"

"Right. You got it." I put my hand on his shoulder; I moved the other one under his balls.

"Oh, yeah…that's nice. I wanna come for you, cocksucker. I wanna come for you a lot—a whole lot of times. I wanna come in your mouth; I wanna come in your face; I wanna come all over your nigger-nappy hair—" He looked down at himself; his hand was moving fast enough now so that the details had vanished.

I felt something cold; he'd put the beer can up against my face, to pull me closer.

"It feels real good, jerkin' off for you, man—this is probably the biggest fuckin' dick you'll ever suck on. And I been learnin' how to make cocksuckers feel good ever since I was a fuckin' kid, man. Since that's about all I fuckin' can do, I'm really into doin' that good. Jesus, playin' with this big dick feels so good!" He looked up at me again. I could see his jaw shaking with the movement in his right shoulder. I could feel his quickening rhythm through his foot against my groin. "I love to jerk on my dick, man—all the fuckin' time, all day long, all year long. That's all I ever wanna ever do, man—jerk off and fuck some cocksucker's face. Comin' feels so fuckin' good, man! It feels *soooo* fuckin' good! Lemme see some tongue, lemme see that hole I'm gonna be stickin' this big old fucker in, that's right—open it up and lemme see that nasty black suck-hole. Show me how you gonna lick around under it, and tickle my balls with your tongue—that's right. Oh, man, that's fuckin' hot! That's fuckin' hot, 'sucker—that's really turnin' me on. Man, this fucker's gonna shoot in a goddamned minute, 'sucker! It's gonna shoot like a motherfucker!" Now his face was down, now it was up. He was hunched over, beating hard as he could, only then the beating got even harder. "Oh, shit! Oh, fuckin' shit…that's so fuckin'…fuckin' horny, man! Fuckin' horny motherfucker!"

If somebody took a two-thirds-cup measure from the row of decreasing-sized aluminum cups I have hanging over my sink, filled it half up with egg white and half with heavy cream, mixed them, then—just as if I weren't there sitting in front of him—flung it on the kid in three tosses—splurt! splat! splop!—that's what his triple shot was like.

Like four BBs, hot drops hit my jaw and chin.

Cum ran down the kid's forehead from his hair. A big blob of it covered the left corner of his mouth. A line of it beaded from his right eye's upper lashes to the lower, to streak on down his cheek. His chest was splattered all over—a glob covering his left nipple eased away from his teat, down his ribs. I looked at his bronze bush, speckled and draped with mucus. Still stiff, his whole dick was slick with it. Pearls of cum rolled over his knuckles, down the back of his fist. Cum puddled under his balls, in my palm.

Breathing hard, opening his green eyes, he grinned at me again. "…and you got about half a dozen more of them loads to come, the next one right inside your face!" He thrust out his tongue to lick cum from the corner of his mouth. "What you laughin' at, nigger? You got cum on *your* face, too!" He took three more deep breaths. "You can have this load, if you wan—somebody's gotta eat it. You, me…" He sounded matter-of-fact about it. "Go on. Stuff's too good to waste—and it makes you healthy. Some guy told me that when I was a kid. Go on—eat it off me."

I looked down. On his jackknifed leg, cum slid in two trickles down his calf. On the instep of his foot, and strung across the dirty knuckles of the first three of his big toes, still working on my crotch, were two globs of it.

I felt the beer can, still cold on my neck, pull me forward. And looked up—and licked the blob off the corner of his mouth. His breath was bologna and something else. And he turned to stick out his tongue against mine. The heel of his thumb slid—rough as some cement worker's—over the back of my neck as I lowered to lick some of it off his chest. He was salty—strong salts, too. Above me, I heard him say, "You're gettin' close to the good part, now."

The beer can left my neck. I saw him set it on the cardboard. A moment on, he reached between his legs with his free hand (the other, cum-bright, worked slowly on the base of his still-erect meat) and pulled my hand out from beneath his nuts. As he sat back, he raised my melanin-dark fingers in his dirt-grayed ones, to drop his face into the pearly smear roiling there. I felt his tongue, warmer and softer than any cat's, lap the pinker palm. And lap again. And again. His lips dozed together, now at the heel, now at the ball, and now in the pooled center. The wet wad of his tongue nudged between my knuckles, slipped across the skin stretched from forefinger to thumb, flicked my wrist where some had rolled. Looking up as he licked, he blinked. Then he raised his face, slick from nose to chin. "You eat cum, and it keeps you from gettin' sick. I guess that's why cocksuckers suck cock, huh? And livin' out in the park, you gotta keep real healthy. I don't suck no cock, man. I am *not* a cocksucker! But I'll eat cum—especially my own. Sometimes I drink my own piss, too. Though somebody else eatin' it and drinking for me is really better, you know?" He chuckled suddenly. "I'm a fuckin' pervert, like the guy said!" Dropped his face to my hand to lap once more, then let it go.

I reached down to take his foot in my hands—and lifted it from my crotch. The sole was rough as board. Inside my pants, my groin tingled where the pressure of him had been. As I raised his big, dirty foot, he went back, to lean on one elbow. (The other hand was still at his own cock. And that cock was still slick with cum and hard and curving toward me.) His toenails were the same worn-down length as the nails on his fingers, with the same dirt beneath. I glanced up at him. Quite seriously, he watched me as I dropped my mouth to eat the cum off his foot.

"You wanna suck my toes, man, that'd be great. I love to get my toes sucked."

"I know someone who really would have liked you," I said. But, then, how would I have explained to a kid like this about Hasler? (But then, maybe I wouldn't have had to.) His toes were rough—and salty, too. I moved on up to what drooled his calf.

He was leaning back on the cardboard, waving his cock from side to side—"See, it's waitin' for you, 'sucker. And it ain't gone soft at all. Get the cheese first, now—oh, shit!"

That was when I dropped my mouth over his cum-slicked head and pushed beneath his skin with my tongue. Troweling smegma from where it was packed thick in the trough circling beneath his glans, I took him all the way down to his scummy fist. (Above, I heard him gargle more beer.) His hand left his cock. And I went down another inch, to where his wet hair pushed against my face—and though my throat was completely blocked, it still wasn't all the way. With wet fingers on my right cheek and dry ones on my left, and his thumbs over my brow, he held my head, and we rolled to the side. He began to hump, at first only filling my throat with half or three-quarters of that fifteen-inch shaft. But after a few plunges, I got a big breath in and thrust my face all the way into his crotch, taking it to the base—"Oh, *shit*, man!" and let him get in four, five, six total thrusts, before I backed off again, to get in another breath.

Pretty soon, we got this pattern, with him taking five or six three-quarter thrusts, while I breathed—and then six or seven full thrusts, to the root—while I didn't. About the second cycle of that, he grunted, "Don't let me kill you now, cocksucker! You're too fuckin' good; and I done almost choked a couple of cocksuckers by accident!"

I just nodded, and we kept it up that way. It was pretty intense. But the kid knew what he was doing. I guess if you have meat on you like that, you learn—or you *do* kill a few cocksuckers!

His speed increased.

Then one hand came away from my head, the other slipped behind it; he grabbed the base of his cock and began to slam in hard with each blow. His fist made a collar I couldn't get past, but even so I was taking nine of fifteen inches, each thrust, every thrust. You just assume—at least I do—that most guys' second loads are going to take twice as long as their first one. But it wasn't the case with this kid. He shot—I felt it in the back of my throat. He pulled out, squirted twice in the front of my mouth—and, I swear, fucking filled it up. Then he went deep in and squirted again. I swallowed, and gasped, and come rolled out over the bony knot of his fist.

He was taking big, deep gasps—when he released his cock and brought his hand up to his face. Without letting his shaft go, I looked up. Lying on his side, he licked the stuff off his fingers; maybe, with him, there was always going to be some extra. Near his shoulder, two beer cans lay on their sides, empty, by a half-eaten roll. A little ways away, another stood upright on the cardboard. Finishing with his fingers, he reached over, got the upright can, and took a long swallow—while I wondered where the hell he'd gotten time to drink a whole second can of beer.

But then, I'd been pretty busy down there.

He put the can down, got my head in both his hands again, and rolled over on his back—not letting me go, so that I rolled over on top of his legs. I had gotten my jeans open and they were halfway down my ass, but that was all. Now he brought one foot up against my cock, so that it lay up along the crevice between his rough sole and his calf. I began to rub—but gently—while he moved his hands, again one wet and one dry, over my face. "Man…now that was a…good suck," he said between gasps.

I took his cock in my hand and came off it (he gave a little grunt), and began to run my hand up and down it, holding it pretty tight. (He let the gasp out, in a comfortable sort of sigh.) "You said you used to drink your own piss," I said. "How did you do that?"

"What do you mean, how?"

"Tell me about it."

He raised his head to look down at me; then he put it back on the cardboard. "I dunno. I'd get me an old cardboard milk container, and open it up, rinse it out—and go down where all the benches are, by the river. I'd sit there, with all the people, usually not too far from the comfort station. Then, when I had to take a leak, I'd stand up, take a couple of steps from the bench out in the road, flip my dick out, and piss into my container. Usually I'd have a fuckin' hard-on but I'm lucky; I can piss pretty much just as easy, whether it's hard or soft. I don't know why, but somehow if you're pissin' into something—a bottle or a milk carton or something, nobody ever stops you. You can be in the middle of the goddamn street. Policemen can even be walkin' by, and as long as you're pissin' into something, they won't say nothing. I wonder why that is?" Lying on his back, he thrust a forefinger, thick as some plumbing tool, into his nostril, dug around, came out with something, and, while I watched, ate it. "Anyway, I'd fill up my milk carton with piss—for me, it's gotta be a quart container. A pint won't hold all my juice, most of the time. Then I'd go back, sit on the bench, wait a few seconds, then take me a big drink out of my carton." He dug in his nose again, found something else in there, and ate that. "You don't wanna wait too long, so it'll still be hot. But then I'd kind of look around and see who was watchin' me." He went back to digging in his nose again.

"What the fuck are you doing?" I asked, from where my head was, down at his crotch.

He glanced down, paused, finger in nose. "What do you mean?"

"What the fuck are you doing?"

"Huh? I'm eatin' my fuckin' snot. What does it look like? You want some? It's good—it's real salty."

"Oh, shit!" I said.

"Naw, come on," he said; this time, with what he scraped out, he thrust his big hand down toward me. "There you go—I just forgot for a moment. I know how to take care of my cocksuckers, man."

I was actually going to take it. But I didn't get a chance to. He pushed his finger into my mouth.

And it was salty.

And it *was* good.

"A couple of years ago," he went on, "there was one guy I used to see in the park here—always dressed real nice. Older guy. He lived right up on Riverside Drive, he said. Said he was an executive in a bank or something." He pulled his big finger out of my mouth and went back up to digging in his nose. "About the second time I did that—pissed in a milk carton, down by the benches, well, he comes over to me, sits right beside me, and says, 'Sure is hot today. I could use a drink of that, if you wouldn't mind.' I asked, 'You know what it is?' And he said, 'Sure. I saw you pissin' in there. That's your piss.' I said, 'Okay, motherfucker. Have a swig—on me.' So he took a long swallow, and said, 'Good stuff.' Then we sat there, passin' it back and forth and shootin' the shit; we talked all sorts of crazy stuff, he was a pretty interesting guy. He tried to gimme some money, too, the first time. But I said, 'Shit, how'm I'm gonna take ten bucks for a couple of swigs from a milk carton full of piss?' We did that about five or six times, too—but that was a few summers ago. I ain't seen him in the park this time. I wonder if he's still all right. But maybe he don't live there no more."

"Did you ask *him* to suck your dick?"

It's funny how even when you can't see somebody's face, sometimes you can hear them grin. "Yup! He said he'd try, and we went into the comfort station there, together. He was kind of scared, though—which is fuckin' stupid 'cause that's what everybody in the place is there for. Only, when it cleared out, he couldn't get it in his mouth. My dick was too fuckin' big! For him to get it in his mouth. I peed on him, though. He said he'd like that, so I did it. But you see, he was this white guy—he wasn't no big-mouthed, woolly-headed nigger like you!" He reached down and roughed my hair; and laughed. "Hey, you rubbin' like that on my leg—don't come yet, will you? Wait till I shoot another load, huh? You come, and you gonna wanna take a rest for a while—I know how you guys are. But I still gotta go some before I can really relax. Here, I got something for you!" And from the head of his cock, still stiff in my flexing fist, from its loose collar of skin, water lifted in a sparkling arch!

I went down on his full yellow stream—and he was holding my head again, wrapping one leg around my shoulder. "Let it spill a little, man, like I told you—all over my balls." Both his hands were wet, now. But I think that was my face. "That's right…that's right…" By now I had both my hands full of his scrawny ass, too, fingertips in his crack (something dry crumbled under them and powdered out), but, hugging him into my face, I didn't care.

Even before his urine ran out, he'd begun to hump. He remembered our rhythm, too. And in three more minutes, he'd shot *another* load—I swear it was as big or bigger than his first. Cum exploded out my mouth, even as I tried to swallow it.

His hands were down there, fingering what ran down his balls up and back up into my mouth, or lifting his big, dripping knuckles to his own mouth. "Oh, shit, man—that was real good. That was fuckin' beautiful, cocksucker!" Once more he rolled me on top of his legs; once more he pulled his foot up against my cock. "You can shoot now…I'm ready to take five." He was breathing hard. I mean the kid put twice the energy most guys do into shooting; and then shot three times as much as anyone I'd ever seen before.

I began to rub—and tasted urine again.

I shot all over his foot.

Yeah, I thought; this kid could have made Tim—or, I suppose, *anyone* who didn't mind a little grub and grunge—happy.

Finally his cock lost about half its hard. I came off him; his whole belly was wet.

There was a little puddle of urine over the blackened whorls within his belly button.

So I licked it out.

Which made him laugh.

He was sitting up now—drinking his fifth can of beer. Again, I hadn't seen him get through the fourth, but four lay empty on the cardboard.

Soon as I rolled off him, the first thing he did was reach down with all his fingers together and wipe my jism from his blackened instep and then run his fingers into his mouth. (He could only get three into it at a time.) "Some black kid was lookin' down over the wall at us, a little while ago. I guess you didn't see him. But that's what got me off the last time. I guess I'm kind of an exhibitionist, sort of." He said it like a considered admission.

"Yeah," I said. "I'd noticed."

He thumbed up some more of my cum off his leg and ate that. "Nigger cum, man—that's the best kind. That's gotta be the healthiest."

I was breathing pretty hard, too, though it was only my first load. "Glad you like it."

"I mean, for makin' you strong and keepin' you from gettin' sick and stuff. Don't you figure?"

"Well, I never—"

But he was pulling over the grocery bag. He jammed another slice of bologna into his mouth. "You want a beer?" He pulled another can loose from its plastic loop and thrust it toward me.

"Sure." I took it.

"And some bologna?"

I opened my mouth and leaned forward.

He started to put it in, then looked down and laughed. Arching forward over his big nuts, his dick was still half-erect. He draped the bologna slice over the head of his cock. "Eat it off my fuckin' dick!"

So I went down between his legs—and while I was getting it in my mouth, he started peeing again. So I got piss down my neck and on my shirt; and the bologna was pretty salty. When I came up, we were both laughing; I popped my beer can and took a swallow.

He looked around, found the roll, and ate more of that. "Hey," he said. "Tell me something."

I was scratching between my legs, where it had grown sweaty with my pants still on. (I was thinking about taking them off.) "Sure."

"What's your name?"

"John," I told him. "What do they call you?"

"Crazy Joey," he said. "That's 'cause I was in the fuckin' crazy hospital. Out on the street, you been in the crazy hospital, and they call you 'crazy.' Crazy Joey. A couple of years ago, one guy used to call me Joey-who-needs-a-bath. Every time he saw me, that's what he'd call me: 'Hey, Joey-who-needs-a-bath!' Which is funny, 'cause my name ain't even Joe. It's Mencus. But just like they call everybody 'crazy' who's been in the crazy hospital, they call everybody who's got a hard name or a funny name or a foreign name Joe or Joey—or John. So they call me Crazy Joey. I don't mind it…. Hey, John?"

"What?"

"I wanted to ask you something—that I don't ever ask nobody till after I dropped my third load in 'im—Mad Man Mike, he told me that. Mad Man Mike and me, we're real tight, see. But I wouldn't even mention his name to you till I'd come three times with you—at least. He told me, sometimes the second time you shoot a load into a cocksucker's face, then they've had enough and they're gonna get up and run off, and you never see 'em again. Guys like him and me, see, we can't take shit like that. Mad Man Mike, he says I'm just like him, when he was a kid. And he told me, don't even bother sayin' anything personal to somebody before the third load—with me, it's three loads and some piss, too. Maybe it's that way with him—he ain't never said. But we're just alike, him and me. Anyway, I wanted to ask—"

"What did you want to ask?"

"Can I turn you out?"

I took another swallow of beer. "What do you mean?"

"Would you like for me to turn you out? Don't you know what it means to turn somebody out?"

"I'm not sure," I said. "I don't think so."

"You know, like when a guy's workin' a bitch, see? And he wants to show her what a good whore she is; so he goes and gets all his friends, see? And they all come up and fuck her—they take turns. Or sometimes they do it all at once. After that, the bitch knows she's really a part of everything that's goin' on with 'em, 'cause she's fucked all the guys at the same time. That's turnin' a bitch out."

"I've heard the term," I said. "But I'm still not exactly sure—"

"I got friends." He nodded deeply. "I got some friends in this park. I could go get some of 'em, bring 'em back here—I could be back in twenty minutes, I bet. And we could all party down—'cause you're a good cocksucker, man. I mean, I know they'd like it. Mad Man Mike—like I say, man: you like me, I know you'd like him. We're real tight, and we like pretty much most of the same stuff, him and me. He knows a whole lot, too, about how to get over, if you're after this kind of stuff. And I was tellin' you about my friend, who likes to eat shit? And Big Buck? He's another black guy—but he's real nice. He's got a big black cheesy dick. You like to suck me, you'd like to suck him—wouldn't you?"

"Well, I don't know," I said. "It sounds kind of complicated, for right now—"

"It ain't complicated. I'd put my pants on, and run right down there—I know where these guys hang out. They like to party just as much as I do." He was standing up now and reached down for his filthy trousers.

"Hold on, now," I said. "Come on, Crazy Joey—there." I reached up and took hold of his cock.

With his pants on one leg, he stopped and grinned down. "Oh, shit…," he said. "The nigger done got me by my fuckin' dick again!"

It had gone down halfway, but not all the way. As I rubbed it though, it began to swell. "You're supposed to be able to come ten times. Let me see you make number four."

"*Awwww...*," he said, real fondly. He turned around to face me, still holding his beer. "Suck it, nigger..."

So, on my knees in front of him, I got his fourth load in what, I swear, had to be under an hour and a quarter since we'd been together.

Sometime in it, his pants came off again. Sitting beside me, after he was finished, he flung an empty beer can off into the trees and asked me: "You ready to go again?"

"Are *you?*"

"*Yeah*, man!" He put his arm around me, and pulled me over. For about three minutes we sat there, wiggling our tongues inside each other's mouths. Then he was pushing me down on him, and his schlong rose up again to prod my face.

We did it three more times after that! Between numbers six and seven, we both lay down beside each other on the cardboard and talked awhile—him mostly about being in the "crazy hospital" and some about living on the street. But he didn't bring up turning me out anymore—for which, I guess, he got points.

"I have to take a leak," I told him.

"Go ahead," he said. "The world's your fuckin' toilet, nigger! And don't forget it—that's what Mad Man Mike says."

Laughing, I got up, went to the edge of the cardboard, and began to pee off the edge into the leaves. A minute later, I felt something behind me; then Joey's hands came around in front of me and joined in my stream. His chin was propped up on my shoulder behind me (and the downcurve of his dick was pressed between my buttocks), and he was washing his hands in my piss. It was a little messy, but it was kind of sweet.

Afterwards, he told me, sucking first one finger, then another, "I piss on my hands every day, man—makes 'em hard. You ever notice how most homeless guys, they have real soft hands, man? Real soft—that's 'cause there's nothin' for 'em to do out here."

(Indeed, it was something I *had* noticed.) "But you piss on 'em, and it keeps 'em rough. For jerkin' off. But sometimes you gotta use someone else's piss besides yours—to change the chemical and stuff, I guess. That makes sense, don't it? Nigger piss, if you can get it. That's cause it's stronger, or something... Like nigger cum. You know anything about that?"

I had to allow I didn't.

"Now, man, I love a nice soft, wet mouth to stick my dick into. But when I beat off, I need me a little friction, know what I mean? That's why I got to keep my hands on the rough side. You gonna suck me off again, now?"

Before we did it this time, I told him, "My jaw is sore, guy!" And it was, the whole underside—but, for some reason, more on the left than on the right.

"Yeah," he said. "But you love it."

"I do."

"And you wanna see if I can really make another load—all in one afternoon, don't you?"

I nodded. "Yeah."

"So you're gonna suck on my big, nasty dick one more time before you go."

"If you're really horny, why don't you beat off one more time—"

"I will if you'll get down there and make love to my balls and dickhead while I'm beating, man. I wanna see you lickin' on it and lovin' it for me."

So I did. And ten minutes later, lying there, grunting and bucking his butt up from the cardboard (dried shit in a kind of black powder on the cardboard made a line beneath his ass), while I pressed my face into his groin and his fist banged at my mouth and cheek, he shot all over my forehead and left eye and ear. Again his heavy, rough fingers wiped it off my face and pushed it into my mouth. He didn't seem to want any of his own anymore.

By this time, I'd noticed, there was hardly any dirt left on his hands—I mean even his nails were clean. Which was a sobering thought.

He rolled a little to the side and slid his cock into my mouth again along with his scummy fingers; after I'd sucked them clean, his hands came up to cage my head and he started humping my face *again*—and, hugging my head practically into his stomach, ten minutes later grunted out *another* load!

When we got our breath back, I told him, "I think I'm going to have to go. I mean, if you're okay...?"

"Sure," he said. "I can stand it now, I guess. I'm gonna have to jerk off a couple of times more before I go to sleep tonight. But at least now I won't get all sick and crazy." We sat together on the cardboard, him still naked; I'd pulled my pants up to go with the last one—then come inside them, when he'd really got to working on this last one. He said, "But you're going to look for me again, ain't you?"

"I...yeah, I think so."

"'Cause now you know what I can do. Right? I ain't bad for a fuckin' pervert, am I?"

"No," I said. "You're pretty good."

"You'll see me around, in the park—sometimes out on Broadway, panhandling sometimes. If they don't clap my ass in the crazy hospital again, for pullin' on my dick. But Mad Man Mike, he says I just gotta do what he says, and they'll stay off me.... They ain't caught me now for a whole long time—almost three months."

"Yeah," I said. "Well, then, you probably should listen to him." I stood up.

"Got something for you, to take with you. For a present." He stood, too. Now he bent down and picked up one of the beer cans, emptied it over his mouth, then turned it up and shook out the last few drops.

Lowering it between his legs and holding his schlong, he aimed for the hole and let his glittering waters go, into the opening; pee roared on the can's bottom. As it filled, the roar grew higher, rising like something not quite a musical note. Then it bubbled over the top, wetting his fingers; so he just moved it aside—dropped his dick—and kept on pissing, stream swinging back and forth from splattering from his right foot to the puddling cardboard between.

He held up the can. "Since we're out of cold ones, you just gonna have to make do with a hot one." He took a swig from the can, then held it out to me. "I'll tell you"—his urine still chattered on the cardboard—"it don't taste like nothing though."

I took it. The can was wonderfully warm. I drank some. "Beer piss." I shrugged. At this point, yeah, it was like drinking hot water. "But at least it's yours."

He pointed off behind me. "You go down along the wall about a hundred yards"—and his dick was just dripping now from the skin: drip-drip-drip-drip-drip-drip…drip-drip…drip-drip…drip…drip… drip—"and it gets low enough so you can climb right back over it."

"What are you going to do?" I asked him.

"Beat off…a couple of more times. Maybe take a nap. Whatever."

"Okay." I looked down at his feet, the left one wet with urine— standing on the piss-darkened cardboard where we'd just been lying. In one large stream and three small ones, urine rolled off the edge. And, yes, I thought about Timothy Hasler. But I didn't get down and kiss his foot or anything, which is probably what Tim would have done. Or thought about doing.

I turned, stepped off the cardboard's frayed edge, and started along beside the park's inner wall. Once I looked back.

He'd stretched out on the cardboard—again doing push-ups!

Crossing Amsterdam Avenue, I was drinking the last of his urine from the can, when, in the middle of the street, one of the homeless Hispanic guys always hanging around the church down the block called to me, "Hey! You ain't supposed to be drinking that on the street…!" It was the heavy guy, who always wore the filthy red cap with the visor pointed backward; he kind of startled me, staggering unsteadily toward me. I got a face full of his winey breath. "You ain't suppose to be drinkin' no beer on the street! Gotta have it in a paper bag—or the cops'll bust ya', man…! You got to go to the bodega over there, ask him for a little paper bag, he give it to you, man. He's nice. You put that in the bag, now— then you be all right, you hear me?"

I just grinned, shook my head, and walked on. (Where those aluminum-colored clouds had come from that now grayed half the sky, I didn't know.) I tossed the can in the wire basket on the corner, and some other homeless black guy in a red cap with a plastic garbage bag over his shoulder swung around and went in after it.

The first raindrops peppered my face and the brown-painted stoop as I reached the door.

By the time I got upstairs and looked out my kitchen window, it had become a real cloudburst. It wasn't six o'clock yet, but it was dark enough for late evening, on its way to night. Outside, Amsterdam Avenue simply exploded with rain.

I made myself a cup of coffee, sat at the kitchen table, and thought about going to look for Crazy Joey, offering the guy at least a place to stay out of the wet. But, frankly, it was raining too hard for me to go back out. And I'd probably have no more luck finding Joey in the rain than I'd had finding a Piece o' Shit that first night five years ago.

I took my coffee in the front room, sat down by another streaked window, picked up the receiver, and punched some buttons on the phone. "Hi, Phel? I'm sorry I didn't get by. But it was such a nice day out—and then the rain and everything—"

"That's okay, babes," Phel told me. "I was out for about an hour myself, earlier. I thought maybe you'd come by when I wasn't here and I'd missed you…"

After we hung up, I sat by the water-beaded pane, thinking: That was about the most interesting, if not the best, sex I'd had in three or four years. I'm not going to put it in a journal. I'm not going to write about it in a letter—and I probably won't even mention it to Pheldon. So how would you go about researching something like that in someone's life?

I looked over at the eleven plastic file boxes—maroon, blue, gray—in two rows along the foot of the bookshelf: more than half of them were filled with material on Hasler.

Suppose I was researching, not the life of some genius philosopher with his books and articles and a wake of articulate friends and acquaintances, but rather, a homeless kid in and out of mental hospitals for chronic masturbation and indecent exposure? (I mean, maybe twice in my life I've seen some guy with a dick that big, jerking off at the movies; but, without making a big thing of it, Crazy Joey's was—yes—the largest I'd ever gotten a chance to wrestle with, as it were, in person.) How would I even start?

A notice in *The New York Times Book Review*? ("I would appreciate hearing from anyone with letters or reminiscences of a mule-dicked white kid called Crazy Joey, or—sometimes—Joey-who-needs-a-bath, late of Brooklyn by way of the state mental hospital at Hyde Park, with green eyes, a broken front tooth, and shit in his asscrack.") Did you go back to the Burger King and ask the manager: "That young man you tossed out of here for masturbating over in the corner last week? While you were throwing him out, he didn't happen to mention his last name or his patient file number from when he was last confined a year or so back, did he?" His real first name, he'd said, was something beginning with M?

Researching Crazy Joey would make researching Mike Ballagio—much less Tim Hasler—look like (my dad would say) "Chopsticks."

As I drank my coffee, gazing out at the streetlights behind the glittering slant of droplets, the downpour smashed into Amsterdam's tarmac, and an unsettling image came to me: naked on his cardboard, the rain decomposing it into mulch around him, Crazy Joey, cross-legged, jerked furiously—rainwater running out his hair, pouring over his shoulders, cascading down his hunched-over back, washing his vertebraes' knobs away, softening his weasely featured face, blunting his knees, dissolving his peach-sized testicles, leaching the green from his eyes, melting away the whites like LifeSavers, sucking at him till he was running, flowing, washing away in the downpour, till there was nothing but his dick and his fist around it, pumping, then only the pistoning of his fist on his cock, when even cock and fist had dissolved to just the pulse, pulse, pulse...

The rain went on all night: really, lying in bed, listening to it—it smacked on the loose window glass at the foot of my bed—I decided that the image was worthy of one of the farther-out entries from Hasler's journals:

A pulse, faintly but firmly repeating, inches from the ground, over some decomposed cardboard below the park's wall, through the night, under sluicing leaves...

Yes, I knew it was only to compensate for the impossibility of the real task I'd envisioned, had anyone ever thought to undertake it. And yet...

# The J Poems
*Walta Borawski*

## Things I Cannot Bring You:

An unsullied past—not that I'd
want to; an uninfected bloodstream
—would that I could—a person

scraped of memories—No, simply
scarred & frightened, a spirit
that waivers, a mouth fearful

of deep kisses, a list of
don't-do's at the ready but also
me, do-do-do, at the ready

*1 January 91*

## I Know Your Name

I see you on your bicycle, it's

a night too cold to ride, I'm
walking briskly with my

train-bound lover I don't
shout your name you turn

into our street you know
where I live Do you

want to see me or
are you picking up

take-home at Cremaldi's?
How do I muster

romance in the face of
HIV infection, daily

terrors & uncertainties,
after several years of

moving in a haze and getting
silly over no one? And what do

you want? You're rather a mystery,
you appear not really happy but

complete in yourself, you smile
at me but no more than you

smile walking or riding by yourself
I've told you more about me than you

have about you, this only feeds my
hyperactive imagination

What are you thinking?
What are you needing?

You coolly say when you've
finished your local studies

you'll move to
New York or L.A.

*New York or L.A.!*
I've not experienced

the interior of your
mind or even your

apartment We've
shaken hands, what we

take away from these
encounters is, I

suppose, our individual
businesses, take-outs,

nourishments we
separately fancy

## Tribute

Flowers you bring me have too
much significance surely you

didn't intend the heather to
root in my heart. Why did

white tulips last two weeks
in aseasonally warm weather?

—Just because I cut their
stem bottoms biweekly, kept

their water clean, lukewarm?

*19 February 91*

## Dishes

Michael left the dinner table
to drive to the airport, his
brother was back from St. Croix.

I looked at you across the
empty dishes & said, I have the
AIDS virus, I'll never

open my mouth flowerlike for
rain to enter another. You had
already made your decision, & I

had clearing to do

*20 February–21 March 91*

## 7 Embarrassments in the Wrong Key

### 1. Impeccable, not Peckable

Catholic University or
repressive parents taught you
posture you can't forget You

don't easily sit or
squat or lie down. Free
weights & Nautilus have

defined rigidity. True,
you are something to behold,
as fine-featured & polite

as any of my acquaintance.
Maybe you'd say Thank You
for a blow job, it's

happened before. Were I
the trigger of your desire
I'd still need the stamina

to unravel the knots
of your good manners

### 2. Amtrak ticket holders
are folders depicting a

toothbrush captioned *Have
you forgotten anything else?*

I remember my name, my address,
my telephone number, the way your

figure gets smaller & your black &
white check trousers turn soft gray

as you retreat. Your wardrobe was
chosen to assist your disappearance

but your eyes & smile belie
understatement of Ralph Lauren

You might as well be wearing
a red silk dress
I cannot forget you

3. Chant

There is no limit
to unrequited love

4. Postcard

Three crows on a winter-
naked tree, Keely Smith
singing Cole Porter's
"I'm in Love Again"

5. Abyss

Sometimes the gap
between who you are

& what I need & made
of you is so wide
so deep I drown

## 6. Remind Me

The image of beloved:
the serious man in beige
trousers standing on the
pedals of his bicycle
hatless on a cold night.
Only a romantic could
be him. Only a romantic
could see him.

## 7. Travel Journal

I was able to follow
all the directions, though they
changed thrice daily & the goal
& the players, too

I was able to find the local
soft rock station to ensure
mushy songs that would
make me think of you

Emotions sprawled
slatternlike on a soft
tired mattress once
the stage of my teenage ecstasy

## Outlaws of Love

I used to think the woman who
repeatedly broke into David
Letterman's home claiming to be

his wife was odd. Now I pretend
you impregnate me before you
leave Cambridge.

*21 February 91*

## Simple Gifts

Many years ago at the Club Baths
in Manhattan I met a dark youth
after hours of lovemaking. He too

was sated before he met me, and we
asked an attendant for a blanket,
it was coarse and gray, and this

young man and I lay on a dormitory
bleacher, with a mirror on the
bottom of the upper tier, four

feet above our heads. As we drifted
off I looked at our reflection and
I knew, this is all that I need.

On Thursday night you returned the
phone message I had left on your
machine, & I glowed for hours.

*21 February 91*

# On Your Guard

The first time you came to see
me at home the Christmas tree

was up, it gave me the will
to insist you not leave until

you had climbed the stairs;
Ginger Rogers and Fred Astaire

glided through my mind:
your secrets I'd find

before the season was over
—I didn't blow your cover—

You were off on a skiing vacation
only I had the motivation

and nothing occurred,
though I grinned and purred

invited you across the moat
suggested you remove your coat

but you didn't desire
I couldn't aspire

to make your cock sing
You now study boxing

instead of romance
your opponent's no chance

to floor this golden boy.
I can still see your leap of joy

after your curtain call as Pangloss
in *Candide*, you've no albatross

but you still go to mass
with your marvelous ass

I confess need to steal
a glance as you kneel

*27 February 91*

## Therapy

Unravel the obsession.
Begin here: he never
encouraged me. When I
feel pain he has not
called, when I feel
jealousy toward men he
may have slept with, may
be having sex with, this
has nothing to do with
him, he's never opened
that part of himself to
me. The man probably
knows nothing beyond I
am infatuated, write notes,
leave messages, get a silly
smile whenever I see him,
and suffer varying energy
levels

*18 February 91*

## Wardrobe

I choose my clothes carefully
in case I run into you I wear

gray, I like gray but I wear it
so often now because you so

underdress, and a lot of your
muted earthtones are beige or

gray. Of course the one time
you praised something I wore it

was an agate and crystal ear-
ring hanging to my shoulder,

and you've touched me through
silk shirts twice, once aubergine,

once slate blue. When one cannot
be naked with someone it is good
to be appropriately clothed

## Incorrigible

The last thing I did the
night I thought I'd be

joining you at the Brattle
to sit three hours at your

side watching Fellini's
*La Dolce Vita* was take two

condoms and two packets of
portable lube from my

dish on the dressing table.
Incorrigible is the word.

*20 February 91*

## 8:30 A.M.

Walking past your house
while your shades are

drawn I assume you are
asleep I tap the seat of

your bicycle locked today
to the street sign at the

corner instead of in its
alcove under the fire

escape I think about being
inside you & your apartment

it's time to go to work
I've never been invited

*27 February 91*

## Last Year

I remember when it first snowed
in winter 1990-91, it started

almost midnight, I dressed for
a storm and entered one. Others

had preceded me, it is a college
town filled with the young,

skidding and making snowballs,
I cannot say there was that near-

silence of rural snow. I only
had two city blocks to go, one

to Mass. Ave., one to Remington
and there like the setting of a

Henry James story stood the
rounded corners of Ware Hall,

the mammoth apartment building
that for two years housed you.

The story ends there. You were
not outside, romping in the snow,

I did not ring your buzzer, you
did not come to the door in

some garment you sleep in, there
was no shared hot cocoa or two

brandy snifters or the suggestion
I remove wet things. In my head

this scene would be replayed many
times, with alternate middles and
endings, only my walk into the
midnight snow actuality, but

all the variations honest, based
in desire, told in the right spirit.

*17 December 91*

## Muscle Psyche

Maybe it's that you are still
in complete control of your
body; I watch you sometimes

from the pedestrian side of
the free weights room, you
so intense about your exercise

it becomes meditation: you, the
weights, the motion and the
mirror. And look what it's done:

you must, by now, be the image
you wanted, the man of your dreams
in the way in which you are the

man of mine. Times you've
instigated hugs your back seems
a barrier warriors require

*7–20 March 91*

## In the Order

Sometimes when I'm feeling
crazy I pretend we're
monks, singing

Gregorian chant like "Enigma"
& staring into each other's
eyes so intensely we

almost miss Vespers but you've
got this discipline & we
two-step in on time.

I would hate for your body
always to be obscured by
a robe, I'd miss your hooded

hair, but maybe our monastery
would have a swimming hole

*28 February 91*

## Sanctus

I thought I would not be
in a state of grace I went

to the Paradise to look for
you, drank club soda alone

Talked to someone Positive
but he cringed at the mention

of my shingles. I thought I
would not be in a state of
grace I went to Catholic mass

My doctor took communion I
bought bagels after the service
and as I drove home on my bike

my pocket bulging and fragrant
another bicyclist called out
my name. I stopped. I was

apparently in a state of
grace. It was you.

*3 March 91*

## Worship

At Saint Paul's that Sunday
they did the *I am a jealous God,*
*put no gods before me* ultimatum.
I sat there in increasing
alienation, thinking, I am in
this church because of the
possibility of running into You.

*12 March 91*

## Figurant

It's almost as if I expected
someone else to make the remainder

of my life extraordinary. Take my hand,
marvelous creature, lead me to

the rest of my life. An actor lover
would have been so apropos to the

terminally ill: the roles one could
play before oblivion took stage center, but

would pain not be pain despite persona?
No matter—it is not how the actor cast

himself, and the dramatis personae
of my dwindle returned to normal:

no last minute stars; all creative
temperament—mine

*7 March 91*

## After Reading an Alfred Chester Story

Here it is Springtime & you not needing to take one walk with me the nights not balmy but pleasant & I with this clay-colored sweat shirt, taupe almost, no color at all but that of the earth & not even normal earth, & you never calling or dropping by unexpectedly, me never running accidentally into you. Today at the computer at work, tired & worn out an instrument of another's words I suddenly looked at the open door & thought You could find out where my office is & come by as a surprise. Isn't it odd how even anger & a too intimate familiarity with neglect never totally do in hope? I wear the gray shirt with a colorful tee underneath, thinking daily, well, maybe, all the tirades my heart choreographs against you make me mad but never do I stop thinking oh, maybe, not even now that it is spring & if you had any viable juices they'd flow & the knowledge I was so constantly available might mean something on the night of a day made you too tired to roam for someone who'd look to you like you look to me

*23–24 April 1991*

## Never Ever

Never wanted to own you
Never wanted to keep
you naked in a small
space Never wanted to
straddle your chest and
shit on your pectorals,
never wanted to piss on
your face. Never wanted
to shave your pubes, tattoo
my initials in their absence.

Never wanted to see your
wardrobe diminished to a dog
collar, never cared to hear
your already limited vocabulary
reduced to Woof! Woof!
Never wanted to stand coolly
detached while my mean dyke
friend pierced your nipples,
never wanted to tug on the
subsequent chain.

Never wanted to take you to
Kenmore Square in your thong
and a raincoat, and leave
you there, in the rain. Never
wanted to supplant your God,
never wanted to take you to
Paradise on a leash, pop
Ecstasy in your mouth,
put you on all fours, have

you hum "I Could Have Danced
All Night," my fist filling
your excellent mouth. Never.

*6 June 91*

## Occluded Front

Though I've never had you
I've become a master of giving

you up. The first time I saw
you I wanted you to have sex

with me. I wasn't expecting
miracles, I didn't assume

you'd reverse my AZT impotence,
I merely saw my brother in you,

and anticipated a great intimacy.
I did what I had to do to meet you,

discovered you had this hectic
schedule, I could not see you except

when I managed to meet you at our
mutual gym, or chance encounters in

our shared neighborhood; even there
I had to guard the distance between

us from me so as not to frighten
you with my intensity, my obvious

desire. I danced in place for you,
allowing my gestures and words to

express fondness, but with great
respect for your detachment. I feared

losing you altogether, you're transient
in the community of my living and

dying, but oh in my head we live in a
rural haven where time is immaterial,

my inappropriate infatuation, your
lack of it matters

little. We're both gentlemen, we
periodically lock eyes, sharing what

cannot be scheduled or misinterpreted.
We've never fucked, but the print of

you's tattooed on my soul, someday
you'll be in the shower or alone or

with someone else on your bed, you'll
notice odd markings on the insides of

your eye-lids the private places no one
goes, you'll see me

*8–9 March 91*

## Riverside Cambridgeport, Winter

Two women with
children are feeding
the ducks. They waddle
out from under the
footbridge for bread
crumbs. Some hungers
are satiable; the thought
softens the ice they
slip on

A motor boat churns
through the icy Charles
in the hopeful thrust
I would bring towards

you

*19 February 91*

## Reality Check

Don't memorize
what he wore during
chance encounters You'll

always conjure his image
in flesh tones—the brown

eyes that seemed happy to
see you—the summer glow

on skin stretched over
those muscles; his clothes

so tight, so often black
or white, sometimes blue,

the blue you favor, and
favors you. How frequently

you've worn the same
combinations—as if you'd

dressed together. Other
than that you were rarely on

the same, as some call it,
wavelength. You wanted, he

didn't. Now he's moving to
New York—he giggles, he'll

rent in Spanish Harlem. You
don't know when you'll have

energy for Amtrak. You know
he wouldn't meet your train.

*12–13 August 1991*

## Fin

There is a little U-Haul
doubleparked outside Ware
Hall, Harvard Street

entrance. Who is moving
out? Who is moving
in?

*30 August 91*

# Transformations

Life is a series of changes; transformations. We often change our ideas, our actions, our geographic location, our physical appearance, even our sense of identity. But how does change happen? What prompts or permits it to occur? To paraphrase Mao Tsetung: "How does change happen? Does it fall from the sky? Does it grow from the ground? No, it comes from within ourselves, from our ability to imagine how life could be different and make it so." Our imagination offers us the chance to change our lives, for only by imagining new options, scenarios, and possibilities can we even think about altering how we live now.

And what role does the sexual imagination play in these transformations? Because our sexuality infuses, influences, so much of our life—thoughts, actions, desires, appetites, dreams, fears, terrors, and longings—the sexual imagination is, in many ways, the key that unlocks the secrets of where we have been and where we are going. The sexual imagination—and the energy it embodies not only stirs our hearts and our cocks, but makes us rethink, recharge, and renew our lives as well.

When the sexual imagination manifests itself in sexual writing, personal thoughts become public fantasies; private energy is transferred to a broader arena. In each of these stories a character goes through a transformation fueled by sexual experience or longing: Desire instigates change, passion ignites action. But there is another dimension at work here. In each of these stories, the writer's private sexual imagination has entered the broader social arena of thinking and action. We read these stories and are moved—emotionally, sexually, physically—by them. They might make us think, give us a hard-on, or allow us to think about our lives in new ways: They will stir our sexual imaginations and those imaginations will never be the same.

Tom Caffrey's "Becoming Al" charts the journey of a man that starts with his finding an advertisement for a gay strip show and ends with some surprising self-discoveries and changes in his life. Caffrey's forthright, even humorous, style is the perfect counterpart to his tale of sexual adventure. While much sexual writing is set in urban environments, Caffrey is one of the few writers really to capture what it is like to live as a gay man in the city, and here the sense of sexual self-adventure is perfectly matched by a milieu that both excites and dislocates simultaneously. As Caffrey's Albert begins his journey to becoming Al—and having new sexual adventures along the way—we see the myriad forms the process of personal transformation can take.

"The Song of the Reeds" by Brian Scott Hoadley details how the pain of loss—a break-up, a death—can be mitigated by the healing powers of sex. In the context of cruising, the potential of queer-bashing, and the lure of anonymous sex, Hoadley's protagonist finds that the emotional complications of his life are addressed in ways he never suspected. Sex here is both restorative and a little frightening, healing and slightly strange.

In Matthew Walker's "Harper's Fairy" the narrator is, at first, annoyed by the changes that have occurred in his physical world: Once-filthy men's rooms, so conducive to cruising, are now sparkling clean and immaculately tidy. But the narrator is in for even more surprises as he discovers that the perpetrator of this cleanliness is perhaps not quite so fastidious about his erotic behavior (the floor's "clean enough to eat off of," Walker's protagonist notes; little does he know.) "Harper's Fairy" is a fantasy about sex and possibilities, about the lure of the unspoken erotica of everyday life and the transformations that occur when those desires are articulated.

# Becoming Al
*Tom Caffrey*

Albert Grant sat in the balcony of the Showtime All-Male Theater wondering if he was expected to jerk off. Just in case, he had stuffed several tissues into the pocket of his jacket as he left the house, and they made a small lump against his side that rustled lightly when he moved his arm. Also in his pocket was a crumpled advertisement that he had found three days earlier while walking from the grocer's back to his apartment. The ad, printed on a small square of blue paper, was twisted around one of the iron rail posts of his steps, and he had nearly stepped on it as he was ascending to his door. He'd picked it up not because he was interested in what it said, but because it annoyed him to have his freshly swept stoop dirtied.

He hadn't actually read it until he'd unpacked the groceries and put them away, the cans martialed in neat rows behind the glass of the cabinet doors, the milk tucked neatly into the refrigerator. Then he'd taken the piece of paper from the counter where he'd dropped it and started to throw it away, stopping when he noticed that there was a picture of a nude man on it. The man

- 387 -

had an unusually large penis, and Albert found himself staring at it helplessly, amazed at the way it hung between the man's legs demanding to be noticed. The ad had been very well printed, and Albert could see every curve of the man's big cock clearly, his eyes following it down from the man's neatly clipped bush to the point at which it flared into a fat, inviting head.

He'd looked at the prick for several minutes before moving his eyes up to scan the rest of the man's body. He appeared to be Italian, with a muscular body that had not been overworked and a chest covered in short, dark hair. The man's face was what Albert thought of as handsome. Too rugged to be considered pretty, his dark eyes looked out from under sleepy lids, the brows over them thick and arched. The shadow drifting over his cheeks suggested that his beard would be heavy.

He looked like any one of the construction workers Albert often saw standing around roadwork sites, their hands resting confidently on their waists and their deeply tanned torsos filmed with sweat as they gazed down manholes or off into the distance at something he himself could never quite see. He was both attracted to and afraid of them, and if one of them chanced to look in his direction, it took him several hours to forget his face.

Apart from his big cock, what interested Albert most about the man was the easy way in which he stood in the picture, as if he'd just stepped out of his dusty work clothes and was headed for the shower or on his way to bed after a long day. There was nothing self-conscious about either his stance or his expression, and Albert wondered if the man was thinking at all about the many men who would see his picture and want to make love with him. He could not imagine exposing himself like that before a camera, and the idea that someone might look at his picture the way he was looking at the man's made him distinctly uneasy.

According to the ad, the man's name was Tony Gioconda, and he was going to be appearing live on stage at the Showtime three times a day for one week starting the next Tuesday. Albert had no intention of going anywhere near the Showtime. It was in a section of town frequented more by drunks and prostitutes who crawled out of the city's smaller cracks when dusk settled in than by architects who lived in brownstones. But he kept the ad anyway, folding it carefully and tucking it into his wallet behind his American Express gold card.

Over the next few days Albert found himself thinking often of the man. His face would drop into Albert's mind suddenly and without warning while he was doing something completely unrelated, like washing the dishes or drawing up the floor plans for a new restaurant. Once, in the middle of giving a presentation to a client, the image of Tony Gioconda's prick rose up before him, eclipsing the face of the corporate president sitting across the table, and he'd had to excuse himself for a few minutes to go into the bathroom and jerk off thinking about the big cock sliding into his throat.

These interruptions of his usually ordered routine had a surprising effect on him, similar to what would occur if he turned a corner on a familiar road and suddenly found himself in a new place. At first they annoyed him, the way they rippled the smooth surface of his life in unexpected patterns. But then he began to welcome, even invite, them. Every so often he would take the ad out of his wallet and look at it. It pleased him to have the man's picture folded and resting in his back pocket, as if somehow they knew one another and shared some kind of a history. After repeated foldings, the paper was crossed by pale, thin lines that neatly sectioned Tony Gioconda's body into squares. Albert liked the way the different parts of Tony's body were framed by these windows, especially the way his cock hung in the center square like a fine cut of meat in a butcher's display, something for hungry men to gaze at longingly.

Once he had stood naked before a mirror and compared his body to Tony's. He would examine one part of himself and then look at the corresponding area of the picture, noting the differences between them. At thirty-seven, he was in very good shape. His stomach, while not as ridged and tight as Tony's, was flat. His chest was smooth and fairly hard, if not sculpted into the twin rises of the Italian's, and his arms were evenly muscled. His face was strong, his blue eyes intent beneath light brown hair.

Assuming the same pose as Tony held in the ad, he noted the way his cock and balls hung. In school he had often sneaked glances at the penises of other boys as they stood awkwardly in the showers trying to focus their eyes anywhere but where they really wanted to look. He had been especially intrigued by one boy, the son of a local politician, whose cock seemed always to be half hard, rising slightly up and away from his balls in a thickening arc. The boy seemed either not to notice or not to care that anyone saw his erection, soaping himself as if he were in his own shower at home. Albert had stood next to him several times, and once the boy's dick had brushed his leg when he turned to rinse himself. He had made no apology, and Albert had been forced to cut his own shower short to avoid being caught with the hard-on that was beginning to rush up from between his legs. That night in bed he had masturbated furiously, his hand rubbing over the burning spot on his thigh.

He looked at his cock as it was reflected in the mirror's face. The head, rounded to a blunt point, hung a little way beyond his balls. He was always amazed when he became hard how much larger his cock became. Soft, it always appeared slightly small, like it belonged to a teenage boy instead of a grown man. But hard, it stiffened out to well beyond seven inches, sticking straight out from his body in a thick line. He knew from his limited experience that men enjoyed it, but he had never been able to ask any of his partners how it compared to others they had had.

After inspecting the rest of himself, he had gone to bed, where he dreamed that he was once again in the school shower room. Someone was standing very close to him, and because it was very steamy, he couldn't tell who it was. Then the steam opened up and Tony had stood before him. Albert had looked on in surprise as Tony reached out and took his cock in his soapy hand, jerking it slowly until it was hard. Then he had dropped to his knees and begun to suck on it while Albert put his hands in Tony's shiny wet hair. The dream had been very realistic, and when he woke up he saw that he had come all over his stomach, and he decided that he would go to the Showtime that evening.

Having made his decision, he was able to work the whole day without thinking about it. Then he had come home, changed his clothes, and taken the bus to a stop near the theater. The driver had not even looked twice at him, and Albert, who imagined that the man must know exactly what it was he was about to do, told himself that it was because the driver saw this kind of thing all the time. After walking several blocks past stores that sold liquor, cheap clothing, and videos catering to every fetish imaginable, he'd found the Showtime. The panes of glass on the doors were blackened, and there was a poster outside of Tony Gioconda, crouching so that the head of his penis nearly swept the floor.

He gave his money to a tired-looking Asian woman who sat behind a thick screen of Plexiglas, wondering if she knew that she was collecting the fare for men's most secret dreams, and went through the door into a stale, smoky hallway carpeted in red. There were several other men leaning against the walls, and they looked up hopefully when he came in. He glanced briefly at their faces. One, a silver-haired middle-aged man still wearing his suit from work, attracted him briefly, but he moved on. He quickly found the stairway to his left and went up into the balcony. It was empty except for three or four men scattered among the seats like grains of rice after a wedding.

Choosing a seat in the middle of the row directly behind the railing, he'd settled into the sagging blue velvet cushion, checking carefully first to make sure there was nothing still wet on it. As he waited for the minutes to pass until the show was scheduled to start, he looked around at the men he could see from his vantage point above the main floor. He had expected the population of the theater to be composed of the old and the unattractive, and was surprised that most of them looked very much like himself.

Behind the small stage at the front of the theater was a large white screen, on which was flickering a picture of two men, one white and one black, fucking on a bed. The bed appeared to be in a hotel room, and Albert was amused to see that the filmmaker had put a small Bible on the bedside table. The black man was fucking the white one, who was on his hands and knees with his head on a pillow. The black man was thrusting savagely at his asshole, and Albert wondered why it was that men in porn movies always slapped the asses of the men they were fucking. The image made his dick stiffen slightly in his pants, and he shifted his position to lessen the pressure at his crotch.

Just as the black man started to shoot his load onto his partner's back, the film was cut abruptly. The lights dimmed to inky blackness, and the house was swallowed by shadows. A white light swept over the stage, and the sound of music spat out of the mouths of tinny speakers set throughout the house. A curtain behind the screen parted, and Tony Gioconda walked onto the stage wearing a policeman's uniform and carrying a billy club.

Albert found himself very attracted to the uniform, and his attention was riveted to Tony, imagining the way the material would feel under his hands. As the music thumped and growled, Tony moved around the stage, grinding his body along with the beat. He was shorter than Albert had imagined, and wore dark glasses that hid his eyes. Still, as he watched Tony come to the edge of the stage and run the billy club between his legs, he felt his balls tighten.

The first thing Tony took off was his shirt, slowly unbuttoning it and then turning to let it fall down his back to the floor like a great blue leaf. When he turned back to the audience, he was rubbing his hands over his chest, pinching his nipples and then pushing his hand into the front of his pants. After a few more minutes, he undid those as well, pulling them down and off in one surprisingly fluid movement.

Wearing only a pair of small dark blue briefs and black leather motorcycle boots, he began to tease the audience, pulling the underwear down until the top of his bush was exposed, then cruelly pulling it back up. He turned around and let them see the firm globes of his ass, bending over as though waiting for one of them to run on stage and begin to fuck him. Finally, he yanked the briefs off, revealing his cock.

From the balcony, Albert could not see in great detail, but he could tell that Tony's prick was beautiful. Long and thick, it swung heavily as he continued to move around the stage. Like the boy's in Albert's high school gym class, it swung half hard over his balls. Then he began to jerk off, stroking his cock slowly as he stood on the stage. His eyes were fixed on a point somewhere in the audience, and Albert wondered if he was looking at someone in particular. His hand made long pulls on the big dick, his fingers squeezing the head and holding it out toward the men sitting in the seats before him.

Making sure that no one was watching him, Albert unzipped his pants and pulled his cock out, leaving his balls inside. He was filled with a peculiar excitement as he sat back and started to play with his prick, all the while keeping his eyes on Tony. He heard the quiet sounds of men moving in the darkness around him, and this made him even more aroused, knowing that if they looked closely they would see him taking part in this most personal pleasure. He kept his hand moving in time with Tony's, enjoying the feeling of his hot flesh beneath his fingers.

He brought himself to the edge several times, feeling a swelling in his groin and slowing his hand just enough to prevent his load from escaping. His balls were starting to ache, but he was determined to wait. Finally, when he saw Tony's eyes close, he knew it was almost time, and he began to pump himself quickly. As Tony grabbed his balls tightly and thick bursts of white streamed from his cockhead, tumbling onto the stage, Albert came in a rush of pleasure, squirting his come onto the floor between his legs with a soft, wet sound.

Then it was over, almost as abruptly as it had started. The music ended, and Tony disappeared behind the curtains. The lights rose slightly and the men on the screen started in right where they had left off. The black man's face twisted into a grimace of pleasure as he finally released his load in a great white arc that covered the other man in a sticky sheet. Albert tucked his cock back into his pants and zipped up quickly. Standing up, he left the balcony and, pushing past two men kissing in the stairwell, exited the theater, and rushed into the dark mouth of the evening.

The next night he found himself once again boarding the bus that would take him to the theater. When he got off at his stop, he walked briskly down the street, this time knowing exactly what it was he was looking for. As he handed his money to the old woman behind the window, he started to blush, thinking that perhaps she remembered him from the night before. But if she did, she made no indication, and he forgot about her as soon as he pushed through the doors and found himself once more in the red-carpeted hall-way and felt a tightening in his stomach.

He paused at the stairs that led to the balcony and then moved on into the lower area of the theater. This was more crowded than the balcony had been, with each row occupied by at least two, and sometimes three, men. As Albert walked down the aisle, which was sticky with layers of dried and fresh come, he noticed the silver-haired man he'd seen the night before having his dick sucked by a young man in shorts and a Mickey Mouse T-shirt, his prick sticking up from the zipper of his suit pants as the other man moved up and down it soundlessly. The man looked at Albert and smiled in recognition, then pushed his partner's face further down onto his cock.

Albert took a seat in one of the few empty rows, on the aisle several rows away from the stage. He looked at his watch, saw that he had a twenty-minute wait, and began to watch the movie that was playing itself out on the screen. In this one, a thin man with bad skin and a prick at least eleven inches long was sticking it into the ass of a short, dark-haired man, who was in turn being blown by another man, who had a crude tattoo of a woman with enormous breasts on his arm. Over the course of twenty minutes, the trio changed positions several times before the man with the big dick and the man with the tattoo came on the dark-haired man's face.

Then the lights dimmed again and the familiar music blurted into the room. It was louder, because he was nearer the speakers than he had been before, but he was able to tune it out as Tony emerged from behind the screen. This time he was dressed as a construction worker, wearing a tight white T-shirt tucked into jeans.

Albert watched him go through his routine, holding his breath as each article of clothing came off and more of Tony's body was revealed to him. Sitting so close, he was able to see the delicate swirls made by his chest hair and the sweat that gleamed on his skin as he danced under the lights. When Tony had stripped down to his briefs, which were white this time, Albert was able to see the outline of his delicious prick where it curved along his groin, the head threatening to burst from the waistband.

Despite his close proximity to the stage and the presence of a man across the aisle, Albert was preparing to jerk off along with Tony when Tony came to the edge of the stage, paused, and then, much to Albert's surprise, moved forward into the aisle. Albert turned and watched as he walked past him, the smell of his sweat hanging on the breeze he caused, and sat on the lap of a fat man six rows back. The fat man put a heavy paw on Tony's crotch and squeezed, a wet grin crossing his fleshy face. Albert wanted to run back and slap him, but Tony got up and moved further up the aisle.

After stopping at a few more seats and letting the men in them touch him briefly, Tony turned and moved back toward the stage. Albert sat very still, not wanting the man to see he had been watching or, God forbid, to sit on his lap. When he felt a hand on his shoulder, he jumped. Looking up, he saw that Tony had stopped at his seat. But instead of sitting on his lap, he took Albert's hand and pulled him to his feet.

Albert allowed himself to be pulled forward, unable to say or do anything. When Tony urged him up the stairs to the stage, he followed, thinking that perhaps he was still at home in his own bed and dreaming what was happening. Standing under the hot lights, he looked into the eyes of the man whose picture he had in his pocket and listened to him say, "How about helping me out here?" Tony was smiling, and Albert nodded at him.

Tony took Albert's coat and tossed it aside, then began to unbutton his shirt. When it was hanging open, he started to rub Albert's chest, his fingers massaging the skin. He pressed forward, and suddenly the hair of his chest was against Albert's skin, soft and inviting. Instinctively, he put his hands on Tony's back and pulled him closer until he could feel Tony's cock pressed against his own.

Tony pulled Albert's shirt off and then fumbled with the buckle of his belt. Albert helped him, oblivious now to the fact that he was undressing on a stage in front of a room filled with other men. He knew only that he wanted nothing more than to be naked with Tony, to feel his flesh against his. In a few seconds he was standing in only his briefs, and Tony was kissing him. Albert kissed him back, his tongue forcing itself into Tony's mouth, his hands finding Tony's nipples and rubbing them roughly. When they broke apart, he looked into his dark eyes and knew that he would go along with whatever Tony wanted.

Tony took Albert's hands and slid them down to his waist. Albert felt soft material under his fingers and pulled at it. Tony's cock fell into his hands, and he held it tightly. Then he dropped to his knees and put the head in his mouth. It was leaking precome, salty and thick, and Albert was soon working up and down the shaft as it stretched to its full length. As he sucked, he worked Tony's balls with his hand, stretching them out and letting them fall back.

When Tony was completely hard, he began fucking Albert's mouth in long slow strokes. Albert watched the inches of flesh pass his lips, felt the head as it pressed against him. His own prick was hanging from his shorts, and he jerked off while he sucked Tony's tool. The lights on his back were hot, and he could feel rivers of sweat beginning to run down his skin.

Tony put a hand on his chin and urged him to his feet, then turned so that Albert's cock was pressed against the crack of his ass.

He started to grind against him, so that Albert could feel the heat from his skin as it moved along the length of his prick. When Tony bent over, exposing his fresh pink hole in a forest of dark hair, Albert knew what to do. Spitting into his palm, he slicked his cock and pressed the head against the tight opening.

Pushing roughly, he plowed into a warmth as sweet and welcoming as a hot bath. Tony pushed back against him and slid onto his crank until Albert's balls were slapping his asscheeks. Closing his eyes, Albert began to fuck him, putting his hands on his waist to steady himself. Tony groaned as the walls of his ass stretched to accommodate Albert's thickness, but he never slowed the speed of his thrusts.

Before long, Albert was slamming his cock into Tony's willing ass, the sweat on his belly making wet slapping sounds whenever it came together with the other man's reddening asscheeks. He was aware that none of it should have been happening, and that made him fuck Tony even harder, as though if he slowed down Tony and the whole theater would dissolve in a pile of dust. He opened his eyes and saw that Tony was jerking his big prick as he was getting plowed, and he was vaguely aware that in the front row another man was busily beating his cock as his neighbor sucked on his balls.

When he finally came, after what seemed like hours of moving in slow motion, he pulled out of Tony's ass and turned him around, letting his load stream over Tony's hairy stomach in four long spurts that drained his heavy nuts and left him breathing raggedly and his legs weak. Tony was still stroking his cock, and he waited until Albert was able to stand behind him and pinch his tits before coming himself, his flood gushing over Albert's hand where it held his balls and falling onto the stage in thick threads. When he was finished, he took Albert's hand and led him behind the screen into a dark room.

"Thanks a lot, man," he said, putting his hand on Albert's back. "I don't always know if that's going to work. Sometimes you get guys up there and they freeze up—can't get it up and all. But you looked like you'd be into it, so I risked it."

Albert couldn't think of anything to say, so he said simply, "Thanks."

Tony handed him a towel, and he wiped himself off. "So, what's your name?"

Albert paused momentarily, then heard himself say, "Al." Then, more confidently, "My name's Al." He liked the way it sounded, short and barked from the throat like a declaration.

"Good to meet you, Al," Tony said. "I have to go get showered before the next show. But if you want to stick around, we could get together after I'm done."

Albert looked at Tony's expectant face, and started to put his pants back on. "I'd like to," he said. "But I have to go home."

Tony smiled. "Too bad. Well, come by whenever you feel like it then. I'll be here."

Albert nodded, and started toward a door that looked like it led to the outside. He found himself in the lobby again. As he walked out the door and onto the street, he fumbled in his pocket. The ad was still there, and as he walked to the bus stop he unfolded it and looked at Tony's picture. As he did, a feeling of deep satisfaction rose up in him, blooming into a warmth that filled every pore, and he decided that it might be nice to walk.

# The Song of the Reeds
### Brian Scott Hoadley

At night, sounds unsettle the soul. Cars flash past as I walk on the sidewalk. Too fast for me to see the occupants, too late for me to care what they look like. Every once in a while one slows down and I can see the taunt on the passengers' lips, the mischief in their eyes. The street lamps cast a yellow glow upon their faces, embellishing their already hate-twisted looks. Once, I thought I saw Jason. But I had heard that he'd left the city.

"Hey, faggot! Remember to wear a condom."

"Where's your dress, little girl?"

"Fucking queer!"

It's easier to turn your collar up against a chill night air than to close your ears to the verbal bashing. Sometimes it's too easy to believe what they say. Every once in a while my boots scuff against the pavement, and I turn to look around. Predators in the night make this walk a dangerous form of exercise. Bashers thrive on single and seemingly innocent men. Men like me, kindred spirits.

Sounds, like maracas, reach me from the tall reeds brushing

together in the light breeze. As I cross the old, arched granite bridge, I can see the moon reflected on the surface of the river. Stopping for a moment, I gaze out across the water to where the reeds are jumbled in great masses along its edge. Their sound is lulling, inviting. In the moonlight I can see shapes crossing from one mass of reeds to another. I met Jason among those shapes. Standing here, now, in the cool night air, it seems so long ago.

A red sports car slows. It holds a lone occupant. He cranes his neck to get a good look at me. After a few seconds, he pulls away without a single insult. Just cruising, I guess. Someone coughs, startling me. I turn quickly as two men walk past and down a dirt path beyond the bridge and into the park. Their footfalls recede into the distance. The gardens are beyond the path, in shadow. Between the water and the gardens, the open park is accentuated with trees and the tall stands of dark green reeds at the river's edge. Reeds that are just deep enough to hide the paths upon which the shapes walk. I can see my breath in the crisp night air. It reminds me of all the people smoking in the bar earlier tonight.

As usual, it was really crowded. I love to dance on a packed floor, eyes closed, rubbing against the sweat-soaked bodies. I somehow manage to lose myself for a period of time. There is no opportunity to feel lonely. But then, I ran into some friends. They even introduced me to a few really nice single guys. The feeling wasn't right. I liked the anonymity of a crowded bar and their presence had grounded me, made my emptiness seem real. It was. Loud music, too many beers, and this empty feeling in the pit of my stomach sent me out into the night for some fresh air. Now standing here on the bridge I've gotta piss, too.

Looking around, I'm not sure if I should wait until I get home or stalk down into the reeds to find a quiet place to release. I feel the temptation, though I know I've gotta avoid the pockets in the reeds. There are too many hungry mouths. I glance around, feeling torn inside. The darkness both mirrors my emptiness and holds the answers to my current loneliness. My bladder presses me to action. I can't wait. I've gotta find a place and hope no one follows me. I walk down a dirt path I've used before, on similar occasions. Farther ahead of me, the shapes continue their shuffle. Faceless, nameless, they search for something warm and inviting. Empty shells look to fill a few moments with something physical. They feel familiar somehow.

I find a dense stand of virgin reeds. There are no discernible paths. Parting them, I carefully pick my way into their darkness. At twelve feet tall, they have a tendency to block the moonlight. Darkness greets me. Squeezing the bulge in my pants, I know I can't hold out much longer. Shit! Forgot that the reeds butt right up against the river. Third time this year I've walked into the cool water. I back up, glance over my shoulder to see if there is anyone around, and unzip my jeans. I'm almost erect from the pressure. Touching the warm flesh of my cock excites me. The pressure forces the hot piss out through the reeds and into the water. The sound of my piss striking the surface of the water startles me. It will attract attention. I angle it onto the dirt- and moss-covered ground at the water's edge. It strikes the moss and is muffled. The hot piss runs off the moss and into the cool water of the river, causing steam to rise into the night air. I shake the last remaining drops from the tip of my cock and stuff it, semi-erect, back into my jeans. Finished, I realize that I feel compelled to head deeper into this park.

The faces of the people walking about begin to take shape as I near them. I recognize some from the bar and some from previous nights out. They all have that hungry, unfulfilled look. Is that the look on my face, I wonder. I pass people leaning against the fence surrounding the gardens. This close, the moonlight makes it easy to see their features. Plain. Average. Watch out for that one. Hello, who's this in the baseball hat? Of course, I don't stop. I keep walking down the path. About fifteen feet past him, I casually stop and look back. He is looking at me. I decide to stand there and lean against the fence like the others. Wonder what the passersby are thinking about me.

Men walk slowly, as if possessed by their emptiness. They search for something to fill the void and provide meaning to their late-night walk. In part, that's why I'm here, I guess. Here he comes. I can tell, by the baseball hat and the army sweatshirt. As he nears me, he looks right at me, smiles, and nods his head to follow him. Catching the baited hook in my groin, I follow.

We walk silently, me slightly behind. His shoulders are broad. His back tapers to a thin waist. He seems muscular, but the sweatshirt hides the details. He searches out a vacant spot. It is difficult. The night is clear and, though, cool, the park is active tonight. I follow him into a small stand of reeds. The center is trampled down from much passage. We are the only ones here. I feel the tension, the sexual buildup. Our bodies hasten the feeling. The moonlight angles in, partially lighting the area. He heads toward the shaded part.

Our lips meet tentatively. My hands roam over the muscled hardness of his body. His features are soft, like Jason's. His blond hair spills out in a curl from the brim of his hat. His face is smooth. He smiles, revealing beautiful, straight, white teeth. His eyes are light, perhaps blue or gray. I can't tell in the darkness. His tongue darts out and his eyes close as my hand massages the hardening flesh in his groin. I can feel the heat of his body.

Our bodies grind together, our tongues battle for supremacy. I kneel onto the reed-trampled ground. My hands fumble clumsily with his button-flys. He is not wearing any underwear. I can see the solid flesh. I carefully remove it from the denim. A foreskin encases the tip. Its small pucker of wrinkled flesh points toward my eager mouth. My tongue reaches out to taste it. Suddenly, I'm aware of someone else. I ignore them. Then there are hands on my shoulders. Not his hands. Others seek to join in our pleasure.

I push away. Gotta get out of here. This is not right. I leave the open stand. All around me, the song of the reeds fills the air, suddenly sounding more deadly, like rattlesnakes' tails. I can see now that at least four people had joined us in the reeds. The blond guy pulls away from the others in exasperation, covers his hard flesh, and follows me. We walk in silence toward the main path that leads out of the park. We pass the shapes, the mouths, and the reeds.

"I'm Ethan," he finally says.

I've always liked that name, his type. Ethan reminds me of him, the other.

"Matthew. My friends call me Matt." I find myself hoping that he likes me.

"I'm not very experienced at this," Ethan says.

I'm not sure if he means the scene, the park, or something else. I'm not sure if it matters. Tonight I don't feel very experienced at this either. I'm not used to coming here anymore. Not used to filling a void. To being lonely.

We make small talk and walk out of the park, up onto the street lamp-lighted walkway. I lean on the granite railing of the bridge and stare out into the park. Beyond the tree line, the Prudential Tower stands vigilant guard over the city. It suddenly strikes me that the tower peers out over the park like some large, cold, metallic voyeur. It makes me shiver. Perhaps it's the cold.

Ethan talks about being lonely and scared. He talks to me, a stranger, as if I have all of the answers. And he reopens my wounds. Not too old, too scabbed over to bleed here in the cool moonlit night. We agree that the night is filled with people like us. That we are all looking for something. Something we can't find in the daylight or in the still quiet of our homes.

He says he came to town with friends and that they left him at the bar. No ride home, subways stopped running for the night, and no place to stay. And now I worry. In my need to satisfy my emptiness, do I become a predator as well?

"My place is large enough," I say (the bait).

"I really don't want to impose on you," he replies (the nibble).

"Really, it's no imposition," I counter (the hook).

"All right. Thanks, I really appreciate it," he answers (the catch).

I almost feel ashamed. But we walk to my home anyway. Once inside the apartment, I turn on the hallway light, a conveniently dim fifteen-watt bulb barely lighting the narrow passage. I take him on the ten-second urgency tour that ends in my bedroom. A picture of Jason glares at me from the bureau. I turn the lights out. We strip, make love, and go to sleep.

I wake up in the morning to an empty bed. His clothes are gone. I begin to panic. Then I remember he's not here anymore. The sheets are intermingled with the smells of last night and the fading scent of Jason. The emotions of Jason's leaving feel much the same, fading toward the edges of my consciousness, mingling with the pleasure of a single night. I confuse their faces, their scents. I push myself out of bed. On the dresser I find a note with a phone number and the name Ethan scrawled across its rumpled surface: "Had to run. Call me. Thanks for last night."

Simple. To the point. I look carefully at the picture of Jason, trying to fix the image of his face in my mind before I place it facedown in the top drawer of my dresser. I begin to feel edgy, as if there's something I have to do. I glance around for some clue as to what it is. Laundry perhaps, and the place needs to be cleaned. It's been a mess since he left. I quickly shower, dress, and leave the apartment.

I realize it's noon. I start walking, trying to figure out where in the hell I am going. The sky is overcast. Everything sits in shadow. I pass people who look just like me. In a hurry, dazed and confused, but progressing toward something. I think about my walk from the bar to the park last night. The loneliness. The futility. I feel the need to see the park during the day. It takes a few minutes to get there.

The park seems just as active now. People work in the gardens, preparing them for the spring. Others simply walk among the gardens enjoying the last of the season's blooming. It occurs to me that those who come here during the day fill some physical space with an expression of love, while at night others fill an emotional space with something physical. At least that's what I do. I look out over the trees. In the daylight, the Prudential Tower looks less threatening. The tall steel old man sleeps during the day, or at least, like the park, takes on a different role.

No one shouts at me now. I can hear the deep throaty call of bullfrogs coming from the reeds as the river flows lazily onward, disappearing beneath the bridge on which I stand. It doesn't seem so complicated now. I don't feel so dirty. As I gaze across the park, I realize that the reeds are just simple stalks lining the river. I know what makes them seem dirty.

I think about Jason. The darkness from the cloud cover weighs heavily on my mind and my heart. I had met Jason here. In those reeds. I imagine him to be there even now. It is difficult to resist the temptation to walk into the reeds. In my pocket, I feel the piece of paper with Ethan's number. I have the urge to call him. To see if he wants to go out with me tonight, to dinner, to the movies. I pull his number from my pocket and jog to the phone in the park. My hand shakes slightly as I push a dime into the coin slot.

The phone rings once. I think about last night. The texture, taste. My desires fulfilled for the moment. The scent and feel of his naked body. The phone rings a second time. I glance toward the reeds. The memories of Jason try to edge out the feelings of last night. Jason's lithe body had moved as fluidly under my hands, my lips, and my tongue. The phone rings a third time. I look around the park. I think about Jason. I think about last night. An answering machine picks up. Ethan's voice calms me, reminds me where I am. I hang up before the tone. Last night was too perfect. My pursuit could ruin the moment, the memory.

Under the cloud-filled sky, I make my way home. To my home. As it was before Jason. A good cleaning will remove the familiar scent, the things that remind me of him. New memories will help ease the pain of his leaving. As I walk toward home, I think I finally accept that he's not coming back. And in an odd way, I welcome the time when I will reflect upon his memory with a fond nostalgia.

# Harper's Fairy
### Matthew Walker

Rest areas on the interstate used to be things of beauty. They stank of piss and shit. The floors were slick with come. The walls were crammed with obscene poetry. You could slip your sweat-stinking, road-weary, throbbing fuckstick through a hole in the wall and get it sucked till you shot a week's worth down the slick wet throat of some pussy-wimp cocksucker. Or, if you were of a mind to, you could bend over and nestle your preslicked fuckchute against the splinter-fringed opening and get your queer ass plowed by a burning hot, come-loaded shooting iron thicker than your forearm and longer than your granddaddy's firsthand account of D-Day.

Nowadays, rest areas are inviting, well-lit, *sanitary*. Parents bring their kids into them. Attendants lurk in hidden storerooms full of cleansers and mops, blaring Alan Jackson or Guns N' Roses through the vents so you know they're there. So you know they're itching for some graffiti to scrub away. You can't even jack off in a place like that; scoring a trucker is next to impossible.

A pair of these monstrosities lurk on either side of I-94 just east of Menomonie. They look more like televangelists' cathedrals than rest areas. Their arched marble roofs and tall mullioned windows bask in the glow of fluorescent tubes. Tiled floors and walls repel even the thought of jism. Against the burnished partitions between the stalls, penknives dull and felt tips wither.

Ordinarily, as I pass these monuments to good hygiene, I nudge the gas pedal a little nearer to the floor, but this time, on impulse, I stopped. On my way home from Madison—where I grew up and my parents still live—to Saint Paul, I had begun waxing horny for the years of raunchy, uninhibited, reckless, gorgeous sex that would never come again. I thought I would spend a few moments to reflect upon the great tradition which had passed away on this site. Also I had to take a dump.

According to my dashboard clock, it was already a few minutes past midnight when I stepped from the car. The sodium lights buzzed and hummed and cast a pinkish pall over the parking lot. The November wind was bitter. I left my coat and wallet in the car and raced toward the door.

Inside, the air was swirling with stifling currents of hot, dry air. There were two separate men's rooms—the locked one was a spare, kept in reserve so the attendant always had something to polish. I ambled into the other. There were three stalls; I chose the middle one. Shit-kicking country music played somewhere behind the tiled walls.

I took my dump staring at blank stainless steel. Bobbing and craning, I tried to read the random scratches on the walls. Only one fragment of graffiti etched into the glittering surface of the partition had not yet been buffed out: "Go Twins '94."

Disheartened, I stood, making ready to leave. My Swiss army knife dropped from my hip pocket and clattered on the floor. That gave me an idea. Leaving my pants puddled at my ankles, I snatched up the knife. With the pointed end of the corkscrew, I scratched a message on the wall to my right: "Tap foot for BJ." That was all I could manage; the slick steel didn't take the scratches easily, and the scraping set my teeth on edge.

Without even pulling up my jeans, I changed stalls. I clutched my cock—it nearly burned my hand, it was so hot for action. My Prince Albert was slick with my precome. I waited.

An hour or more passed. Men came and went—as many as four or five at a time—but few used the stall where I'd scratched my message. Each time someone stepped in next door, I leaned forward, watching his feet, waiting for any movement that could be called a tap. All in vain.

After a long dry spell, someone came in. The restroom door closed softly. As the newcomer walked past my stall on squeaky shoes, the dark blue of his clothing darkened the crack between the stall door and the frame. He moved slowly, and I saw the china white of one eye as he peeked in at me. My heart racing, I plumped my dick and scrunched forward on the seat so that he could see it.

By then he'd already stepped into the middle stall, where I'd left my message. He neither sat nor closed the stall door. I leaned forward for a look at his shoes. Scuffed dark brown work boots, the soiled laces loose and untied. My cock jumped in my hand. The polished tiles of the floor reflected the color of his clothing, but not the shape of his body.

For a long time, he stood facing the toilet. His feet were firmly planted, but his legs made small back-and-forth motions. Was he jacking off? His reflection in the floor wasn't clear enough to tell. I waited for the sound of his piss, but it never came. I slid my foot toward him. He still didn't move. Standing, I pulled up my jeans, stuffing my boner down my right pants leg.

Forcing myself to go slowly, I opened the door to my stall and poked my head around into his. He leaned to one side, bending slightly at the waist. On his head he wore a dingy red bandanna; the dark blond hair that spilled out of it was just long enough to cover his neck. He wore ugly blue coveralls. The heavy twill fit his ass and thighs so snugly that I could see the perfect dimpled roundness of his asscheeks. Through worn denim I squeezed my cock.

Half-turning, he glared at me. He had a brush and a spray bottle of something in his hand. Oh, shit. He was the fucking attendant.

"You the one that did this?" he said. His voice was a throat-heavy rumble, a surly growl. Dazed, I shook my head, but my hand still clutched a smoking gun: my cock. I was caught rod-handed. He turned to face me now, and took a step in my direction. "Well? Are you?"

According to the patch above his left tit, his name was Harper. He was far from handsome, especially now, with his face pinched in a dark grimace. His narrow cheeks flexed as he gritted his teeth; brown stubble shadowed the pale skin. A thick, raggedly trimmed mustache emphasized the snarling curl of his upper lip. His pale forehead furrowed in anger, split unevenly by a crooked vertical scar over his left eye.

"You a faggot or not?" he said.

I blinked at him until he must have thought I was the stupidest man on earth. "Fuckin' queer," he said, setting the brush and bottle on the toilet paper dispenser. He stepped toward me. I cringed, and I hated myself for it. He was a small man, really—the top of his head reached only to my chin, which meant he couldn't be much taller than five and a half feet—but the street-scrapper's brawn of his body over-matched the office-worker's softness of mine. And I couldn't stop staring at that scar on his forehead; in some way, it proved he was a dangerous man. I stumbled back against the wall, my fingers scrambling against cold tile.

Grinning at my cowardice, he brushed past me and stepped into the stall where I'd last been sitting. "Jesus. You fuckin' queers come in here and sit around all goddamn night with your shitty lubed asses all over my goddamn toilet seat. I'll bet if you sat there long enough you'd carve a friggin' glory hole in my goddamn wall. Look at that. Don't even know enough to flush."

In one swift move, he grabbed me by the scruff, dragged me into the stall, and forced me to my knees. His strong fingers held my head inches from the toilet seat. Where I'd been sitting, sweat and ass-slime marred its gleaming black surface. The seat was the standard U-shaped kind, with the open end of the U at the front of the toilet. In the gap, a puddle of piss made a perfect circle of lemon yellow on the white porcelain. The water in the bowl was the same pale shade of yellow.

"Is that yours?" Harper said, pointing at the piss on the bowl's rim. Under his nails there were half-moons of grime.

Fighting against his grip, I nodded.

"You think this is some latrine out in the woods, and you can just piss all over the place in here? I just cleaned this up tonight. Maybe I didn't do a good enough job. Maybe it looks like a fuckin' outhouse to you."

"No," I said. That didn't seem good enough, so I babbled something more: "It's clean. The toilet's clean, the walls're clean, the floor's clean. It's all clean enough."

"Clean enough for what?"

"Clean enough—clean enough to eat off of."

He smiled. An evil smile. He wiped the piss off the toilet rim with two fingers. Before I could guess what he intended, he had them both deep in my mouth. I gagged on them, struggling and sputtering.

But then something changed. Harper's fingers softened inside my mouth in some way. Almost without my knowing it, my tongue moved against him, seeking more of their callous surface. He tasted and smelled of sweet, strong sweat. The taste of the piss was lost in his salty savor. I closed my eyes and let him take me. His fingers slid deeper, all the way into my throat, fucking me. I let him.

He chuckled. Opening my eyes, I looked up at him. The scar on his forehead split his left eyebrow; the white gap in the dark hair was oddly luminous. A smile—or maybe it was my sudden desire for him—changed his face entirely; he barely resembled the angry hoodlum I'd first taken him for.

"Fag," he said, taking his fingers away from me. Clutching harder at the back of my neck, he pressed me toward the toilet. "Lick," he said. He spoke softly, so that his lion's voice seemed full of affection. I licked the toilet seat, letting him guide me from one end of the U to the other.

When the seat was clean enough to suit him, he lifted it. I guessed his next move, but I didn't fight him. I let him push my head into the bowl. My nose barely touched the icy, piss-smelling water. He flushed and, at the same moment, shoved my head all the way in. Water swirled around me—into my hair, into my mouth—as my forehead struck the smooth porcelain.

He hauled me out of the toilet before clean water replaced my piss. The smelly water in my hair drenched my shirt and splattered the floor and walls. Its stink overpowered the restroom's raw stench of disinfectant and deodorizer.

"Is your cock hard, queer?" Harper said.

I couldn't remember when it had been harder. "Yes, Sir," I said, wiping the water from my eyes.

"So's mine. Wanta take care of me?"

"Yes, Sir."

He let go of my neck and reached back to lock the stall door. Turning to face him, I pressed my face against the bulge between his legs. The sweet, unmistakable fragrance of unwashed crotch rewarded me. I breathed deeply.

"I go three or four days at a time without showering," he said. "Sometimes a week. I can't stand all this fuckin' pine-scented shit. Bet you like it rank, too, don't you, dicklicker?"

"Oh, fuck, yeah," I whispered. Through the heavy fabric I tasted his musk, his piss and jack-off juice. He leaned over and, grabbing me again by the hair, lifted my face into his armpit. I breathed a deep stew of dirty, hard-working sweat.

He unzipped the coveralls. Except for a few brown hairs around each of his tiny, shell-pink nipples, his chest was hairless. His pecs were round and firm, his belly flat. A shallow cleft from collarbone to navel split him evenly.

I crushed my face against him, breathing and tasting his skin— it was salty and bitter from his sweat, and would be even more so now, after I wiped my piss-wet hair and beard across it. I gnawed his nipples, making him groan. Curled, damp hair, the color of corn silk, lurked under his arms. He peeled back the coveralls, and I lurched at his bare left pit.

Except for a filthy jockstrap, he was naked underneath the coveralls. The uniform fell heavily to the floor. His shoulders were rawboned. His arms and legs were burly and sparsely furred. High on his left arm he bore a tattoo: a jailhouse-blue band of thorns. Two of the needle-thin thorns dripped cartoonish crocodile tears of crimson blood. I covered the tattoo with my hand and squeezed. He flexed. The way the muscles moved under my hand—smoothly, with grace and power—made me sigh and shiver like a teenaged girl.

When he dropped the jockstrap, his cock unfurled like a banner, surrounded by matted brown hair. It was bigger than the molded-from-real-life, illegal-in-Texas dildo I'd been practicing on at home. Cut, with a heart-shaped head the same color as his nipples. The pisshole was ragged at the edges; it was more like a wound than a slit. His balls were fat; the hairy, veined sac hung low and heavy. His gold-brown pubic hair was long enough to be combed.

Pulling me to my feet, he clutched his naked body against me, clutching at my ass with sharp fingers. With his coveralls and jockstrap hobbling his ankles, he half squatted to fit me between his legs. He found the place where my stiff cock lay against my thigh, and he humped his own big dick against it. The rough fabric of my jeans chafed my skin. I was hot and eager to get naked.

He stroked my chest through my thin cotton shirt. "It's hairy under there, ain't it, daddy? Huh?"

"Yeah. Fuckin' hairy."

He shuffled back a step, unlocking the stall door. "Come here," he said. Pulling his coveralls up to his knees, he led me to the handicapped stall. It was three times bigger than the other stalls; we had room to move. Harper snagged open two zippers at his ankles and slipped his coveralls off over his boots. The jockstrap went next. When he bent over, the bandanna slipped off his head. Dark blond hair, parted in the center, fell smooth and straight to his shoulders. He kicked the bandanna, jockstrap, and coveralls aside.

"Now you," he said. "You strip."

I stripped slowly. I opened my shirt and peeled it away from my hairy round belly. I kicked off my sneakers, shooting them into a corner. I rolled my socks off my big, hairy feet and, holding them in my mouth to suck out the sweet smell of sweat, I slid my jeans over my furry hips and legs.

My skin wasn't so perfect as Harper's, and the muscles in my arms and legs weren't so firm, but he seemed to like what he saw: a forty-something, potbellied, daddyslave with a graying pelt, a meaty, pierced, rock-hard boner, and a pair of ready holes. My pink-brown nipples were as thick and hard as fingers.

He nodded, smiling. "Not bad, shithole," he said. "Get that hairy fag ass over here, daddyslut."

Shivering in anticipation, I stepped away from the bundle of denim on the floor and opened my arms for him. He stroked my chest and belly. His hands found my ass, ruffling the hair there. I squeezed my asscheeks together, trapping his fingers in the crack. Yanking them free, he smacked and plumped my ass some more, then let his hands roam over my back and chest. I closed my eyes, pressing my body against his.

He plucked the socks from my mouth. "Not bad at all, fuckhole. You don't look like a fairy. You like someone's favorite teddy bear."

"Right now I'd rather be a fairy, Sir." That word—*fairy*—didn't come easily.

"Damn fuckin' right. Get ready to be my dicklickin' fairy suckhole. Big fuckin' bear daddy," he said. "Big fuckin' hairy cocksuckin' papa bear faggot. Ain't that right? You're a queer daddy, ain'tcha? A cocksuckin' cunt fairy."

While he rubbed his stubble-rough face against my graying beard, mingling our mustaches together, I would have admitted to anything: shooting JFK, liking Andrew Dice Clay, writing for *Hard Copy*, anything. "Yes. Fuck, yes," I said.

"Then suck me, daddy. Gag on that fuckin' unwashed dick, papa bear."

I sank to my knees again, and, gripping the silky skin of his ass, forced him down my throat. He slipped in easier than Mr. Latex and tasted better. His crotch hairs stank of whatever he never washed off: piss, shit, come, sweat. Heaven.

He held my face against his crotch. The pulse in his cock drummed against my tongue and throat. Soon—too soon!—I gagged on him, choking on the rising gorge. At the last second he let me go. I slumped over, hugging his booted feet. He squatted over me and pounded my back with his fist.

"Fuckin' daddy fudge-packed shithole cocksucker. Fuckin' fuckhole."

I jerked away from his fist and, pushing him against the nearest wall, slammed my face hard onto his cock. I fucked myself with his fat, fat pole, forcing myself to take him until tears blinded me and I could barely breathe.

With the toes of his boots he prodded my own stiff pole, bending it back between my thighs. My PA nicked softly against the tiled floor; that and my frenzied slurping could have been the only sounds in the world. Harper kicked lightly at my balls until I writhed from the growing pain. He reached under my arms to twist my tits and smack my chest.

"Fuckin' papa-bear butthole," he said.

Stepping away from the wall, he drove his fuckstick into my mouth. I struggled to adjust my breathing to the new cadence; he didn't care if I could breathe or not. I clawed at his ass, scraping at his moist hole with the fingers of both hands.

"Yeah, fucker," he said. "Yeah. You want a glory hole, fucker? There it is. I got that hot fuckin' hole just waitin' for a daddy fuckbear to tongue-gouge it."

Abruptly he pushed me away from him. The suddenness of it caught me off guard and I sprawled backwards onto the cold tile. My head landed on the forward edge of the toilet. Before I could stop him, he stepped over me and I saw his round, dimpled asscheeks spreading over my face. The deep, raunchy tang of his butthole filled my world. Without thinking I reached my tongue out for him, but he stopped short, squatting just out of range while he poured a gust of foul air over me.

"Like that, fuckbear slutdaddy? Like that rank fart?"

"God, fuck, yes," I said, swallowing his stench.

"Like that fuckin' glory hole, shitface?"

"Fuck, yes, shit, yeah."

"Sure wish I could feel your fuckin' tongue on it, dickhole. Next time bring a dam or some Saran Wrap or somethin'. You got a safe?"

I groaned. "In the car."

"No sweat. You can suck me some more."

Squatting over my chest, he rammed his pole down my throat again. Just then, the restroom door opened and closed. Harper froze, balls deep, listening to footsteps approaching. The newcomer approached our stall door. Harper's pound of flesh plugged my gullet; I struggled not to gag or gasp or sputter.

"Open up," the newcomer said. "State police."

My heart stopped, but Harper laughed. Pulling his cock from my mouth, he stepped to the stall door and unlocked it. The newcomer was no cop. He wore a flannel shirt, filthy jeans, and scuffed engineer boots. He was about Harper's height, but slimmer and more wiry. He could have been my age or ten years older; it was difficult to tell. He kept his black hair swept to one side, as though to cover a bald spot. His skin was dusky and smooth, but when he smiled it crinkled and buckled into crow's feet and laugh lines.

Ignoring me, the older man sank to his knees. "I need it real bad this time, Sir," he said, and he handed Harper a fistful of foil packets: rubbers and lube. "I locked the door when I came in."

Harper nodded. "You know what to do, shithole."

Standing, the newcomer kicked off his boots and jeans. His cock, which was as average as my own, pointed to the ceiling. It was deep purple. A small, veined wattle underneath the head served as a souvenir of a faulty circumcision. At its base, his big balls seemed to stretch their sac to the limit, as if he were already in the middle of coming.

Motioning toward me, Harper said, "Billy, this is my new fuckbear daddyslut. Make nice."

With a hand on each of our shoulders, Harper pushed Billy and me together. Billy wrapped strong, thin arms around me and, pulling me against him, fucked my mouth with his slick, cool tongue. I opened to him, and he pressed harder. He didn't seem to mind the smell of piss on me; tangling his fingers in my wet hair, he sniffed my face and neck and licked me clean.

Billy's hands moved to my asscheeks and squeezed. I unbuttoned his shirt and slid it off his shoulders. Our pulsing cocks rasped against each other.

Kneeling, Harper reached between us. His rough hands gently forced our hips apart. Thick fingers clenched around my balls, and I felt him wrap something around them. Whatever it was, he pulled it so tight that I gasped into Billy's mouth. When Harper was done with me, Billy's balls got the same treatment, and Billy moaned softly against my tongue when the noose tightened.

Harper stepped away, and Billy and I stopped kissing long enough to see what he'd done. Using one of his own bootlaces, he'd tied our nut sacs together. In unison, we tried to pull apart. The slightly painful drag on my balls and the intimate connection to Billy made me weak with passion.

While I drove my tongue so deep into Billy's mouth that he gagged, Harper pulled my hands around behind my back and cinched his other bootlace tight around my wrists. Precome dribbled from the two holes in my cock into Billy's pubic bush.

Again, Harper pried us apart, and he pressed the width of his body between us. To make room for him, Billy and I stretched our ball tether to its limit.

Together, we feasted on Harper's fat prick. There was plenty to go around. We licked up and down the shaft, our hot tongues slicking the cockflesh with spit and meeting on the underside. I gorged myself on Harper's balls and the rank, gooey sweat that collected underneath them, while Billy forced the throbbing prick down his clutching throat. We switched. Harper moaned, rubbing his hands through our hair.

Gasping, Harper pulled away. "You ready to get fucked now?" he said to Billy.

Billy was already struggling to free his balls. Harper helped him. Once Billy was loose, Harper tucked the free end of the lace into my mouth. "Don't let go of that, fagdaddy," he said.

Still kneeling, Billy put his shirt back on, but didn't button it. He tore open one of the packets he'd brought and edged a lubed rubber over Harper's fat member. The older man rolled onto his back and grabbed his ankles. Harper knelt over Billy's body and, in the same motion, drove home the full length of his prick.

Harper threw Billy a legendary fuck. It was the kind of marathon that porno directors shoot for three days to capture. Harper bucked and stroked and rammed and spooned and poked and slammed, cursing all the while. Billy, sliding on the worn fabric of his shirt, edged out the door of the stall, then across the rest room floor. I crouched in the open doorway of the stall, watching. Harper shoved him from one end of the room to another and back again, literally wiping the floor with him.

At last, they slid my way again, stopping when Billy's shoulders hit my knees. My hard cock throbbed an inch from Billy's face. I edged forward, and Billy gobbled my balls. He squeezed them between his lips and pulled on them, and I felt the dragging sensation all the way up in my belly.

Just then, Billy leaked a deluge of fuckjuice down his chest. Harper stopped cold, and I could tell by the way his eyes rolled back in his head that he'd shot. My heart sank.

Billy tucked and buttoned and zipped; in less than a minute he was at the door and ready to go. He smiled at me and gave me a thumbs-up. Then he kissed Harper's boots and left. Harper stood over me, his still-rubbered cock dripping with Billy's ass-scum.

"You next?"

"You just came," I said, still holding the bootlace in my teeth.

Smiling, shaking his head, he plucked the string free. Almost absentmindedly, he yanked on it, stretching my balls. "I faked it. I wanted to save it for you. Hell, Billy can't tell the difference. He only cares about his own load anyway. You want it doggy-style or like Billy?"

"Like Billy. I want to see your face."

He smiled. "A fuckin' romantic. Can you take it that hard?"

"Yes, Sir." I paused. "But go easy at first."

Freshly raincoated, Harper forced my body into the tight pretzel that Billy had slipped into so easily. He left my hands bound under me. He stuffed the end of the bootlace in my mouth again.

All the lube Billy had brought with him Harper now sprinkled on his cock and my asshole. Kneeling over me, he took aim. He stuffed the fat dickhead in slowly, almost gingerly, but however slowly he went, it was still like forcing a plum through a drinking straw. By the time I had the whole column of fuckflesh in me, I thought I'd swallowed a baseball bat.

And once I had all of him, Harper slammed me as tirelessly and as mercilessly as he had Billy. The weight of his body held my legs against my chest. His wrist-thick rod stabbed my hole, burning and branding and stretching me until, suddenly, it felt good. My head spun and my heart lurched. I howled like a dog until Harper stuffed his hand in my mouth to shut me up. Squeezing his fat pole with my pussyring, rocking on the small of my back with my bound hands like a hobbyhorse, I met and matched his strokes.

Chest heaving, his face twisted into the angry grimace he'd been wearing when I'd first seen him, Harper collapsed against me, his cock buried deep inside me. I held my breath. He was so still that I felt him shoot into the rubber: five strong spurts, muted by the latex but all perfectly discernible. Sliding a hand between his belly and my ass, he held the rubber in place. For a few minutes more, his cock throbbed inside me.

Then he left me, with a light slap on the ass.

I still held the bootlace in my teeth, and my balls and cock had twisted around each other so that my shiny red nut sac pointed toward the ceiling and my heavy-hard cock lay sideways along my thigh, pointing toward my feet. "You look hot, daddybear," Harper said. "I ought to leave you trussed up like that for a while." But even as he said it he leaned down and rolled me over to untie my hands.

While I recovered from the freight-train-sized fuck, he carefully pulled the rubber off his shrinking prick. He tied it off and took it to the sink to clean the slime off it. As I hauled my body to its knees, he picked up my piss-soaked shirt and dropped the rubber into the breast pocket. "A little snack for later," he said.

I smiled. I collected my socks from the corner where they'd landed. Balancing against the spotless tiled wall, I slipped my feet into them; the left one was still damp at the toe from my spit.

He glanced over at my clothes. I followed his eyes to a spot of red on the floor—my Swiss army knife had fallen from the pocket of my jeans again. Squatting, Harper snatched it up and opened it. "Is this what you used to scratch up my wall?" I nodded. "Come here."

Nervously, I obeyed. He lifted the knife. He did it without menace, but I flinched, intending to back away. Before I could, he had my balls in his hand. Gingerly, he slipped the knife between my skin and his bootlace. The blade split the worn cord easily. Standing, Harper lifted my jeans and dropped the knife into the pocket. While his back was turned, I gave my balls a panicky grope; there was no blood.

"One more thing," he said, turning to face me. "You ain't come yet, and I'd hate to let my new fagdaddy go unsatisfied. So let's see you shoot." He flung my jeans to the floor.

I shook my head, looking at my soft cock. "Thanks, but I don't need to."

He was adamant. His face darkened with anger and he stepped toward me. "It wasn't a fuckin' request, shithole. Get the fuck on your knees and make it shoot, fuckwad."

When I still wouldn't move, a light kick to the back of my knees with one foot and a simultaneous jab to my nuts with the fingers of one hand brought me swiftly to the floor. My boner made a sudden comeback.

"Move it, daddy. Beat it. Come on. I gotta get back to work."

Trembling and spreading my knees a little wider, I stroked my throbbing rod with one hand and my blue balls with the other. Harper enjoyed the show. His own prick got its second wind because of me, and his hips swayed as though he were still fucking one of my holes.

"Yeah, that's it," he said. "Stroke it off, daddy fuckbear cuntface."

A few more minutes of dirty talk and I was ready to go. I caught a whiff of his crotch-stink, and that sent me over the edge. "I'm gonna shoot," I told him. "I'm gonna fuckin' cream my guts out."

"Do it, fuckdaddy."

I did it. I sprayed the toilet bowl and the tile with my fuckbear daddy-cream. The last volley veered to one side and landed smack between Harper's boots. As soon as it landed there, the boots moved. Even before I'd dribbled my last, one of the grubby soles was on the back of my head, pushing me toward the floor.

"Lick it up," he was saying. "Lick up your fuckin' cockspit, daddyslut. Lick it off my clean floor, fuckbear. Gotta keep it clean enough to eat off of, don't we, shitwipe?"

I slurped away my own spicy juice, snorting and moaning, following the sparkling snail tracks up the side of the toilet. I said, "Yes, Sir. Yes, Sir, clean enough to eat off of. Yes, Sir."

After I'd swallowed all of my jizz, he shoved me to the floor again with his boot. "Keep goin', papa bear. Clean it all up," he said. "Lick up those fuckin' butthole drippings, daddyslut. Gotta keep my clean floor clean, fuckbear."

"Yes, Sir."

The fabric of his coveralls rustled as he stepped into them. "Good work, shithole," he said, zipping the coveralls up the front. "Keep that up. And when you're done here, don't forget to lick up the piss you left all over the other stall."

"Yes, Sir."

"I work ten P.M. to six A.M. Sunday to Thursday. Get your shitty ass back in here sometime."

"Yes, Sir."

He left. I kept licking for a few minutes, until I felt foolish doing it. I reached for my clothes, but they were gone. The bastard had taken them. I had clothes in the car, but how the hell was I supposed to get there? I stood, turning.

A man stood in the doorway of the stall. A hulking black behemoth nearly as wide as the doorway itself, his neck and forearms and calves were all thicker than my head. He wore a baseball cap with the bill at the back. As he locked the stall door behind him, he took off the cap—his shaved head gleamed in the garish fluorescent light—and dropped it onto the hook on the back of the door. When he moved his arms, his shirt gaped at the front, its buttons threatening to pop. In the gaps I saw smooth fields of ebony skin.

With two fingers, each as thick as my dick, he fumbled for the zipper pull at the fly of his faded jeans. As he unzipped, I gulped, imagining the massive prong that would suit this man's build—it would have to be registered as a deadly weapon. He hauled it out; a little smaller than Harper's, it was well within legal limits. The skin was the black-purple of a king's velvet robe.

"Harper says you give good head," he said. His voice was as thick and heavy as his body. "Says you like to get pushed around, too. He gave me some scumbags." He dug a half dozen foil packages out of his back pocket and showed them to me. "I been driving a while, so I'm horny as shit, and I intend to use 'em all. There's a whole lobby full of guys out there, so when I'm done with you," he said, "there'll be plenty more where I came from. You'll get your clothes back when you've finished us all."

I fell to my knees. Before his thick pole split my throat, I barely had time to say, "Yes, Sir."

# Biographies

**Walta Borawski** is the author of *Sexually Dangerous Poet* and *Lingering in a Silk Shirt*. His poems have appeared in *Fag Rag, Gay Community News, RFD, Mouth of the Dragon, Outweek, PWA Coalition Newsline, Christopher Street*, and *Radical America*. His work has been anthologized in *Son of the Male Muse, A True Likeness, Gay & Lesbian Poetry in Our Time, Poets for Life, The Name of Love: Classic Gay Male Love Poems, Jugular Defences, Ex-Lover Weird Shit*, and *The Badboy Book of Erotic Poetry*. He died of AIDS-related causes on February 9, 1994 at his home in Cambridge, Massachusetts.

**Randy Boyd** is a native of Indianapolis, Indiana and a 1985 graduate of UCLA. His fiction has appeared in *Blackfire* magazine and the anthologies *Certain Voices, Flesh and the Word 2*, and *Sojourner: Black Voices in the Age of AIDS*. His nonfiction has been featured in *Frontiers, Au Courant, The Washington Blade*, and the anthology *Friends and Lovers: Gay Men Write About the Families They Create*. Randy acknowledges a great debt to the late John Preston for believing in Randy's work.

**Christopher Bram** grew up in Virginia and attended the College of William and Mary. He is the author of *Surprising Myself, Hold Tight, In Memory of Angel Clare, Almost History,* and *Father of Frankenstein.* He lives in New York City.

**Tom Caffrey** is the author of the erotic story collections *Hitting Home & Other Stories* and *Tales From the Men's Room.* His fiction appears regularly in magazines, including *Wilde, Advocate Men, Freshmen, Torso,* and has been featured in *Flesh and the Word 3, The Best American Erotica 1995,* and *Ritual Sex.*

**Tom Cole** is a writer and artist living in Cambridge, Mass.

**Samuel R. Delany** is the author of *The Mad Man,* as well as the autobiography *The Motion of Light in Water.* His science-fiction novels, including *Dhalgren, Stars in my Pockets Like Grains of Sand,* and the Neveryon series have won four Nebula Awards. He is Professor of Contemporary Literature at the University of Massachusetts, Amherst.

**Philip Gambone** has published short stories in over a dozen magazines and anthologies and has been listed in *Best American Short Stories, 1989.* His collection, *The Language We Use Up Here,* was published in 1991. His essays have appeared in the anthologies *Hometowns, A Member of the Family, Sister & Brother,* and *Wrestling With the Angel.* Currently he teaches in the Park School in Brookline, Massachusetts, and in the writing program at Harvard, where he has received two Distinguished Teaching Awards.

**Brian Scott Hoadley** is a fiction writer and poet. He is currently pursuing an MFA in Creative Writing at Emerson College in Boston. He has read his work at the Cantab, the Claremont Reading series, and in the OutWrite '95 Gay and Lesbian Writer's Conference. Brian currently resides in Boston.

**James C. Johnstone** is a writer, editor, bon vivant based in Vancouver, Canada. His written work has been published in *Sister & Brother: Lesbians and Gay Men Write About Their Lives Together*, edited by Joan Nestle and John Preston. He is the co-editor, with Karen X. Tulchinsky, of the anthology *Queer View Mirror: Lesbian and Gay Short Short Fiction*.

**David Laurents** is the editor of *The Badboy Book of Erotic Poetry*, *Wanderlust: Homoerotic Tales of Travel*, and *Southern Comfort*. His own erotic stories and poems have appeared in many magazines, including *Honcho*, *Overload*, *First Hand*, *Steam*, *Gay Scotland*, and elsewhere, and in the anthologies *Stallions and Other Studs*, *Barely Legal*, *Sportsmen*, *Wired Hard*, *My Three Boys*, *Meltdown!*, and others. He lives in Manhattan.

**Will Leber** is a native Californian and graduate of Stanford University. He worked for many years in the garment industry in New York and now lives in San Francisco. His erotic fiction has appeared in the anthologies *Flesh and the Word 2*, *Flesh and the Word 3*, and *Looking for Mr. Preston*. He is currently working on a collection of erotic short stories and a novel about fashion models.

**Stan Leventhal** was a novelist, editor, activist who organized gay people in the publishing industry, and was a founder of the Pat Parker/Vito Russo Center Library. He was the editor-in-chief of the Mavety Media Group, publishers of *Inches*, *Mandate*, and *Honcho*, as well as the founding editor of the now-defunct Amethyst Press, publisher of Bo Houston, John Gilgun, Patrick Moore, and others. His published writings include two volumes of short stories, *A Herd of Tiny Elephants* (1988) and *Candy Holidays* (1991); two mystery novels, *Faultlines* (1989) and *The Black Marble Pool* (1990); and two autobiographical novels, *Mountain Climbing in Sheridan Square* (1988) and *Skydiving in Christopher Street* (1995) that detail gay male life in Manhattan, as well as the forthcoming *Barbie in Bondage*. Stan Leventhal died of AIDS-related causes on January 15, 1995.

**William John Mann** is a journalist and fiction writer whose work has appeared in numerous publications, including *The Boston Pheonix*, *Men's Style*, *Wilde*, and *The Advocate*. His essays and fiction have appeared in the anthologies *Sister & Brother*, *Looking for Mr. Preston*, *Shadows of Love*, *Wanderlust*, and the forthcoming *Queerly Classed*. He won the 1994 Porn Press Award from PDA Press. The former publisher of the award-winning *Metroline*, he is currently completing a novel, a collection of ghost stories, and a biography of the film star William Haines.

**Edmund Miller**, author of the legendary *Fucking Animals* and other books of poetry, is chairman of the English Department at the C.W. Post Campus of Long Island University where he teaches British literature and historical linguistics. Among his scholarly works are three books about the seventeenth-century poet George Herbert. His stories have appeared in *Playguy*, *Blueboy*, *Honcho*, and numerous anthologies. Dr. Miller is currently working on a sonnet sequence about the go-go boys of New York City.

**Michael Rowe** is the author of *Writing Below The Belt: Conversations With Erotic Authors*. He is a contributor to *The Harvard Gay & Lesbian Review*, as well as numerous nonfiction anthologies, including *Friends and Lovers* and *Sister & Brother*. Some of his most recent fiction appears in *Flesh and The Word 3*, *Queer View Mirror*, and the Canadian horror fiction anthology *Northern Frights 3*. His first novel, *Darkling I Listen*, will be published in 1997. He makes his home in Toronto with his life-partner, Brian, and their adopted nephew, Patrick.

**Charley Shively** has written for *Fag Rag*, *Gay Sunshine*, *Straight to Hell*, *GCN*, *Polished Knob*, and *Gayme*. Professor of American Studies at the University of Massachusetts, Boston, he has written two books on Walt Whitman and *A History of the Conception of Death in America* (1987). He is the author of a long study, *Cocksucking as an Act of Revolution*, a work without an ending or a publisher.

**Dik Staal/Nigel Kent** is an Australian artist/leather guy, born 1933, living in Europe since 1960. His erotic art on s/m themes is world famous and has been exhibited in Holland, Germany, England, France, and New York. His art has been published extensively in Europe and the U.S. in such magazines as *Mr. SM*, *Toy* (Sweden), *Magazine* (France), *Amigo* (Spain), *Revolt* (Finland), and *Drummer* (USA). Since June 1994 he has been writing erotic stories, including "What's in an Inch."

**Wickie Stamps** is a writer whose published works appear in *For Shelter and Beyond—Ending Violence Against Women* (MCBWSG); *Sister & Brother*, edited by Joan Nestle and John Preston (Harper SF); *Looking for Mr. Preston*, edited by Laura Antoniou (Masquerade); *Dykescapes: Short Fiction by New Lesbian Writers*, edited by Toina Portillo (Alyson); *Doing It for Daddy*, edited by Pat Califia (Alyson); *Leatherfolk*, edited by Mark Thompson (Alyson); and *Queer View Mirror*, edited by James Johnstone and Karen X. Tulchinsky (Arsenal Pulp Trash). Presently, Ms. Stamps is the editor of *Drummer* magazine.

**Don Shewey** has written extensively for the *Village Voice*, taught theater at New York University, and published three books, including *Out Front*, the Grove Press anthology of gay and lesbian plays. His 1991 interview with Madonna for the *Advocate* was syndicated around the world to 19 countries in 11 languages. He lives in Manhattan, where he also works as a professional bodyworker, and he is currently writing a comic novel about sex as spiritual practice.

**R. S. Thomas** has been writing male-male erotica since 1991. His work has appeared in *Manifest Reader* and in the anthologies *Sportsmen*, *Wanderlust*, *Southern Comfort*, and *Western Trails*.

**Aaron Travis** is the pseudonym of Steven Saylor, who has been a newspaper and magazine editor, porn author (the almost complete works of Aaron Travis in six volumes from Badboy Books), desktop self-publisher, literary agent (Lars Eighner's *Travels with Lizbeth*), essayist (most recently John Preston's *Friends and Lovers*), award-winning short story writer (with frequent contributions to *Ellery Queen's Mystery Magazine*), and historical/mystery novelist (*Roman Blood, Arms of Nemesis, The Venus Throw*, and the Dashiell Hammett Award nominee and Lambda Literary Award winner *Catilina's Riddle*). He was born in 1956 and divides his time between homes in Berkeley, California, and Amethyst, Texas.

**Matthew Walker** lives in Minneapolis/St. Paul with his daddy. He's been published in *Drummer* and *Manifest Reader*.

**H. L. Wylie** is the pseudonym of David A. Nichols, who, encouraged by his family, decided upon the use of his grandfather's name for publication purposes. David shares his love of the Jersey shore and writing with his lifemate of twenty years, Michael. From college days to the present, David and Michael have created a large circle of gay and straight friends alike—friends who lend and stimulate creativity for a million ideas. David is busy putting all those ideas to text. H. L. Wylie will be around for years to come.

This constitutes an extention of the copyright page:

## EURYDICE

### f/32

*"Its wonderful to see a woman...celebrating her body and her sexuality by creating a fabulous and funny tale."*—Kathy Acker

With the story of Ela (whose name is a pseudonym for orgasm), Eurydice won the National Fiction competition sponsored by Fiction Collective Two and Illinois State University. A funny, disturbing quest for unity, *f/32* prompted Frederic Tuten to proclaim "almost any page ... redeems us from the anemic writing and banalities we have endured in the past decade..."                    $10.95/350-3

## LARRY TOWNSEND

### ASK LARRY

Twelve years of Masterful advice (and the occasional command) from Larry Townsend (*Run, Little Leatherboy*, *Chains*), the leatherman's long-time confidant and adviser. Starting just before the onslaught of AIDS, Townsend wrote the "Leather Notebook" column for *Drummer* magazine, tackling subjects from sexual technique to safer sex, whips to welts, Daddies to dog collars. Now, with *Ask Larry*, readers can avail themselves of Townsend's collected wisdom as well as the author's contemporary commentary—a careful consideration of the way life has changed in the AIDS era, and the specific ways in which the disease has altered perceptions of once-simple problems. Any man worth his leathers can't afford to miss this volume from one of the tribe's most celebrated and trusted scribes.                    $12.95/289-2

## RUSS KICK

### OUTPOSTS:

### A Catalog of Rare and Disturbing Alternative Information

A huge, authoritative guide to some of the most offbeat and bizarre publications available today! Dedicated to the notion of a society based on true freedom of expression, *Outposts* shines light into the darkest nooks and most overlooked crannies of American thought. Rather than simply summarize the plethora of controversial opinions crowding the American scene, Kick has tracked down the real McCoy and compiled over five hundred reviews of work penned by political extremists, conspiracy theorists, hallucinogenic pathfinders, sexual explorers, religious iconoclasts and social malcontents. Better yet, each review is followed by ordering information for the many readers sure to want these remarkable publications for themselves.    $19.95/0202-8

## WILLIAM CARNEY

### THE REAL THING

*Carney gives us a good look at the mores and lifestyle of the first generation of gay leathermen. A chilling mystery/romance novel as well.*                    —Pat Califia

Out of print for years, *The Real Thing* has long served as a touchstone in any consideration of gay "edge fiction." First published in 1968, this uncompromising story of New York leathermen received instant acclaim —and in the years since, has become a highly-prized volume to those lucky enough to acquire a copy. Now, *The Real Thing* returns from exile, ready to thrill a new generation—and reacquaint itself with its original audience.                    $10.95/280-9

## LUCY TAYLOR

### UNNATURAL ACTS

*"A topnotch collection..."* —Science Fiction Chronicle

The remarkable debut of a provocative writer. *Unnatural Acts* plunges into the dark side of the psyche, past all pleasantries and prohibitions, and brings to life a disturbing vision of erotic horror. Unrelenting angels and hungry gods play with souls and bodies in Taylor's cosmos: where heaven and hell are merely differences of perspective; where redemption and damnation lie behind the same shocking acts.                    *181-0*

## LOOKING FOR MR. PRESTON

Edited by Laura Antoniou, *Looking for Mr. Preston* includes work by Lars Eighner, Pat Califia, Michael Bronski, Felice Picano, Joan Nestle, Larry Townsend, Sasha Alyson, Andrew Holleran, Michael Lowenthal, and others who contributed interviews, essays and personal reminiscences of John Preston—a man whose career spanned the industry from the early pages of the *Advocate* to various national bestseller lists. Preston was the author of over twenty books, including *Franny, the Queen of Provincetown,* and *Mr. Benson*. He also edited the noted *Flesh and the Word* erotic anthologies, *Personal Dispatches: Writers Confront AIDS*, and *Hometowns,*. More importantly, Preston became a personal inspiration, friend and mentor to many of today's gay and lesbian authors and editors. Ten percent of the proceeds from sale of the book will go to the AIDS Project of Southern Maine, for which Preston had served as President of the Board. $23.95/288-4

## EDITED BY MICHAEL LOWENTHAL

### THE BEST OF THE BADBOYS

*"...What I like best about Badboy is the fact that it does not neglect the classics.... Badboy Books has resurrected writings from the Golden Age of gayrotic fiction (1966-1972), before visual media replaced books in the hands and minds of the masses...."*
—Jesse Monteagudo, *The Community Voice*

A collection of the best of Masquerade Books' phenomenally popular BADBOY line of gay erotic writing. BADBOY's sizable roster includes many names that are legendary in gay circles. Their work has contributed significantly to BADBOY's runaway success, establishing the imprint as a home for not only new but classic writing in the genre. The very best of the leading Badboys is collected here, in this testament to the artistry that has catapulted these "outlaw" authors to best-selling status. *233-7*

## EDITED BY AMARANTHA KNIGHT

### LOVE BITES

Vampire lovers, hookers, groupies and hustlers of all sexual persuasions are waiting to entice you into their sensuous world. But be prepared! By the end of this book, you will have not only succumbed to their dark and sexy charms, but you will also have joined the swelling ranks of humanity which understand on a very personal level that Love Bites —from the Introduction by Amarantha Knight

A volume of tales dedicated to legend's sexiest demon—the Vampire. Amarantha Knight, herself an author who has delved into vampire lore, has gathered the very best writers in the field to produce a collection of uncommon, and chilling, allure.

Including such names as Ron Dee, Nancy A. Collins, Nancy Kilpatrick, Lois Tilton and David Aaron Clark, *Love Bites* is not only the finest collection of erotic horror available—but a virtual who's who of promising new talent. *234-5*

## BIZARRE SEX

### BIZARRE SEX AND OTHER CRIMES OF PASSION
#### *Edited by Stan Tal*

Stan Tal, editor of *Bizarre Sex*, Canada's boldest fiction publication, has culled the very best stories that have crossed his desk—and now unleashes them on the reading public in *Bizarre Sex and Other Crimes of Passion*. Over twenty small masterpieces of erotic shock make this one of the year's most unexpectedly alluring anthologies. Including such masters of erotic horror and fantasy as Edward Lee, Lucy Taylor, Nancy Kilpatrick and Caro Soles, *Bizarre Sex and Other Crimes of Passion*, is a treasure-trove of arousing chills. *210-2*

## GUILLERMO BOSCH
### RAIN

"*The intensely sensual descriptions of color and light, the passionate characters, the sensitive experiences of love and pain depicted in* Rain *moved me a great deal.* Rain *is really a trip...*"
—Dr. Timothy Leary

"Rain *definitely pays homage to the European tradition of an erotic literature which stimulates intellectual and moral questioning of social, economic and political institutions.* Rain *is an important book.*"          —Robert Sam Anson, author of *Best Intentions*

"Rain *is a vivid novel that transcends its genre. Only Guillermo Bosch could blend the political and erotic with such ease.*"          —David Freeman, author of *A Hollywood Education*

"*It was Bosch's poetic language which first attracted me to* Rain, *but his unprejudiced mixing of ethnicity, different sexual persuasions and diverse personalities is unique and most refreshing.*"
—Meri Nana-Ana Danquah

An adult fairy tale, *Rain* takes place in a time when the mysteries of Eros are played out against a background of uncommon deprivation. The tale begins on the 1,537th day of drought—when one man comes to know the true depths of thirst. In a quest to sate his hunger for some knowledge of the wide world, he is taken through a series of extraordinary, unearthly encounters that promise to change not only his life, but the course of civilization around him.          *232-9*

## MICHAEL LASSELL
### THE HARD WAY

"*Michael Lassell's poems are worldly in the best way, defining the arc of a world of gay life in our own decade of mounting horror and oppression. With an effortless feel for dark laughter he roams the city, a startling combination of boulevardier and hooker.... Lassell is a master of the necessary word. In an age of tepid and whining verse, his bawdy and bittersweet songs are like a plunge in cold champagne.*"

—Paul Monette

*Virtually all of the material in this book was written and published between 1983 and 1993, although it covers all the years I can remember. The focus, of course, is on the post-Stonewall Liberation Years.... I am, like most writers, horrified to read work written as recently as ten days ago, much less ten years ago, but I have bitten the bullet and made few changes, except when some reference is so out of cultural currency as to obscure my own obscure point, or when I can't remember what the hell I meant by something. But what you see here, is pretty much the way it was the first time it appeared in black and white....*

—from the Introduction

The first collection of renowned gay writer Michael Lassell's poetry, fiction and essays. Widely anthologized and a staple of gay literary and entertainment publications nationwide, Lassell is regarded as one of the most distinctive and accomplished talents of his generation. As much a chronicle of post-Stonewall gay life as a compendium of a remarkable writer's work, *The Hard Way* is sure to appeal to anyone interested in the state of contemporary writing.          *231-0*

## SAMUEL R. DELANY

### THE MAD MAN

For his thesis, graduate student John Marr researches the life and work of the brilliant Timothy Hasler: a philosopher whose career was cut tragically short over a decade earlier. Marr encounters numerous obstacles, as other researchers turn up evidence of Hasler's personal life that is deemed simply too unpleasant. On another front, Marr finds himself increasingly drawn toward more shocking, depraved sexual entanglements with the homeless men of his neighborhood, until it begins to seem that Hasler's death might hold some key to his own life as a gay man in the age of AIDS.

*This new novel by Samuel R. Delany not only expands the parameters of what he has given us in the past, but fuses together two seemingly disparate genres of writing and comes up with something which is not comparable to any existing text of which I am aware.... What Delany has done here is take the ideas of Marquis de Sade one step further, by filtering extreme and obsessive sexual behavior through the sieve of post-modern experience....* —Lambda Book Report

*The latest novel from Hugo- and Nebula-winning science fiction writer and critic Delany... reads like a pornographic reflection of Peter Ackroyd's Chatterton or A.S. Byatt's Possession.... The pornographic element... becomes more than simple shock or titillation, though, as Delany develops an insightful dichotomy between [his protagonist]'s two worlds: the one of cerebral philosophy and dry academia, the other of heedless, 'impersonal' obsessive sexual extremism. When these worlds finally collide ... the novel achieves a surprisingly satisfying resolution....* —Publishers Weekly
**hardcover 193-4/$23.95**

### THE MOTION OF LIGHT IN WATER

*"A very moving, intensely fascinating literary biography from an extraordinary writer. Thoroughly admirable candor and luminous stylistic precision; the artist as a young man and a memorable picture of an age."* —William Gibson

*"A remarkably candid and revealing...study of an extraordinary and extraordinarily appealing human being, and a fascinating...account of the early days of a significant science fiction writer's career."* —Robert Silverberg

The first unexpurgated American edition of award-winning author Samuel R. Delany's riveting autobiography covers the early years of one of science fiction's most important voices. Beginning with his marriage to the young, remarkably gifted poet Marilyn Hacker, Delany paints a vivid and compelling picture of New York's East Village in the early '60s—a time of unprecedented social change and transformation. Startling and revealing, *The Motion of Light in Water* traces the roots of one of America's most innovative writers. **133-0**

## KATHLEEN K.

### SWEET TALKERS

Kathleen K. is a professional, in the finest sense of the word. She takes her work seriously, always approaching it with diligence, imagination and backbone; an exceptional judge of character, she manages both customers and employees with a flair that has made her business a success. But many people would dismiss Kathleen's achievements, falling as they do, outside mainstream corporate America.

Here, for the first time, is the story behind the provocative advertisements and 970 prefixes. Kathleen K. opens up her diary for a rare peek at the day-to-day life of a phone sex operator—and reveals a number of secrets and surprises. Because far from being a sleazy, underground scam, the service Kathleen provides often speaks to the lives of its customers with a directness and compassion they receive nowhere else. **192-6**

## ROBERT PATRICK
### TEMPLE SLAVE

*...you must read this book. It draws such a tragic, and, in a way, noble portrait of Mr. Buono: It leads the reader, almost against his will, into a deep sympathy with this strange man who tried to comfort, to encourage and to feed both the worthy and the worthless... It is impossible not to mourn for this man—impossible not to praise this book*          —Quentin Crisp

*This is nothing less than the secret history of the most theatrical of theaters, the most bohemian of Americans and the most knowing of queens. Patrick writes with a lush and witty abandon, as if this departure from the crafting of plays has energized him.* **Temple Slave** *is also one of the best ways to learn what it was like to be fabulous, gay, theatrical and loved in a time at once more and less dangerous to gay life than our own.*          —Genre

**Temple Slave** tells the story of the Espresso Buono—the archetypal alternative performance space—and the wildly talented misfits who called it home in the early 60s. The Buono became the birthplace of a new underground theater—and the personal and social consciousness that would lead to Stonewall and the modern gay and lesbian movement. **Temple Slave** is a kaleidoscopic page from gay history—a riotous tour de force.          ***191-8***

## DAVID MELTZER
### THE AGENCY TRILOGY

With the Essex House edition of **The Agency** in 1968, the highly regarded poet David Meltzer took America on a trip into a hell of unbridled sexuality. The story of a supersecret, Orwellian sexual network, **The Agency** explored issues of erotic dominance and submission with an immediacy and frankness previously unheard of in American literature, as well as presented a vision of an America consumed and dehumanized by a lust for power. This landmark novel was followed by **The Agent**, and **How Many Blocks in the Pile?**—taken with **The Agency,** they confirm Meltzer's position as one of America's early masters of the erotic genre.

*...'The Agency' is clearly Meltzer's paradigm of society; a mindless machine of which we are all 'agents' including those whom the machine supposedly serves....*          —Norman Spinrad
***216-7***

## CARO SOLES
### MELTDOWN!
**An Anthology of Erotic Science Fiction and Dark Fantasy for Gay Men**

Editor Caro Soles has put together one of the most explosive, mind-bending collections of gay erotic writing ever published. **Meltdown!** contains the very best examples of this increasingly popular sub-genre: stories meant to shock and delight, to send a shiver down the spine and start a fire down below. An extraordinary volume, **Meltdown!** presents both new voices and provocative pieces by world-famous writers Edmund White and Samuel R. Delany.          ***203-5***

## GAUNTLET
### THE BEST OF *GAUNTLET* Edited by Barry Hoffman

*No material, no opinion is taboo enough to violate* Gauntlet*'s purpose of 'exploring the limits of free expression'—airing all views in the name of the First Amendment.*—Associated Press

Dedicated to "exploring the limits of free expression," *Gauntlet* has, with its semi-annual issues, taken on such explosive topics as race, pornography, political correctness, and media manipulation—always publishing the widest possible range of opinions. Only in *Gauntlet* might one expect to encounter Phyllis Schlafley *and* Annie Sprinkle, Stephen King *and* Madonna—often within pages of one another. The very best, most provocative articles have been gathered by editor-in-chief Barry Hoffman, to make *The Best of Gauntlet* a most provocative exploration of American society's limits. ***202-7***

## JOHN PRESTON

### MY LIFE AS A PORNOGRAPHER
#### AND OTHER INDECENT ACTS

The erotic nonfiction of John Preston. Includes the title essay, given as the John Pearson Perry Lecture at Harvard University, and the legendary "Good-Bye to Sally Gearhart," and many other provocative writings.

*...essential and enlightening...His sex-positive stand on safer-sex education as the only truly effective AIDS-prevention strategy will certainly not win him any conservative converts, but AIDS activists will be shouting their assent.... [My Life as a Pornographer] is a bridge from the sexually liberated 1970s to the more cautious 1990s, and Preston has walked much of that way as a standard-bearer to the cause for equal rights....* —Library Journal

*Preston's a model essayist; he writes pellucid prose in a voice that, like Samuel Johnson's, combines authority with entertainment.... My Life as a Pornographer...is not pornography, but rather reflections upon the writing and production of it. Preston ranges from really superb journalism of his interviews with denizens of the S/M demi-mond, particularly a superb portrait of a Colt model Preston calls "Joe" to a brilliant analysis of the "theater" of the New York sex club, The Mineshaft.... In a deeply sex-phobic world, Preston has never shied away from a vision of the redemptive potential of the erotic drive. Better than perhaps anyone in our community, Preston knows how physical joy can bridge differences and make us well.*

—Lambda Book Report     *135-7*

### HUSTLING:
#### A GENTLEMAN'S GUIDE TO THE FINE ART OF HOMOSEXUAL PROSTITUTION

John Preston solicited the advice of "working boys" from across the country in his effort to produce the ultimate guide to the hustler's world. *Hustling* covers every practical aspect of the business, from clientele and payment options to "specialties," sidelines and drawbacks. No stone is left unturned in this guidebook to the ins and outs of this much-mythologized trade.     *137-3*

## SKIN TWO

### THE BEST OF *SKIN TWO*     *Edited by Tim Woodward*

For over a decade, *Skin Two* has served as the bible of the international fetish community. A groundbreaking journal from the crossroads of sexuality, fashion, and art, *Skin Two* specializes in provocative, challenging essays by the finest writers working in the "radical sex" scene. Collected here, for the first time, are the articles and interviews that have established the magazine's singular reputation. Including interviews with cult figures Tim Burton, Clive Barker and Jean Paul Gaultier.     *130-6*

## MICHAEL PERKINS

### THE GOOD PARTS: An Uncensored Guide to Literary Sexuality

Michael Perkins, one of America's only serious critics to regularly scrutinize sexual literature, presents an overview of sex as seen in the pages of over 100 major volumes from the past twenty years.

*I decided when I wrote my first column in 1968 that I would take the opportunity presented by Screw to chronicle the inevitable and inexorable rise of an unfairly neglected genre of contemporary writing. I wondered if I would remain interested in the subject for very long, and if the field would not eventually diminish so there would be nothing to review.... Every week since then I have published a thousand-word review, and occasionally a longer essay, devoted to discovering and reporting on the manifestations of sexuality in all kinds of fiction, nonfiction, and poetry. In my columns I cast a wide net (a million words so far) over a subject no one else wanted to take a long look at. It has indeed held my interest.*     186-1